The Ultimate
Fishing Book
Strategies for Success

About the Editor

Spence Petros is a regular contributor to *North American Fisherman* magazine, and has made a living fishing and writing about it for over three decades. He is uniquely suited to editing and updating this limited edition, 10th Anniversary collection of NAFC fishing classics.

Mike Vail
Vice President, Product Marketing/Business Development

Tom Carpenter
Director of Book and New Media Development

Steve Pennaz
Executive Director, North American Fishing Club

Dan Kennedy
Book Production Manager

Michele Teigen
Book Development Coordinator

Becky Fitch
Editorial Assistant

Amy Boxrud and Julie Lindemann
Text Production

Beowulf Ltd.
Book Design and Production

9 8 7 6 5 4 3 2

ISBN 1-58159-015-6

North American Fishing Club
12301 Whitewater Drive
Minnetonka, MN 55343

Photo and Illustration Credits

Bill Lindner, Don Wirth, Jerry Robb, Soc Clay, Spence Petros, Gary Borger, Creative Publishing International, Keith Sutton, Kurt Beckstrom, Doug Stamm, Dick Sternberg, David Rottinghaus, Bill Marchel, Bill Vanderford, Kevin VanDam, Scott Ripley, Steve Pennaz, Tim Tucker, Richard Franklin, Louie Stout, George Barnett, Denver Bryan, Michael Jones, Jeff Samsel, Bob Cary, Dave Vedder, Clark Montgomery, Ed Park, Gary Nelson, Greg Bohn, Jim Saric, Ray Hansen, Scott Liles, Sylvia Bashline, Bill Schmid, Dave Mull, F. Eugene Hester, Grady Allen, Greg Silker, Jason Borger, Jim Bashline, Joe Bucher, Larry Larsen, Mark LaBarbera, Mark Romanack, Roger Peterson, Sam Curtis, Ted Takasaki, Tina Walski, George Ostroushko, Joe Tomelleri, Larry Mishkar

Table of Contents

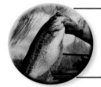

• Chapter 1 •
Largemouth Bass

• Chapter 2 •
Smallmouth Bass

• Chapter 3 •
Bluegill

• Chapter 4 •
Crappie

• Chapter 5 •
Catfish

• Chapter 6 •
Walleye

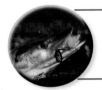

Creating the Ultimate Fishing Book

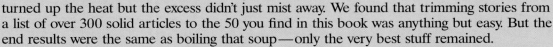

*W*hen our 10th Anniversary rolled around here at the North American Fishing Club, we took a good look at all the work we had done through those years. Our thought? Now there is some of the best and most solid freshwater fishing information you'll find anywhere. A perfect way to celebrate would be to put the "best of the best" together in one ultimate fishing book.

That challenge was simple in theory: select the best, most-informative feature articles published in *North American Fisherman* the past 10 years. Oh, and break them down by species, because club members fish just about everything that swims.

It should have been simple—like boiling down soup to enhance the flavor and condense to the good stuff. So we turned up the heat but the excess didn't just mist away. We found that trimming stories from a list of over 300 solid articles to the 50 you find in this book was anything but easy. But the end results were the same as boiling that soup—only the very best stuff remained.

So in your hands is a compilation of the best articles ever to appear in your club publication, *North American Fisherman.* These stories cover all the popular species—largemouth and smallmouth bass, trout, walleye, catfish, pike, crappie, bluegill and more. And these stories will treat you to a variety of looks at fishing for each of these wonderful species, bringing you time-honored strategies and techniques that will bring more and bigger fish to your net.

The authors? The best in the business, from both yesterday and today. Guys like Larry Dahlberg, Kurt Beckstrom, Spence Petros, Don Wirth, Gary Borger, Tim Tucker, Joe Bucher, Kevin VanDam, Dick Sternberg and others. Long-time NAFC members will also recognize names like Jim Bashline and Otis "Toad" Smith who have since passed away but left us a legacy of their fishing expertise.

Speaking of expertise...what better editor to pull all this together than our own Spence Petros? Spence was the guy reviewing, reworking and updating all these stories. You'll be surprised at how well each of these stories remains sound in its basic strategy (a tribute to the original writers), and pleased at how updated the information is to today's expanded understandings and improved equipment (a tribute to Spence and his fish-catching knowledge).

That's what makes a great fishing book—the knowledge you will take away from it, and then utilize to improve your own fishing success. You'll find species that are your passion in this book, and you'll learn, from the best of the best, how to handle some other species you may have been thinking about pursuing.

To us, that makes this *The Ultimate Fishing Book.* We hope you treasure it, and the *Strategies for Success* it offers. We're proud to bring it to you.

Steve Pennaz
Executive Director, North American Fishing Club

chapter 1

Largemouth Bass

NAFC members love their large-mouths, and for good reason. What other fish is so widespread—North, South, East and West—from huge reservoirs to the farm pond down the road? What other predator is so willing to smash a crankbait, slash a stickbait or suck in a spin-nerbait? And what other fish can stump us so badly, until we finally locate that magic formula for the day....

Here's the best of *North American Fisherman's* best on how to catch bass under a variety of conditions. Use this knowledge to do battle with more bigmouths than ever.

The Duclos Diaries

by Kurt Beckstrom

Think extreme details really don't make much of a difference? You'll be amazed at what NAFC member Paul Duclos (pictured below) does to catch giant bass!

*U*ntil March 1997, North American Fishing Club member Paul Duclos was an angling unknown, quietly going about the business of catching overstuffed largemouths on an extremely regular basis.

Unlike a handful of other big-bass specialists, however, this owner of a carpet-cleaning business in Santa Rosa, California, didn't have a national following of bass anglers whose ears pricked at every rumor of another big bass being caught.

But that changed when North American Fisherman broke nationally a story that knocked the bassin' world crossways, and illustrated it with a picture of Duclos holding what very likely could have been a new world-record largemouth ("Fisherman News Update," May/June 1997). Within a few weeks, millions of anglers knew about Duclos' catch, and most formed strong opinions about the angler as a result.

Hero Or Fool?

Their convictions stem from his decision not to risk killing the monster bass by transporting it to a certified scale. Instead, he called his wife and asked her to deliver the household's bathroom scale to the lake.

He weighed himself with and without the fish in his arms, and came up with a difference of 24 pounds—almost 2 pounds more than George Perry's long-standing world record. Afterward, he snapped a few photos, released the bass and watched her swim strongly away.

Because of that decision Duclos has been labeled a hero by the conservation-minded and branded crazy by those who say he threw away guaranteed fame and fortune.

Either way, it makes little difference now. Duclos says he'd do the same thing again, and the rest of us will have to catch a bass just as big before we can be sure about what we would do in the same situation.

No doubt, Duclos came to the forefront of the national scene because of "the fish," as he calls it. But what most people don't know is that the catch wasn't a fluke. Duclos has taken a number of giant bass over the years—the ones shown in the accompanying photo were caught recently. He'll dedicate days to connect with one truly huge fish rather than spend hours on a hot bite with 5 and 6 pounders.

Duclos caught "the fish" while casting a 9-inch Castaic Trout, a plug especially designed to attract

---

"He'll dedicate days to connect with one truly huge fish."

California's rainbow-fed, Florida-strain bruisers. But tossing and trolling giant plugs isn't the only way he takes oversize bass. He has developed an entire big-bass system using giant plastic worms, live crayfish, jigs and, of course, magnum crankbaits. What's more, he fishes them with an unrivaled attention to detail.

On the following pages, in a North American Fisherman exclusive, he discloses to his fellow NAFC members all he's learned about targeting the biggest largemouth bass in the waters he fishes. Not typical behavior, perhaps, but then Duclos doesn't fish competitively and has no reason to keep his unique methods secret. In fact, he enjoys seeing other anglers experience success. As he explains, "If I can help someone catch the biggest bass of their life, I'm happy."

Hunting For Trophies

When Duclos goes bass fishing, he's more hunter than angler, he says.

Although the structure he fishes is the same as what other bass anglers seek—drop-offs, points, humps, etc.—he spends more time studying those spots than the typical fisherman.

"You've got to find out where they live," he says,

DUCLOS' 12 DEADLIEST TIPS

1. Study the lake until you know all the potential big-fish hotspots.

2. Use top-quality gear that's sensitive enough to detect subtle pickups, yet strong enough to handle big fish.

3. Make sure you have everything ready to go—rods, anchor lines, etc.—before you approach the target zone.

4. Double-anchor the boat to keep it from swinging over the target zone. Use dark-colored anchor lines.

5. Fish as quietly as possible.

6. Always apply a good quality fish scent to mask human odors.

7. Fish low-memory monofilament and stretch the first seven to 10 feet before you start fishing. Coiled line spooks fish.

8. Frequently check the line for nicks and weak spots. Once you hook a big bass, you don't want to lose it.

9. Keep hooks razor sharp.

10. Keep the presentation as natural as possible. Don't give the fish a chance to reject your lure.

11. Be patient. You're basically fishing for one strike a day. A second one is a bonus.

12. Release trophy bass unharmed.

"and that means you've got to study the lake. The hardest part about catching big fish is finding them. After that, it's just a matter of applying yourself."

The waters Duclos favors aren't very far from his home. And because his bass rig is a tiny 8-foot, Water Scamp pram powered only by a Minn Kota transom-mount electric motor, they're not very big. The lake that produced "the fish" has only 75 surface acres.

One luxury Duclos enjoys is that the water levels on these lakes often drop during the summer. If they drop low enough, he can actually identify likely spots with his own eyes.

"Most of the time, I just make mental notes and keep them in my head, but I have photographed

---

and videotaped some of the structures I've located this way."

When the water is high, he does it like anyone else—with his sonar unit, a Lowrance X-85. But when he's scouting, that's all he does.

"I leave the rods at home when I'm on a scouting trip, and spend five or six hours running over a section of the lake with my eyes glued to the screen.

"I don't bring fishing gear because I don't want to be tempted to fish. I want to concentrate on learning the lake."

That's considerable willpower, considering the fact that Duclos' time on the water amounts to roughly nine hours a week. Like anyone else, he must balance fishing time with business and family time.

There's no secret as to what Duclos looks for—drop-offs, points and humps sprouting weeds or timber—with adjacency to deep water. There is one thing that will cause the adrenaline to flow, however. Boulders. "If I find boulders on a piece of structure, I know that sooner or later, I'll catch a big bass off them. "There's just something about large rocks that attracts trophy-size bass."

Boat positioning is another huge factor in his program. We'll get into where he sets up later, but for now, he says it's absolutely critical that the boat remain motionless for his wormin' and jiggin' styles.

"The boat is always double-anchored at the bow and stern," he says. "If it swings with the wind, I can't put my casts in the strike zone. Plus, I want the retrieves to be slow and controlled; you can't do that when the boat is drifting."

Castaic Softbait

Worms And Jigs

The most famous of the California big-bass lures, of course, are the giant cranks—Castaic Trout, A.C. Plug, Z-Plug and others. Worms and jigs, however, are aspects of Duclos' program that are just as important.

The worms he fishes measure monsters—Tightline and Muscle worms that are 16 to 21 inches long. So is the rod he uses—an 8½-foot G. Loomis model (HSR 1021 C).

"It's long enough and has the backbone to make a strong hookset, but it's also sensitive enough that I can feel a pickup."

His Shimano Chronarch Bantam 100 baitcaster is spooled with Berkley XL—8-pound when he's fishing clear water and up to 12-pound line if the water's stained. Not overly stout stuff, but Duclos doesn't want the fish to see the line. Consequently, he goes with the lightest he can get away with, and even camouflages it by alternately coloring short sections with a permanent marker.

When he's finished, the pattern looks like a series of dashes a few inches long, which breaks up the mono's outline underwater. Clear line is colored with

Tightline Worm

Castaic Hardbait

"I don't sing out loud. It's all in my head. I know it takes me, say, three minutes to mentally sing a certain song, so after I've done it three times, I know I've been fishing approximately nine minutes. By that time I should nearly be finished with the retrieve. I can also judge the pace and slow down or speed up if I have to."

When he does feel a bump (huge bass usually strike surprisingly light, he says), the hookset is immediate and "big." Hence, the long, stout rod.

a green marker; green line requires a blue marker.

Instead of the traditional bullet weight, Duclos buries a couple of 1½- to 2-inch lengths of thick wire solder into the worm's head. The added weight is just enough to make the worm fall slowly to the bottom. And to add a bit of noise, he inserts two or three glass rattles into the head, between the solder sticks.

The worm is Texas-rigged on an Eagle Claw Featherlite 2.5/0 worm hook and cast to the fish zone, but his retrieve is a far cry from what most anglers are used to. Describing the speed at which he brings the worm back as "slow" would be a gross understatement.

"Duclos' jigging program takes the slow approach."

"I rest the rod between my knees and just roll the spool with my thumb. Each roll drags the worm about two inches, at most, and one retrieve takes between seven to 10 minutes."

Duclos believes that trophy bass are loners, and mostly in a neutral to negative mood. The slow-moving bait allows the bass an extended look and plenty of time to strike.

To enforce the discipline it takes to fish this way, and at the same time break the monotony, Duclos sings to himself.

Working Jigs

Duclos' jigging program takes the same slow approach. He dresses an ⅛- to ½-ounce rubber-skirt jig with a 5¼-inch Strike King Pork-O that's been split with a razor blade from the tail to about an inch from the head for added action.

Black and purple are personal favorites, but red and crawdad see their share of service. After splitting the tails, Duclos adds the appropriate color food dye to the container so the newly exposed white edges take on the color of the bait.

As a final touch, both the jig-and-pork combo and his huge plastic worms get dosed with a special scent mixture to mask any human odors that may linger.

"I mix about equal parts of BaitMate Crawdad gel and multicolored rainbow glitter, the kind you buy at the drug store," says Duclos, "and apply it to the jigs and worms. As the lures fall and move through the water, the pieces of red, blue, green and silver glitter come off and look like the scales of a rainbow trout."

The angler's jiggin' stick is the same length but a bit heavier than his worm rod (Loomis HSR1025C), making it better for launching the heavier jigs. The reel is still a Bantam 100, but spooled with 14- to 20-pound P-Line or Berkley Big Game monofilament (14 in clean water, 20 in stained).

Again, his retrieve is slow and along the bottom, a technique he calls "plowing."

"When the jig bottoms out, I slowly lift the rodtip from the 3 o'clock to the 2 o'clock position

CASTING CRANKS

Wind Direction →

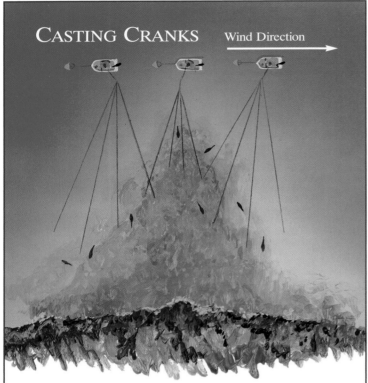

A wind-blown point is prime territory for casting magnum crank-baits. Duclos starts on the upwind side and drops a drift sock off the bow. It slows the boat and keeps the nose pointed into the wind.

As the boat drifts backward past the point, he fancasts first one edge, then over the top, and finally the trailing edge of the point. Retrieves are slow, with the lure running close to, but not bumping, the bottom.

and just crawl it along over obstacles on the bottom."

Between lifts, he picks up line slack and repeats the process until the retrieve is complete. The whole process takes about three or four minutes on a 50-foot cast, he explains.

Bubbling Crawdads

Live crayfish are a big-time favorite among California's bassin' corps, and Duclos is no different.

On his wormin' rig, he ties a Gamakatsu or Owner bait hook and punches it through the very front of the rock-like "horn" between the eyes (you'll have to work the hook back and forth to get it through). Hook size depends on the crayfish—normally a size 1, size 2 or 1/0 for the big five-inch craws he prefers. About 18 inches from the hook he pinches on one

BB-size split shot to help keep the bait on the bottom. He also removes the small claw on each pincer to keep the crawdad from grabbing onto weeds.

Sometimes, when the bass are extremely inactive, Duclos says even a live crawdad can't buy a strike. In that case, he breaks out his secret weapon—half of an Alka-Seltzer tablet, wrapped in a small piece of pantyhose material and Super Glued to the crawdad's shell.

"The bubbles attract bass," he explains. "I think they see or hear the fizzing and swim over to investigate. Then, they find the crawdad moving slowly across the bottom.

"This is a great big-fish technique all year, but it's especially good in February, March and April. I caught my first truly big bass on a live crawdad."

Monster Cranks

Because of California's ongoing trout stocking program, huge rainbow-pattern crankbaits are a staple item in many trophy bass anglers' arsenals. While there are a number of different models available, Duclos prefers 7- and 9-inch Castaic Trout lures, both the hard- and soft-body versions, for most applications.

These big lures require the same stout rod he uses for jigs, but the reel is a Shimano Calcutta 400 spooled with 17- to 30-pound Berkley Big Game monofilament.

As with his worm, jig and crawdad presentations, Duclos uses a few tricks to make the crankbaits more appealing.

"First off, I take red and black permanent markers and make the lure look a little more realistic. I accentuate the red side stripes and add more black spots, especially on the front half."

From that point, he further modifies the lures, depending on where they are to be used. On each side of the soft-body baits he cuts two slits, about two inches long and ¼-inch deep, and one along the top. The night before a fishing trip, he packs each slit with Rainbow Trout Bait Butter, a commercial fish attractant/masking scent in paste form.

"I'm a real believer in covering human scent," he explains, "so in addition to the Trout Butter, I also dunk the entire lure into a container of Reel Craw or Kick N' Bass liquid scent."

Like the gel scent he uses on jigs and worms, the liquid attractant gets a liberal dose of multicolored glitter before being applied.

Duclos throws the modified soft cranks when fishing the shallows (three to seven feet deep) and retrieves them slowly just below the surface. Stocker trout, especially the newly-planted fish, tend to hold close to shore, he explains, and giant bass target them there.

Further modifications are required for fishing shallows that are choked with tules or hydrilla. His weed bait is a hard- or soft-body trout that has had the diving lip removed and the solitary treble replaced with two single hooks equipped with homemade wire weedguards.

"With this lure, you just have to walk-the-dog through the weeds," Duclos says.

If he needs to probe a point or drop-off that is deeper than 20 feet, Duclos weights the big lures with wire solder. He inserts two to five 1½-inch pieces into the soft-body lures, or wraps them around the hook shanks on the hard-bodies.

"When I wrap the hooks, I over-wrap the solder with black thread, then cover that with a layer of epoxy to seal in the solder odor."

Wooden A.C. Plugs are another story. With these, he drills three ⅛-inch holes, ½-inch deep, along the top and bottom of the head. He fills each with molten lead and seals them with epoxy.

"The goal is to add just enough weight to make the lure sink very slowly when you put it in the water," he says.

Duclos casts and trolls the big lures. His trolling rig is a Loomis rod (SWR108-20C) and a Calcutta 400 reel—beefier than the casting rod because it has to handle the drag of the big plug as it moves through the water. The reel is spooled with 17-pound lead core line when he's dragging a soft bait; 20- to 25-pound Big Game for hard baits.

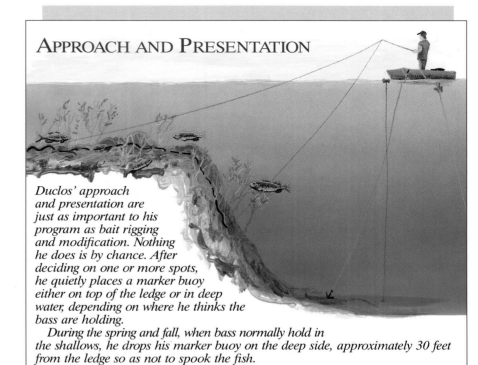

APPROACH AND PRESENTATION

Duclos' approach and presentation are just as important to his program as bait rigging and modification. Nothing he does is by chance. After deciding on one or more spots, he quietly places a marker buoy either on top of the ledge or in deep water, depending on where he thinks the bass are holding.

During the spring and fall, when bass normally hold in the shallows, he drops his marker buoy on the deep side, approximately 30 feet from the ledge so as not to spook the fish.

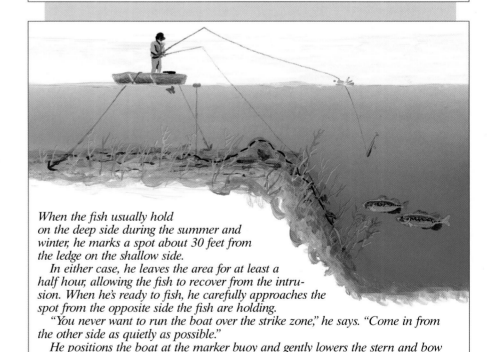

When the fish usually hold on the deep side during the summer and winter, he marks a spot about 30 feet from the ledge on the shallow side.

In either case, he leaves the area for at least a half hour, allowing the fish to recover from the intrusion. When he's ready to fish, he carefully approaches the spot from the opposite side the fish are holding.

"You never want to run the boat over the strike zone," he says. "Come in from the other side as quietly as possible."

He positions the boat at the marker buoy and gently lowers the stern and bow anchors, and makes the first cast. If he's anchored deep, he casts past the lip and crawls the worm, jig or crawdad through the shallows, over the edge and down the drop. When anchored shallow, he casts over the lip and allows the lure to hit bottom on the deep side before crawling it up the slope.

Duclos' strategies and tactics consistently fool monster bass.

"With the lead core, I put 15 to 25 feet of 15-pound fluorocarbon leader in front of the bait. Fish have a hard time seeing the fluorocarbon, so the lure looks more natural. I run it anywhere from 75 to 150 feet behind the boat, and can keep track of it because I mark the main line every 25 feet."

Target zones are the deep sides of drop-off points, and deep flats. When trolling structure, Duclos runs close to, but not touching, bottom. On a clean flat, he allows the bait to bump bottom, kicking up clouds of silt as it runs.

"The reason I don't run the lure on bottom when I'm fishing structure is simple," he explains. "Each bait costs about $30 and I don't want to hang one."

In both cases, trolling speed is slow, just fast enough to impart an enticing wobble. "You want to keep the speed as slow as possible. These big fish won't usually chase down a fast-moving lure."

Versatility, innovation and meticulous attention to detail are the keys to Duclos' success. You may not be able to make everything he does work on the waters you fish, but you can certainly adapt his techniques to your program—maybe even improve on them.

VanDam On...
Cold Front Bass

by Kevin VanDam

Here's a solid game plan that will teach you how to make the most out of those dreaded cold fronts. Armed with these strategies, you can fish through a full cold snap...if you don't let it shake you.

While no other weather condition can affect bass fishing as negatively as a cold front, it doesn't always have the terrible impact most anglers think it does. In fact, I've seen situations where an autumn cold snap actually improved fishing for me. It would have improved for other anglers as well, but they were convinced the conditions were going to make fishing tough, and went out to prove it.

That's something every NAFC member should aim to avoid, regardless of the season, because bass never do the same thing every time a cold-front passes.

There are no hard-and-fast rules for patterning cold front bass.

Furthermore, a cold front has stages, and each stage affects fish differently. For example, bass often become more active—and the fishing action picks up as a front approaches.

But they seem to disappear altogether the day after the front passes, when you're faced with high, bright, skies, and the wind is either blowing strongly, or there's no wind at all.

If it's calm after the front, bass are usually spooky. On the other hand, a strong wind makes it difficult to present lures that must be kept in the strike zone longer. Unless the front lingers, bass gradually become more active on the second day after it passes.

Form A Plan

When I compile a game plan for a cold front, I consider the clarity of the lake, water depth, temperature, season, the part of the country I'm fishing and what weather patterns may have occurred prior to the front passing.

COLD FRONT BASS ON NATURAL LAKES

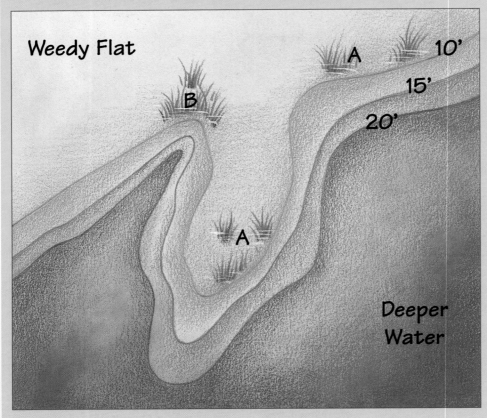

Weedy Flat

A

B

10'

15'

20'

A

A

Deeper Water

During earlier fall, bass often duck into the thickest patches of weeds on a flat (A). In later fall, when most weeds have begun to die, still-green weeds on inside turns are often key areas where the bass will bunch up. Turns that are more slot-like and are adjacent to deeper water (B) can be magnets for schools of larger-than-average bass.

bass are the least bothered. I've proven this several times on Michigan's clear, natural lakes. During the fall, when the largemouth bite may be off because of a front, I can still find small-mouths that blast my lures.

Preceding weather patterns are a major consideration, yet one most anglers overlook.

For example, it has been overcast for a couple days prior to a cold blast, and the ensuing front delivers bright sun, bluebird skies and an abrupt drop in water temperature, it's going to affect the bass more adversely. Had the skies been bright prior to the front, there would be less negative impact on fishing.

Falling water temperatures are less of a factor in fall than they are during spring or summer.

A spring cold front that causes water temps to fall fairly dramatically can chase bass out of shallows, sending them back to wintering areas. During the summer, a major drop in surface temperature can shock shallow-water bass rather severely. They may leave the area, or simply become inactive.

But by mid-fall, the bass are not only accustomed to falling water temps, they seem to welcome them. Cooler water drives baitfish shallower and triggers a feeding binge in the bass. These fish can sometimes find a comfort zone and stay active for longer periods of time.

Fronts tend to affect stained, shallow lakes less severely than they do clear-water lakes, so given a choice, avoid clear waters under cold-front conditions.

The part of country you're fishing can make a difference, too. Cold fronts have less of an impact on Northern waters than they do on Southern lakes because Northern bass are more accustomed to them. Believe me—I know.

Central Michigan, where I live, gets blasted by cold fronts on a regular basis, and our bass don't seem to be as bothered by them as much as fish in Southern impoundments.

Fronts distress Florida-strain largemouths more than other types of bass, while smallmouth or spotted

"Most bass are caught on 'reactionary strikes' during cold-front situations."

Now, a cold front can slow them down temporarily, or will push them tighter to the cover, but it doesn't always stifle their desire to feed. On several occasions I have caught bass on the same lures and in the same spots I had caught them before a front approached.

My first major tournament win, on Georgia's Lake Lanier, is a good example. The fish were in a fall pattern and gearing up for winter. The area received a lot of rain the week before practice, so the water was muddy. The lake was cooling down and the fish were starting to move shallow and toward the creeks.

By targeting deep bluff banks upriver on the main channel, I actually caught more fish during the competition than I did during the entire practice session.

That's because the cold front stopped the fish from roaming up and down the banks. Instead, it locked them onto structure, and tight to fallen trees and rock points along the bank. I caught most of my big fish by repeatedly casting a slow-rolled spinnerbait and crankbait to each spot.

Lure Presentations

Whether it's caused by a jig dropping in front of their face or by a spinnerbait whirling nearby, most bass are caught on what I call "reactionary strikes" during cold-front situations. Although bass may not feed as often, you can still make them strike.

When I'm fishing a reservoir after an early-fall cold front, I head for the creeks, turn the trolling motor on high and cast either a spinnerbait or shallow crankbait.

The key is to make as many casts as possible to solid objects—logs, stumps and rocks—to determine whether the front had a positive effect on the fish, which it can at that time of year. If the high-speed approach doesn't work, I'll slow down and fish each piece of cover more thoroughly with jigs and worms.

Later in the fall, a front may push the bass halfway out of the creeks, or closer to the drop-offs in the same types of areas they used during the pre-spawn staging period.

Then, I'll slow the presentation and toss more suspending-type crankbaits, jerkbaits or slow-roll a spinnerbait through likely spots.

I like lures that have action built into them, or allow me to impart action to them. I use a lot of stop-and-go presentations this time of year, because an erratic, yet enticing, retrieve gives the fish more time to look at the bait and a better chance to catch it.

Suspending baits work best because a lure that hangs right in front of the fish on the pause will attract many more strikes than one that floats away.

Although jigs and soft-plastics are popular and productive cold-front baits, I don't think you can beat a crankbait for triggering reactionary strikes from sluggish bass in cold water. The crankbait's action and the way it deflects off stumps, logs, brush and other hard cover triggers a lot of big, neutral largemouths into biting.

BUMPIN' COVER

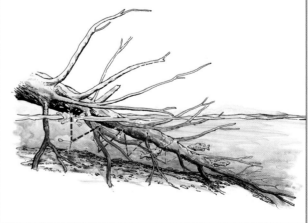

On post-front, bluebird days, make multiple casts to fish holding tight to cover. Allow the crank or spinnerbait to bump the cover, then stall or fall slowly.

VanDam's Tips for Fall Cold Front Bass

RESERVOIRS

Early Fall

1. Cast spinnerbaits or shallow-diving cranks to solid objects in the creeks. Lots of casts, cover water.

2. If the high-speed approach doesn't work, slow down and fish objects with jigs and worms.

Late Fall

1. Cast suspending cranks and jerkbaits or spinnerbaits to structures halfway out of creeks, or to drop-offs.

NATURAL LAKES

Early Fall

1. Weedbeds on shallow flats—Fish jerk baits over the thickest part of the bed. Erratic retrieves are best.

2. Weedbeds on deep flats—Grubs and Carolina-rigged worms fished as close to the bottom as possible.

Late Fall

1. Look for bass in weedbeds on deep inside turns close to the bank or a major flat.

However, if I have to slow down or believe the bass are in thick cover, I'll go to a jig-and-pig or a lizard. These are good lures for stained water because their bulk displaces a lot of water, which means more vibration to help the fish find them more easily.

I also consider the lake's forage base when choosing a lure. If I catch a bass that has a shad sticking from its mouth, I'll fish crankbaits, spinnerbaits and jerkbaits. I know the bass are keying on that type of forage and I will choose colors accordingly.

Now, if I see a crawfish in a bass' throat, or find pieces of regurgitated crawfish in my livewell, I switch to a jig-and-pig or another type of lure I can keep right on the bottom.

Whichever lure you choose, make multiple casts to heavy cover. Never give up after one or two casts, especially when fishing after strong cold fronts. I've seen times when it took 10 or more casts to the same spot to produce a fish.

Lake Bass

Bass in natural lakes don't have creeks or a lot of woody cover available, so they hold in weedbeds on shallow flats during the fall feeding period.

A cold front may push them into the thicker part of the weedbed, or move them to weedbeds on deeper flats. Later in the fall, a front will often force them even deeper into the weeds where they stack up in inside turns. I target turns that are closest to the bank or closest to a major flat.

Under normal conditions, crankbaits and spinnerbaits produce best in clear, natural lakes during the fall, but after a cold front, I tend to do better with jerkbaits and soft-plastic lures.

When I suspect fall fish in a clear lake are holding shallow, a jerkbait is typically my first choice. Because I can work one of these lures erratically and keep it in the zone longer, it definitely increases my chances of triggering a strike. In fact, it's the best "reactionary" lure you can use in clear water.

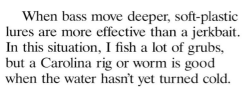

When bass move deeper, soft-plastic lures are more effective than a jerkbait. In this situation, I fish a lot of grubs, but a Carolina rig or worm is good when the water hasn't yet turned cold.

Bass in cold, clear lakes are driven toward deeper cover by a cold front, and tend to spend more time on the bottom, so keep your lure as close to the bottom as possible.

I also downsize lures, opting for 4-inch, straight-tail worms, tube jigs and centipede- or french fry-style baits that have little or no built-in action. I simply drag these lures along the bottom. Natural colors like browns, greens and various translucent hues are more subtle and seem to work best on these negative fish. In clear water, the object is to disguise the lure so the fish sees and is attracted by the movement of the lure, but doesn't get too good a look at the bait itself.

Thin-diameter monofilament helps, too, especially when you're fishing these smaller baits. Heavy line dampens the action of light lures, making the motion appear less realistic.

I also think about line color, especially when I'm faced with clear, shallow water. When bass are fussy, I can't afford to take any chances that might spook them. In my opinion, clear line is the only way to go in this situation.

When the water is stained, though, I'll fish a superline, like Berkley's FireLine. The low-stretch quality allows me to feel soft, subtle strikes from bass that aren't very aggressive. And the water color helps hide the line from the fish's view.

Finally, it's also important to keep a positive attitude when faced with a cold front. In fact, it may be the most valuable tool you have. If you truly believe you will catch fish no matter what the obstacle, you're much more apt to be successful.

Also, it will help to keep in mind that a cold front may even make bass bite better this time of year. If you think positive, you'll be surprised at the number of largemouths you can catch.

VanDam keeps all options open by rigging a number of rods with various lures. When cold-front bass are holding shallow, though, he reaches for a jerkbait, which hangs in the strike zone like no other lure, he says.

Big Bass ... Little Waters

by Spence Petros

*Sometimes you've got the urge to fish but only have an
hour or two to spare. No problem...thousands of small waters all over the
country hold outsized bass, and here's how to catch them.*

When I slid into my car, the first natural heat I had felt in four months hit me. The sun's radiant energy on this unseasonably warm mid-March day had raised the temperature inside my vehicle, and at the same time, got my bass-fishing juices flowing.

In spite of numerous outstanding fishing trips I've taken to exotic places, and even though a fully-rigged boat was sitting in my garage, I knew it was pond time—a period when pint-size waters offer king-size bass-fishing opportunities.

You say you're not interested in catching 1- or 2-pound bass? Good. Neither am I. These small waters, whether natural ponds in Ohio, dammed creeks in Alabama or stock tanks in Texas, can produce surprisingly large fish. Just take a look at a list of the state-record bass and you'll see that an awfully high percentage of them came from ponds.

I've caught hundreds of pond bass in the 2- to 5-pound range, and dozens more that topped 5 pounds, including my largest-ever northern-strain large-mouth—a 7¾-pound brute.

Another great advantage is that you can often fish a pond on short notice. Even if you don't have a full day, you can experience a successful pond outing after supper, during a lunch break or "on the way to the store" (sorry it took so long to pick up the milk, honey).

> "A bass doesn't need much
> space to pack on pounds."

Another plus: pond fishing is inexpensive. A rod and reel, a small box with a few lures, a short drive and you're in business.

All you have to do is find water to fish. Many pond owners will grant access to a courteous, relatively neat-looking angler. For your part, just remember to abide by the owner's fishing rules and make sure you leave the spot cleaner than you found it.

Many states stock private waters with the stipulation that the public be allowed to fish. Check with your state fisheries or conservation department to see if a list of participating pond owners is available for your area.

While farm ponds are top prospects, "Forest Preserve" waters, highway excavation ponds, retention ponds around housing projects, park ponds, water hazards on golf courses and cemetery ponds all hold excellent potential. A bass doesn't need much space to pack on pounds.

Think Warm!

Catching bass while other anglers are just thinking about it is a lot of fun, but there's more to it than finding a pond and casting a line. Certain guidelines will help make your trips more productive. For one, think warm! Fish during the warmest parts of warm days in areas where the water temperature rises first.

No need to start early. When water temperatures are in the low 50s or below, the hottest action usually occurs in the afternoon, with warm, sunny days being the best. As the sun sets and its rays begin to strike the water at a low angle, action slows quickly.

What you're looking for are areas where the water is warmer than anywhere else in the pond. The ultimate spot is a sun-drenched bay that has a

Small ponds can produce some trophy bass. Trophy bass are caught each year in small ponds across America.

dark bottom, stained water and is protected from the wind. Usually, all these conditions don't exist in one spot, but you should be able to locate areas where most factors are present.

Many times, an incoming creek will pour warm, stained water over a shallow flat. If you find such a spot, fish cover such as wood, weeds, overgrown banks or anything else that presents a casting target.

I've also caught bass that were relating to shopping carts, milk crates, bed springs, pallets, broken docks, sunken boats and assorted car parts from ponds in or near urban and suburban areas. While it's never good to have such things discarded in this way, it does prove that just about any cover located in the right area can hold large bass.

Shallow, protected bays, marshy backwaters and canals are also prime spots in the early season. By "protected," I mean areas that are necked down to reduce water movement into them or aren't exposed

Edges, whether found in a big lake or a small pond, offer the best chance at a big bass. Don't pass up any shot at fishing an edge.

to prevailing winds. An area ringed by high weeds might be just such a spot.

Ponds in low areas often have shallow, swampy, dark-bottom bays. These muck-bottom, marshy areas heat up fast in the spring sunshine and draw early-season bass like magnets. Those that have at least 1½ to 2 feet of water are best. Bass won't spawn on the soft, silty bottoms, however, so they draw fish only during the first few warming trends of the year.

Man-made canals are another great early-spring spot, especially if they dead-end in a T or L shape. The back ends, which are protected from most water movement, heat up quickly and draw hungry bass looking for forage fish. Canals often have firmer bottoms, at least along the banks, making them prime spawning sites.

Vegetation in an early-to-warm bay can also produce fish. An old reed or rush bank, especially when the stalks are broken and laid over, may harbor a school of aggressive pre-spawn bass. A cattail or willow-lined bank, fallen tree or remnants of old submerged weedbeds are also good bets.

An "erosion cut" or small feeder creek that funnels water into the pond can draw bass anytime a hard rain or heavy snow-melt produces a lot of runoff. In clear-water ponds, I've seen strong mid-summer rains muddy the water around a feeder mouth. The bass come right into the shallows and gobble up everything in sight.

Also remember to check rocky banks near the pond's outflow, especially when the sun is shining and the water is calm. Even though this rock-studded bank usually borders the pond's deepest water, it still holds great potential. Another often overlooked spring hotspot is a deeper hole or pool in the outflow creek below the spillway.

Some well-manicured ponds lack wood, large rocks or thick weedbeds. Here, bass usually hold tight against a bank overgrown with vegetation, and will also suspend in the shaded area under a large willow growing on the shoreline. Cast parallel to the grassy bank and maneuver small, slow-moving lures under the overhanging branches.

Ponds commonly have bottoms covered with sandgrass, a short (six to 18 inches) weed that looks like dill. This plant, which never really dies off, starts to draw bass when the water temperature reaches about 50 degrees. Pre-spawn bass will cruise the sandgrass flats and may even use them for spawning.

Managing Your Own Pond

Catch-and-release is critical if you want your pond to yield big fish consistently.

*E*ver thought of owning your own bass pond? It's surprisingly simple if you have the space and the right soil type. A local excavator will charge a couple thousand dollars to dig a quarter- to half-acre pond, or you can be a bit more extravagant if you have the budget. I know a guy who spent a hundred grand to build his dream pond.

Assume your pond should be at least 10 to 12 feet deep, otherwise it could freeze out during a harsh winter (in areas of extreme temperatures), or become oxygen starved during a long, hot summer. Installing an aerator is often a good idea, north or south.

When digging your pond, make sure it has a 3- to 4-foot deep bay to serve as a spawning area for a variety of fish. Spread gravel, pea stone or No. 6 rock in the bay to maximize spawning potential. The rest of the pond can have sharper-breaking banks to inhibit weed and algae growth.

A new pond can be stocked with 3- to 4-inch bass, while an established pond should get 6- to 8-inch bass. About 100 bass per acre is generally recommended, unless you're trying to create a trophy fishery. Then, reduce it to 75 bass per acre so there's less competition.

Also, when the time comes, release any bigger fish you catch. It's relatively easy to fish out smaller waters.

It's also important to feed the bass to get maximum growth. Fathead minnows are inexpensive and will spawn several times a year. Shiners are also excellent forage that big bass love, but they cost considerably more than fatheads.

If you want a bass/bluegill pond, stock hybrid bluegills (cross between a male bluegill and female green sunfish), which are more easily controlled than standard 'gills since nearly all are males. When stocking standard 'gills, use only five pairs per acre. Any more and you risk overpopulation.

To maintain the correct predator-to-prey balance, remove four pounds of bluegills for every pound of bass taken from the pond. This is also important to keep the 'gill population in check.

Many pond owners would like their own catfish fishery; plan on about 50 cats per acre if you plan on harvesting them. If not, go with 25 or so per acre.

Cover is essential to any fishery. Weighted hardwood trees and pallets tied together make excellent hiding areas. Avoid evergreen trees because they can turn the water acidic.

A lot of what you need to learn about managing your own pond can come from your state department of conservation. And chances are they will have a list of hatcheries in your area.

I also recommend you get your pond-building plans approved by them prior to building. That way, you can conform to whatever regulations apply in your area.

—Spence Petros

FINDING BASS IN PONDS

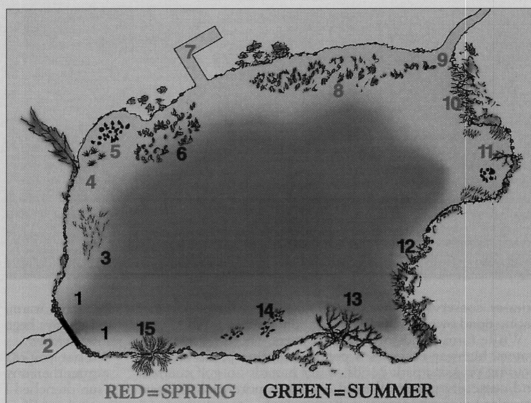

RED = SPRING   GREEN = SUMMER

1. Riprap bank (all season), **2.** Hole below spillway, **3.** Sandgrass flat close to deep water, **4.** Mouth of an erosion cut, **5.** Shallow, marshy area, **6.** Submerged weedbed (cabbage, milfoil) bordering deep water, **7.** Man-made canal, **8.** Sandgrass flat, **9.** Inflowing creek, **10.** Overgrown bank near creek mouth, **11.** Shallow, dark-bottom bay, **12.** Overgrown bank near deep water, **13.** Fallen trees near deep water, **14.** Weeds near deep water, **15.** Big willow tree.

Many ponds, especially in the South, offer all the fish-attracting features of this example. Even if the pond you fish is smaller, it's sure to have some of these characteristics. Target these key areas and you'll catch bass on any pond.

Sandgrass flats are also major nighttime hot spots in the summer.

Summer Success Strategies

As the seasons change and water temps rise, switch your focus from warm-water shallows to the best-looking cover near the deepest water. Bass may still be found on the flats under low-light conditions or at night, but it's a low-percentage game.

Cover in the cooler half of the pond, for exam-ple, would be more productive during the warm months than that in the half that warms first in the spring. Check the overgrown bank, weeds, wood, etc. that are close to deep, cool water.

Deeper bays can draw bass, particularly early or late in the day. If there's no cover, cast parallel to overgrown banks. Banks adjacent to at least a few feet of water can be hot. If high water levels submerge a grassy or weed-lined bank, keep a tight grip on the rod handle when working the edge. This is a real hotspot.

To learn the depths of a pond and to locate any concealed cover, quietly walk the bank and make casts with a sinking lure. A slip-sinker worm rig, spinnerbait or jig-and-plastic combination works well. Begin counting each cast after the lure hits the water. Stop when it settles on the bottom and the line goes slack. The longer your count, the deeper the water.

Because of their tremendous sensitivity, the new low-stretch superlines work well for pinpointing underwater jewels. Not only can you tell rocks from wood, you'll note size differences, too. With practice, you'll also be able to differentiate between various types of weed growth.

> *"In clear-water ponds, the best summertime action usually occurs very early or late in the day."*

During the hot months, tall weed-beds or thick slop may cover areas of a pond. These isolated patches of extremely heavy vegetation are prime hideouts for summer bass, but I generally avoid waters that are totally choked with weeds. The fishing is much too frustrating. Hit these ponds early in the year, before the weeds get too thick.

In clear-water ponds, the best summertime action usually occurs very early or late in the day, or at night. Once the sun penetrates the surface, it's often a waste of time to challenge gin-clear waters. If you can't fish during the low-light periods, stick with dark-water ponds that shield bass from intense sunlight.

Catching Pond Bass

My bread-and-butter lure for early-season bassin' is a ¼-ounce spinnerbait with a silver Colorado blade. I start with a white skirt in clear water; chartreuse in stained water.

A slow, bottom-brushing retrieve usually tempts the most strikes in the chilly waters of early spring. Rolling the bait over cover typically pays off a few weeks later. A fast, near-surface retrieve may be best for active, warm-water bass. Once the water warms up, larger, tandem-blade baits are best for fishing around cover in stained, shallow water.

Flooded shoreline grasses and thick, matted weedbeds require weedless lures. My top two choices are an unweighted, 6-inch Slug-Go and a Snag Proof Tournament Frog.

The jerkworm is highly versatile and can be dragged over cover, darted through open areas and allowed to sink into holes. I particularly like the Tournament Frog for pond fishing because it doesn't disturb the surface when cast, and you can activate its rubber-skirt legs with a slight twitch of the rodtip. Plus, there's no plastic behind the hook that might interfere with the hookset.

I fish both lures on superlines, and get plenty of distance and hooksetting power with a 6½- to 7-foot spinning rod.

Topwater lures work great in ponds, but fast, erratic actions usually don't produce well in waters that have had much fishing pressure. In this situation, success usually comes early or late in the day on prop-type surface lures retrieved at a slow to medium-steady pace. No jerks or twitches—just a straight retrieve, with the blades bulging the surface.

Want to catch the "king" of the pond? Fish a muskie-size Jitterbug after dark on a warm, calm, summer night, with heavy baitcasting gear to match this oversize lure. Be sure to wait at least 30 seconds after the lure's monstrous splashdown to give the bass a chance to regroup, then use a slow, steady retrieve.

For rooting fish out of cover, go with a jig-and-worm, jig-and-pig or Texas-rigged worm. They're also good for teasing less aggressive bass into hitting. I prefer ⅛ to ¼ ouncers.

Shallow-running minnow imitators such as a Rapala, Rebel Minnow, Rogue or ThunderStick can be twitched next to cover to draw a bass out, or with the rod held high, reeled over submerged vegetation.

About the only popular bass lure that I haven't had much success with when fishing ponds is the lipless, vibrating crankbait. It swims past cover too quickly for the bass to react, and it hangs up easily.

First Of The Year

Whether they give you a jump-start on other anglers, or simply allow you to take advantage of limited free time, ponds can fill a void in your fishing calendar. The bass are there—all you have to do is go catch 'em.

Big Bass: Rivers

by Clark Montgomery

Throughout our country, somewhat secretive "river rats" slide boats into unheralded rivers and catch big bass. You too can get in on the action.

Some mornings you just know the bass are gonna bite. A fishing buddy describes it as "that spooky feeling," an undeniable electricity crackling through the ozone just before the big one logs on. I felt it when I saw the narrow passageway through dense shoreline trees. Even before I got a close look at it, I knew a pot o' largemouth gold lay at the end of this trail.

A shallow river cove became evident as I pulled my aluminum boat out of the current and killed the outboard. Dropping my trolling motor in, I maneuvered carefully through the shallow cut, ducking to avoid the tangled tree branches.

> *"... a slow, rolling wake oozed out of the sunken timber. A huge bass swirled ..."*

Soon the tunnel opened to reveal a miniature lake, actually the remnants of an old phosphate mining pit. Here the water was three feet deep, tannic-stained and studded with ancient cypress stumps. If Webster had a listing for "bass hole" in his dictionary, a picture of this place would be next to it.

I picked up a baitcasting rod rigged with an old wooden topwater prop bait, the kind that gurgles on the surface like a bullfrog with the shakes when you chug it. As I cast, a great blue heron took off from a tree beside me, squawking as its broad wings slapped the thick morning air. Surprisingly, my cast landed exactly where I wanted it to—right next to a fallen tree—but I was so rattled that I backlashed the reel. Cussing under my breath, I laid the rod lengthwise across my knees and began picking at the bird's nest.

The ripples from under the plug hadn't even subsided before a slow, rolling wake oozed out of the sunken timber. A huge bass swirled beneath the lure, then sucked it in.

All I could do was lift the rod and jerk weakly as the bass, too massive to jump, churned on the surface. I tried to crank the reel handle, but the backlash had the spool locked tight. The fish bulldozed back toward the sunken tree, parting my line with a loud pop.

I sat there a moment to regain my composure, then straightened the backlash before I went back to fishing. I managed to catch and release six fat largemouths that day, with a total weight of nearly 30 pounds. When the bite ended around 2:30, I trailered my boat and drove to the marina at a nearby reservoir, where some friends were competing in a team bass tournament. My buddies weighed in four bass totaling about 12 pounds; the winning team had seven weighing 18 pounds, 3 ounces.

I didn't bother to tell my pals about the fish I'd caught in the river pit that morning, nor about the 11- or 12-pounder that had snapped my line. Wouldn't have done any good anyway—they were already planning for next weekend's team tournament being held at another reservoir.

Underfished Treasures

Nationwide, rivers are underfished bass treasures. Today, many bass anglers focus their efforts on big reservoirs or lakes, where they race around in high-powered bass rigs and cast for cash, not lunkers.

River bassin' is a different ballgame. Some of the best bass rivers are too shallow for a 20-foot tournament boat to navigate. Others are hundreds of miles long, intimidating to all but the most dedicated anglers. Still others flow right through major metropolitan areas and most anglers figure any place that close to home couldn't possibly hold big bass. They don't know what they're missing.

"River bassin' is a different ballgame."

"I started fishing rivers 20 years ago," Murfreesboro, Tennessee, bass expert Joey Monteleone told me recently. "I bought a 10-foot aluminum johnboat at a yard sale, slapped an electric trolling motor on it and began exploring some of the small, shallow rivers near my home. To my surprise, I started catching big bass."

Monteleone had never caught a lunker largemouth before he started fishing moving water, but he quickly realized he was on an untapped mother lode of big fish.

"About a month after I bought my boat, I caught a 7-pound largemouth from a river running right through a subdivision in town. I went back the next afternoon and caught an 8¼ pounder."

WORKING COVER LIKE WOOD IS IMPORTANT FOR BOTH LARGEMOUTHS AND SMALLMOUTHS.

River bass specialist Joey Monteleone was shocked by the size of the bass he found in small rivers. He's taken largemouths as big as 10 pounds in waters just like this, as well as huge smallies.

At first, Monteleone told fishing acquaintances about his success, but was taken aback by their reaction.

"They thought I was blowing smoke," he recalls. "One of them said, 'I've been fishing Percy Priest [a nearby 14,000-acre reservoir] since it was impounded and have never caught an 8-pound largemouth. Do you expect me to believe you caught one that big from some piddlin' river?'"

Since then, Monteleone hasn't bothered to talk river bassin' with nonbelievers. He's been too busy learning all he can about moving-water largemouths and has become an expert at catching them in the process.

Unpressured, Not Remote

Many of the rivers Monteleone fishes are totally unpressured, but that doesn't mean they're remote—quite the contrary. Most of them run right through metropolitan areas.

The Tennessee basser recalls a trip that he made last spring to a river near Nashville. "One fall afternoon, I was floating a river that flowed right through a residential development. As I rounded a

bend, I could hear a football game on the radio. A group of neighbors had gathered at one of the riverside homes and was listening to the game on the back deck, which hung out over the river. It is one of my favorite spots."

Monteleone drifted silently past them, cast a spinnerbait at a dock piling and hooked into a big bass.

"Most of the places I fish don't even have launching ramps!"

"I stuck my rod in the water so the fish wouldn't jump and make a big commotion," he laughs. "I didn't want the people on the deck to know the size of the bass that were swimming in their backyard."

Joey finally lipped the bass, a 9 pounder, and quickly slid it back into the river.

"Just as I was drying my hands, I heard someone call from the deck, 'Catchin' anything?' I replied, 'Just one.' They went back to their football game and I went back to my fishing."

The river expert mentions this episode to make an important point: "Today, fishing pressure is the number-one enemy of big bass. Lunker largemouths aren't common to begin with, and when you have a lot of experienced fishermen gunning for them, their population dwindles even more.

"The nice thing about rivers is, you rarely see anyone with a great deal of bass fishing skill on them, especially the small ones that I like to fish. I may float past dads and kids on the bank soaking crickets for bluegills or weekend catfishermen anchored in a cove, but I encounter very few knowledgeable bass anglers. Today, big lakes and reservoirs are the chosen venues for the vast majority of skilled bassers."

Many bass anglers start out fishing neighborhood streams and local rivers, but quickly abandon the pursuit once their interest and expertise in the sport grow.

"The lure of bass boats and tournaments pulls most bassers away from moving water," Monteleone figures. "When a guy decides he wants to get into bass fishing, the first thing he normally does is go out and buy a bass boat with all the bells and whistles. Then he joins a club with other like-minded fishermen and starts fishing their weekend tournaments. Before long, he's locked into big-water fishing. You sure as heck can't run a bass boat 60 mph in a shallow river. Most of the places I fish don't even have launching ramps!"

Targeting Stream Bass

You may have some exceptional bass fishing right in your own backyard, says George Verrusio, an Indiana basser who has caught trophy-class bass from water you can jump across.

"Bass streams are even less pressured than rivers. They're sometimes hard work to fish, but they're worth it."

Verrusio says finding the right stretch of water is the stream basser's first challenge. "Largemouth streams run slower and are more stained than smallmouth streams. Often both species will occur in the same streams, but smallies like rock cover more than weeds."

Both species like wood, however.

"I've often caught a largemouth on one cast to a submerged tree and a smallmouth on the next."

Deep holes are a big plus for both species, Verrusio finds. "They provide sanctuary for bass, especially in clear streams and when the stream runs low in summer."

Fisheries personnel can get you off to a good start by recommending the best bass streams in your area.

"Talk to biologists," says Verusio. "They often electro-shock streams as part of their studies, and can tell you which ones hold the biggest bass."

Get a detailed county map of the area you plan to fish and study stream access points. "Streams can be easily fished out, so you need to stay away from heavily pressured stretches if you want to catch quality bass," George notes.

"Most fishermen access a stream where it runs close to a road or under a bridge, so avoid these areas. If there are no other access points, I generally wade a long distance from the road or bridge before I'll bother to start casting."

This stream basser has caught big fish wading both with and against the current. When he spots a likely piece of cover, he'll saturate it before moving on.

"Stream bass are like muskies—sometimes you just have to tick 'em off before they'll strike."

George doesn't use ultra-light gear in streams, favoring a long, stiff spinning rod and 8-pound mono instead. His favorite lures include soft plastic grubs on weedless leadheads, short finesse worms, tube jigs, small spinnerbaits, minnow imitations and buzzbaits.

Just a Select Few

Experienced river bassers know you needn't bring along a zillion lures to score big on bass. Joey Monteleone cites the following as his favorite artificials for lunker largemouths:

• **Jig-And-Pig**—"If I could have but one lure for river largemouths, this would be it. The combo is deadly in all water temperatures." Monteleone targets shallow shoreline wood with the jig. Favorite color? Black and red.

• **Floater/diver minnows**—"These are highly realistic lures that mimic small shad and creek minnows. Silver, gold and perch are usually the best colors. Cast them upstream, close to the bank, and retrieve with the current using erratic twitches to make the lure dart."

• **Small soft-plastics on leadheads**—"Grubs and shad bodies on leadheads are excellent in current. Not only are they the size of small river baitfish, they sink into the strike zone quickly."

• **Big crankbaits**—"Big plugs are better than small ones for river bass. They're more visible in murky rivers and their long lips bump off potential hangups like rocks and stumps."

• **Spinnerbaits**—"I'll fish these in the same woodsy places as jigs, and over shallow submerged grassbeds. They're especially good as the water warms into the low 60s. Use a chartreuse or yellow lure with a Colorado blade in murky water; a white, clear or green skirt and a willow-leaf blade in clear water."

• **Topwaters**—"Highly effective in smaller rivers. A buzzbait is awesome when fished around logjams, fallen trees and current-breaking rocks."

Potential For Giants

"A good river has far more potential for producing giant bass than most lakes," believes Bud Lawson, a big-bass expert from Dunnellon, Florida. He ought to know, he's caught scores of monster bass from the warm, slow-moving rivers on Florida's west coast, including fish up to 17½ pounds. "Rivers suffer from what I call the 'disbelief factor.' Anglers don't associate largemouth bass with current, and simply refuse to believe a river can hold big bass. The fishing media back up this belief by focusing 99 percent of their bass articles and video segments on big lakes and reservoirs."

Lawson encountered a potential world-record largemouth several years ago in a Florida river. "The bass was hanging around a shallow cove off the main current in clear water, and I got a real good look at her. I had a 15 pounder in my livewell when I saw her, but this fish was totally beyond that class—at least 24 pounds. It wouldn't surprise me at all to see a new world record come from a river some day."

What makes river bass get so big? Some scientists believe there are factors beyond lack of fishing pressure that can lead to the production of giants in moving water. Birmingham, Alabama, fisheries biologist Chris Stephenson cites a few:

> *"What makes river bass get so big? Fewer ups and downs, superior habitat and ample forage."*

Fewer Ups And Downs—"A river is a relatively stable environment year-round. It undergoes fewer temperature extremes over the course of the year than a lake or reservoir might. This lack of wide temperature swings can produce longevity in river fish. The temperature of a river is typically higher than that of a lake in winter and lower in summer. Plus, some rivers flow from springs which may fluctuate very little in temperature from month to month."

Superior Habitat—"Many rivers offer superior bass habitat. In the spring, high waters often flood remote backwater areas, providing good places for bass to spawn unmolested by fishermen. Their banks can be a tangle of submerged wood and aquatic grasses that provide excellent cover. Water quality is often superb, and rivers don't stratify in summer as do lakes and reservoirs—there's oxygen from the bottom to the surface. And well-oxygenated water allows a bass to feed heavily and grow all summer. Bass in shallower, oxygen-starved lakes will slow down, or even stop feeding when the levels get low."

Ample Forage—"Rivers offer a veritable chowder of forage, as anyone who's ever thrown a cast net into moving water can tell you. Bass don't have to move far to find a meal."

Where River Bass Lurk

Although bass are abundant in many rivers, they aren't everywhere. Our river experts agree that moving-water largemouths are relatively easy to locate, however. "Current concentrates bass," Joey Monteleone has discovered. "It puts them in predictable places. Once you know how to target these key spots, you can catch river bass anywhere. I've caught bass from the exact same kinds of places in rivers all over the country."

Largemouth bass don't cotton much to current, Bud Lawson adds. He says river largemouths are found in slack water places like:

Weedbeds—"Many rivers have abundant aquatic vegetation, and this is the first place I'd look for big largemouths. The weeds serve as a current break, provide cover and attract prey species."

Wood—"Shoreline stumps and bushes become submerged as the river's level rises; bass use these for current breaks. Trees and other driftwood that wash into the river during floods provide ideal bass cover. Docks and pilings serve as overhead shade and current breaks."

Backwater Pits and Ponds—"Some rivers have an adjacent network of pits or old ponds dug out for mining or agricultural needs. These offer a sanctuary

RIVERS WITH LARGEMOUTH ONLY

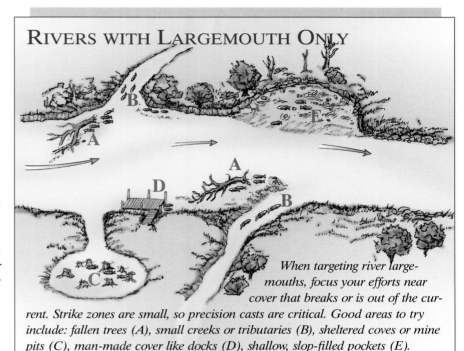

When targeting river largemouths, focus your efforts near cover that breaks or is out of the current. Strike zones are small, so precision casts are critical. Good areas to try include: fallen trees (A), small creeks or tributaries (B), sheltered coves or mine pits (C), man-made cover like docks (D), shallow, slop-filled pockets (E).

RIVERS WITH BOTH LARGEMOUTH AND SMALLMOUTH

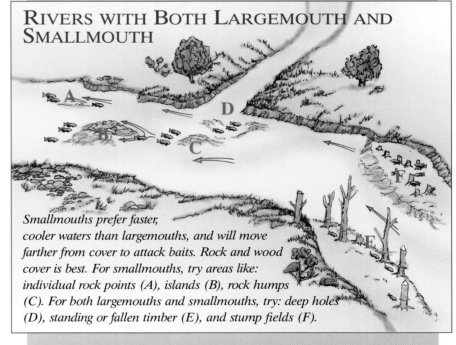

Smallmouths prefer faster, cooler waters than largemouths, and will move farther from cover to attack baits. Rock and wood cover is best. For smallmouths, try areas like: individual rock points (A), islands (B), rock humps (C). For both largemouths and smallmouths, try: deep holes (D), standing or fallen timber (E), and stump fields (F).

Make sure you check various edges around any piece of cover or structure. Bass may hold tight to and just upcurrent from cover, in addition to the area immediately downcurrent. Check the upcurrent and downcurrent edges of holes, humps, bars and bridge pillars. Anglers often ignore the thin band of slack water just upcurrent from a structure or piece of cover; that's where a bigger bass often holds to get the first shot at forage coming at her with the current.

Many of the best rivers lack improved landing sites, limiting the number of anglers. Small, lightweight boats shine on these waters.

from current and provide tremendous spawning grounds for river bass."

Shallow Sloughs—"These areas of diminished current are super bass spawning places. They run off the main river channel."

Bars—"These are shallow main-river structures subject to a thorough sweeping by current. The best bars have stumps, logjams or big rocks on them, which serve as current breaks."

Critical: Top Presentations

Presentation is the factor that most stymies new river bassers.

"Most bass fishermen just don't know how to deal with current," believes Monteleone. "Current can drag your lure way off its mark in a river, and that's a problem. River largemouths stay very tight

to cover. They may move only a few inches to grab passing prey. In moving water, the strike zone is often half the size of what it is in a lake or reservoir. Consequently, an accurate lure presentation isn't merely desirable, it's critical."

Monteleone calls pitching the ideal presentation for river largemouths.

"Generally, you can't reach the best spots with an overhand cast," he explains. "But you can easily pitch a lure beneath overhanging limbs or into the middle of a logjam.

"The pitched lure (generally a jig-and-pig) also enters the water quietly—another critical factor to river success. When you cast a heavy lure overhand, it slaps the water loudly and puts every bass in the area on alert. A pitched lure slides into the water gently.

"You can also pitch a lure farther than you can flip one, which comes in handy in clear water where bass may be spooky."

Boat Control

Boat control can be tricky in heavy current. NAFC member Jim Moyer, a bass guide on Kentucky's Cumberland River, uses two basic methods. When working shoreline cover, he points the nose of his boat into the flow and drifts downstream using his bow-mounted electric motor to both correct the drift and to maintain the proper speed. He works close-in, making short, accurate casts to shoreline cover or current breaks.

Moyer will also anchor, especially if he plans to fish a specific piece of midstream structure with live bait.

"I'll graph a mid-river hump, and if I spot bass on top, I'll circle back around and drop anchor well above the structure," Moyer indicates. "Once the anchor catches (Moyer uses a 35-pound hunk of iron train track), I'll let out just enough rope to allow me to reach the target zone with drifted bait."

Current Affair

River bassers are a special breed. They'd rather catch one wall-hanger than a livewell full of keepers. If you're tired of flogging your area lake or reservoir and catching nothing but small bass, why not explore a river near you? And when you catch more big bass than you ever dreamed possible, don't be surprised if you fall in love with current.

High–Low Largemouths

by Tim Tucker

Top pros discuss how they "go with the flow" to stay on bass despite shifting water levels.

*I*t can occur gradually, like seasonal clockwork—or it can happen overnight. The comfortable lake, river or reservoir level of today is transformed into a sea of mystery as rising or falling water completely changes life for bass and bass fishermen.

It then becomes a challenge for even the most experienced anglers to relocate concentrations of bass and coax them into striking.

Faced with such daunting situations, many bass anglers never even take their boats off their trailers. Going home is easier than trying to decipher water-level fluctuations. But those who tough it out are often rewarded; good fishing can be had with the proper approach, even during the most radical water-level changes.

"A bass is a bass and it will adjust to any environment—and fishermen must, too," says Gary Klein, a Texas pro who grew up on northern California's Lake Oroville, which typically fluctuates an amazing 90 feet a year.

Coping with water-level changes is often a matter of gauging the bass' reaction to them.

"Everything responds to fluctuations in varying degrees. With bass, it's a major reaction," explains Ken Cook, noted bass pro and former fisheries biologist. "Of course, a lot depends on how large—and fast—the fluctuation is."

It's therefore very important to make the distinction between gradual, seasonal fluctuations and the more drastic day-to-day transformations.

Seasonal Fluctuations

When spring rains slowly boost lake levels or the fall drawdown lowers a reservoir, anglers have time to fine-tune their responses to the fluctuating water table because bass make gradual changes in their location as the water rises or drops an average of

three to six inches per week.

Most man-made impoundments are lowered five to 15 feet in the late fall to prevent shoreline erosion and to serve as a buffer against spring flooding from seasonal rains.

Daily Changes

On large reservoirs, changes are usually more abrupt. This is particularly true of those managed by the U.S. Army Corps of Engineers on rivers like the Tennessee, Ohio, Kentucky, Mississippi and others.

The main purposes of these river lakes are commercial barge navigation and the creation of electricity, and fluctuations are the rule rather than the exception. Naturally, bass have learned to put up with the changes.

"The Ohio River—my home water—fluctuates two to three feet all the time," explains Joe Thomas, former Red Man All-American champion and NAFC Bass Advisory Council member. "So it doesn't really affect the fish as much as it does on lakes like Dale Hollow or Mead, which rarely fluctuate."

"On rivers like the Ohio, you can count on the water level fluctuating several times a week," he adds, "so you automatically adjust to it. Anglers quickly learn that when the water goes up, both bass and baitfish will go farther up into the milfoil beds. Conversely, when levels drop, bass predictably move to the outside edge of the grassline."

> *"Bass make gradual changes in their location as the water rises or drops."*

In a fast-changing waterway like the Ohio River, bass react instantly to the swift rise and fall of their environment. In lakes that fluctuate more slowly, however, bass are unaccustomed to such changes and may take longer to begin feeding.

Rising Vs. Falling Water

Most anglers prefer rising water conditions over the times when the bottom falls out of their lake.

"Rising water isn't much of a problem," Klein contends, "but falling water can be a nightmare, particularly on some types of impoundments at certain times of the year. The problem is locating the fish; dropping water moves them out of obvious places, and you really have to hunt for them."

Rising water creates some unusual structure—from picnic tables to roadways—but can also produce great bass fishing.

The Ultimate Fishing Book: Strategies for Success

Extremely low water can cause bass to suspend offshore—making it very difficult to locate and catch them.

Joe Thomas concurs.

"I think rising water is easier, because bass seek the new shoreline when the water goes up," he says. "They move into newly flooded areas where food is entering the water—and they're usually in a feeding mood."

But Cook emphasizes that there is a bright side to dropping water levels: current concentrates bass in narrow places or around main-lake points—where they can ambush forage and still access deep water.

Bass seem to adjust to rising water more quickly than to falling levels. Dropping water usually must stabilize for a day or two before bass begin feeding again. Not so with rising water.

Rising-Water Tactics

Several years ago, a national tournament on Texas' Sam Rayburn Reservoir was won by a pro targeting a group of recently submerged picnic tables. In 1995, Jay Yelas captured top honors in a major tourney on the Illinois River by working a newly flooded field of milo.

Those are just two examples of rising-water success stories. Why did they happen? As the water level climbs, it unleashes a massive bass migration

into the shallows. Once the water stabilizes, the fish scatter and utilize various forms of flooded cover.

"With rising water, bass' habitat is swelling, and their shallow-water comfort level increases," Cook says. "I think bass follow rising water into the shallows because the baitfish are drawn there. It is simply an enhanced opportunity for bass to eat."

This is good news to anglers because it concentrates bass in the shallows.

"Rising water is generally a positive thing because it eliminates a lot of areas to fish," says top pro and NAFC Bass Advisory Council member Kevin Van-Dam. "For example, in the middle of summer, a majority of bass will be offshore on deep structure. But if the lake comes up a foot or two and floods the bushes, most of the fish will move shallower. This allows me to concentrate on just the new cover—and forget about the old."

Increasing water levels can also improve fishing conditions when heavy rains warm the water temperature; cold rains have the opposite effect.

The proper tactical approach to most rising water situations involves fishing the newly flooded areas, although dense trees and brush sometimes make it difficult to reach relocated bass. Thomas works hard to penetrate such places with his boat,

RISING WATERS

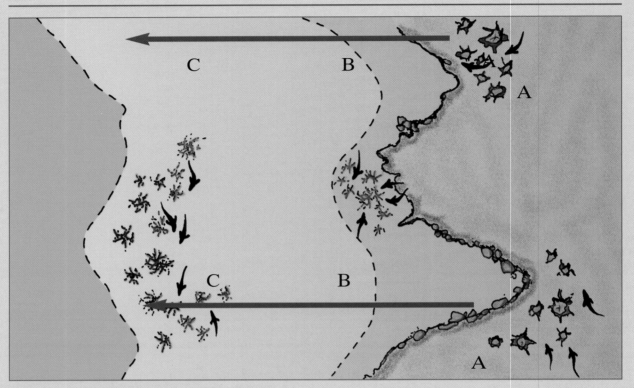

Largemouths quickly take advantage of the increased feeding opportunities rising water levels offer, moving from stable-level locations (A); into newly flooded cover (B); then to timber, brush and other forage-rich habitat (C) near the high-water mark. Fish are active, so fast-moving baits like spinnerbaits and buzzbaits are good choices.

but also looks for any vertical piece of shoreline like a levee or rock wall that will stop the fish's movement.

Other prime spots include cow pastures, grassy fields, and the extreme back portions of tributaries, where the flooding opens up new habitat, yet offers the clearest water.

This is especially important when rapidly rising water carries mud into the shallows, which dulls the fish's senses. Under these conditions, it is also wise to target shoreline brush and other vegetation that filters most silt.

"Clean water is a magnet for bass when a reservoir is rising," maintains Illinois pro George Little, who has his own tricks for finding such areas. "I always check my map for little pockets and inlets that are out of the current and likely to have the

clearest water. During increasing water levels, bass usually avoid main-lake areas, where the current is strongest and mud is thickest."

Since rising water usually requires covering new ground with fast-moving lures, the primary tools of both VanDam and Thomas are spinnerbaits and buzzbaits. For ultra-heavy cover, they switch to rubber-skirted jigs (also worked quickly).

Facing Falling Water

The annual autumn drawdown on most lakes pulls bass off of the banks, makes them suspend and forces baitfish into deeper water. This decrease in viable shoreline cover creates a major problem for anglers.

"Falling water can make the job of locating bass more difficult, because they will suspend off the bank—at times making them almost impossible to find and catch," VanDam says. "But it often positions bass in obvious places like points, the deepest pieces of cover or the deep end of a laydown."

As the water drops and the fish lose the cover they've been relating to, bass will become "insecure," according to Thomas. These fish are usually not aggressive and will hold as tightly to cover as possible before abandoning it. Bass in dropping water will relocate to deeper cover, bluffs, vertical points and banks, where they can more easily adjust to the changing water column.

To intercept these bass on their way to deeper water, the experts combine personal experience with a quality map and depthfinder in an attempt to locate structure at different depths.

The most likely stopping points include: long points, creek mouths that empty into main channels, the edge of flats, creek channels that touch a point, channel bends, ledges, humps, the outside edge of standing timber, stump fields and grass beds.

"Falling water demands using slow-moving lures to tempt cover-hugging bass."

Gary Klein has found that any structure or breakline which serves as an "edge against open water" is likely to attract bass adjusting to falling water.

VanDam keys on isolated objects, "like boat docks, fallen trees or long, tapering points that stick way out into a creek." But he cautions: "You have to spend time studying your map and running around looking for this visible cover, which might be one key dock on a point, or a couple of trees that have fallen into a channel bank."

Falling water demands using slow-moving lures to tempt cover-hugging bass. These include jigs, plastic worms, methodically fished crankbaits and slow-rolled spinnerbaits. Crankbaits and Carolina-rigged soft plastics are excellent tools for paralleling major points (from shallow to deep) to catch bass on their way out from shore.

FALLING WATERS

As water levels recede, bass abandon traditional shore-line cover (A); for slightly deeper cover (B); before making the transition to deep-water locations such as old creek channels (C).

When the fish are suspended and sluggish, the most productive tactic usually involves vertically presenting a jig, worm or jigging spoon.

All The Time

The bottom line is: Don't give up. Water-level changes can be confusing to fishermen. But with the proper outlook and an understanding of bass movement, rising and falling water situations won't seem so mysterious after all.

Super Shallow Bass

by Tim Tucker

Nothing is quite as thrilling as watching a big bass suck in your lure.
But these big fish don't come easy in shallow water.

Cruising out of the shoreline shadows, the big bass' back was barely covered with water. In the bow of our boat, Guido Hibdon snapped to attention as he studied this super-shallow largemouth, calculating its path.

It was late-winter on Alabama's Lake Tuscaloosa and this bass was taking a shallow stroll during the warmest part of the day. A 5 pounder or so, the fish slowly finned its way along the sandy bottom, cutting between a pair of boat docks that were about 40 yards apart.

As luck would have it, the bass was swimming away from our boat, oblivious to us. Hibdon quickly kicked his trolling motor into high gear to gain ground on the fish.

After closing the distance, his whip-like cast sent a tiny tube jig about 12 feet in front of the still-cruising fish. With deft precision honed by years of experience, he somehow managed to scoot the tube across the bottom so it intersected the bass' path.

One subtle twitch and the bass made an instinctive, but major, mistake.

"Can you believe how shallow that bass was?" Hibdon said, smiling, after landing and releasing it. "There was no more than 18 inches of water where that bass was swimming. That just goes to show you that sometimes we overlook bass in real shallow water. But there are shallow bass year-round in some lakes.

"For some people, shallow-water fishing—particularly sight fishing—is like hunting," Hibdon says. "We travel around and actually hunt for shallow, visible bass."

Stalking bass in skinny water is almost all visual work that involves casting to fairly obvious cover (the only cover where bass can hide in a given area) or to the fish itself.

"In super-shallow water, you have to take every-

thing into consideration, particularly sound and movement," says Claude Fishburne, a Georgia angler who has developed a reputation for catching bass in ultra-shallow water. "It forces you to take precautions that you hardly ever think about at any other time.

"Like down-sizing the blades on your trolling motor to eliminate the noise and amount of propulsion. If your prop is too big, it makes too much noise and pushes too much water, which can disturb the lake bottom," he continues.

"The clothes you wear can also make a difference. I usually wear dark clothes when I know the bass are real shallow and the water is fairly clear. I also worry about where my shadow falls on the water and whether the fish can see my rod or body movements."

Fishburne's concerns are valid because super-shallow fishing usually means dealing with good visibility—for both the fish and fisherman.

Shallow Seasons

Most experienced anglers agree that almost every lake will have some shallow-water bass throughout the year. But spring and fall are the seasons when thin-water bass will be most prevalent. And the early-to-late spring pre-spawn through spawn period is the absolute best time to gain some experience in dealing with the shallowest bass of all.

When bass hit the flats, it's much easier to pinpoint their location. Except for cruising fish, most bass will be near some type of cover or object—particularly vegetation and wood. Spawning bass are even easier to find, since they hold near cover with any hard-bottom openings.

Although it's not always possible to sight fish for super-shallow bass—especially when a steady wind

Big fish plus skinny water equals fun fishing!

puts ripples or waves in the water—veteran anglers will search an area for visible fish before working various pieces of cover.

Begin by scanning from the bank out to the point in the water where visibility decreases significantly. This is the zone you should concentrate on before moving deeper.

Super-shallow flats close to deep water are often the shoreline stretches where bass tend to congregate most, nearly any time of year. This combination of shallow and deep water allows resident bass to quickly switch depths in response to weather changes; it also offers fish easy access to shallow water for periodic feeding forays.

Here's something else to keep in mind: Shallow-

water fishing usually means coping with bass that are either stationary or cruising. Each requires a different approach.

Stationary Bass

Bass that are positioned tightly to cover are considerably easier to coax into biting than are moving bass. The best strategy is to cast a small lure well past the bass or cover and attempt to bring it in front of the fish with measured, subtle movements.

With spawning fish, the wisest method is to maneuver the lure (usually a tube jig or small rubber crayfish) onto the bed and allow it to remain there with only slight, occasional movements.

Anglers like Shaw Grigsby and Guido Hibdon understand the allure of such a presentation during this protective period and stress the importance of

immediately releasing male and female bass so they can return to their spawning duties.

"What you prefer to find is a fish that is stationary," explains Grigsby, an NAFC Bass Advisory Council member from Florida and an expert on catching bass in thin water. "You either see the fish by picking out a silhouette or shadow, or by picking out a slight bit of movement of the fin or tail. If you find a stationary fish, obviously, it is very much at ease. Those are the fish that you know you can catch."

An overlooked place to find stationary bass is in the shade created by large shoreline-growing trees. The bass use shade as cover while waiting for something to swim by. Overhanging willow trees are particularly productive, but make sure you gently pitch an unweighted plastic lure under the limbs.

Proper boat positioning is critical when fishing the shallows. When working cover that is likely to

SUNGLASSES: EYE ON SUCCESS

The newest breed of fishing sunglasses are light-years better, and more durable, than your old Foster Grants. And for shallow-water fishing, quality sunglasses are required equipment.

Quality polarized sunglasses help you see fish and cover under the water's surface. They also provide important protection from ultraviolet rays, which can cause eye strain or damage.

Here's what to look for in choosing a pair of quality fishing sunglasses.

Construction: Today's lenses are made of such materials as glass, polycarbonate, space-age resins and plastic. Resins are the most scratch-resistant, but glass still offers the absolute best optical clarity.

Lens color: Lens colors perform differently as light conditions change. In fact, you may consider switching sunglasses throughout the day to cope with different light intensity.

Gray is the least effective color; it slightly darkens the light and is only useful in the brightest sunshine.

Brown enhances the existing light conditions, making this a good, all-around lens color for fishing.

High-quality polarized sunglasses will help you see fish you never knew were there.

Amber is preferred for sight fishing and is the best choice for low-light conditions.

Vermillion intensifies colors and creates more contrast; good for foggy or hazy days.

Photochromic lenses lighten or darken depending on the amount of light entering the glasses. Photochromic brown is a good choice for fishing.

Price: Fishing sunglasses can range from $10 to $100 and more, especially if you need prescription lenses. It's worth it to pay more for quality lenses, but make sure you're not paying too much for style.

Keep a low profile, approach slowly, carefully scan.

harbor stationary bass, Fishburne keeps his boat at least 25 feet away (farther in super-clear water) and anchors the bow and stern in place.

"In real clear water, I position the boat far away from the bass so that the smallest amount of the boat is visible to the fish," he says. "I also try to anchor or position my boat so the glare on the water works in my favor and not the fish's."

Intercepting Cruisers

Most anglers sing a different tune, however, when it comes to shallow-water fish that are on the move.

"A cruising bass that is moving fast has probably been spooked and you might as well give up on it," says Grigsby.

If you think that a fish hasn't been spooked, it's worth a cast. Especially if it's moving slowly through the shallows, where it might be on the prowl for food.

"The key to catching a cruising bass is to try to get your boat in front of the fish and lead him. Don't try to throw your bait at the fish or just in front of it. I'll usually try to lead a cruiser by about 10 feet and try to make the bait cross the fish's path right when the fish gets there," Fishburne instructs.

The ideal boat position for a cruising bass is away and slightly in front of the slow-moving fish. According to Fishburne, this puts the angler in an ideal position for casting well in front of a cruiser.

"One trick I use is to skip a tube lure or a little grub across the water to get a strike from a cruising bass," he says. "A cruising fish will see and hear the commotion and think it's either an injured shad or another bass chasing a shad."

Another way to catch cruising bass is simply to wait and watch the fish, according to Dion Hibdon, a tournament pro who excels at shallow-water fishing. Dion resists the urge to make an immediate cast to a bass on the move; instead, he tries to predict the fish's path before jumping into action.

In off-colored water, when the bass is not visible, Dion uses the direction in which shad, perch or other forage are fleeing to gauge where the aggressive bass is likely to be heading. Then he picks a spot and casts well in front of the fish.

In crystal clear, northern smallmouth waters, bronze-backs can often be spotted like bonefish cruising the flats, often 50 yards away, or farther.

"If you think that a fish hasn't been spooked, it's worth a cast."

Savvy anglers rig up with 7–8 foot spinning rods and long-cast-type reels spooled full of quality 4-pound test line. Extra-long casts are made to intercept moving fish. Long range strikes are nearly impossible to feel, so when the bass goes down and turns, set the hook hard and reel like crazy to get a tight line.

Shallow-Water Baits

For super-shallow fishing, water clarity usually dictates lure selection.

When water is off-colored and sight fishing is not possible, surface or shallow-running lures that cover water quickly are the best choices. These include small topwater plugs like the Rebel Pop-R or Storm Rattlin' Chug Bug, soft-plastic jerkbaits like

GRIGSBY ON SHALLOW WATER

Although he's shown impressive versatility over the last 15 years of tournament fishing, Florida's Shaw Grigsby is considered one of the country's best shallow-water bass anglers. Here's the gear he uses.

TACKLE AND GEAR
Rod: Six-foot medium-action graphite Quantum Tour Edition model 604 spinning rod. "This is the perfect rod for shallow water because of its versatility. It is short enough to make skip casts beneath docks and overhanging trees, yet long enough to provide good hook-setting power with light line."

Reel: Quantum Bluerunner 20 or 40 spinning reel. "A no-frills reel that has the right size spool for making long casts and taking up line on the hook set. Also, it has a great front drag, which is important with light-line, shallow-water fishing."

Line: 10-pound-test green Stren. Use a Palomar knot.

Lures: "By far the best sight-fishing lure I've ever used is a G-4 tube made by Luck "E" Strike. I rig it with a No. 1 or 1/0 High Performance hook, with both internal and external weights."

Special Equipment: X55 Lowrance liquid-crystal depthfinder, Lowrance temperature gauge, Hobie polarized Sightmaster sunglasses (amber/yellow lenses), Drift Control Sea Anchor.

SPECIAL TIPS
Basic retrieve: "I usually cast the lure, engage the reel and watch my line as it falls. "The fish are not usually aggressive, so you often won't feel the strike; your line will just move off to one side.

"Once my bait hits the bottom or a ledge, I lift it up and allow it to fall again. Then, I'll bring it back by slowly swimming it. Most of the strikes occur as the fly starts to drop."

Sighting bass: "I scan from the bank out to about as far as I can see the bottom. And that's it. I'm not going to try to look (for fish) in five feet of water if I only have two feet of visibility."

Rigging tubes: "Pegging a ¹⁄₁₆- to ³⁄₁₆-ounce bullet weight above the tube bait gives it a fairly straight descent that is best suited for open water or for targeting individual cover when bass are fairly active. To make the tube spiral as it falls, I use a ¹⁄₃₂- to ⅛-ounce Quick Clip internal weight. That's a good motion for triggering strikes from inactive bass."

—Tim Tucker

the Slug-Go or Shad Assassin and even down-sized buzzbaits and spinnerbaits.

Another good bait in this situation is a floating worm. A simple, buoyant plastic worm can be used to cover lots of water, as well as to finesse individual bass into striking. The subtle qualities of floating worms (like the Zoom Trick Worm, Charm Assassin or Jawtec Rippin' Rattler) are perfect for working the shallowest bass habitat.

Floating worms are also an excellent choice in clear water.

The undisputed champion of ultra-shallow baits, however, is the small tube jig. This is particularly true for stationary bass, which can be badgered into biting with the subtle but tantalizing action of these over-grown crappie jigs on a light (¹⁄₁₆- to ⅛-ounce) leadhead or with a pegged bullet weight.

For cruising bass in shallow water, Guido Hibdon prefers a small crayfish imitation like his Baby Bug in natural shell or pumpkinseed. Other productive lures include a small plastic lizard, ringworm, grub, soft- or hard-plastic jerkbait and a straight finesse-type worm (rigged with a split-shot a foot or so above it).

But selecting the right lure is just one part of the overall strategy for probing super-shallow water effectively.

By studying the water and using the right approach, fishing the shallowest of bass waters doesn't have to be intimidating, it can be downright fun and productive—any time of year.

Timberrrrr Bass

by Tim Tucker

*Savvy anglers don't look at a stand of wood and just see a bunch of trees.
They've learned how to pinpoint the key areas and the best ways to fish them.
Here are the strategies and techniques you need to know.*

You know the names—Toledo Bend, Livingston, Santee-Cooper, Rodman, Truman, West Point, Rayburn—all world-class lakes that have provided a classic southern brand of bass fishing for several decades. Timber bass. These lakes are renowned for their fields of flooded timber.

There are others, of course.

Although aquatic vegetation has been the modern-day savior for many aging reservoirs, those lakes with the vast stands of bass-rich timber gave birth to several generations of fishing tales. Most are probably true.

The nucleus of these great bass fisheries began when huge forests were left intact as the reservoirs were flooded. The result is outstanding bass habitat because the timber provides excellent cover for bass as well as the food chain that supports them.

In fact, it's likely a bass will spend most or all of its life in timber—if the water is deep enough that the fish can adjust to changing weather conditions. In many cases, there is no reason to roam elsewhere since many largemouths even spawn on the horizontal limbs and fallen trunks of larger trees.

The beneficiary of this behavior is, of course,

bass fishermen who know how to mine flooded timber for its hidden treasure. An impressive example of what's possible occurred in October a few years ago on famed Sam Rayburn Reservoir in Texas, when veteran tournament pro David Wharton caught three 9 pounders (part of a five-bass, 32.97-pound limit) in a single day from a patch of standing timber.

"Standing timber is productive all year long," says tournament king and NAFC Bass Advisory Council (BAC) member Roland Martin, who guided on South Carolina's Santee-Cooper Reservoir before he moved to Florida. "Whatever the month, there is some type of pattern at some depth that will catch fish."

Giant fields of flooded trees can be overwhelming to some anglers, however. Many simply settle for fishing the outside edge instead of cashing in on the

riches hidden inside. That's a big mistake, according to experienced timber fishermen.

"Many people are intimidated by all the trees," says Harold Allen, a guide and top pro who has spent most of his life fishing the timbered reservoirs of Texas and Mississippi. "Intimidation will make them start running and gunning rather than setting

"Bass in flooded timber strongly relate to changes in the bottom contour."

up a game plan from the beginning. Fishing a timbered lake is quite a challenge, but certainly not impossible. Your success increases as you learn more about the cover and how bass relate to it."

Reading Flooded Timber

"The best thing about flooded timber is that it offers such a variety of places for bass to hide," says NAFC BAC member Shaw Grigsby, who learned to fish standing timber in Florida's Rodman Reservoir. "But that's also the worst thing about it. The first step to locating bass in flooded timber is to apply seasonal patterns just like you would with any other type of lake."

Harold Allen applies skills he learned while roaming the backcountry of East Texas.

"My ability to fish timber is based on my ability to read it. While walking through the hills and hollows one day, I noticed that certain kinds of trees grow in certain places. By learning what kind or particular size of trees are located in various places, like ditches and creek banks, you can zero in on the places where bass live."

Veteran Mississippi pro Paul Elias emphasizes that pinpointing the areas of flooded timber with the greatest potential begins by trying to understand what's below the water's surface. That process starts before he even gets into his boat.

When fishing new waters, Elias first drives around the lake to determine which type of terrain holds which size trees. He also likes to know where bigger trees grow.

A variety of baits, including soft plastics (pictured), spinnerbait, crankbaits and jigging spoons, will take timber bass. The key is selecting the right bait for the conditions.

SEVEN TIPS FOR HONING IN ON FLOODED TIMBER BASS

Here are seven ideas for eliminating unproductive water and focusing in on the best, likeliest spots:

Standing willow trees in southern reservoirs are usually found adjacent to a ditch or depression.

Barkless cottonwood trees are often found along an old creek bank.

Oak trees grow on hard, clay bottoms, while pine trees are rooted in sandy soil (and often indicate ridges where bass will spawn in the spring).

Cypress trees are almost always located along sloughs, bayous or small creeks. A clump of cypress trees usually indicates a shallow depression, while larger, scattered trees can mark a deeper slough.

A group of trees towering over others may indicate the presence of an underwater hump.

The way certain trees lean can indicate the bends of a creek channel that winds through the timber.

The size of trees can be a clue to the location of unusual features on the reservoir bottom. For example, a line of large trees may be growing on the edge of an old fencerow since farmers often leave bigger trees intact to serve as windbreaks. Also, the largest trees in an area may pinpoint an old hollow. They grow tall because of the extra nutrients that wash into the depression.

Sometimes you have to get right in there with them.

As with any type of lake, bass in flooded timber strongly relate to changes in the bottom contour. So this information comes in handy when Elias spots similar trees among the flooded timber. (See "Seven Tips for Honing In on Flooded Timber Bass" sidebar.)

"The key with flooded timber is to look for irregularities in areas that are otherwise uniform," continues Roland Martin. "Bass will roam throughout the timber, but hold on anything that's different, like a leaning tree inside a group of standing trees, for example.

"Probably the easiest way to find fish in standing timber is to locate a point, which, in itself, is an irregular feature and could have irregular features on it—like the edge of a creek channel. And if you can find a timbered point with the wind blowing in, you can bet there will be a bunch of baitfish and bass on it."

Two of Martin's favorite timber strategies involve targeting isolated patches of trees and individual trees of a different species from the surrounding wood. Any lone tree positioned off the prominent tree line is worth checking.

On large flats without significant variance in depth, pro angler Robert Hamilton of Mississippi is drawn to the bigger trees, which often hold the largest concentrations of bass. "Bigger trees are an irregular feature in themselves and any kind of irregularity is always a good spot to find fish, whether you're fishing timber or not," he says.

"Timber is one of the more interesting situations for fishermen," emphasizes Rick Clunn. "You have to learn to recognize the types of trees and then learn where those kinds of trees grow.

"You learn that cypress trees grow on sludge bottoms and birches grow around creek channels. Gradually, by looking at the trees, you learn to quickly recognize what type of situation you have beneath the water."

Shaw Grigsby uses a combination of his visual and electronic skills for seeking out bass hotspots in tree-laden waters. While he utilizes the clues that the visible trees provide, much of his searching time is spent weaving through the timber with his eyes

glued to the screen of his Lowrance LMS 350. He looks for changes in the lake floor, bottom structure at particular depths (depending on the season) and more subtle cover like an individual stump or rock pile.

Lures And Tactics For Flooded Timber

A variety of artificial lures can entice strikes from bass hiding in heavy timber.

The long-time standard timber bait is a plastic worm. Grigsby's favorite is an 8-inch version with a curlytail and enough bulk to swim through the tree limbs. He rigs it Texas style.

Other timber experts prefer even larger soft plastics.

Accomplished guide and tournament pro Chet Douthit, who learned the basics of bass fishing among the trees in Missouri's Truman Reservoir, relies on an 11-inch plastic worm summer through fall. He concentrates his efforts near larger trees positioned along creek channel edges in 25 to 30 feet of water and looks for big bass suspended about 10 feet below the surface. Swimming a large worm down along the trunks and through the limbs of these huge trees is a reliable way to catch fish during the warmest months.

It was in 1993 that Roland Martin discovered that a giant 9-inch Slug-Go was the ticket to catching the largest fish swimming in the timbered water of legendary Lake Baccarac in Mexico. Rigging the cigar-shaped lure with an 8/0 hook and tiny ⅛-ounce Florida Rig screw-in sinker, Martin fished the Slug-Go in the conventional fashion of a plastic worm at the base of trees in 5 to 10 feet of water.

Each morning, this tactic produced at least five bass weighing 6 to 9 pounds.

"A big ¾-ounce spinnerbait is also an incredible tool for fishing this kind of heavy cover," adds Rick Clunn. "It's a bait that you can work through the trees, limbs and brush, and it can be fished at almost any depth. Its versatility makes it a good bait for standing timber because you usually have to determine where the bass are positioned in the water column."

Crankbaits are surprisingly good tools for locating and catching bass in flooded timber, according to Paul Elias. And it is the type of lure that tree bass are least likely to see on a regular basis. They don't become conditioned to the sight and sound of crankbaits because so few anglers fish them.

"Crankbait fishing in timber is so aggravating that

most people won't stick with it," explains Elias, one of the country's foremost cranking authorities. "But there are a lot of benefits, especially in the hotter months.

"The main mistake people make when they're trying to crank timber is that they don't choose their casts carefully. If you just throw your bait into a mess of flooded limbs, you're going to have a hard time getting it back out. But if you pinpoint your casts, say, throwing along the side of laying timber or trees that are a little more horizontal, or in the small lanes between standing trees, you will have fewer problems."

Elias, whose favorite timber crankbait is a brown-and-chartreuse Mann's Model 79 Accu-Trac, emphasizes that a big-lipped diving plug will deflect off most limbs. If not, simply pause and allow your lure to float free before continuing your retrieve.

"Crankbaits are surprisingly good tools for locating and catching bass in flooded timber."

A buoyant lure with a large lip won't float straight up, but will back away from a wood snag. Make sure the hooks are razor-sharp, as bass will often suck them in as they are rising. Watch the line for a sign of a hit. If your larger lipped lure seems to be plowing into the wood too hard, go to heavier test line to reduce the lure's running depth, plus hold the rod top a little higher. Some anglers bend in or cut off the lead prong on the front treble hook to help reduce snags.

Two other potent timber lures are jigging spoons and jig-and-pork combinations. Jigging spoons are effective for catching deep, sluggish, suspended bass in cold weather because they can be fished vertically through the limbs and along the trunks with considerable precision. The jig-and-pig is a good choice for working trees growing on ridges and drop-offs, as well as for working fallen trees and stumps.

Nature provides the road map and technology supplies the tools for solving the mysteries and enjoying the bounty of flooded timber. With the proper approach, flooded forests don't seem so intimidating after all.

The Sun ...
How It Affects Bass

by Tim Tucker

Many bass anglers view bright sunlight as the "enemy."
But in reality it can help us catch more bass.

*I*t may be the most misunderstood and over-looked aspect of bass fishing. It has spawned some time-hardened wives' tales and half-truths that won't go away. Yet, it can provide anglers with a strategic edge too important to ignore. What could be so all encompassing when it comes to bass fishing? The sun.

Although we may not give it proper consideration as anglers, the sun is the center of the bass's world—just as it is in our universe. If you don't understand the relationship between bass and the sun, you are not taking advantage of one of nature's best guides to better bass fishing—if you will just follow it.

The Myths About Sunlight

Some myths die hard, particularly in fishing. Perhaps the most believed commandment in bass fishing is that fish are more active during the low-light hours of early morning and late afternoon, or during overcast conditions. Indeed, many bass anglers believe the best times to fish are when the sun is on the horizon or when skies are overcast.

A Texas research group conducted a several-month study that showed catch rates are considerably higher when the sun is shining compared to cloudy days. During the study, which was conducted over a span of several months, about 85 percent of the fish were caught on sunny days—which was disproportionately high for the amount of sunshine during the test period.

The results of this study do not surprise big-bass authority and noted naturalist Doug Hannon. The vast majority of his more than 500 10-pound-plus bass were caught between 10 a.m. and 2 p.m., the

brightest hours of the day.

"I caught them in the highest light time of the day," the Florida angler says, "and my overall success on fish of all sizes has been better on sunny days than on cloudy ones."

"My own studies have shown that bass feed much more during the daytime and especially toward the middle of the day. And when I question anglers about when they caught the biggest fish of their lives, nine out of 10 answered the middle of the day when the sun was the brightest. People have no trouble remembering the details of their biggest bass."

Although many large bass are caught during the midday hours, water color is a big factor. In heavily stained waters bass may feed best under sunny conditions. Yet in gin-clear lakes, lower light conditions can be the key when trying to encounter active moving bass. But even on these lakes, sun can be your aid, as it drives bass into shade where they can be pinpointed.

Another great fallacy about bass is that they "don't like" or avoid the sun because they lack lids to protect their eyes from bright sunlight.

"Bass are sunfish," says Ken Cook, a former Oklahoma fisheries biologist and past Bass Masters Classic champion. "They don't shy away from the sun simply because sunlight bothers them. But you would be surprised at the number of fishermen who believe that."

The Biological Facts

With the major myths out of the way, it is important to consider some biological facts about bass and the sun that you can utilize to a strategic advantage.

The most critical fact is that, when given a choice, bass will relate to shade on sunny days because it gives them a visual advantage over their prey.

"Most fishermen will be surprised to learn that the eyes of most gamefish, particularly bass, are very much oriented to bright light," Hannon explains. "Most people think bass can't see in the sun, so they seek the shade to protect their eyes. Pretty much the opposite is true."

"Bass have excellent color vision—almost as highly developed as our own. We lose almost all of our color vision in the dark. The same thing is true for bass, which tells you that they are primarily daytime feeders and hunters."

Sunlight can make bass easier to locate … by making them retreat to shade.

The biggest reason bass relate to shade is because the shadows provide a visual advantage, according to Cook. While a bass can see perfectly well in bright sunlight, shade actually enhances their ability to see sun-oriented prey like shad and bluegills. This improved visual acuity—not relief from direct sunlight—is one reason bass often hold in the shadows.

Another factor to consider is that shade provides protection from overhead predators like ospreys and herons, which cannot spot a stationary bass as easily in the darker water.

"Bass are primarily daytime feeders and hunters."

It is also important to understand that there are many different things that provide the shade bass utilize. It can be the shade created by physical objects such as docks, lily pads or surface mats of aquatic vegetation, or simply water depth. In clear Western reservoirs like Lake Mead, where submerged cover is minimal, bass will go deeper to reduce the amount of sunlight that reaches them.

The photo above clearly shows why bass prefer to hold in shady areas. Their prey, like these sunfish, is clearly visible against the light background while the bass itself remains well hidden in the shadows. Knowing how bass relate to cover is critical for fishing success.

Sun Strategies

"One of the most crucial things to understand about bass fishing is that bass, like most animals, relate to edges," Cook says. "Shade makes a very definite edge and bass will move along this edge to ambush baitfish from the shade."

Knowing how bass relate to both sunlight and shade provides an insight that all bass anglers can utilize to their advantage. Bright sunlight puts bass in pre-dictable places and even provides a hint of how each fish will likely be positioned—information that can help you make the proper lure presentation.

Cook always starts his fishing day by gauging the amount of sunlight penetration in his fishing waters before formulating his game plan for the day.

To measure it, he simply drops a white spinnerbait into the water and stops its descent when it disappears from sight. If the spinnerbait fades at the 10-foot mark, he knows that this depth is about 50 percent of the current light penetration (in order for him to see it at 10 feet, the sunlight has to reach the spinner-bait, reflect off it and travel another 10 feet upward—thus maximum light penetration is about 20 feet).

"Bass relate to edges. Shade makes a very definite edge."

That is a vital piece of information because he knows that the most active bass are likely to be holding around cover or structure in water shallower than the "50-percent" point of sunlight penetration.

When looking at shade from a strategic point of view, it is important to examine it similarly to the way you would survey a grassline or stump field.

"The shadow cast by an overhanging tree or a row of overhanging trees is seldom a straight line," says all-time tournament king Roland Martin, one of the first pros to use shade as the basis for entire patterns. "There will be parts of the shadow that stick out. Wherever that shadow intersects with other structure, like a grassline, is a key spot. That is an edge-on-edge situation.

"Whenever I look at a grassline, I always look for a point or pocket. And when a big shadow of a tree intersects with a weedline, that's a good ambush point for bass. Another thing to look for is any irregular feature on the shade line itself. If you have a line of overhanging or tall trees putting a shadow on the water, always look for little irregular-ities in the shade line. You want to fish any spot in a fairly uniform shade line where it forms a point or has a cut or sunny pocket in it. These irregularities can hold bass like a point or cut in a grassline."

Bankside Shade

The uniqueness of Martin's thinking toward sunlight and shade was clearly illustrated during a tournament

on Alabama's Lake Guntersville. Martin qualified by working a shade pattern that was completely different from the tactics of the rest of tournament field.

After checking a topographic map to pinpoint high, steep banks that were likely to cast a major shadow during certain hours of the morning, Martin put together a strategy based on fishing shallow milfoil patches that grew in the shade. Using a buzzbait and a plastic frog imitation, he targeted the shadows created by the largest trees over the milfoil and enjoyed a strike or two every 20 trees or so. All of his 25 bass came from these shady spots.

"No one ran a shade pattern the whole tournament," Martin adds, "despite the fact all you had to do was figure the angle of the sun, then look for the steep banks with the biggest trees, and follow the shadows of the trees. I followed the shadows out into this grassbed to find the concentrations of shad. The bass were nearby."

> *"The shade created ambush*
> *points for the fish."*

"It was a classic situation that I've seen in lake after lake. The shade created ambush points for the fish. Knowing that gave me an advantage. A lot of the fishermen were throwing frogs and buzzbaits in the grass early in the morning, but once the sun got up, they abandoned that method and went to flipping. But by working the shade on different banks, I was able to enjoy good fishing for several hours."

Into The Sun

For pro angler Joe Thomas, bright sunshine forces some automatic adjustments, as it usually moves bass tighter to cover, practically eliminating long casts and quick retrieves. For Thomas, it usually signals the time to begin flipping heavy brush, grass or docks. He moves his boat closer to the structure than usual and concentrates on dropping a jig, worm or plastic crayfish as quietly as possible into every shady spot.

Bass using shade will almost always face the sun, a fact to keep in mind when casting to that dark area beside a stickup, dock piling or log.

One of the most common mistakes made by fishermen working sun-drenched structure is allowing their shadows to fall near the shade. Thomas believes that a shadow from above creates the fear of an overhead predator in the fish, causing them to flee.

"Since the fish is looking into the sun and because your shadow naturally falls away from the sun, I like to fish into the sun or at least cross-sun," Thomas advises.

"Fishing into the sun, you have some visual problems yourself. Cross-sun is the ideal situation. For instance, if you are fishing a shade line, you can parallel it like you would a grassbed. That way, you present the bait to more fish. You can cast parallel to the shade line of a dock the same way. Another tip is to work these spots by bringing the lure through the sunlit edge and then the shade edge to determine which will trigger strikes.

"Little things like determining the fish's position at the shade edge or sunlit edge is the key to catching more fish than other people around you."

Understanding the relationship between bass and the sun, and putting that information to use, will help lead you to consistent bass-fishing success.

The old wives' tale about direct sunlight hurting a bass' lidless eyes is bunk. The truth is they can see very well in bright sunlight; a fact that should change the way you fish.

Too Thick To Fish

by Don Wirth

Don't let muddy water ruin your day. Sure, it can change things, but bass keep on feeding.
All you've got to do is adjust. Here's a good game plan for dirty-water success.

"Forget fishing tomorrow, Don. We got four inches of rain last night and the lake's turned to mud. It's too thick to fish!" The sad voice breaking the seemingly bad news over the phone belonged to Glenn, my bass fishing partner. Weeks earlier we had made plans to get together for some great bass action.

After telling Glenn we'd fish after conditions improved, I proceeded to finish packing my rods and hooked up my bass boat.

I knew Glenn hates to fish muddy water, so I didn't even try to talk him into going. Instead, I slipped down to the lake early the next morning and caught 50 bass by noon, a mixed bag of largemouths and smallies, some of which topped 5 pounds.

Muddy water doesn't make me sing the blues. In fact, I've grown to love chocolate-brown reservoirs and rivers. It took some mighty savvy bassin' men to show me the ins and outs of fishing dirty water.

If your heart sinks when your favorite bass water is rolling with mud, this article is for you. That's exactly the way I used to be, until I saw the light.

Not every body of water turns muddy after a heavy rain, but enough of them do to make this one of the most common, most frustrating conditions avid bass anglers face. Some lakes stay

muddy and some river-run reservoirs are chronically stained.

Of course, spring is one of the rainiest seasons of the year in many regions. Combine the dramatic decrease in water clarity with the normally low temperatures of early spring water and you've got tough conditions indeed.

The location of a body of water has a lot to do with how often, and to what extent, it may turn muddy. Lakes and rivers in low-lying areas tend to have especially silty bottoms, and may be so muddy that few anglers fish them for anything but catfish or carp.

If a river or lake is usually clear, but turns muddy following a heavy rain, chances are it's located in an agricultural area with intense runoff. Indeed, enough topsoil washes into our waters each year that it's a much larger problem than merely being an annoyance to avid anglers.

Deep, rocky reservoirs clear up the fastest. Weedy, natural lakes also clear quickly, as aquatic vegetation filters out suspended particles.

But instead of standing around waiting for a muddy lake or river to clear, a better tactic is to arm yourself with the knowledge needed to catch bass — mud or no mud.

Dance'n Lesson

The first time I really got excited about bassin' in the mud was during a trip to Pickwick Lake, Alabama, with famed fisherman and NAFC bass columnist, Bill Dance. Due to Bill's intense schedule, I'd been forced to book my trip with him months in advance, with no hope of last-minute rescheduling.

When I arrived and saw the lake was high and the color of a Tootsie Roll, I was extremely disappointed. I had looked forward to this trip for weeks and now my hopes of catching a bass — let alone photographing it — were low. "Don't worry!" he grinned as I shook my head. "These fish'll hit — just watch!"

Dance motored 20 yards from the launch ramp to some basketball-sized riprap near the dam. He cast a big, fat, metallic-blue crankbait up against the rocks. The first sound I heard was the lure clanking across a rock; the second was Bill grunting, "There he is!"

Immediately a 6-pound smallmouth bolted for the surface, then jumped. The fish crashed back into the water like a sack of spuds, shot under the

boat and fought deep for what seemed like an eternity. Bill eventually coaxed it to within lipping distance and boated the bronzeback.

"Cast right next to the bank," he instructed as he released the fat bass. I did, and a fish nailed my crankbait with the first turn of the reel handle. It jumped three times and nearly pulled the hooks out of the lure before I managed to swing it into Bill's boat. Dance was already into another big fish, a largemouth that rolled on the surface and threw the hooks. We guesstimated its weight to be 7 pounds.

"The fish crashed back into the water like a sack of spuds, shot under the boat and fought deep for what seemed like an eternity."

"Okay, now cast 10 feet from the bank," Dance said. When this cast failed to elicit a strike, he grinned. "See? They're right smack against the bank. They won't move out to grab anything! You've got to chunk it right where they can see it!"

What had started out to be one of the more disappointing fishing trips of my career had suddenly and remarkably turned into one of the most exciting. In all, Bill and I boated more than 100 bass, including a 7½-pound largemouth and a 6¾-pound smallie. And I broke off the biggest bronzeback that ever blasted my lure, a fish that pulled like a freight train before snapping my monofilament.

Of Baloney And Mud

Most bass fishermen abhor muddy water. Clear is good; stained even better. But mud? No way.

After that first experience bassin' in water that looked too thick to fish, I've changed my mind about fishing muddy water. Not only is it possible to catch quality fish, it's downright likely if you know what you're doing.

But succeeding in the mud requires that you dispel a couple of myths about bass behavior, such as:
• Bass hate muddy water and will leave it to seek out clearer water.

Don't stay home when the water is muddy. The bassin' can be superb!

• Bass rarely bite in muddy water and if they do, they are rarely aggressive.

Baloney!

Bass are not prone to migrate. One reason bass are the most popular gamefish nationwide is that they're capable of surviving (and thriving) under an amazing array of conditions. Rather than swim 25 miles down the lake in search of clearer water, bass will adapt to muddy conditions. And, as Bill Dance proved to me, once you locate the fish, it's easy to get them to bite — and bite hard.

Finding The Fish

I've caught big bass in muddy lakes in a foot of water. But once the water clears, these same fish move deeper. Why do they move up when it's muddy? Simple! So they can see better. There's more light penetration in one or two feet of muddy water than in 12. And—never, ever forget this — a bass is first and foremost a sight feeder.

Here are some more tips that will help you locate bass when your waters turn muddy:

Fish tight to objects. Remember what happened when I cast that crankbait 10 feet from the riprap? I hauled water! But nearly every time I laid it tight to the rocks I had a strike!

I've seen this scenario repeated time and again when fishing muddy lakes and rivers. You've got to fish tight to cover or the fish won't hit. When visibility is severely limited, a bass won't wander far from its home.

Shun current. Muddy conditions are often accompanied by increased current because of the sudden infusion of runoff into the lake or river. Largemouth bass are slack-water fish, and smallies can handle heavier current; but neither fish will stay in a rush of water.

When current increases after a torrential rain, concentrate your efforts on slack water.

Trigger other senses. Although bass are primarily sight feeders, they will call upon other senses for input when feeding. The lateral lines are sensory organs that pick up vibrations, and the fish's sense

of smell is surprisingly refined. Bass can hear, too. Bass researcher Dough Hannon says they can pick up the sound of an electric trolling motor at a distance of several hundred yards! That's why rattling baits, or others that produce strong vibrations, are so productive in dirty water.

Bass aren't the only fish affected by muddy water. Baitfish often head to the shallows. When you see shad or other forage species flipping in extremely shallow water, so much the better.

Flash And Noise

Knowing where bass go in muddy water, and why, makes the task of locating them much easier, but you still have to catch them. You know they're going to be shallow and close to cover, and that they won't be able to see very well. This makes proper lure selection and placement paramount. In muddy water, bass need an easy target— one they can see with little trouble. If you had been using a ¼-ounce crankbait when the water was clear, move up to a ½- or even a ¾-ounce crank when it turns muddy. If a grub was the hot bait, switch to a jig-and-pig, which has more mass, moves more water and is easier to detect. Likewise with a spinnerbait or any other lure for that matter. Always use bigger lures when the water looks like chocolate milk.

Make sure, however, the big baits you choose are capable of banging into stumps, rocks and other objects without hanging up on every other cast. Plastic worms, weedless jigs, spinnerbaits and big-lipped crankbaits are all good choices.

Big lures close to cover also mean using a meaty rod and reel, and stout line. Don't worry about spooking fish. Muddy water will conceal heavy line.

As for color, I like "shock" colors—chartreuse, fluorescent orange, bright blue—that bass can see, even in the murkiest water. A big, fat chartreuse crankbait may not produce in clear water, but it can be your ticket to lunkerdom when it's muddy!

Don't forget the other senses. A big spinnerbait with cupped blades is a tremendous muddy-water lure. It sends out vibrations that bass can zero in on. In fact, lures that chatter, rattle or buzz produce better in dark water.

I'm not one to advocate the use of fish-attracting scents much of the time, but I'll use 'em when it's muddy, especially if the water is cold. Research has shown that bass pick up scent easier in cold water.

FINE-TUNING YOUR APPROACH

*I*n bass fishing, it's the little things that count. Here are some tips I've learned over the years that will help you catch bass in muddy water.

1. **Match Lure Color To Light Intensity**— Lure color can make a tremendous difference in your success rate when fishing muddy waters. Base your selection on light intensity. On a bright, sunny day, I usually choose a reflective bait, like a chrome-sided Rat-L-Trap. The muddy water diffuses the flash given off by the lure and makes it appear more lifelike. If the sun goes behind the clouds, however, reflective lures tend to disappear in the murk.

2. **Work Spinnerbaits Near The Surface**— Work a spinnerbait faster in muddy water than you might in clear. My favorite presentation is to retrieve the line very close to the surface so the rotating blade makes a wake on top. This is a tremendous warm-water presentation on a muddy flat or in the back of a stained creek arm. The best blade for this retrieve is a big, round Colorado.

3. **Go With Noisy Topwater Baits**—Forget finesse topwaters like floating minnows and soft jerk baits. Go with the noisy lures! Big prop baits, buzzbaits, poppers and Jitterbugs. I like 'em when the water temperature tops 70 degrees.

4. **Think Crayfish Baits**—I really like a crayfish-type artificial in muddy water, whether the water is hot or cold. Granted, I've caught more bass on lures that imitate baitfish, but my biggest bass have come on crayfish-imitators, such as weedless jigs, brownish crankbaits and the ever-popular jig-and-pig. Insert a worm rattle into the plastic body to produce a clicking sound that imitates a crayfish scuttling across a rocky bottom.

One advantage of fishing muddy water is that bass aren't easily spooked. Very often you can flip jigs into stumps and laydowns and catch fish right beside the boat. Indeed, flipping and pitching are great presentations where the fish's visibility is restricted.

These short-line techniques allow you to thoroughly saturate cover and put your lure in front of the fish. When casting to a bank, I'll first routinely move 50 percent closer to structure or cover than I would if the water were clear, then I'll try to lay my lure against every good-looking rock, stump or brushpile.

Bass are primarily sight feeders, but they also rely on their lateral lines and sense of smell to target prey. Appealing to these senses, as Bill Dance is doing here, will improve your odds of success.

Primary Targets

I've fished muddy waters in a number of areas and have found that no matter where you are, bass tend to concentrate in key areas. These areas are now my primary targets in muddy conditions.

Shallow flats are major feeding areas for bass just about anytime, but especially when the water's muddy. In early spring and fall, a flat will warm quickly, providing a more suitable temperature for active bass and a drawing card for baitfish. Use a spinnerbait, big crankbait or noisy topwater lure.

Following a heavy rain, creek arms will have increased current flow. Bass will avoid the strong rush of water, so look for pockets of slack water out of the main current. Run a spinnerbait or rattling crankbait through them and hang on to your rod!

The back ends of tributaries may hold numbers of fish, too. When it rains, worms and insects wash into the water sparking a feeding spree among all fish species. When bluegills and small bass start picking off these critters, the lunkers won't be far behind. Conversely, tributary headwaters are the first to clear up, so bass in these areas will be far more likely to run down a fast-moving crankbait.

Points are always a good bet for bass, whether the water is clear or muddy. When visibility is limited, however, bass move shallower and hold tighter to the point. I choose a big, bottom-bumping crankbait on this type of structure.

Bass will hang in eddies created by the current in rivers and some reservoirs. If you find this situation, tie on a jig-and-pig combination and use a slow, enticing presentation.

In early spring, when bass are staging for the spawn, they naturally move to the edge of shallow water. But when it's muddy, they're likely to move all the way up and hold tight to a stump, rock or brush pile. You can't beat a saturation approach with a plastic worm or jig-and-pig here.

Rocks and riprap are best on sunny days. The rocks heat up quickly, perhaps making the surrounding water a degree or two warmer. That can make all the difference

during the early spring.

I've also found that bass are more likely to feed on crayfish in muddy water than in clear, probably because the crustaceans crawl out of their holes when sun penetration is diminished. Use a bottom-bumping lure like a crankbait or a jig-and-pig combo that clicks and rattles as it hits rocks.

In weedy lakes, muddy water usually doesn't stay that way for long. The water will clear first where weeds are most prevalent. As the water begins to clear, you can enjoy a predictable bass bite by hunting small, isolated, offshore weed clumps and fishing a worm or jig, or a topwater lure if the water is warm.

While larger bass in many lakes may favor the deep edge of the weeds during warmer weather, muddy water may push them to the "inside edge" where the growth begins. As waters clear, a movement back to deeper weeds can be expected.

Love The Mud

Clear water is a joy to behold, but if it's big bass you're after, learn to love the mud. Once you adapt to it, you'll find fast fishing—and a shot at a lunker as well. Best of all, you'll probably have the lake to yourself.

chapter 2

Smallmouth Bass

There's nothing quite like a smallmouth for fishing excitement. The places we go to chase smallmouths are part of the attraction—clear lakes, swift streams, rocky shorelines and more. The fight is the other chief attraction. Ounce for ounce and pound for pound, absolutely nothing in freshwater fights like a bronzeback that has felt the hook. Who can say their heart hasn't leaped with a green-and-tan smallmouth hurtling through the air, then diving down so fast you thought your rod was going to snap?

But forget about landing him for a second. You've got to get him to hit first. Here's some of *North American Fisherman's* best advice on hooking brown bass; then you're on your own.

Springtime Smallmouth

by Spence Petros

*For years the author has been using water temperatures
to clue him in on where the smallmouth are—from ice-out to
post-spawn—and what presentations should work best.*

"Forty-degree water; that's the coldest opening day I've ever seen," I shouted as my partner was pulling the trailer out from under my floating boat. To make matters worse, I had all but guaranteed smallmouth action on this early-May bass opener.

Four hours later we had only one 15-inch smallie to show for our efforts. Still, after a quick lunch, we continued with our game plan—jigging piers, sunken cribs and sandgrass-studded, hard-bottom flats. A controlled drift allowed us to fish the desired four- to 10-foot level. If we started catching only the smaller males in that depth range, the plan was to move deeper to adjacent inside turns and points along the drop-off.

Experience on this lake had taught me it was best to first fish active bass on flats that had some cover, then move to adjacent deeper water, if necessary, to locate larger fish. If we worked the deep water first, with slow presentations, we wouldn't cover much territory. And on this type of lake, where 30 to 35 percent of the shoreline had bass-holding potential, we had to fish in a fast and effective manner.

The early-afternoon winds picked up, as they often do, and when one particularly strong gust blew the boat too shallow, I stopped the retrieve to adjust the electric motor. After a few seconds, I moved the jig again and immediately felt tension. A quick wrist snap connected me to a chunky smallmouth.

After that, we landed 18 bass; 17 hit the "dead jig" off the bottom in that numbing-cold water. A two- to three-second pause every 10 feet or so was the key. We never felt a strike or saw the line jump. When we resumed the retrieve, the bass was there.

This unique experience, which occurred years ago, actually offered five lessons concerning cold-water, pre-spawn smallmouth bass—lessons that have proven their worth many times through the years. Here's what we learned that day.

Not Too Early

Until the water temperatures reach the 50-degree range, or are at least in the high 40s during a sunny, warming trend, the best smallmouth fishing is usually limited to the warmer, afternoon hours. At such times, I rarely get on the water before 9 a.m., and even then the action generally doesn't pick up until midday.

The exception is when the weather has been consistently warm and a cold front starts to close in. This often triggers a strong, but short-lived, flurry of morning activity before the front arrives.

Sunlight can warm the waters a few degrees during the course of a day, but did you know a smallmouth might physically warm up even more? The dark color on the fish's back absorbs radiant energy from the sun and warms its body.

This explains why the bite usually picks up as the day progresses, or why bass may hit only slow-moving jigs earlier in the day, but jump all over crankbaits in the afternoon.

First, Eliminate Water

There are several types of natural lakes that commonly hold numbers of smallmouths. One is relatively fertile with fairly extensive weedbeds, usually in bay areas, but is mostly sand and rock based. These waters may have largemouths in the weeds, while the smallies favor areas sprinkled with sand and boulders (fist-size or chunk-rock); short, dill-like sandgrass; or combinations of all these features.

SAND/ROCK SMALLMOUTH LAKE

This common smallmouth lake is sand/rock based, but will often feature weedbeds, generally in the bay areas. Most of the springtime action will occur along banks bordering deeper water, but the sides of the bays and the bay points can also be productive this time of year.

The key to catching cold-water bass shallower than the edge of the flats is to fish flats with cover (A). Any warm trend after ice-out will usually pull smallies to these areas where they will hold in just about any type of cover. Bass will move across clean flats (B) when the water temperatures rise to the magic 55-degree mark.

Many times one or two stretches of the bank offer consistent action, while you draw a blank at similar sites. Be sure to revisit productive stretches several times a day as fish will continue to filter up from deeper water.

Springtime smallmouth spots in this type of lake typically lie in the same general areas. Motor around the lake to find shorelines with potential, and focus on the stretches that look the best (C, D and E). Smallies will also hold on deeper turns, points, and rock structures adjacent to spawning flats (F).

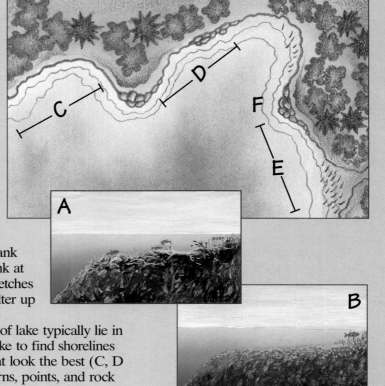

SHIELD LAKES

Shield lakes commonly feature large, shallow bays and/or long flat arms that smallmouths must cross before reaching the spawning grounds. Before migrating into the shallows, however, they typically bunch up on structure or cover adjacent to the closest, deep water. Spots such as a boulder-studded point (A), rock- and reed-covered reef (B), rocky point (C), and chunk rock bank (D), are all prime pre-spawn areas.

The reef (B) features rock, gravel plus emergent and submerged vegetation. Thus, smallies may spawn near this structure, and may hold there during summer if depths of at least 20 to 25 feet are available in the immediate area.

Once water temperatures in the bays reach the mid-50s, bass will move in and cruise around looking for spawning areas. Cast to any cover available until you discover a pattern. Skinny, limbless trees (E), provide too little cover unless several of them are bunched together, or are intermixed with rocks.

Bulrushes or reeds (F) can be good, too, especially if they contain large, scattered rocks. Large logs (G) provide cover and shade, and can be prime sites. Cruising bass often rest up on isolated rock piles (H) and may bed adjacent to their bases. Crevices between large boulders (I) can also hold bass.

Watch for a deeper slot or run (J) that heads into a beaver lodge. This deep cut in the shallow bay can hold a school of big bass, and is usually overlooked by most anglers.

A combination of logs, rocks and reeds (K) is another prime spot, and one that could just hold a trophy. Finally, don't pass up an opportunity to fish any hard- or soft-bottom reef (L), or large scattered rocks (M).

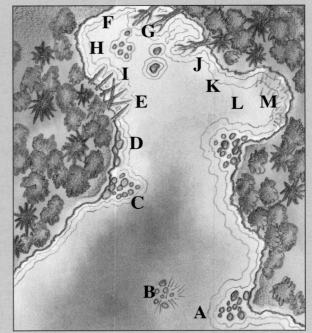

Lakes like this typically don't have bays with large, shallow back ends that draw smallmouths. They generally feature weeds, which make them more suited to largemouths.

Smallies, however, often hold along the sides and around the points of the bay, areas that generally have firmer bottoms. They can make fairly short migrations into the shallow water from the drop-off, which usually starts in the 10- to 16-foot range.

When first starting to fish a lake of this type, whether it's 500 or 5,000 acres, I generally motor around the shoreline, looking for submerged rocks. Visible rocks often mean the presence of deeper rocks.

Even gravel shores bordered by muck, marl or sand banks can hold smallies, especially if there's sandgrass on the adjacent flats.

Relatively infertile shield lakes are also good spring smallmouth producers. Unlike the more-fertile mesotrophic lakes, the amount of productive shoreline on a shield lake is limited. In a way, that's good, because large numbers of spring smallmouths concentrate in these small areas.

Shield lakes often feature large, shallow bays and/or long arms that warm much faster than the main lake. This means many of the good springtime spots are often hundreds of yards away from

deeper water. However, bass won't cross expansive, featureless flats to get to spawning areas until water temperatures rise above the mid-50s.

This is an important gauge that tells you if the bass have moved shallow. Many times I've checked the water temperature in a shallow bay, found it to be less than 55 degrees, and the bass weren't there. But a day or two later, after the temperature climbed to 55 or higher, aggressive smallies were everywhere.

Because the water is often fairly clear in such bays, I do much more looking than fishing when trying to locate bass. I first investigate bays, or small coves within bays, that are protected from the north wind, and look for fish or signs of fish. Clean spawning beds are a sure sign. It means the fish have been spooked, or moved deeper because of fishing pressure or weather conditions.

Sight-fishing like this is fun. I start scanning the water after the sun has climbed fairly high (about 10 a.m.), which makes it easier to see into the water. I try to keep the sun at my back to reduce glare, but you have to be careful that your shadow doesn't fall across the fish. If you see puffs of silt, it means you have spooked the fish.

Wear polarized glasses, a long-billed hat and go as fast as possible while still being able to see the bottom—probably from 2 to 8 mph, depending on depth and water clarity.

If the water is in the 55- to 60-degree range, expect the bass to be on the move, searching for spawning sites. If the water is warmer than 60 degrees, watch for bass bedding around cover.

Cover In Fertile Lakes

Lakes that are easily accessible generally receive heavy recreational use, so rough, unkempt shorelines (fallen trees, overhanging brush, broken down docks, etc.) are rare. Consequently, smallmouths and anglers frequently look to man-made cover.

Favorite cover on these well-manicured lakes include fish cribs, rock piles, foundations, pillars, deep edges near a launch ramp, as well as moored boats and the cinder blocks or concrete-filled tires that hold the floating boat markers in place.

Basically, anything that provides cover along a stretch of shoreline can harbor fish. Naturally, deeper cover, or cover that's more difficult to find will tend to hold more and larger smallmouths.

Smallies move shallow as water warms during the spring. Areas featuring cover such as rocks, wood and grass are best.

Many of these lakes will be ringed with piers and docks belonging to the homeowners. The bases, or foundations, that anchor these structures to the bottom, if they are located on a firm bottom, are also prime holding spots for smallmouths.

One of my favorite patterns occurs in early spring, before docks are installed. The permanent foundations that support these structures can be smallmouth havens. I motor along the shore, looking for stretches of gravel, sand or rock, and note spots where docks will soon be set up. Usually the telltale sign is a path (stone, wood planks, worn grass or dirt) that leads to water's edge. A cement slab on the shoreline is another indication.

With a little practice you can also tell which dock systems will extend the closest to deep water. Simply, the more dock sections stacked on shore, the better.

Sandgrass is another type of cover to keep in mind. The presence of sandgrass around any structure or cover usually makes it a better option for the fish, and this can help you eliminate a lot of water that has less potential.

Anglers who target spring smallmouths should release fish immediately in case they're protecting spawning beds. Bedding smallies aren't heavily harassed by panfish, primarily because their preferred habitat is not favored by these species.

Heavy fishing pressure will often chase bass off isolated pieces of wood and rock cover, causing them to shift to adjacent sandgrass-studded flats. Smallmouths will also spawn on these flats, clearing the brittle weeds with their tails until they've formed a bed.

Retrieves And Tackle Tips

In the cold waters of early spring, I like to fish a Fuzz-E-Grub jig using a swimming, bottom-brushing retrieve. Keep the rodtip low to the water and pointed toward the lure. This keeps the wind from moving the line around, and allows you see a strike more easily. Plus, it puts you in good position for a fast, solid hookset.

I favor a 5½-foot spinning rod with a fast tip when fishing jigs, and spool up with 6-pound mono, which is usually strong enough to pull jigs with light-wire hooks free from snags.

Execute the swimming retrieve with the reel, not the rod. Make two or three medium-slow cranks with the reel, pause a second or two until the lure hits bottom (line goes slack), then repeat. In very cold water, or after a cold front, let the jig set a couple extra seconds between movements.

As the water warms, popping a jig such as a tube or twister off bottom often triggers strikes when nothing else works. A "double jump," which is a

snap followed by another short, quick snap before the lure drops more than a couple of inches, can be very effective.

When fishing is tough—strong winds, neutral fish, or heavy fishing pressure—dress your jig with a minnow and use a slower lift-and-drop, or a bottom-dragging retrieve.

When using crankbaits in cold water, it's important to make at least two casts to each spot; three or four to exceptionally good-looking cover. It's very common for smallmouths to ignore the first presentation, but hit the second or third. The first is simply a wake-up call.

Normally I prefer a sensitive, yet fairly stiff rod when casting cranks so I can feel the lure's vibration or watch the rodtip vibrate. But when tossing smaller crankbaits long distances on light line, a 6½-to 7-foot spinning rod with a softer tip works better. I watch the longer, more flexible tip for sign of a strike.

Targeting Big Bass

When fishing clear lakes, especially those that have a lot of high-potential areas along the shore, I almost always start on the banks that are on the receiving end of a stiff breeze. The more wind the better, as long as it doesn't make casting too difficult.

Wind and wave action roils the bottom, stirring silt and sand, giving the water some color. It cuts light penetration, and gives the smallmouths more confidence. This is where you'll find the biggest fish.

Also, find out what the wind direction and velocity was on the day or two before your arrival. Often areas will still have some color from previous high winds.

Rains can also improve water color on deep, clear lakes. Rarely can you get too much rain or stain on these types of waters.

Watch for soft ground, erosion cuts or feeder creeks that can all contribute to darker water color.

Remember, too, that larger bass sometimes hold a little deeper than smaller fish. While the 1 to 2½ pounders are up on the flats, the 3 to 5 pounders often locate on the drop-off bordering the shelf. Or, maybe on nearby cover that's closer to deep water.

Whether you're going for numbers or targeting trophies, spring smallmouths are predictable, fun to catch and will test the limits of your light tackle. If you haven't already, it's time to put them on your early-season agenda.

WHAT TO USE WHEN

From Ice-Out to 43 Degrees

At this stage, throw small tube jigs, Fuzz-E-Grubs and sparse hair jigs with thin, flexible pork or plastic trailers. All these baits will have enough action, even at slow retrieve speeds.

A slow, bottom-brushing retrieve usually works, but remember to pause the bait for a few seconds—allowing it to lie on the bottom—when the fish won't react to the moving lure. Adding a small minnow or leech is also an option.

Water Temp: 44 to 49 Degrees

As the water warms, hop, lift and jump the jig on the retrieve. You can also start fishing neutrally buoyant minnow plugs (jerkbaits), and crankbaits retrieved at moderate speed, especially during an afternoon warm spell. Slow-rolling a ¼-ounce spinnerbait over or into wood cover or weed clumps can be productive.

Water Temp: 50 to 58 Degrees

Bass start responding to more active presentations. Go to a heavier jig (³⁄₁₆-ounce and up), and add a curlytail or other plastic body that vibrates as it moves through the water.

Lipped crankbaits are also deadly in this temperature range, as are lipless, vibrating cranks and in-line spinners (Mepps, Panther Martin, Blue Fox, etc.). Fish lipless cranks and spinners over flat, shallow (two to six feet) areas, especially if the water is stained.

Jerkbaits can be hot, and in clear lakes they can pull smallies up from a depth of five feet and deeper.

If fish are active, lures that allow you to cover ground quickly—crankbaits, spinnerbaits, jerkbaits—will help you locate scattered fish in a hurry.

In clear-water lakes with lots of fishing pressure, a large, lively minnow on a live bait rig slow trolled or drifted along the deep edges of spawning flats may be the best method for taking big bass. If you locate a concentration of fish, stop and cast.

Water Temp: 59 Degrees Through Spawn

As water temperatures in the spawning areas approach the 60-degree range, faster presentations usually produce smaller bass. Large fish, generally females, begin to bed and rarely chase a fast-moving lure. Instead, they'll hang near the beds and aggressively protect them from intruders.

I target these spawning smallies only if there are no panfish around the beds. Panfish often invade largemouth beds if the bass is caught, but this problem often doesn't exist with smallmouths.

Plastic-body jigs in the ¹⁄₁₆- to ⅛-ounce range are tough to beat for bedding bass. And if the jig has to be lifted over wood or snaked through weeds, a thin, wire weedguard will help. Six- or 8-pound-test mono usually works best.

Surface lures like a small shallow-diving minnow plug, downsized topwaters, or even popper flies are other options. Cast them over the beds and retrieve them with a soft twitch.

Live bait behind a split shot will catch virtually every bass you see, unless you come into a bedding area like a moose in rut. Carefully lip-land each bass—no net—and quickly release it.

Rockin' Smallmouths

by Don Wirth

Gravel, chunk rock, boulders, shoreline-related rocks, offshore structure, slow tapers, fast drops—it sure can get confusing. But this story sorts it out better than any other we've seen.

There's a scene in a low-budget prison movie where a newly incarcerated inmate steps from a bus and stares in disbelief at an enormous pile of rocks before him—rocks he's expected to bust into tiny fragments with a sledgehammer. You know what he's thinking just by the look on his face, and it's the same feeling many smallmouth anglers get when they first fish a rocky lake: "Where do I start?"

Some lakes have so much rock that pinpointing the places where bronzebacks are most likely to lurk seems impossible. Breaking down all that rock into a workable pattern appears almost insurmountable.

But cracking rocks is what this story is all about. And the savvy smallmouth angler knows that knowledge, not a sledgehammer, is the best tool for the job.

Tough To Crack

Rocky lakes can be prime habitat for smallmouth bass. But these waters are notoriously tough to crack. Fred McClintock, who regularly guides smallmouth

anglers on Tennessee's Dale Hollow Lake, has fished rocky smallmouth lakes from Canada to Alabama. He can attest that although they all post unique challenges, these types of waters have several factors in common:

- **Depth**—Most rocky smallmouth lakes are deep. That's okay—smallmouths thrive in deep water. "I've caught fish down to 76 feet, but most often they'll hold at 15 to 30 feet," McClintock says.
- **Clarity**—Rocky lakes are typically clear—some nearly transparent. Tributaries feeding rocky reservoirs often run very clear as well. Even if the creek arms flow with mud for a day or so following a hard rain, they clear up quickly.
- **Fertility**—Compared to typical bass waters, rocky lakes are relatively infertile.
- **Shoreline cover**—Rocky lakes, especially reservoirs, don't usually offer much shoreline cover in the form of submerged wood or weeds. This often pulls the food chain, and the smallmouths, offshore.

> *"Once you understand how smallmouths and their prey relate to a rocky environment, you can begin establishing some patterns."*

"To an angler used to lakes with lots of cover, it's pretty discouraging," McClintock admits, "but once you understand how smallmouths and their prey relate to a rocky environment, you can begin establishing some patterns."

Rock Connection

What function do rocks serve in the smallmouth's world? While they don't provide thick shelter, like the big weedbeds preferred by largemouth bass, they supply enough cover for smallmouths.

"Like all predators, smallies try to use cover when hunting prey," says McClintock. "They keep a low profile, using the rocks for concealment."

In deep, open water, he adds, smallmouths may use rocks for another purpose—as reference points or landmarks. "Some biologists think rocks may provide smallmouths with visual markers to help keep them oriented. They suspend over rocky structure, including large individual boulders, rock ledges and rock piles, usually when they're less active."

In moving waters, rocks also protect smallies from the current. The fish often hold tightly behind, between, in front, even under big rocks, then dart out into the current to feed.

Multiple Faces Of Rock

Various types of rock and rock structures will, at certain times, hold smallmouth bass. Each type has its own special appeal, and you should always keep them in mind when fishing a rocky lake. If one type doesn't produce, try another. Rocks are the primary structure in such lakes, and the fish have to be somewhere.

- **Sheer bluffs**—Smallmouths are not as vertically oriented as spotted bass, but more so than largemouths. They will suspend off sheer rock bluffs, especially where bluffs border a river channel with some current flow. Baitfish run the bluffs, which puts the gamefish in a good position to pick up an easy meal. Smallies will also forage for crayfish in the rock rubble near the base of the bluffs.
- **Boulders**—Most commonly found in Western reservoirs and Canadian Shield lakes, boulders provide hiding places for smallmouths and forage.
- **Ledges**—Call them platforms, stairsteps, whatever— they serve as a transition from one depth level to the next. Smallies may suspend over a ledge, or simply sit on top of it. Either way, they have quick access to forage above and below.
- **Chunk rock**—Many banks and points are composed of chunk rock, which provides plenty of hiding places for crayfish, a preferred smallmouth forage.

Steep bluff banks will hold smallies in late spring and fall. Twitch a minnow imitation on the surface or go deep with a jig or crankbait.

- **Gravel**—Nothing more than rock broken into small chunks, gravel is most productive during the spring, when smallies use it as a spawning surface. Look for gravel on main-lake flats, in the lower half of tributaries and on long points that taper slowly from the shore.
- **Rock piles**—These isolated mounds of chunk rock can be submerged or may poke through the surface. They're sometimes just rock rubble that was pushed aside during dam construction or channelization. Here again, they offer good cover for forage.
- **Rock islands**—Common in Canadian Shield lakes, they're usually small and may take the form of a single massive rock, or a group of huge boulders.
- **Reefs**—These offshore rock ridges may rise close to the surface, and are typically found in natural lakes. They offer tremendous appeal to predators.
- **Riprap**—This is rock dumped along the banks of a causeway or near a dam to protect the shoreline. It's best for smallies in river-run reservoirs where current is present.

Year-Round Attraction

Smallmouths have a year-round attraction to rock structure. Trouble is, the type of structure they prefer varies from season to season, according to small-

mouth guide Jack Christian of Goodlettsville, Tennessee. He has been chasing smallies for the better part of his life, and knows when to find them on specific rock formations. More importantly, he knows how to catch them.

- **Spring**—Smallmouths begin spawning on gravel flats and long, slow-tapering gravel points when the water temperature rises to around 58 degrees.

"Spawning takes place in both the main lake and in the larger tributaries, but usually not too far back into the creek arms. The biggest females will be the first to bed, moving in early to claim the best spots."

Spawning takes place in three to 12 feet of water, depending on its clarity, and continues until the water reaches about 68 degrees, he adds. While this is the best time to catch the smallie of your dreams, you can shift the odds even more in your favor if you do some homework.

"Most fishing pressure will be directed at the biggest, most visible concentrations of gravel, but even isolated patches will attract spawners," explains Christian. "If you fish a reservoir, cruise the lake during winter drawdown to find these smaller patches, and while you're at it, look

"You can shift the odds even more in your favor if you do some homework."

for isolated stumps, small patches of grass and large pieces of chunk rocks peppered on the gravel.

"These can really enhance a spawning area because smallies often make their nests right next to such objects."

Christian's favorite spring lures are the fly-n-rind (a hair jig with a pork trailer) and a jig-and-grub combo. He fishes both on a stiff spinning rod with 6- or 8-pound mono.

"Position your boat in eight feet of water. Fancast the area, allowing the lure to hit bottom. Hold the rodtip at 10 o'clock and reel slowly and steadily, swimming the bait back to the boat. Spawning smallies, unlike bedding largemouths, are super-aggressive—I've had 'em rip the rod clean out of

my hands!" Christian swears.

• **Summer**—Smallies move offshore during the day, sometimes suspending above the thermocline. At this time, they may be uncatchable except by trolling. Consequently, most smallmouth anglers in Christian's region nightfish during the summer.

"Big smallies move up shallow at night, searching for crayfish on main-lake rock piles, and chunk-rock and gravel points," he says. "The key is finding the right depth. Don't be afraid to begin fishing the shallows at night. I've caught big fish from just a foot of water. But if you aren't getting bit, by all means move deeper—15 to 25 feet should do it."

Leadhead jigs rank high at night when smallies are deep. "Use spider jigs, hair jigs and grubs on rock piles and deep chunk-rock points, but expect to lose some lures in the rocks," Christian says.

Jigs equipped with weedguards will keep hangups to a minimum, as will moving the lure as soon as it touches bottom. "Don't let a jig just sit there, or it'll fall down between the cracks in the rocks. Instead, pop the rodtip sharply so the lure hops as soon as it hits bottom." Christian prefers stiff spinning gear and 10-pound mono for fishing leadheads at night.

In river-run reservoirs, Christian relies on a spin-nerbait to catch smallies after dark. "The fish move onto gravel bars and hold tight to stumps and big rocks, using them as current breaks. Short, accurate casts to these objects will produce jarring strikes."

A short-arm spinnerbait with a Colorado blade works best. Christian fishes it on a stiff 6-foot bait-casting rod with 15- to 20-pound mono. "Smallies hold shallower and are more active in fast current. When the gates are open at the dam, the fish can be in just a foot of water at night and incredibly vicious. I've had 'em pull the blade clean off a spinnerbait."

• **Fall**—"This is a tricky time to fish a rocky lake," Christian warns, "because it's difficult to establish a consistent depth pattern. Sometimes smallies hold extremely deep on bluffs and 45-degree rock banks. Other times they'll be quite shallow on main-lake points."

As a rule of thumb, fish shallower when the wind blows because it often pushes microorganisms, baitfish—and hungry bass—onto windward banks.

You'll need a more varied selection of lures in the fall, he adds.

"Early in the morning, it's common to see schools of smallies chasing baitfish on the surface over a rock pile, gravel point or open water. Stickbaits and floating minnow-imitators are ideal for schooling fish."

As the sun rises, however, they move deep. "Target 45-degree chunk-rock banks with leadhead grubs and metal blade baits. I've caught 'em 55 feet deep on blade baits like the Silver Buddy in October."

INSIDE TIPS FOR ROCKY LAKES

Rocky lakes can be tough to crack. Here are some shortcuts from expert smallmouth anglers:

1. **Target transitions**—Small pockets, gullies, washouts, veins of dissimilar rock, transitions from one size rock to another and other seemingly minor variations in bank composition are especially important in rocky lakes that offer little else for the smallmouths.
2. **Off-colored water**—Rocky lakes are often exceedingly clear. Where murky water enters the system from a tributary, or where a mud-line has formed against the bank on a windy day, smallies may move shallow and become highly aggressive.
3. **A good wind**—Smallmouths in rocky lakes often move very shallow on windy days, especially on main-lake points. This pattern is viable in fall and winter on days when the wind blows out of the south.
4. **Suspended fish**—Bronzebacks in clear, rocky lakes are notorious for suspending. Several tactics can call 'em to the surface, even if they're 15 to 20 feet deep. Cast a big chartreuse spinnerbait to main-lake points, reeling it quickly so it runs just beneath the surface. Or, throw a soft jerkbait near a bluff bank or 45-degree rock bank and twitch it gently on the surface.
5. **Topwaters**—Topwater lures can be surprisingly effective in rocky lakes. In calm water, twitch a subtle topwater like a minnow lure close to rock banks or points. In choppy water, switch to a more aggressive lure, such as a stickbait or prop bait.

If the wind is blowing, it's crankin' time, he adds. "Big schools of baitfish move onto the points, and smallies will be close behind. Use shad- and crayfish-imitating lures with long diving lips. Many strikes will come on the first turn of the reel handle."

The guide uses a 6-foot, medium-action baitcasting rod with 14-pound mono for stickbaits, a 6-foot spinning rod with 10-pound line for blade baits, and a 6½-foot, medium-action spinning rod with 6- to 8-pound line for minnow imitators and crankbaits.

GOOD EATS

Crayfish are abundant in most rocky lakes, venturing out from their stone homes mostly at night. Smallmouths, with their sharply-pointed snouts, are highly adept at rooting the crustaceans out from under or between rocks. Lures such as diving crankbaits, hair jigs with pork trailers and soft-plastic spider jigs are good crayfish mimics. Fish them close to the bottom on points, flats, ledges, etc.

Hellgrammites are another popular smallmouth forage abundant around rocks. These fearsome-looking critters are the larval stage of the dobsonfly; they're most likely to be found in gravel-bottom streams and in the flowing headwaters of rocky reservoirs. Smallmouths eat 'em like candy.

Stream anglers fish hellgrammites as live bait, but a small spider jig will serve as a close approximation of the real thing.

Several varieties of baitfish are attracted to rocks. Shad, shiners and newly-hatched gamefish fry feed on the soft algae that covers submerged rocks like a fur coat. Shiny silver lures like blade baits and reflective crankbaits mimic these fish. Darters, small stick-like fish that sit on the bottom and dart away when alarmed, are common in rocky waters. Match them with short, straight plastic worms fished on a Carolina rig.

• **Winter**—"This is another prime time to catch a giant smallmouth in a clear, rocky lake, provided ice isn't a factor," Christian says. "These fish are typically far more aggressive in cold water than largemouths."

Where to start? "My favorite winter structure is a deep, steep, rocky point on the main lake or in a large tributary," he explains.

"Smallmouths relate to this structure in several ways—they may sit on the bottom at the end or sides, suspend off the end or sides, or suspend in the hollow area between two rocky points. The farther they are from structure, the more difficult they'll be to catch."

For fish holding fairly close to the point, Christian recommends a leadhead lure (fly, spider jig, lizard, etc.) or blade bait. For suspending smallies, try a jigging spoon. "Sometimes baitfish gang up in huge schools in the hollows when the surface temperature drops below 50 degrees. Vertically jigging the lure into a school can produce a lot of big smallmouths."

Stair-step ledges on a 45-degree chunk-rock bank are another hot winter structure. "These are especially prevalent in reservoirs with a limestone base. The ledges are often short outcrops that drop about five to eight feet at a time. Smallies will park on them at whatever depth is most comfortable."

"Smallmouths are typically far more aggressive in cold water than largemouths."

Here, Christian recommends leadheads and blade baits. "Start by casting into shallow water and bumping the lure out to the various depths along the ledge. But once you locate a concentration of fish, position your boat along the bank and target the preferred depth zone with parallel casts."

Once you understand how smallmouths relate to rocks, you can have a rockin' good time catching 'em. Take the advice of our experts and learn to target rock structure in your local lakes. Adjust your lures and presentations to the smallmouth's depth and mood, and soon you'll have a real string-stretcher on the end of your line.

Rock Solid Smallies

by Spence Petros

Forget about gossamer-thin lines and finesse presentations.
Autumn is the time to break out the heavy artillery for big smallmouth!

Somehow, our fishing tactic reminded me of a movie about the Old West. But instead of outlaws on horseback surrounding a circle of covered wagons, we were in a boat going round-and-round a wind-battered rock hump, firing crankbaits at our targets—big fall smallmouths.

I had a feeling it might be an especially successful trip when my partner caught a 5-pound smallmouth on his first cast. And I was right—over the next few days, we boated dozens of large bass.

Though this experience occurred nearly 20 years ago, the pattern we developed then still takes fall smallmouths today. In fact, it's as close to a sure bet as you'll find because smallmouths change their habits as water temps fall. Night-feeding, for example, grinds to a halt and bass begin to concentrate on rock structure, where dwindling forage forces them to feed throughout the day.

So, instead of trying to connect with wary, tight-lipped bass, scattered at a variety of depths and feeding in short bursts, you've got them right where you want them—bunched up on rocky structures and feeding on a limited forage base during the daylight hours.

Early fall, bright sun and shallow rocks—a perfect combination for smallmouth action. The sun heats the rocks, which warm the water, which draws the fish.

Surprise Bonanza—Shallow Lakes

You usually think of a natural smallmouth lake as being deep and relatively clear, with a sand, gravel and rock bottom. While this is an ideal situation, some of the heaviest smallmouth bass are caught in shallow lakes where smallies are considered a minority species.

In some cases, these fish get virtually no fishing pressure because they are usually scattered and difficult to find during most of the warm-weather season. But come fall, the smallies bunch up on the few decent structures these lakes have to offer.

Since shallow lakes are normally fairly fertile (with at least some weed growth), and generally lack classic, deep-water structure, smallmouth bass aren't overly abundant in these waters. But the fish that are there grow to enormous sizes. In fact, 5 to 7 pounders are fairly common.

In these shallow lakes, the deeper the rocks, the better. Rock points extending far out into the lake, and rock piles at least 7 or 8 feet deep are prime areas. Rock humps or rocky areas on sand/gravel humps also hold excellent potential, as do rock-studded banks.

A real sleeper spot for big smallmouths in a shallow lake is a fallen tree along a steep bank. I first discovered smallies using this type of cover while working tree-studded banks for muskies and walleyes. Now it's one of my favorites.

Wind is important. If you fish these shallow areas when the weather is calm and the water clear, you'd swear there wasn't a smallmouth in the lake. However, if a strong wind blasts onto a shallow point or roars over the top of a rock-capped hump near the surface, big, aggressive smallies will knock the paint off your lures.

Timing And Tactics

The fall bite on shallow lakes normally begins a couple of weeks earlier than it does on classic (i.e.: deep) smallmouth waters, and stays hot right up until turnover. As water temperatures approach the turnover range—58 to 54 degrees—I start thinking about shifting to deeper waters, which will be at least a week or two behind in temperature progression.

After the turnover, I still explore some shallow lakes, but concentrate most of my efforts on deep, clear waters that hold larger numbers of smallmouths. These fish are usually bunched in key areas and are generally easy to catch.

Before the lake turns, crankbaits are tough to beat for covering water in a fast and effective manner. Lipped divers bouncing off rocks trigger a lot of strikes, especially from larger fish.

If the bass have been pressured, or if weather conditions curtail the action, I switch to jigs. A tube or curlytail jig hopped or glided over the top of structure and down its sides works great.

The ultimate presentation for neutral fish, however, is a good-size chub or sucker worked slowly behind a split shot, or a jig-and-minnow combination. I prefer a fairly light jig, such as an ⅛ ouncer, with a grub body, tipped with a 3- to 4-inch minnow. If one of these presentations doesn't trigger strikes, it's time to move on.

If you must fish shallow lakes during the post-turnover period, crankbaits are a good choice during

ROCK HUMP

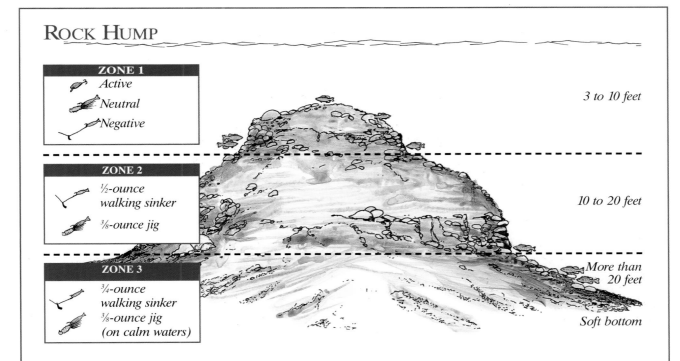

ZONE 1
- *Active*
- *Neutral*
- *Negative*

3 to 10 feet

ZONE 2
- *½-ounce walking sinker*
- *⅜-ounce jig*

10 to 20 feet

ZONE 3
- *¾-ounce walking sinker*
- *⅜-ounce jig (on calm waters)*

More than 20 feet

Soft bottom

Actively feeding bass can be anywhere, but most of the time they'll hold near projections, corners in the contour, heavier concentrations of rocks, lips, and bottom transition areas that change from hard to soft.

Use these tips to target fish in specific zones:

- *Zone 1 is best fished with crankbaits for active bass, jigs for more neutral fish and live bait rigs under the toughest conditions.*

- *Zone 2 is best worked with a jig-and-minnow combo or live bait rig with a ½-ounce walking sinker and a large minnow.*

- *Zone 3 features deep ledges, the base of the structure, and the transition area. Use a ¾-ounce walking sinker on a live bait rig or a ⅜-ounce jig tipped with a minnow, if it's not too windy. A 10- to 14-pound superline provides great sensitivity and hooksetting power. With a live bait rig, search for bass with a lip-hooked minnow. But once you locate fish, hook the bait behind the dorsal fin. The minnow won't dive into the rocks, plus you can make a quick hookset, which means more smallies are lip-hooked for easy release.*

a warm spell, or when the sky is bright and the wind is calm. Sunlight warms the shallow rocks and the surrounding water.

For the most part, live bait rigs and jigs work better when the fish are holding deeper, or if the water is cold and they won't chase a fast-moving lure.

Classic Smallmouth Lakes

Clear, deep lakes with lots of sand, gravel and rock are ideal waters for smallmouth bass.

Unfortunately, these lakes will humble almost any angler who tries to consistently pry "smalljaws" from its depths.

Savvy anglers hit these waters hard during prime times—early or late in the day, when it's windy and/or cloudy, and right after the fall turnover.

During pre-turnover on these clear, deep lakes, I usually take a run-and-gun crankbait approach, especially when it's windy or cloudy. This is a time of transition when bass generally hold on a variety of structures. They'll relate to shallow rock piles,

fallen trees and reed beds, deep humps and points, over scattered large rocks in a variety of depths, and may even suspend off of or between structures.

In this situation, it's imperative that your plan of attack cover a lot of water. Bouncing crankbaits over rock-studded humps and points is most productive for me, provided there's enough structure in the depth range of my deep-diving crankbait. If the majority of good-looking structure is too deep for casting a crank, jigs and live bait rigs matched with 4- to 5-inch minnows get the nod.

Crankbait Savvy

Sometimes the fishing's easy, as it was on that lake so many years ago. Dozens of near-surface rock humps were marked by buoys to warn boaters.

If the humps on the lakes you fish aren't marked, then investing in a GPS unit, or at least a good lake map, is essential. Punch the locations of off-shore structures into your GPS, or mark shoreline sightings right on your map.

Crankbaits should bounce across the top of a hump or point, then make contact down the side for as long as possible. Hold the rodtip high, slow the retrieve when the lure bangs the bottom hard, then drop the rodtip and speed the retrieve when you lose bottom contact.

Generally, I'll cast from deep to shallow water, but may snug up to the structure and cast parallel to its edge if I feel the bass are holding deeper along the breakline. You'll find active bass anywhere along the structure, but when the action slows, rocky fingers, eroded cuts or ledges will be the keys. Switch to a jig when faced with nonactive fish.

After the turnover, when surface waters cool and sink, they mix with the bottom layers and the whole lake becomes fairly uniform in temperature—usually around 52 to 56 degrees.

Big bass will then abandon shallower water and school on points, humps and sharp ledges that are in or closely related to the main lake basin, or the deepest water in the area.

It's usually no problem catching these bass, as long as you have several good presentations in your bag of tricks. Your biggest enemy is not bright skies, cold fronts, rain, or even snow, but strong winds that make boat control difficult. But even the wind can be overcome on most occasions.

BOTTOM BOUNCING CRANKS

Rodtip high, slow retrieve...

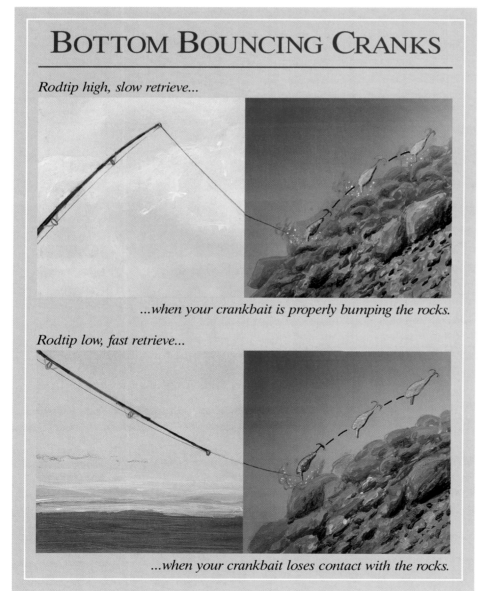

...when your crankbait is properly bumping the rocks.

Rodtip low, fast retrieve...

...when your crankbait loses contact with the rocks.

Smallies can be caught high on structure (4 to 10 feet or so), under warming conditions, especially if the sun is shining and waves aren't diluting light penetration. At this depth range, try crankbaits first, but always follow up with a jig, jig-and-minnow or a lively minnow worked slowly behind a split shot.

The amount of time you spend fishing the top of a structure depends on its reputation for producing fish, and the amount of potential fish-holding cover it offers.

Generally, the sides and base of a hump or point are the key areas after the turnover. When probing water deeper than 12 feet, I'll generally troll into the wind. Back-trolling with a small outboard or stern-mount electric motor, or forward-trolling with a bow-mount electric motor, allows me to follow tight contours much more effectively than if the boat is being pushed around by the waves.

If the waves become too big, running a boat against them can be virtually impossible.

Rather than getting soaked by the backsplash off the transom, try this trick: Drop a few highly-visible marker buoys slightly shallower than the area you want to fish. Motor upwind and turn your outboard against the waves to slow your drift speed as you float through the zone.

This tactic allows a slow, vertical presentation as you "slip" through the hotspot. Many times I've used the "downwind backtroll" tactic to stay on fish while the other boats either left the lake or were blown all over the structure.

On deep-water edges like these, the bread-and-butter pre-sentation for big smallmouths is a live bait rig with a ½- to ¾-ounce walking sinker and a 5- to 6-inch minnow. If that's too intimidating for you, go to a 3- to 4-inch minnow.

We've all heard that big baits catch bigger fish—well, it's never more true than for big fall smallmouths. Big crankbaits produce big bass when they're holding shallow, and big smallies love big minnows when they're holding deep.

I'll generally slow-troll a lip-hooked minnow around the perimeter of a structure that

Tip—tank every smallmouth you catch (but don't go over your limit) until you plan to move. Releasing a fish back into the school will shut the entire school down.

offers rocks near a drop-off. My feeling is that if you're not getting snagged occasionally, you're not fishing a good area.

The heavy walking sinker allows you to fish nearly vertically for ultimate feel, minimal hang-ups and maximum hooksetting power. I use 14-pound-test FireLine, with a 3-foot mono leader of 10- to 14-pound green mono, and a size 1 or 1/0 hook.

A 7-foot spinning rod with a gradual taper is the ideal stick. You need power to move the weight and hook the fish, so you don't want a fast tip that will collapse before the power is applied to the fish. My two favorite 7 footers are the South Bend System 10, which is my own design, and Quantum's Tour Edition model.

This fall, give smallmouths a go. Most lakes receive little pressure and the fish are bunched on key structures. More importantly— they're eager to bite!

Anywhere you catch one fall smallmouth, you're likely to catch a bunch. Double, even triple hookups are possible if you find the right spot.

Smallmouths, Clearly

by Don Wirth

Giant smallmouth roam the clear-water reservoirs throughout the central portion of the United States. These tactics will help you catch these bruisers in their haunts located near deep bluffs, weedbeds, humps, points … even when they are suspended.

"Winds light and variable," the forecaster on the 10 o'clock news had promised the night before. But it wasn't a locomotive howling through the hollows that October morning—it was a 45 mph gale.

Breakers pounded against the rock bluffs out on the main lake where I was fishing, and boat control was next to impossible. Waves sloshed over the bow of my bass boat as I tied on the only lure I could fish effectively under these adverse conditions, a heavy metal blade bait.

I shot out a cast toward the bluff and held my rod high, watching the blade sink quickly into the clear-water depths. It never touched bottom; a solid rap indicated smallmouth intervention.

From the bend in the rod after I set the hook, I knew I was into a big fish—and in big trouble unless I could quickly get the boat away from the bluff. Holding the rod in one hand, I cranked up the outboard motor and shifted into reverse. Water sloshed over the transom as the boat spun around into open water, where I hoped to fight the fish without fear of washing into the rocks.

Just then the monster smallie blew into the air, and burned drag again as it shot back down deep. Seeing the fish spooked me—I'd once seen an 8-plus pounder weighed at the dock, but this fish seemed bigger.

Again the gale forced me toward the craggy bluff. I was finding it impossible to control the boat and fight the bass at the same time. And when I reached for the shifter, the bass took a nosedive.

The rod jerked from my grasp and slammed against the gunwale. The line caught around a mooring cleat, stretched and popped with the sound of a .22 gunshot. That one hurt.

No question, smallies grow big in gin-clear waters like the reservoir I was fishing that day, and hooking them—or landing them—isn't easy. But some high-percentage approaches will tip the odds in your favor, especially in autumn. If you give them a try, you'll be in for some amazing smallmouth action not only this fall, but all through the year.

In The Clear

In clear lakes, the entire chain of life—smallies and their forage—is usually located somewhere offshore. Bass hold on long points, prowl mid-lake humps, hang off steep bluffs and suspend in open water, sometimes at extreme depths. There's really no reason for smallies to hang around shallow banks in a clear lake, where there's precious little cover and not much for them to find in the way of food.

Autumn can be an especially frustrating time for anglers fishing clear water because smallies are often in a transitional mode. You may pick up one fish super-deep, another relatively shallow. What gives?

In a clear-water reservoir smallmouth spend much of the fall suspended. That's because their major forage is shad, which commonly roam the open water. This doesn't necessarily mean the bass are a mile from the nearest bank (although they might well be), but it does mean that traditional bottom-bumping, bank-probing approaches that pay off in murkier lakes at other times of the year will usually come up empty.

Unlike most die-hard bass fishermen, I love to troll. It's a deadly fall tactic for big smallies in deep, clear waters. When the water begins to cool off in October, I'll troll main-lake structure—including points, humps and open bays—with a combination of flutter spoons on downriggers and deep-diving crankbaits on flatlines.

"In a clear lake, smallies spend much of autumn suspended."

The 25-foot zone seems to be especially productive. My favorite trolling crankbaits include Storm's Magnum Wiggle Wart, Bomber's Model A, and slender "walleye plugs" such as Lindy's Shadling and Heddon's Wally Demon. Try chrome on sunny days, perch or fire tiger when it's cloudy.

Trolling's productivity begins to taper off by mid-November in the mid-South as the water cools. Then, chrome and perch patterns are by far the best color choices for crankbaits.

Surface Smallies

Believe it or not, in early fall topwater lures can produce amazing results, even when bass are suspended 30 feet deep! Sloping rock banks and open pockets between main-lake points are your best bets.

The Spinrite tailspinner is a clear-water cult favorite among smart Southern smallmouth anglers. Blade baits and jigging spoons are also ideal for deep smallies in clear reservoirs.

Cast a stickbait like a Heddon Zara Spook or floater/diver minnow like a Rapala, Smithwick Rogue or A. C. Shiner No. 450 close to the bank and twitch it out into open water.

Don't be surprised if you see a whole school of smallies rise out of the depths and chase the lure. I've caught 6 pounders that shot up from 30 feet to nail a Spook bobbing overhead. Baits that cause a surface disruption, such as a Heddon Torpedo, can also draw strikes.

A soft plastic jerkbait fished on or under the surface is powerful medicine on clear-water smallies, as well. This is probably the most realistic artificial you can throw in clear water; it'll draw strikes on the toughest days.

Don't overfish it—a slight bump with your rodtip imparts the right action. A white, chartreuse or shad Slug-Go or similar jerkbait is simply awesome when drifted slowly and gently twitched around rock bluffs or steep banks.

Breezy Pointers

Although I prefer dead-calm conditions for fishing topwater lures, I like a stiff breeze blowing when casting crankbaits, blade baits, tailspinners and leadhead lures, all of which can produce big smallies in clear water. Granted, too much wind can be a problem, but a reasonably stiff breeze, especially one from the south or west, can move fish suspending in open water closer to points or sloping banks.

On a windy day, seek out long, tapering gravel or mud points, especially those where a mudline has built up, and burn ¼-ounce crankbaits like the Model A, Rapala Fat Rap or Luhr-Jensen Hot Lips Express in the one- to 10-foot zone. Smallies may be very shallow, perhaps rooting out crayfish under the cover of discolored water.

Metal blade baits, tailspinners and jigging spoons are ideal for deep fall smallies. Locate baitfish schools and/or suspending smallies on your graph and work these lures down to the level of the fish.

I recall one brisk October day when a buddy and I boated 32 fat smallies and 15 bonus spotted bass in a clear-water reservoir on Silver Buddy blade baits dropped down steep chunk-rock banks. The fish were suspended off these cavernous banks; some were nearly 60 feet deep! A week later, we found smallmouths in the same lake suspending 40 feet deep off a channel point and popped 15 nice fish on heavy jigging spoons.

Spinning Success

Tailspinners can also work well in the fall, although few smallmouth anglers fish them. My favorite is the Spinrite, a marabou-dressed tailspinner that's a cult favorite among Southeastern small-

CLEAR PATHS TO SMALLMOUTHS

Points: When the wind blows, the hottest fish hold in shallow water right at the end of points—a good time for crankbaits. On calm days, actively feeding smallies move to the deep edges off points. Switch to blade baits or jigging spoons.

Humps: The best humps rise out of deep water and top out at about 10 feet below the surface. Hot smallies hold right on top of the hump in all weather conditions. Jig a grub directly on top of the structure, or troll a crankbait across the hump.

Weedbeds: Clear-water bronzebacks typically suspend over or outside deep weed-beds, rather than hide inside weedy jungles. The most active fish will suspend tight to weed tops or weedlines. Work a 1-ounce spinnerbait down to 20 feet, or jig a grub with a weed guard.

Bluff banks: Fish suspend off rock structure or hold around boulders at the base of the bluff. Hot smallies often hold at extreme depths of 50 feet or more. Fish blade baits or jigging spoons, deep. On slow days, when fish aren't biting, switch to topwater baits or soft plastic jerkbaits to attract smallies from deep water.

River channels: Hot fish will hang over the river channel, above the thermocline. The best fishing is where your sonar screen shows "balls" of baitfish; when baitfish appear as a horizontal line, fishing can be tough. Troll a crankbait directly over the channel, or try vertical jigging at night.

mouth addicts. I'll fish it horizontally like a crankbait, only with a retrieve that's about 10 times slower. Working the lure slowly will cause its spinner blade to flash and spin; it's a killer presentation in clear water.

Small hair jigs dressed with pork rind and soft plastic grubs are always reliable fall lures. Their compact profile and realistic darting action makes them easy for a shy smallmouth to bite in clear water. I fish brown or black "flies" (hair jigs) and chartreuse grubs on overcast days, but switch to a white fly or smoke grub when the sun's shining.

OK, now for the most amazing tactic for suspended smallies I know of: move out to the end of a long point and chuck a big spinnerbait, preferably one with tandem chartreuse willow-leaf blades, then retrieve it quickly just under the surface. Suspending bass will rise up long distances to blast the lure.

This is a big-fish tactic that has won several pro-level bass tournaments with limit catches of bronzebacks. Spinner-baits are good, too, around deep weedbeds and weedlines.

Clear lakes offer ideal habitat for smallmouth bass—especially for trophy-size fish—but you've got to understand where the smallies are located to fish these waters right. Follow the tips I've presented here and you'll be on the clear road to success. Guaranteed.

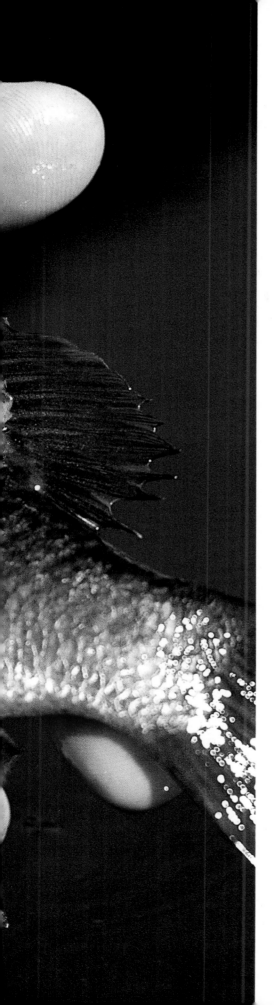

chapter 3

Bluegill

Bluegill, sunfish, bream, brim, shell-cracker and a host of other panfish... they all bring warmth to our fisherman hearts. Maybe it's because we started out catching these pint-sized but delicious battlers long ago. Maybe it's because we still love catching them—what's wrong with some simple fun and good fishing action? But it's also because, when it comes right down to it, catching good-sized panfish is a real fishing challenge.

Here is some of the best advice we've ever seen on the subject. The results —hefty panfish challenging your lightweight equipment— are worth the fishing effort.

Bull Roundup

by Spence Petros

Recent successes have proven that big 'gills suspend a lot more than anglers think.
Here's how to target the biggest bluegills in any lake.

Visions of digging into a steaming platter of crispy, golden bluegill fillets were beginning to evaporate from my mind. I had fished all the places these delectable panfish were "supposed" to be—to no avail—and I was getting frustrated.

Canals, small bays, piers, moored boats, trees, stumps, the remnants of last year's weeds and even some deeper edges failed to produce a single fish. To top it off, the weather was unseasonably warm, the wind was light and the spring sun was beating on the water—perfect conditions—or so I thought.

The only signs of activity were schools of fish that spooked as I motored past, but they seemed to be small and holding just inches below the surface, always along a sun-drenched, lee shoreline corner.

Curious, I killed the outboard and slowly glided into the next calm corner with the electric motor. I kept the sun at my back, while carefully scanning the water through polarized glasses.

A Swirl...Then Another

I could see fish leaving—and they weren't small. I quietly slid the anchor into the water and baited a small ice-fishing spoon with a live grub.

A long, soft-action rod and a spinning reel with a long-cast spool filled with ultra-thin 4-pound test mono enabled me to get the tiny offering to the fish. Within seconds I was hooked up to a bull bluegill. The rodtip bucked as the big 'gill fought all the way to the boat.

Several more fish followed until the spot burned out, but it didn't matter—I had discovered a new pattern that would allow me to catch all the big 'gills I cared to clean and eat that day.

Since that day about six years ago, I stopped ignoring fish suspended inches under the surface over deep water. I've learned to come in on them quietly and use a two-rod approach to maximize results. Both rods should be at least 6 feet long, and even longer if possible. Long-cast spinning reels are filled with a super-thin clear or low-visibility green mono for maximum casting distance with lightweight baits.

A small "ice-fishing" spoon with a size 6 to 10 hook is baited with a grub or small piece of worm. You may add a tiny split shot to cast a little farther, but place it a few feet up the line to minimize splash when the rig lands.

Rig another ice spoon below a float on the second rod. A lightweight fixed float (non-sliding) such as a Thill Shy Bite or Mini-Shy Bite is best for minimum splash, but when more distance or accuracy is needed, or when fishing a bait deeper than four feet, use a pear-shaped Mini-Stealth slip float.

Both spinning outfits will handle almost all early-season situations.

Big bluegills often suspend. Early in the season, calm, sun-drenched areas draw them like magnets. Besides using protected corners, 'gills also favor small bays or harbors, piers, swimming rafts, lee corners on points or flats, and patchy weed growth. In summer, the big ones will often suspend over open water, but we'll tackle that later on.

Dead-end canals and small bays are other spring hotspots. Fish may be found way back in the canals during early warming trends. After the weather has warmed and stabilized, bluegills may be found throughout the canals and bays.

The keys to how long the fish use these spots are water depth and bottom content. If the bottom has some sand and/or gravel, the fish may use them for spawning purposes. The back ends of bays with soft, dark bottoms warm early and produce insect hatches, while the deeper, firm-bottom areas closer to the main lake are more suitable for spawning.

Sheltered flats can also hold big bluegills. Flats usually have a more fertile bottom than shores that break sharply and are more likely to offer some type of vegetation.

An extended flat with a weedbed can also be good, even if the weeds are old and patchy. As new

Whether on jigs, miniature bait rigs or under slip floats, panfish-size leeches are durable, reliable live baits for catching bull bluegills. Even better, 'gills love to eat 'em.

WHERE TO FIND BIG BLUEGILLS

Best places to check for big, early-season bluegills include areas that are sheltered from the wind and receive direct sunlight (A), man-made canals with dead-end channels (B), sheltered, flat, fertile areas (C), shallow flats with patchy old or new weed growth (D), banks with overhanging brush, tall grass, willows or other trees (E), reed beds (F), stumps and fallen trees (G).

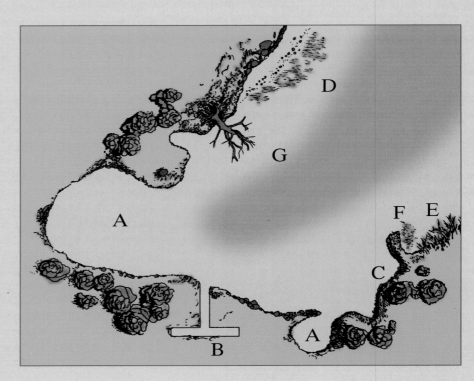

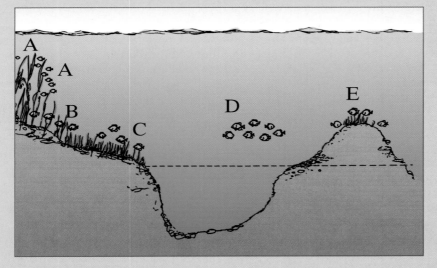

While smaller bluegills hang over the weed tops (A) or suspend along the outside weed edge, the big ones will generally be closer to bottom along the deep edge (B) or down in the weeds. If small fish are in these areas, look for larger ones scattered along deeper short grasses on adjacent flats (C), suspended at or above the thermocline (D), or holding on the sides and tops of sunken islands, humps and other offshore structure (E). Big bluegills that first move into open water from the deep weed edge usually move out on a horizontal plane—from B to D. Later in the day, the fish will move out even farther from the weeds.

weeds begin to sprout, bluegills will hold in them just before spawning along the inside edge (shallower portion) of the bed. Prime spawning areas on natural lakes and ponds are along inside weed edges, in sheltered bays and over shallow flats with patches of weeds.

Banks with overhanging brush, tall grass or willows can hold a lot of fish. The keys are how far the cover extends over the water and the depth of adjacent water. I've seen some willow trees, with their abundance of shade and insects, attract fish until mid-fall … but the key was the proximity to deeper water.

Reeds and rushes can also be hot. In lakes where reeds die in the winter, the remnants of last year's beds draw fish early in the year. Reeds generally grow on sandy bottoms, while rushes usually thrive on a softer, darker bottom. Both may hold fish through summer, but bluegills are more apt to be found along bulrush beds in shallow Southern lakes during the warmer months.

Wood in the water, such as stumps and fallen trees, is an obvious attractor. Visible stumps and the easy-to-fish parts of a fallen tree will generally produce small fish. For bull bluegills, look for deeper stumps, which may only appear as circular patches of darker water.

Quietly slip a bait into the tangles of a fallen tree, and also check outside the tree for deeper, scattered limbs that have been broken off by high water or melting ice. A 20-foot-long telescoping pole like South Bend's SD-20 lets you gently and accurately drop a bait into small openings.

Pattern For Busy Lakes

A special bluegill spawning situation often occurs in clear, deep, heavily used "playground lakes," where water-skiers and pleasure boaters tear up the water as soon as the weather warms.

There aren't many calm spawning areas as boats send waves pounding up against the shore, stirring up the bottom. Even sheltered harbors are a hotbed of activity as boats filter in and out. One of the few places offering bluegills refuge is a large group of moored boats, especially if it features a no-wake zone.

A moored boat is usually held in place by a buoy, which is connected to some type of underwater anchor. Often, this base is a cement-filled tire or a few cinder blocks. Big bluegills will often bed

alongside this cover once the water temperature in the shallows reaches 67 to 68 degrees.

Crawl a small nightcrawler or leech across the bottom behind a medium-size split shot. When you feel it hit the tire or block just wait. If a big 'gill is around, he'll grab the bait. And if you catch one, other moorings should produce additional fish.

Summer Patterns

Once bluegills finish spawning, weed-beds are in bloom and fish movement often involves some type of vegetation.

Most anglers don't understand that while smaller 'gills may hug the shorelines, the big ones prefer deeper water—down in the weeds or along the deep edges. When the medium-size fish are on the outside weedlines, the bulls are deeper along the drop-off, or suspended over deeper water.

"Big bluegills prefer deeper water—down in the weeds or along the deep edges."

Any given body of water usually has some big bluegills in it. I've caught jumbo 'gills out of a lake where only small fish were supposed to exist. The keys to summertime success on bull bluegills are fishing deep, checking for suspended fish and using leeches to bypass smaller fish.

Years ago, I accidentally discovered big bluegills in deep water while slow-fishing 20- to 35-foot depths with live bait rigs. We were using nightcrawlers and leeches for walleyes and smallmouth bass, but we began to catch giant bluegills. And this wasn't an isolated instance, as a number of anglers in our fishing network experienced the same thing in other lakes.

The consensus was that big 'gills on deep structure often became active just before the walleyes started to hit, and the bluegills were consistently being caught off deep flats and the tops of deep humps and bars, while the walleyes held along the edges, generally five to 10 feet deeper.

Author Spence Petros prefers a 6- to 7-foot spinning rod, ultra-thin mono and slip floats for tackling early-season bluegills on flats peppered with scattered patches of last year's weeds.

It was then just a matter of downsizing our presentations and slowing down, with a lot of stop-and-go tactics, to catch more bull bluegills.

Suspended Bluegills

Most anglers experiencing consistent success on big bluegills during the summer are fishing outside weed edges, deeper structure or cover such as fallen trees, stumps, docks or overhanging trees that border deeper water.

Most are missing vast schools of virtually untouched, suspended bluegills that commonly exist in lakes that develop a thermocline.

The reason most anglers get fooled is because they experience big-fish activity early and late in the day on deep weed edges and structure, then assume the fish quit biting after 9 a.m.

I've been catching suspended open-water bluegills for more than 25 years, but Jerry Belz, of Prairie, Wisconsin, really has it down to a science.

"About mid- to late-June the big bluegills start using open water," claims Belz. "I don't rush out in a hurry to start fishing. About 9 a.m., I'll start looking for suspended fish with my sonar. I prefer to motor downwind at a moderate speed, to reduce the amount of boat slap on the water; too much noise will spook fish and you won't pick them up on your sonar.

"Start just outside the weedline, and generally stay over depths of 15 to 35 feet," he continued. "Later in the day, the fish may hold over even deeper water, especially if it's bright and sunny. In late afternoon, a reverse movement occurs, with the big 'gills arriving at the weedline again during the last hour or two of the day."

Once Belz locates a concentration of fish, he sets up a drift quartering through the area. Rather than drifting in from the weedline directly to the deep water, he wants to stay in the fish zone as long as possible, so a little burst from an electric motor may be in order once in awhile, if the wind isn't favorable.

Belz and other open-water experts use as many rods as the law allows. Small spoons and tiny jigs baited with grubs are a top choice, but many experiment with small weighted plastics such as the super-thin Willy Worms, Berkley Micro Power Worms and Power Wigglers, or any other small tidbit that will fit into a bluegill's tiny mouth. A split shot or two is often placed above the offering to get the bait down to the fish. Four-pound test line is a good all-around choice.

"The windier the better," claims Belz. "Calm, bright days are tough. But when the wind is blowing and there's some cloud cover, you can usually catch all the fish you want."

Big, suspended bluegills are not just found in a few select lakes, they occur in a lot of waters where they are vastly overlooked. I've found them in natural lakes and reservoirs—even farm ponds and quarries. And in these smaller bodies of water, shorebound anglers can easily reap the harvest by using properly balanced European-style floats and small baits.

Bait And Tackle Tips

During periods of colder water, tiny spoons and jigs dressed with small baits such as mealworms, grubs, maggots or pieces of worms are top choices. As the waters warm and the 'gills become more aggressive, larger baits like crickets, hellgrammites, pinhead minnows, grasshoppers, catalpa worms,

garden worms and baby nightcrawlers work well.

My absolute favorite bait for bull bluegills from post spawn until early fall is a medium-size leech. Small leeches attract both large and small 'gills, but a larger leech seems to intimidate the smaller fish.

You can also pull a leech slowly away from a small bluegill without ripping it off the hook. I've caught hundreds of big bluegills by sight fishing them with leeches. And it's a rare bluegill that can't be caught on a leech fished with 2- or 4-pound test line and a light-wire size 8 hook.

Small jig-type lures such as inch-long swirltails, tiny tube jigs, little Road Runners and 1/32-ounce Fuzz-E-Grubs also take big 'gills. Put a little bait on them if fishing is slow.

I favor 6- to 7-foot, light-action spinning rods and long-cast reels filled with premium extra-thin mono. Clear line is favored when line watching, while low-visibility green is preferred for other situations. Twelve-foot European-style float rods are particularly effective when fishing from shore, as well as dabbling baits in hard-to-reach spots from a boat.

When big bluegills are in the shallows spawning, or they are feeding near the surface, a fly rod is a deadly tool. I favor a 5-weight fly rod (and matching line) between 7½ to 8 feet long. A floating, weight-forward line is used to cast size 8 or 10 popping bugs, sponge spiders or nymphs.

What Makes Big Bluegills

After 30 years of chasing big 'gills, I've come to the conclusion that no single type of water is best. I've caught bulls in farm ponds, shallow flowages, deep lakes, strip-mine pits and slow-moving rivers.

Any body of water produces a certain amount of bluegill forage per acre. If 1,000 bluegills exist in that acre, each would hypothetically eat $\frac{1}{1,000}$ of the available forage. If half the fish were removed, the remaining half would get double the share. So the first factor is how much forage is available for each fish.

Sterile waters produce fewer pounds per acre than fertile lakes having a lot of suspended forage such as various forms of plankton, tiny freshwater shrimp or "water lice."

Low gamefish populations also hurt the chances for bluegills to reach trophy size. As numbers of bass, pike, muskies, stripers, catfish and walleyes decline, bluegill numbers skyrocket—and individual fish have less to eat, causing over-abundant, stunted 'gills.

Much of my big-bluegill success comes from fishing in lakes where bluegills are a neglected species, fishing deeper waters, and going after that virtually unmolested population of suspended fish. Of course, being able to get into a good fertile farm pond now and then sure doesn't hurt.

'CRAWLER HARNESS FOR BULLS

Most people assume you need small baits for big bluegills, but that's not always the case. Bluegill expert Terry Tuma has spent years studying the ways of trophy 'gills, and he's designed a summertime live bait rig which targets the biggest bulls in any system.

Start with two feet of limp, 4-pound test monofilament, either green or clear depending on water clarity. Tie on a pair of size 8, long-shank Aberdeen-style Tru-Turn hooks, 3 inches apart. Thread on a single size 3mm bead, red or orange, and attach a black barrel swivel to the other end. Use a 1/16- to 1/8-ounce bullet sinker. Rig a 6-inch 'crawler and, using an electric motor, troll it slowly along deep weedlines, the edges of sunken islands, on humps (particularly those with cabbage or other weed growth). Use slow, short sweeps of the rod to trigger strikes.

If the bluegills are extremely tight-lipped, thread a 1½-inch 'crawler section on a single size 8 Aberdeen hook. Pinch a split shot 10 inches above the bait. Two-pound line is best for this rig, which should be "jig-trolled" in the same areas.

—Dan Johnson

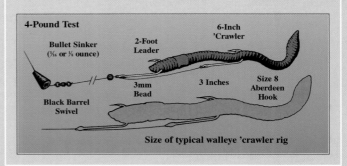

Size of typical walleye 'crawler rig

Suspended Panfish

by Louie Stout

During the hot, midday hours, big bluegills and crappie are usually not shallow, and they don't stop biting! Here's the real scoop on what's going on.

Everyone is an expert when panfish are shallow and hungry. Come summer, however, only the strong survive as schools of bull bluegills and slab crappie vanish from skinny water near shore. Then, the only anglers catching these broad-shouldered fish with even a hint of consistency are those who know where to look.

That means deep water, but it doesn't always mean fishing deep.

The deep weed edge is the starting point for most anglers. Both bluegills and crappie can be found here, especially during peak feeding times early and late in the day, but weedlines hold just some of the fish some of the time.

To find the largest concentrations, you must look even farther from shore—into the murky depths where big panfish suspend.

Sometimes the mother lode is merely a long cast from the weedline. In other situations, the boys of summer are so far offshore you feel odd targeting panfish.

Chasing suspended summer panfish is a game of adjusting your tactics to the conditions. It's a game we'll show you how to win.

Profile Of A Stalker

Don Stevens of Kalamazoo, Michigan, plays the suspended panfish game better than most. In fact, he's so good, if panfish had a post office, his picture would be tacked to the wall.

"Don's the best I've ever seen at catching suspended panfish," says NAFC Bass Advisory Council Member Kevin VanDam, a friend of Stevens. "He catches more fish in late summer than anyone I know."

Stevens shrugs off the praise by saying anyone with good sonar, light tackle and a feel for detecting subtle bites can do just as well.

He stumbled onto his deadly tactic years ago, when he read a magazine article about a Texas fisherman who used a paper graph to find suspended crappie during the winter. "I decided that if he could do it there, I could do it too," Stevens recalls.

The following summer, Stevens put the theory to the test on one of his favorite lakes. "I idled around the middle, watching for fish to appear on my sonar," he says. "When a large, black glob emerged on the screen in 30 feet of water, I couldn't believe it was fish. The blob began 10 feet beneath the sur-

Don Stevens prowls lakes for suspended panfish, a tactic he says any NAFC member can master.

face and was stacked several feet thick."

Stevens quietly backed off, dropped anchor and cast in the direction of the school.

"My bait sank 7 feet and stopped suddenly. I wondered why, so I jerked on the rod and a fish jerked back. I proceeded to catch 25 crappie on 25 casts and have been a believer [in suspended panfish] ever since," he says.

That eye-opening experience taught Stevens several valuable lessons, including the importance of sonar—and the fact that fishermen should never get locked into a weedline pattern for panfish during the summer.

Why Panfish Suspend

Some panfish, especially small fish, never leave

THE DAILY COMMUTE

Panfish suspending in deep water during midday (A) often make an afternoon commute, following zooplankton and minnows in one of two directions. Bluegills and crappie near the deep weedline move in to feed (B), while offshore fish migrate toward the surface (C). Just the reverse occurs in the morning hours. Hint: Depths will be greater than shown here, in clear water.

shallow water in July and August. Young bluegills feed heavily on the abundant supply of insect larvae and other invertebrates that live on aquatic vegetation. The weeds also offer juvenile 'gills protection from largemouth bass and other predators.

A curious thing happens once bluegills reach adulthood, however. Their tastes change. Large 'gills often abandon the sanctuary of the weeds and move out into deeper water to feed on zooplankton such as daphnia. As their diets change, they become dependent upon the movement of zooplankton throughout the water column, and depending on the conditions, may range from near bottom to the surface.

Not all big bluegills make the switch to zooplankton, however. And even when they do, the change may only be for a short period of time. Studies have shown that this behavior varies on different lakes—a mystery fishery scientists are still trying to unravel. But it's still a pattern worth checking out on any lake you fish.

Crappie, too, aren't tied to the weeds. Like bluegills, crappie will feed on zooplankton, but

they're particularly fond of minnows. On lakes with a shad forage base, crappie may follow schools of juvenile shad into open water far from near-shore weeds and other classic habitat such as standing timber. Same thing goes with emerald shiners and other minnow species which rarely relate to shoreline vegetation.

Both bluegills and crappie will also suspend in deep water near the weed edge during the day, then move in to feed at dawn and dusk.

Where To Look

Locating suspended panfish can be as simple as driving around the lake until you mark fish on your sonar. But combing the water with a narrow sonar beam can be a time-consuming task, unless you know where to look.

It's impossible to produce a blueprint that will outline summer panfish locations on every lake. The pattern of summer migration into open water varies from one lake to the next, according to the availability of forage, water clarity, oxygen levels and other factors.

Understand how these variables interact with one another, however, and it's possible to make an educated guess about panfish location on the lakes near you.

On lakes where crappie totally abandon the weed edge to follow schools of minnows, they tend to roam farther from shore than bluegills dining on zooplankton. Your best is to crank up the sonar, set up as many rods as the law allows, and start looking.

To locate bull 'gills, look in deep water off classic weedline haunts, such as long, gradually tapering points. Check the lake map for sunken islands and humps, too. Bluegills may be holding tight or suspending nearby, especially if the top of the structure is covered with weeds.

Forage also plays a large role in the depth at which panfish hold. Consider the relationship between bluegills, zooplankton and their environment, for example. 'Gills feed on zooplankton, which feed on microscopic plants (phytoplankton).

These tiny plants move up and down in the water column according to light intensity. Seeking the sun's rays, phytoplankton tend to move higher during low-light periods such as dawn and dusk. Conversely, they will be deeper on days when the sun shines brightly. Zooplankton follow, as do bluegills.

What about crappie? Same thing. They feed on minnows, which eat plankton. Follow the forage trail and eventually you'll locate the predators.

Since light penetration is greater in clear water than turbid, you can expect the entire food chain to be deeper in a clear lake than it will be in dingy waters. Bluegills could be 80 feet down in extremely clear water, or just three feet beneath the surface in a nutrient-rich, eutrophic lake.

But there's more to the equation than that. Water clarity—or the lack thereof—is generally a function of the amount of nutrients, phytoplankton and zooplankton floating around the lake.

If zooplankton are scattered in a deep, clear body of water, panfish will be, too. Of course, bluegills are less likely to abandon weed-related

WEATHER AND WARMTH

Water temperature and weather play a major role in where bluegills and crappie suspend, says fisheries biologist Jed Pearson. "The fish seek water temperatures that provide them the most comfort, and layers of water that contain the most food."

Both bluegills and crappie prefer water temperatures in the 60- to 65-degree range, though they can survive in warmer or colder water.

Prime feeding opportunities are almost always linked to zooplankton, which move up and down in the water column following their own food supply—phytoplankton. As daylight increases, plankton move deeper, then rise as light levels fall at the end of the day. Look for panfish closer to the surface on overcast days, and when there's a chop on the water.

Pearson notes that oxygen depletion in water below the thermocline also pushes panfish closer to the surface. "The band of depleted oxygen on the bottom increases in depth throughout the summer," he describes. "It just keeps pushing the food chain toward the surface, where there is more oxygen."

Time of year can be a factor, too. In the fall, rising and falling water temperatures affect the depth at which panfish suspend, says Indiana panfish expert Ken Tucker.

"Panfish tend to be more active during warmer periods of the day whenever the water is cooling down or warming up, such as during the fall or in the spring," Tucker adds.

He says fish that were holding in 15 to 30 feet of water during the early morning periods can move within a few feet of the surface on a sunny fall day.

"It's almost like they're sunning themselves," Tucker explains. "On the other hand, a sudden cold front will push them deeper."

Crappie and bluegill can't resist the combination of a jig head, soft plastic mini tube bait, and waxworms.

forage when zooplankton are scarce, so you might not even have to look beyond shoreline vegetation—assuming there is some.

Just the opposite is true in turbid water, where both types of plankton and hungry bluegills will be found in a narrow band near the surface. That's Stevens' preferred scenario.

"The suspended panfish pattern is most effective when light penetration is reduced," he says. "Particularly when the water is clouded by algae blooms."

Oxygen also affects the levels at which panfish suspend. In lakes that stratify during summer, low oxygen levels often prevent bluegills and crappie from venturing below the thermocline.

Catching The Commuters

The deep weedline on many lakes produces a decent panfish bite early and late in the day through-out much of the summer. Though the fishing drops off during the day on the edge of the weeds, these waters can actually offer the best of both worlds.

Both crappie and bluegills will feed along the weeds early in the morning, suspend in deeper water during the day, then return to the weeds to feed when the sun dips low in the horizon.

Catching these commuters in their daytime quarters is a matter of following them into deep water. Rather than going in for coffee after the weed bite cools down, quietly search the adjacent open water.

Electronic Eyes

This isn't weedline fishing; visual clues guide you to concentrations of panfish. This means a good sonar unit and the ability to use it are essential.

"I never wet a line until I mark fish with my electronics," Stevens insists. "Then I know the exact spot and the precise depth at which the fish are holding. It eliminates the guesswork."

Stevens prefers a liquid-crystal display (LCD) unit because it gives him "a better picture of where the fish are," he explains. "Flashers work, too, but you have to pay close attention or you could miss the fish." An LCD with at least a 20-degree cone angle, or better yet, multiple sonar beams, will speed your search both in shallow, turbid waters and when panfish are scattered and suspended in deep water.

Panfish will swim close to one another, but rarely school tightly enough to form a solid band on the screen. Baitfish such as young shad will, however, and you may find crappie in close proximity to such a dark cloud.

Art Of Presentation

When Stevens locates a school of panfish, he tosses a marker buoy into the water ahead of the school, then positions the boat so the wind is to his back and the school is between him and the buoy.

"The wind helps you cast tiny baits farther," he explains.

Stevens ties a long anchor rope to the back of the boat. If he needs to get closer, he lets out more rope; if he's too close to the fish, he shortens the anchor line. Also, by anchoring off the back, the rope is unlikely to interfere with hooked fish.

As a side note, Stevens believes the marker buoy does more than provide him with a visual target in open water. He says fish are often attracted to the buoy string, and sometimes school tightly around it.

"I think it's like a bush sitting on a barren flat," he offers. "This string is the only thing around them in open water. It's natural for them to be attracted to it. Unfortunately, if they hold real tight to the marker you may snag the string with a cast."

Stevens says he's observed another phenomenon of suspended fish. He believes a continuous sonar signal can cause a school to move, so he turns off his electronics once he's pinpointed the fish.

"I've seen it happen many times when I've anchored too close to the fish and forgot to turn off the electronics," he explains. "All of a sudden the fish quit biting and the school disperses."

Stevens uses mini tube jigs for both crappie and bluegills, on jig heads ranging from 1/64- to 1/8-ounce. Day in and day out, 1/16- and 1/32-ounce heads are his favorites.

Crappie typically prefer slightly larger tubes, while bluegills often demand smaller baits. If the 'gills are near bottom in deep water, a small split shot a foot to 18 inches up the line helps take a tiny jig deep.

Stevens experiments with colors, but says chartreuse tends to work best for the crappie on the waters he fishes. Blue and white can be a top producer for bluegills.

The jig is tipped with as many as four waxworms, which he threads onto the hook shank and pushes into the tube's cavity.

"The jig is a vehicle for getting the hook and bait to the fish," he explains. "The waxworm offers a little scent and taste, and the tube provides a more lifelike feel. I suppose you could catch them with waxworms piled onto a plain jig head, but the complete package will catch more fish."

Obviously, tiny baits require light line and longer rods. Stevens uses a 7-foot, medium-light spinning rod and 4-pound test line. In ultra-clear water, or when the fish are fussy, he switches to 2-pound test.

Longer rods provide more hooksetting leverage

In the split-screen mode, the right side of Stevens' fishfinder shows what may appear to be weeds on the bottom. However, the left half of the screen (zoom mode) magnifies the area and shows panfish suspended nearly 10 feet off the bottom. This proved to be a school of crappie.

in deep water, and their sensitivity improves Stevens' ability to detect subtle bites. He says almost any decent spinning reel will work, but prefers larger spools to boost casting distance.

Stevens casts slightly past the fish and counts the bait down. "I know from experience how fast each jig size falls," he explains. "So I can estimate when the jig is in the school."

You can establish sink rates for your jigs by dropping them overboard on a slack line in a known depth of water. Just count them down until they hit bottom, then do the math.

"The most important thing to remember is that you're fishing a depth, not a structure. If I think it's a '20 count' to where the fish are, I'll count to 20 then lift the rod and slowly swim the jig back. If no strikes occur, I'll cast again and count to 30 before I begin my retrieve."

If the fish are scattered, drift or troll through the area with your jigs at the depth you marked the fish. Use your electric trolling motor to stay on course, or hover over a particularly productive spot long enough to pluck a few fish from it.

Trolling deep water may require jigs up to 1/4-ounce, though 1/8 ouncers are generally better. Experiment with mini-spinnerbaits such as Beetle Spins and Super Shysters; the blades may attract fish from a distance. As with Stevens' casting presentation, use a lift-drop technique to swim the bait as you troll.

Where legal, spider rigging (primarily a Southern technique that involves slow trolling with multiple poles, usually 10–16 feet long) is an excellent technique for taking scattered panfish, particularly crappie. The more lines you put in the water, the better your chances of connecting with suspended slabs.

The most difficult aspect of Stevens' system is knowing when a fish has the bait. This is compounded by the fact that many strikes occur as the bait is falling—whether casting or jig-trolling.

"The line becomes your bobber," he says. "Don't expect it to jump or rush sideways unless the fish are really aggressive. With most strikes, the jig just stops falling before it hits bottom."

Like the rest of Stevens' system, strike detection takes practice. However, the payoff is big bluegills and crappie long after the spring fling has faded.

Crickets & Crackers

by Jeff Samsel

Spawning shellcrackers provide some of the season's hottest fishing action.
Here's how to time it right, find the fish and get them to hit.

G erald Mishoe understood exactly what his hands were wrapped around. But on Easter Sunday, it would take nearly two hours for him and his cousin, H.F. Gunnells, to find a certified scale on which they could weigh the monstrous redear sunfish they had just landed.

"I know it sounds like a fish story," Mishoe says, "but the fish weighed 5 pounds, 3 ounces on my Berkley digital scale immediately after it was caught."

That would have tied the current world record for the species. Even at 5 pounds, 1 ounce, registered on the scales at Angler's Mart in Moncks Corner, the fish took South Carolina's state record by more than a pound and was easily among the largest redears ever caught.

Redear sunfish, or shellcrackers, as they're much better known throughout their range, are the big daddies of the sunfish clan. Their top-end potential exceeds that of even bluegills, and while 6- to 8-inch fish represent the norm in most waters, pounders show up frequently in shellcracker hotspots.

Shellcrackers eat insect larvae and a mix of small aquatic critters, just as other sunfish species do. But as their nickname implies, they have a strong preference for fresh-cracked clams, mussels and snails.

A study conducted on South Carolina's Lake Murray showed mollusks made up roughly 70 percent of the diet of two-year-old shellcrackers, and that number increased to more than 80 percent by age three.

The same study showed shellcrackers growing to roughly 3½ inches in their first year and taking three years to reach 10 inches in length, which is consistent with other growth-rate studies done on the species.

The Ultimate Fishing Book: Strategies for Success

TIMING THE SPAWN

*I*n many ways, shellcrackers are similar to other sunfish species, but they can be tougher to catch, on average. That's why most anglers target them during the spawning season. Like bluegills, shellcrackers are colonial nesters. A hundred or more nests may be built in a confined area.

Unlike bluegills, which spawn throughout the summer months in the southern half of their range, shellcrackers spawn most heavily during the spring and fall. Activity is clearly related to water temperature, with most spawning taking place when water temps hover at 72 degrees. However, it appears that spawning ceases when temperatures climb too high. Evidence of this can be found in spawn timing throughout the fish's range.

In the most southern part of its range (Florida and Alabama), the shellcracker spawns heavily in the spring and fall, but sparingly during the summer. In the central part of their range

(Texas to South Carolina), spawning begins in May and continues into the middle of summer.

In northern states like Illinois and Michigan, however, spawning is usually restricted to mid summer and may last only a month.

One study in Florida says spawning peaks coincide with a full and new moon—an important fact to keep in mind as you plan upcoming fishing trips.

Another factor to consider is preferred spawning depth. Shellcrackers may lay their eggs in water just inches deep, or may deposit them up to 10 feet below the surface, depending on water clarity. In relatively clear-water lakes where redear sunfish are most common, spawning beds are often located four to six feet deep. In lakes where they coexist with bluegills, shellcrackers generally spawn deeper than 'gills. They build shallow-depression nests on sand, gravel, or mud bottoms.

—Dr. Hal Schramm

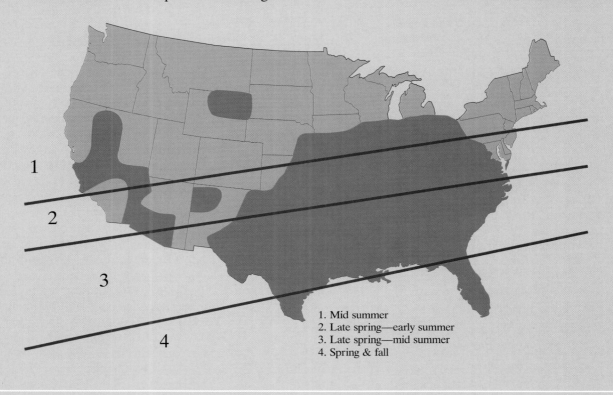

1. Mid summer
2. Late spring—early summer
3. Late spring—mid summer
4. Spring & fall

LAKE FISHING TECHNIQUE

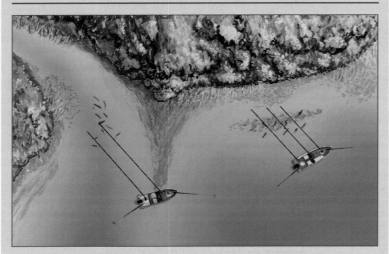

Slowly cast and retrieve when fishing still water. You don't need to impart action to the bait, just cover water. Under the right circumstances (fish location and wind direction), you can also drift over the fish zone. Again, key on submerged grass and clam beds.

RIVER FISHING TECHNIQUE

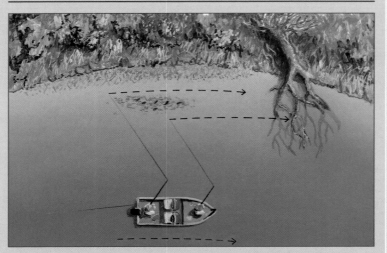

Submerged vegetation near a clam bed is a prime spot for big 'crackers, as are fallen trees along the shoreline. In slowly-moving water, anchor the boat and allow the light current to drift your baits through the fish zone.

However, in controlled pond settings, where the water is heavily fertilized, these fish regularly grow to 8 inches in a single year.

The native range of shellcrackers extends roughly from Florida to Texas to Missouri, but the fish have been stocked in various waters through the Midwest and Southwest. Less prolific breeders than bluegills, shellcrackers are considered good fish to stock in smaller lakes because they are less apt to become overpopulated and stunted.

Gerald Mishoe and H.F. Gunnells, both of Charleston, South Carolina, target shellcrackers and bluegills extensively. The record fish came from the diversion canal between South Carolina's famed Moultrie and Marion lakes, and that is where these two anglers spend the bulk of their angling hours.

They catch more big fish in a weekend than a typical angler catches during his lifetime. Fishing with them recently on the diversion canal, I got in on a mixed catch of 18 shellcrackers and bluegills that together weighed just over 16 pounds. Incredible as it sounds to most anglers, that's a normal day of panfishing for these fellows.

Fish A Fertile System

Like most top shellcracker waters, the diversion canal has a deep, sandy bottom, plentiful wood cover, modest current at most times, and relatively clear water for a very fertile system. It also has a thriving population of tiny Asiatic clams.

Occasionally, a shell will become lodged on a hook as Mishoe and Gunnells are fishing. When that happens, the anglers consider it a very good sign.

"Bring up a clam shell and you should catch some shellcrackers," Mishoe says. "They'll be down there feasting on those clams."

The pair has tried using the meat from the little clams as bait, with minimal success. They also buck popular wisdom that says worms are the best bait for shellcrackers. Their preference is the bait that took the state-record fish—crickets!

Shellcrackers use a wider range of depths

than most other sunfish, commonly holding as deep as 35 feet through the summer. They like little or no current, and are more apt to be found along the edge of a vegetation mat than right up under the grass itself.

In Southern reservoirs and rivers that traditionally produce big shellcrackers, biologists and creel clerks generally find numbers of anglers targeting the species in mid to late spring. That's when the fish move toward their spawning beds. Fishermen like Mishoe and Gunnells, who go after shellcrackers year-round, are the exception, not the norm.

Shellcrackers spawn when water temperatures are in the 70- to 74-degree range, and they stay on the beds approximately three weeks. Shellcrackers favor sandy bottoms when spawning, and tend to choose open or semi-open areas of lakes, instead of the backs of creeks and coves where bluegills prefer to bed.

Bedding 'Crackers

Male shellcrackers scoop out the nests and guard the eggs, but males and females hold in the vicinity of good spawning habitat throughout the spring. Five to 15 feet is a good range to fish from

The all-important slip float allows precise bait placement, whether you're fishing in just 2 feet of water or 20.

MORE ABOUT SHELLCRACKERS

Officially, they're called redear sunfish, but legions of anglers know them as shellcrackers, or simply 'crackers. Others call them, bream, yellow bream, or the all-inclusive "perch."

The fish has a set of highly-developed grinding teeth in its throat which are capable of crushing snails, thus the name.

But shellcrackers also eat crickets, worms, grubs, catalpa worms, insect larvae and other typical sunfish foods. You can catch them on artificials, too, at times.

The gill cover on an adult shellcracker has a whitish border with the tip accented with a bright red (males) or orange (females) margin around it.

Their back and sides are light olive-green to gold, their breast yellow to yellow-orange. There are five to 10 dusky vertical bars on their sides, their pectoral fins are long and pointed.

They can be distinguished from the pumpkinseed, which they most closely resemble, by the lack of spots on the dorsal fin and the missing blue wavy cheek lines. They have the same breeding habits as the pumpkinseed, and have been known to hybridize with bluegill and green sunfish.

Most shellcrackers are caught in the spring while on spawning beds. Later, they move to deeper water or heavy cover and are more difficult to locate. In the summer, they can hold 25 to 35 feet below the surface.

Shellcrackers produce fewer young than other sunfish, but they grow more quickly and usually grow larger than bluegills in the same body of water.

Locating a bed of shellcrackers can produce good sized and good numbers of fish.

mid-March through the end of June. But when the fish are actually on the beds, they can be much shallower.

Shellcrackers hold low in the water column, whatever the water depth, so presenting baits near the floor is essential. Most anglers use split shot rigs to keep their baits near bottom, but Mishoe and Gunnells add a slip float to the system to make their presentations even more precise.

The slip float rig offers instant depth control, allowing them to suspend baits just above tree limbs and sunken grassbeds, regardless of depth.

More importantly, the slip float allows them to drift baits through potential hotspots—looking for fish instead of waiting for them. From an anchored boat, the anglers quarter-cast upstream and allow the current to carry the rigs through the fish zone.

"We cover a lot of water with our rigs, while at the same time, we keep the baits down deep," says Mishoe. "We are able to figure out exactly where the baits need to be. Often, we'll get several hits in a very small area, and if the next cricket does not

pass through that exact spot, at just the right depth, you would think there were no fish in the river."

While shellcrackers are almost always in the lower third of the water column, Mishoe and Gunnells know there's no magic depth that will produce fish every time. If they don't connect with 'crackers at traditional depths, they adjust their float stops until they find the strike zone.

One week the cricket has to tick bottom to draw a strike; the next week it may be ignored unless it's riding two feet higher. "You have to experiment every time," Mishoe explains.

Fly Rod Fanatics

Instead of the typical panfish rig, Mishoe and Gunnells fish 9-foot, 5- or 6-weight fly rods. They're matched with Penn 4200 ultra-light spinning reels and 6-pound clear monofilament. The long, whippy rods allow the anglers to cast lightweight offerings effectively, and provide the leverage needed to finesse big fish to the boat. Plus, they're simply fun to fish because the length and action allows the

'crackers to put up a good fight.

As an added benefit, the long rods serve as gauges to quickly check the depth of the bait up to 18 feet (two rod lengths).

"If I catch a couple fish and Gerald hasn't had a strike, we'll do a depth-check," Gunnells says. By reeling the float stop to the reel, he can show his partner how deep he's fishing.

Gunnells and Mishoe rely on the canal's light currents to carry their offerings through likely areas, but what about anglers who fish still water?

The system works as well, according to the pair, but instead of current, you use wind to drift your boat over the fish zone. In the absence of wind, you can also cast-and-retrieve the float rig slowly over the area.

An occasional twitch of the rod, or crank of the reel handle, is all that's required. You're only trying to cover more of the productive zone, not impart any type of action to the bait.

Remember, go after 'crackers, don't wait on them. And, make adjustments until you find the right depth where the fish are biting.

Whether you fish lakes or slow-moving rivers, take a page out of H.F. Gunnells and Gerald Mishoe's shellcracker book. Next time you could be the one who goes running around looking for a certified scale.

Chapter 4

Crappie

W ho doesn't love crappies? They are panfish extraordinaire — from their widespread range and habitat preferences, to their willingness to bite, to something as simple as how handsome a basket or cooler looks with all those silver and black-speckled crappies flopping around. Whether it's spring, summer, fall or winter... somewhere, somebody's out chasing crappies.

But these panfish are not pushovers. The spawn makes them relatively accessible, but the rest of the year is a different story. Here is sound advice on unlocking the secrets.

Cranking For Crappies

by Gary Nelson

Why not! You can cover a lot of water, and have excellent control over your lure's depth and speed. And bigger-than-average crappies will usually smack your offerings.

When Scott Szafran felt the unmistakable thump of a fish hitting his crankbait, little did he know that the crappie on the other end of his line would land his name in the record book. The slab struck while he and fishing partner Ed Grunst trolled along a drop-off blanketed with cabbage weeds on Lake Elizabeth in extreme southeastern Wisconsin. The 2-pound, 1-ounce black-and-white

hybrid crappie is now the National Fresh Water Fishing Hall of Fame's new all-tackle record.

"There was only one hook in his lip and we didn't have a net with us," Szafran recalls. "I tried to lip it like you would a bass, but that didn't work. Instead, I grabbed the line and lifted. Luckily, the fish didn't fall off until it was inside the boat."

By now, I know many of you are thinking,

"Crappies on crankbaits? No way!" Believe it. Crappie anglers across the country are finding out just how deadly crankbaits are for crappies, especially the new miniature models. Crankbaits allow you to strain lots of water, especially during post-spawn and summer periods when crappies often roam open water, making it difficult to locate them. Warm-water specklesides may also target larger prey than they do in spring—a size perfectly matched by crankbaits that look more real than jigs when fishing at a slightly faster than usual speed.

> ## "Crankbaits allow you to strain lots of water."

Crankbaiting crappies is a new technique, but fish from Florida to Manitoba will hit these baits. It's especially popular in northern Mississippi, where lakes are commonly murky. One weekend last summer, a group of Mississippi trollers I know caught 150 crappies, including some real slabs, on small crankbaits weighted with split shot. At a nearby reservoir, the tactic was successfully employed on main points in 20 feet of water during the same week. While Szafran notes that his record crappie also came from murky water, he adds that crankbaits are effective in transparent water, too.

"I've had great success trolling for crappies in the clear waters of Bull Shoals Lake in June and July," he says.

Choosing Crankbaits

Clear-water anglers appear to fare best with extra small, clear-lipped baits sporting natural colors. Brightly colored, slightly larger baits provide extra visibility in dark water.

E.F. Johnston, a bait shop owner on the Mississippi River's relatively murky Tunica Cut-Off, says he carries locally made, no-name crankbaits for crappie fans. He says chartreuse models work best in winter, but top summer-trolling hues are green-and-white, blue-and-white and black-and-white.

The lure's action is also important. Drag it alongside your boat to check its movement and make sure the lure runs true. If it tracks to one side, bend the line tie a bit in the direction you want the lure to go.

Generally, if the line attaches at the lure's nose, the lure has little side-to-side wobble, a possible advantage in cold or clear water. If the line attaches to the lip, it has more wobble, and is fitting for warm or murky water.

Size is another consideration. Scott Szafran's record crappie smacked a $4^{1}/_{2}$-inch Hellbender, but crankbaits that are smaller than typical bass lures bring more hits, even in murky water. Fortunately, more and more lure manufacturers are offering crankbaits that match the size and shape of minnows, shad, young crayfish and other typical crappie prey.

Deep Divers

Big-lipped crankbait that can be retrieved at slow speeds are the ticket when crappies are 10 to 20 feet down. Crankbaits generally run at the depths the makers claim when casting, but usually run deeper when trolled. You can check running depths by casting or trolling lures through various waters' known depths and noting when the lures hit bottom.

Many deep divers match deep-bellied baitfish and commonly run $1^{1}/_{8}$ to 3 inches long. Good examples are the Rapala Shad Rap SR5, $^{3}/_{16}$-ounce; Cotton Cordell Wee Shad, $^{1}/_{9}$-ounce; C.C. Shad, $^{1}/_{3}$-ounce; Rebel Shad-R, $^{1}/_{3}$-ounce; Bomber Model "A", $^{1}/_{8}$-ounce; and Storm Pee Wee Wart, $^{1}/_{5}$-ounce. Quarter-ounce baits include the Luhr-Jensen Triple Deep, Storm Hot'N Tot, Bomber Model A and Fat A, Cotton Cordell Wally Diver, Bagley Diving Bitty B, and for extra-deep crappies, try the Luhr-Jensen Baby Hot Lips. It dives to 23 feet when trolled on 8-pound-test line.

Thin, minnow-like baits that produce a tighter wobble include the new Rebel Ghost Minnows in $^{3}/_{32}$-, $^{1}/_{9}$- and $^{1}/_{8}$-ounce sizes; and Killer Baits Killer Shiner, $^{1}/_{4}$-ounce.

Shallow Divers

Because shallow-diving crankbaits are commonly floating lures, they're somewhat snag-proof, which is perfect for fishing shallow feeding shelves. You might consider trolling them behind planer boards, away from the boat, to keep from spooking shallow-water fish.

With a little added weight, these lures can be used successfully in deep water, too. Simply attach

Miniature crankbaits imitate the young prey crappies love to eat.

some split shot, an L-armed, "bottom bouncer" sinker to take them down. A 1-ounce sinker is recommended for water 10 to 20 feet deep, 2-ounce for 20 to 40 feet. The leader from sinker to crankbait should be about 3 to 5 feet long. Some of these sinkers can be rigged slip-style, so a crappie hooked on a thin-wire hook is less apt to rip free.

Lures with deep-bellied, shad-type shapes, generally 1 to 2½ inches in length, include the Rapala Shallow Shad Rap SSR5, 3/16-ounce and Mini Fat Rap, 1/8-ounce; Smithwick Bo-Jack, 3/16-ounce; Storm ThinFin Silver Shad T Series, 1/5-ounce; Rebel Super Teeny Wee-R, 1/8-ounce; and Bill Norman Quarter Bug, 1/10-ounce. Quarter-ouncers include the Cotton Cordell Big O; Rapala Fat Rap; Rebel Super Teeny-R and Humpback; Yakima Hawg Boss Mini-Toad; and Bomber Fat "A", 1/16- and 1/5-ounce.

Narrower, minnow-shaped baits (1½ to 3 inches) include the No. 5 Floating Rapala, 1/16-ounce; Jointed Rapala Model J7, 1/8-ounce; Storm Jr. ThunderStick J series, 1/4-ounce; Rebel Minnow, 1/16-ounce; Heddon Hellcat, 1/4-ounce; Acme Nils Master IDR5, 2 inches; Luhr-Jensen Sea-Bee, 3 inches; Gaines Rainbow Runner, 1/4-ounce; and Bomber Long "A", 1/16-ounce.

Banana-shaped plugs include the Yakima Helin FlatFish, 1/4-ounce; Luhr-Jensen Beno, 1/4-ounce and Kwikfish, 1¼ inches.

"Small crankbaits are best when trolling for slab crappies."

Rebel has a series of ultra-light "naturals" that mimic real forage. These lures are Teeny Wee Crayfish, 1/10-ounce; Deep Teeny Wee Crayfish, 1/9-ounce; Wee Crayfigh, 1/5-ounce; Teeny Wee Frog, 1/8-ounce; Hellgrammite, 3/32-ounce; Crickhopper, 3/32-ounce; Creek Creature, 9/64-ounce; Tadfry, 1/16-ounce; and Cat'r Crawler, 5/64-ounce.

Crankbaits That Sink

You can easily retrieve or troll these weighted, lipped crankbaits at a depth of your choice. Examples are the minnow-shaped Rapala Countdown, 1/8-ounce; Storm ThinFin T-S Series, 1/4-ounce; and Rebel Tracdown Minnow, 1/4-ounce.

Lipless Crankbaits

Sinking lipless crankbaits can be trolled, cast or even vertically fished. Choices include the Bill Lewis Tiny-Trap, 1/8-ounce, and mini-Trap, 1/4-ounce; Heddon Bayou Boogie, 1/4-ounce; Bomber Ratl "R", 1/4-ounce; Cotton Cordell Ratt'l Spot and Spot Minnow, 1/8-ounce; Rapala Rattlin' Rap RNR5, 3/8-ounce; Smithwick Water Gater, 1/4-ounce and Tail Gater (the same but with a tail spinner); Bill Norman Tiny-N-Ticer, 1/10-ounce; and the 1/2-ounce Vortex Lightnin Darter, fished like a jig.

"We have fishermen who use our 1/2-ounce Lightnin Darter with a jigging motion for crappies," notes Wes Higgins of Vortex Lures in Montana.

Trolling Techniques

Post-spawn crappies commonly roam from shore, but they stay in the general vicinity of their spawning site. Summer crappies might be found anywhere there's sufficient oxygen and forage. In murky water, that might be just a few feet deep, like on the Tunica Cut-Off, where crappie trolling peaks in June and July. "In summer, the action is usually at two or three feet," says E.F. Johnston, "but in the hot weather, they troll deeper—five or six feet, or more." Many oxbows and other natural lakes have no real structure, which makes trolled crankbaits very important crappie-locating tools. Open water near brushy or weedy spawning areas are good places to start.

Crappies in clear water sometimes swim deeper, at or above the thermocline. The depth varies with the season, but it may be at about 10 feet in early summer and drop to 20 to 30 feet later in the year. As Scott Szafran can attest, weedy drop-offs are excellent starting points and, on weedless reservoirs, you might also consider main-cove and main-lake rocky or timbered points. When Szafran vacationed at Bull Shoals, where the water is clear and there's lots of structure, he met a man who directed him to some submerged points and told him to fish for crappies 90 minutes before dark. "I decided I would use my Hellbender and right away I caught a 1½-pound crappie. That day, my father and I caught about 18 crappies trolling Hellbenders in 10 feet of water over a rock slide. At times, our crankbaits bumped the bottom. We trolled as slowly as we could with a 9½-horsepower outboard."

Having two or more anglers in the boat boosts your chance of finding crappies. You can test-fish various depths more quickly. If each angler can legally fish more than one rod, so much the better.

If you need extra depth but don't want to add lead, try lighter line, such as 4- or 6-pound-test mono. Long-line trolling also takes your bait deeper, though a long line may make a hooksetting difficult.

Some trollers experiment with stop-and-go techniques or jiggle their rods for added action, but often all you need is a steady speed. The best crappie-trolling speed is as slow as you can troll while maintaining lure action. At less than about 1 mph, floater/divers generally rise, and sinking lures fall.

Some bites are definite thumps, but other times they'll be barely detectable. Szafran uses a sensitive graphite rod, sometimes holding the line with his finger. When you do feel a hit, throw out a marker

CRAPPIE CRANKBAITS

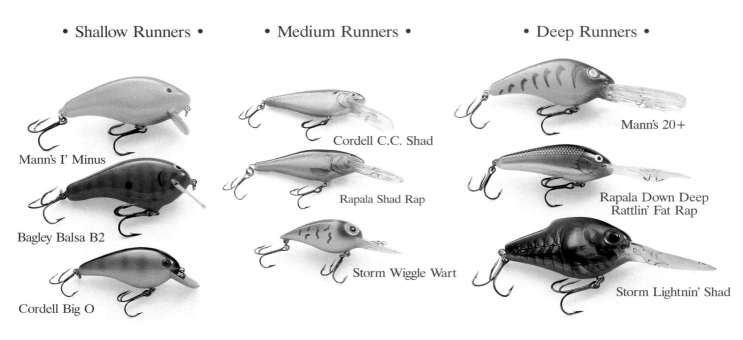

• Shallow Runners •

Mann's I' Minus

Bagley Balsa B2

Cordell Big O

• Medium Runners •

Cordell C.C. Shad

Rapala Shad Rap

Storm Wiggle Wart

• Deep Runners •

Mann's 20+

Rapala Down Deep Rattlin' Fat Rap

Storm Lightnin' Shad

EXTRA TROLLING TIPS

Crappies have very soft mouths, so care must be taken when trolling with crankbaits so the hooks don't rip free. A longer, light-action rod in the 6½- to 8-foot range is ideal, and it must have a soft tip. Fight the urge to make a long, sweeping hookset when you get a strike. A short hookset, or none at all (just keep the motor running an extra 5 to 10 feet), works better. Loosen up the drag a bit so the fight from a large crappie doesn't rip the hooks free.

When reeling a fish in toward the boat, do it at a moderate speed with the rodtip low to the water. This prevents the fish from jumping, something they commonly do in warm weather when brought to a moving boat. Net those big ones! It's heartbreaking to see a slab-sided crappie tear free a foot above the surface. And they can easily do so when hooked on a small treble hook. Some anglers even take off the treble hooks on their favorite small crankbaits and replace them with larger single hooks. Make sure the hook weights are similar, for good lure action.

buoy and note the lure's depth. Knowing how much line is out helps you return to the same depth. You might keep track by marking the line or by clipping a line counter onto your rod. Another useful tool is a trolling chart, such as Bead Tackle's Depth-O-Troll. You hook your line onto this plastic chart then read down the line-length column. The point at which your line crosses the column indicates how deep you're fishing.

Final Words

When you've found crappies, you might switch to a jig or minnow-and-bobber rig for a close, quiet presentation. Whether you're fishing the home lake for some tasty fillets or competing in a Crappiethon tournament for big dollars, crankbaits can effectively accomplish the important mission of first finding Ol' Specklesides. After all, you can't catch crappies until you know where they're hiding.

Crappie — Timing The Spawn

by Gary Korsgaden

Every spring, just like clockwork, certain conditions draw big crappies into the shallows. Here's how to cash in on this early-season bonanza!

Look for shallow bays with lots of cover early in the season.

Conditions were perfect as the electric motor eased us quietly into the dark-bottomed bay. I glanced at the temperature gauge and noted with satisfaction that it read 65 degrees—three degrees warmer than the main lake. Somehow I knew the stump-laden shoreline was going to yield a bumper crop of crappie. One cast confirmed my suspicion.

Setting the hook on the first slab of the season felt good. It meant the spring crappie bite had started and we were in position to take advantage of it. It wasn't long before we reached our limit.

Warm sunshine and active fish—it's a powerful combination that winter-weary anglers find hard to resist. No wonder thousands of anglers flock to known crappie hotspots each spring. Time the spawn properly, and you're rewarded with good fishing. Miss it, and well, there's always next year.

> *"The fish are also triggered by lengthening daylight hours."*

Admittedly, timing the spawn is not always easy. Conditions change from year to year and anglers must adjust to these changes. There are clues to help you solve the riddle, however, ones that I've learned after years of tracking my springtime crappie successes—and failures.

Understanding The Spawn

The peak crappie spawning temperature range is 62 to 65 degrees. However, ideal water temperatures alone will not induce the fish to start spawning. The fish are also triggered by lengthening daylight hours, which stimulate their urge to reproduce.

Then again, light levels don't have to be perfect for you to find crappie in the shallows. Unseasonably warm weather can drive up water temperatures, leading to an early movement of fish to shallow water. Fishing can be good during these times, but more likely it'll be inconsistent because spring's frequent cold fronts will force the fish back into deeper water.

When light finally does reach optimal levels, male crappie move shallow and begin to fan beds, while the female fish hold in deeper water, moving into the spawning area only after their eggs have ripened.

Expect the fish to be spooky during the early part of the spawn. After a few days they seem to settle down. And that's when good crappie fishing really begins.

Your first catches of the year will probably be the smaller, male fish. But with each new day, and as the water steadily warms up, the larger female crappie will begin to appear. Your goal is to get there when both the male and female crappie are shallow, so you'll have access to larger female fish, in addition to smaller males.

The Right Waters

Timing the spawn also depends on where you fish because certain bodies of water warm faster than others. Rivers, for example, typically warm first because they have darker water, are shallower and receive runoff from warm spring rains. Look

for good numbers of fish in shallow backwaters.

Shallow lakes, especially those with stained waters, are also good early in the year because they warm quickly. Crappie in these lakes typically spawn earlier than fish in deep and clear lakes or reservoirs. Save the deep lakes for your mid- to late-spring fishing, and look for shallow bays with lots of cover early in the season.

Spawning crappie seek cover such as reed banks, cattails, brush piles, weedbeds, stumps or brush— almost any area with the right water temperature and depth.

When you find a good crappie spawning site, you're in luck, because it will produce fish year after year. Start your search in bays or coves along the north shoreline of the lake or reservoir you plan to fish. These spots receive warm southern breezes and sunshine. River inlets and outlets are also excellent areas because the water is typically warmer there. Crappie will spawn around nearby cover.

Water clarity is another factor to consider; it influences the depth at which crappie spawn. Crappie in clear waters tend to spawn in deeper areas, often 10 feet or more, while fish in stained or cloudy waters may move into water one foot deep or less.

Pre-Spawn Crappie

In the days prior to the spawn, crappie group in deep-water staging areas close to the spawning sites. In lakes and reservoirs, that can be as deep as 40 to 50 feet, while river crappie prefer the quiet current areas off the main river channel, in about 15 to 20 feet of water.

Large numbers of crappie will often be in these areas, yet few anglers take advantage of the opportunity. If you have trouble locating fish in the shallows, don't hesitate to move deeper and use your sonar to hunt for schools of staging fish.

Marking the school with your sonar allows you to present your bait precisely in front of the fish, which is important because pre-spawn crappie tend to be inactive and will not chase a bait very far. However, once you find the fish and determine the depth, the action can be steady.

One of the best methods for taking pre-spawn crappie is to slowly fish a small jig. I prefer $\frac{1}{32}$- or even $\frac{1}{64}$-ounce jigs with plain hair or marabou bodies, tipped with a small minnow or waxworm.

For the best success, drop the offering to the depth crappie are holding and move it with the boat, slowly working your bait through the school. Keep varying the depth of your offering until you get a hit, then concentrate on that depth.

Or, give the fish a choice: attach a small barrel swivel about three feet above the jig, tie on a 2-foot leader of 4-pound monofilament and a size 8 Tru-Turn Aberdeen hook with a minnow. Toss the rig out and fish it slowly. You'll find that crappie usually key on one of the baits, but don't be surprised by a double, either!

If crappie are spooked by your boat passing over them—especially in clear water—change tactics. Use a $\frac{1}{32}$-ounce jig tipped with a minnow and cast it past the school, letting it sink on a slack line (keep your bail open). Start counting as the jig

SPRING COLD FRONTS

Cold fronts during the spring are usually more dramatic than summer cold fronts because they cause high barometric readings, cold temperatures and strong winds before and after their passage.

Severe cold fronts can change things in a hurry, often kicking fish out of the shallows and back into deep water where they can be hard to find. Once the fronts pass and water temperatures rise, crappie will begin to move into spawning areas again.

Catching crappie after a cold front requires patience. In lakes, crappie will be suspended in deep water close to spawning sites. Reservoir crappie will head for deep breaks off the main river channel. In rivers, look for suspended crappie in slow-current areas along creek channels 15 to 20 feet deep.

HOT RIVER PATTERN

Walleye or white bass "runs" in rivers draw anglers by the thousands. But did you ever hear about the crappie run? Sure, many fish move into the back-waters, but a lot migrate up toward the dam, then back off to bunch in slow-moving eddies just off the main channel. If a flooded, brush-lined bank is present, the fish will be in the cover. Float and minnow rigs, or weedless jigs baited with plastic or minnows, work best. Lower water levels or no cover will cause crappies to suspend in the eddy. Swim a flatter-bodied light jig through the mid depths. A ⅛-ounce swimming Fuzz-E-Grub, Marlyn Puddle Jumper, Tube Minnow, etc., will "glide" better than a more compact, thinner pro-file plastic dressing. Watch for water temperatures in the low- to mid-60s.

sinks, figuring one second for each foot of depth you want to reach. Begin your retrieve at different depths until you connect with fish.

Exploring The Shallows

During the spawn, when fish finally move shallow, I have one tried-and-true method. I start with a long graphite pole—sort of a modern-day version of the old cane pole—with a spinning reel on it.

A natural presentation can get you springtime stringers like this.

Mine is a custom-made 10 footer, but factory-made versions are available in 10- to 20-foot lengths. The long pole allows me to position my bait precisely and quietly, with or without a float.

Jigs are my all-time favorite bait for taking shallow-water crappie. Almost any ½₂- or ¹⁄₁₆-ounce jig with a plastic, hair or marabou body will work. White, silver and gray are good choices for clear water, while orange, pink and yellow are generally better in stained or cloudy waters.

More important than color, however, is a natural presentation. This means using light line and fresh bait. The addition of live bait will tempt the spawning crappie by adding scent, movement and sound to the jig. Use a float, too, because it allows you to fish slowly and work specific depths.

Try sight-fishing for crappie in the shallows. Most times you'll see the fish dart away from you or your boat, or you'll see them holding on or near spawning beds. When you spot fish, work the area by wading the shoreline or anchoring your boat on a deep-water edge, then casting a few feet past the fish or cover. Bring your bait in slowly. If you don't get a strike, change the depth and try again.

After female crappie have laid their eggs, they'll move back out to deeper

water and leave the smaller male crappie to guard the nests. When this occurs, anglers can catch crappie off both sides of the boat.

Your partner can take the smaller male fish in the shallows with a float and a jig, while you fish the deeper side, casting and counting down your jig without a float (you'll want to catch the bigger female fish, of course!).

Keep in mind that there are no absolutes when fishing for spawning crappie. Water temperature is just one part of the equation. Adequate sunlight from longer daylight hours is another. However, toss in the varied weather and water conditions that springtime brings, and it's very difficult to predict the exact time of the spawn. But not impossible.

Once you learn when to hit the shallows, and what to do when the fish are there, your success rate will soar. And after a long winter, a little sun and a lot of action sounds pretty good, doesn't it?

Northern shorelines, backwaters and coves with shallow, warm water and plenty of cover are prime spots for spawning crappie.

FISHING FLOATS

*I*n most spring situations, sensitive balsa floats will help you key on specific cover or depths and help you detect light-biting fish. Few crappie can resist a minnow-tipped jig suspended motionless in front of them—an impossible presentation to make without a float.

However, many first-time spring crappie anglers make the mistake of using a float that is too large. Stick with small, light floats, instead. I prefer the balsa European-style floats (see photo), which are easy to cast, enter the water quietly and are very sensitive.

The key to fishing floats is adding the right amount of shot to balance the float in the water. In windy conditions, I use enough shot to keep the float erect in the water with half the float erect in the water with half of the body exposed. This way I know when I actually have a hit, and when it's just the wind pulling the float under. On calm days, I weigh the float so just the tip sticks out of the water, which signals even the lightest bites.

Casting bubbles that you can fill with water also work great. The added weight in the float allows it and the jig to be cast into strong winds, yet the rig is very sensitive.

Spring Crappie

by Gary Laden

More crappie are caught on jigs than on all other lures combined. But if you're locked into just a couple techniques, you're missing a lot more potential action!

Stump-laden and close to a good spawning flat, the channel ledge was an ideal holding spot for schooling crappie. And when the sonar's liquid-crystal screen lit up with the image of a school of slabs suspended over a standing tree along the ledge, we thought we were in business. Wrong!

For the first 20 minutes, we slowly retrieved a variety of tiny jigs and straight-tailed chartreuse grubs over the isolated, fish-heavy tree. When it became painfully obvious that this technique wasn't the ticket, we switched to live minnows fished six inches below a tiny split shot. Again, we waited—then waited some more.

My fishing partner, Garry Moore, who guides on Georgia's Lake Sidney Lanier, had seen enough. Reaching into the rod locker, he pulled out an ultra-light combination spooled with an almost invisible 2-pound clear line and tied on a $\frac{1}{16}$-ounce tube jig.

"These fish are real spooky today," he said. "When crappie are this inactive, I've learned to fish a jig that offers minimal action. In the kind of mood they're in today, they simply won't chase a bait. They'll eat, but only if the bait is left practically motionless in front of their nose. I call it force-feeding inactive fish."

Moore dropped the new offering directly beneath the boat, mentally calculating the fall of his ultra-light bait at one foot per two seconds. After counting off 20 seconds, he engaged the reel and

Big stringers like this are always possible, even when crappie are finicky. These tips will help you maximize your catch.

imparted a subtle quivering action with the rodtip. When he set the hook on a scrappy 2-pound slab a couple of minutes later, I dove for my tackle box.

Mood Swings

Crappie often take a bait so subtly that anglers don't realize it until the fish begin to swim off. On other occasions, the strike is an intense jolt. Savvy anglers let the activity level of the fish dictate their lure selection and presentation.

"Selecting the proper jig and presentation based on a crappie's activity level is the key to consistently catching more fish," says Larry Colombo of Eufaula, Alabama, a noted deep-structure angler. "We've all been camped over a school of suspended crappie without getting the first inkling of a strike. Whether it is a passing cold front or one of a host of other factors that adversely affect the fishing, crappie activity sometimes just turns off at various times throughout the year, or perhaps during the course of a day.

"When crappie are active, there is usually little difficulty catching them. It's when they're inactive that anglers are faced with the greatest challenge. That's when you need to evaluate your tackle and lure selection and determine whether they are suitable to the conditions at hand. This may make the difference between an unsuccessful trip and a successful one."

"Proper tackle will make the difference between an unsuccessful trip and a successful one."

At times, schools of inactive fish may suspend over deep-water structure, say a river channel ledge, roadbed or submerged hump. You can see them on your sonar, but simply can't elicit a strike from a single fish in the school. At other times, you may find a dozen or so large slabs a foot or so below a large marina dock. Seemingly in a state of suspended animation, they shun your jigs, grubs or minnows.

"One unusual fact is that inactive crappie will many times take an artificial bait more readily than

One unusual fact is that inactive crappie will many times take an artificial bait more readily than a live one.

a live one," points out Tony Couch, a fishing guide from Lake Oconee, Georgia. "These fish instinctively realize that they will need to expend excess energy chasing live forage during times of stress (extremely warm or cool water, frontal changes, etc).

"Remarkably, however, they will more readily strike jigs left hovering in their field of vision for long periods of time. I'm not implying that an inactive crappie will instantaneously pounce on a marabou or tube jig the moment it hits the water. But a jig left almost motionless in front of an inactive crappie will literally tantalize the fish until he decides to eat it or kill it."

One particularly effective class of jigs for tempting inactive crappie is comprised of marabou or those with a combination of plastic and marabou.

Although marabou appears rather bulky and fluffy when dry, it condenses when wet and offers a subtle, unobtrusive appearance and action. The

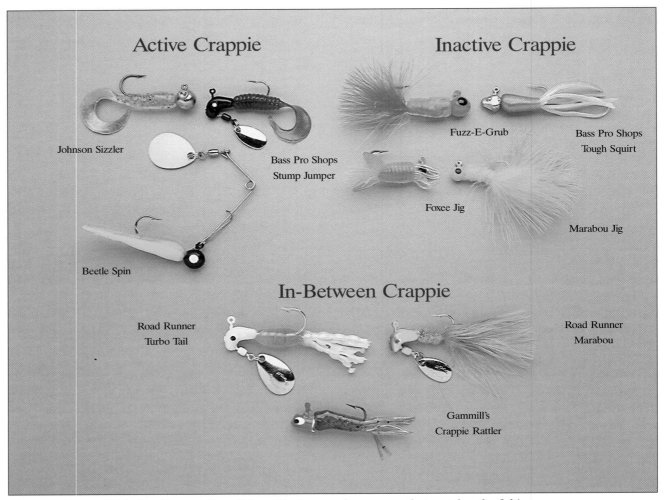

Active Crappie

Johnson Sizzler

Bass Pro Shops
Stump Jumper

Beetle Spin

Inactive Crappie

Fuzz-E-Grub

Bass Pro Shops
Tough Squirt

Foxee Jig

Marabou Jig

In-Between Crappie

Road Runner
Turbo Tail

Road Runner
Marabou

Gammill's
Crappie Rattler

There are jigs available for all types of conditions. For best results, use one that matches the fish's activity level.

combination plastic body/marabou trailer baits, such as the Hal Fly or Lindy's Fuzz-E-Grub, fall very slowly through the water, giving crappie a longer look at the bait.

In Garry Moore's experience, the tube jig is the most productive bait for inactive crappie during all seasons. He prefers a solid-bodied tube rather than a hollow one. He believes crappie tend to nip at the tentacles of tube baits, and often pull the skirt of hollow tubes off the jig head before ever being detected.

"With the leadhead exposed and a loop knot tied to a line tie on top of the head, the jig falls more horizontally," Moore explains. "This is certainly a natural looking target. It also tends to fall more erratically, almost spiraling to the depths

below when rigged in this manner. Injured baitfish are erratic in their movements, not predictable or repetitive. That's why the tube jig is such a dynamite bait; it duplicates the random action of baitfish."

"The tube jig is the most productive bait for inactive crappie during all seasons."

When crappie are inactive, such as during a mid-summer heat wave or a cold winter day, Moore relies on his "vertical hovering" approach. Positioning his boat directly above likely crappie cover or

structure, he works the jig slightly above that structure. His standard line choice is 4-pound test, but he may go as light as 2-pound if the fish are inactive.

Once the bait falls to the proper depth, he allows it to sit motionless for minutes at a time. He may also alter this presentation slightly by imparting a slight hovering action to the bait.

If there are no takers at that depth, he reels the jig up about two feet and suspends or hovers it at that level for several more minutes. With this method, he gradually works the entire water column.

From Below

Contrary to what many anglers believe to be true about crappie behavior, Moore says he gets more strikes by bringing the baits from below crappie than by dropping them on top of the fish. Crappie guide Harold Morgan, who has been fishing on many of the lakes along the Tennessee/Kentucky border for 24 years, concurs with Moore's conclusion.

"When crappie are active, I like to drop my jigs smack-dab on top of the school," says Morgan, "but when they're not in a biting mood, I raise the bait from below their field of vision. They usually won't go down to strike, but seem to be stimulated to attack a jig that's on the rise."

Often, anglers are faced with inactive fish holding in heavy cover in shallow water. A good technique in this situation is to suspend a jig beneath a slip float. This essentially duplicates the technique Garry Moore uses when fishing for inactive crappie in deep water. The float keeps the jig suspended above the cover, and the waves impart a subtle action to the bait. The lighter the float, of course, the less resistance the fish will feel when it takes the jig.

The new, thin-profile, European-influenced floats are ideal for crappie. They are super-sensitive and will register light hits that wouldn't be noted on the old-fashioned, round, snap-on bobbers. Even if fishing heavy cover in shallow water, use a slip-style float. It gives you a compact presentation that can more easily be flipped or dropped into smaller openings. A slip float also allows you to vertically jig the jig to tease crappie into biting.

When Crappie Are Hot

For active fish, such as those congregated on a flat and feeding vigorously in preparation for the spawn, or those ambushing unwary baitfish from the confines of sunken brush piles, baits with plenty of action and/or a vibrating spinning blade seem to generate fast and furious action.

"My approach tends to be more horizontal than vertical when I'm dealing with active crappie," says Couch. "I tend to cast beyond a school of fish— or a target that could potentially hold fish—then slowly retrieve the lure past the fish or target.

"If a straight, steady retrieve fails to generate strikes, I slow down to a swim-and-fall retrieve. This involves reeling the bait back to the boat, but stopping it every few feet and allowing it to fall for a second or two. A crappie that's following the bait, but won't strike while it's swimming, will usually take it on the fall."

"Baits with plenty of action and/or a vibrating spinning blade seem to generate fast and furious action."

Curlytail grubs, like the Berkley Power Grub, are extremely productive baits for active fish. The Creme Lit'l Fishie has a soft-plastic body with tremendous tail action that generates strikes from active fish. A $\frac{1}{16}$-ounce Blakemore Road Runner, with the plastic grub body, is also an excellent bait for fast-biting crappie, as are baits with grub bodies and spinning blades, like the Johnson Beetle Spin.

When fishing for active fish in clear water, try smoke, salt-and-pepper or shad color patterns. Off-colored water calls for brighter, more visible colors like chartreuse, orange and pink.

If you locate a school of active crappie, the best advice I can give is to fish fast. By fast, I don't mean a fast retrieve. Rather, keep casting to the school to keep your lure in front of them.

When active, crappie are very competitive and try to take the bait away from other fish. The more times you cast into the fish-holding cover, the more crappie you'll catch. Often, the action slows down if you haven't put a bait in the strike zone for several minutes.

Jigging Tips

*W*hen vertically fishing over a school of crappie in deeper water, strikes can be noted several ways. Run the line across the index finger on the hand holding the spinning rod for extra feel. Develop a rhythm when lifting and dropping a jig. Always expect the jig to tighten like it did on the last similar lift. If something the least bit different occurs, set the hook. Hits on tiny jigs quivered in deeper water are particularly hard to detect. Watch for the line to tighten a bit or use a very soft-tip rod and watch for a slight bend of the rodtip each time the tip is lifted a couple inches.

In-Between Crappie

Joe Dunaway, a crappie expert with years of experience on Georgia's Lake Allatoona, defines neutral fish as those that will strike a bait if it appears vulnerable and easily taken, but won't pursue a bait or baitfish very far. He believes that a neutral crappie can be turned into an active one with the proper presentation and lure selection.

"I use a presentation that I refer to as a 'reflex-strike' approach," says Dunaway. "I cast to cover and allow the bait to free-fall on a tight line until it makes contact with the cover. Then, I gently hop the lure one or two feet off that cover—depending on the depth of the water—and allow it to fall back again. I maintain this lift-and-fall retrieve all the way back to the boat. Under most circumstances, crappie will engulf the bait on the fall.

"The falling action seems to turn neutral fish into actively biting ones. I think they're aroused when the bait kicks up puffs of silt when it hits the bottom or knocks off a piece of algae from a decaying tree."

Some baits to consider when fishing neutral fish include Blakemore Road Runners, either in the Turbo Tail or marabou tail versions. The turbo tail is a solid-bodied tube jig affixed to the horse-shaped leadhead and paired with a single blade. The marabou-bodied bait offers a small profile, but the blade gives off just enough flash to stimulate mildly interested fish.

Garry Moore has recently found success using Gammill's Crappie Rattler jig heads when fishing for neutral crappie. These jig heads contain a stainless steel rattle that emits a strong sound vibration.

Moore finds them to be highly effective at generating strikes from neutral fish. He pairs a tube body or grub to the head and fishes it vertically to keep the sound right in front of them for long periods of time.

Let The Crappie Tell You

Every crappie angler has a preferred lure design, lure color and retrieval technique. And they all work at times. But for steady action every day, consider an approach that matches the size, color and action of the lure to the activity level of the crappie. Why fish slow-moving baits for crappie that may literally snatch the rod from your grasp?

On the other hand, one can see how inefficient it would be to zip a small spinner or rip a jig through a school of inactive fish. Allow the crappie to dictate what lure and presentation you use.

The Ultimate Fishing Book: Strategies for Success

Reservoir Crappies

by Gary Nelson

Fall's changing weather causes the crappies to frequently shift locations and positions. And then there are their mood swings. Here's how to cope with all the variables.

Shoreline foliage ablaze with autumn colors means one thing to reservoir crappie anglers: the time is right to catch some of the longest, widest slabs of the year. Expect a challenge, however, as fall crappie can be tough to pattern.

As the days get shorter and water temperatures fall, most reservoir crappie leave their summertime haunts in the main body of the reservoir and move toward the creek arms. Some fish will stay in deep water, but the majority congregate along secondary channels and cove mouths to stage for the next leg of the journey.

As fall progresses, the migration surges up the creek arms into shallow timber, producing excellent fishing as hungry crappie feed heavily on shad and other forage in the shallows in preparation for the coming winter.

Before you know it, the fish begin to drop back toward the main lake, but they hang up in cover

"Fall: The time is right to catch some of the longest, widest slabs of the year."

along the way, and that's where you can get in a few more shots at the slabs of fall...before the cold drives them into deep water offshore.

First Things First

The first stage of the fall crappie bite takes place before the reservoir turns over. You'll find crappie in shallower depths than you will in late fall. You'll also see a lot of smaller crappie early on, but don't worry—larger fish soon follow.

GOOD COVE / BAD COVE

As any old-time reservoir rat can tell you, all creek arms are not created equal. Some coves teem with crappie in the fall, while other nearby arms are relatively barren. How do you know where to look?

Fisheries crews often take advantage of the fall migration to assess crappie populations— and they don't care to waste time on dead water, either. Biologists use a variety of clues to help them find the most productive water. You can, too.

"One of the most obvious is timber," says Arkansas biologist Mike Armstrong. "Fall crappie will almost always relate to wood cover such as brush or submerged trees." Trees with limbs still attached are generally preferred over bare trunks.

"Crappie don't do well in coves with steep-sloping, rocky bottoms," he adds. "The best shorelines taper off more gradually into deep water."

A creek channel will help draw crappie into a cove, too, probably because it offers them thermal sanctuary when cold fronts and severe storms hit.

Above all, however, forage is key.

"In our reservoirs, threadfin and gizzard shad move into the creek arms, and the crappie feed heavily on them," says Armstrong. "They also eat other species, such as silversides."

Unless the baitfish are in extremely shallow water, you should be able to locate clouds of them on your sonar. Obviously, larger marks mixed in with the preyfish are a good sign. If you can't find any forage, chances are good you're fishing the wrong cove.

FALL CRAPPIE MOVEMENT

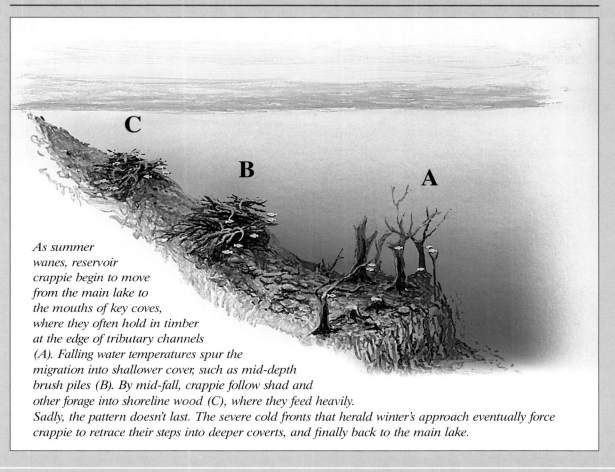

As summer wanes, reservoir crappie begin to move from the main lake to the mouths of key coves, where they often hold in timber at the edge of tributary channels (A). Falling water temperatures spur the migration into shallower cover, such as mid-depth brush piles (B). By mid-fall, crappie follow shad and other forage into shoreline wood (C), where they feed heavily. Sadly, the pattern doesn't last. The severe cold fronts that herald winter's approach eventually force crappie to retrace their steps into deeper coverts, and finally back to the main lake.

The mouth of a cove or creek arm is a good place to begin searching for crappie when water temperatures still hover at or above the high 50s. The fish soon move up the arm onto points or into pockets along the old creek channel ledge. Bridge pilings are known crappie hangouts, too, especially for black crappie. Whites are more often found up on the flats within the creek arm itself.

Fish in these areas relate to cover, just as they do in spring. It might consist of rocks or aquatic vegetation, but most often it's wood—dead trees, stumps and brush piles planted by fisheries personnel or other serious crappie anglers.

"In the fall, I generally find crappie in brushy cover," says Bobby Garland, who has fished crappie in both clear- and murky-water reservoirs across the country during the past four decades. "My favorite situation is when they move into the tops of shallow brush piles."

Garland, a bass fishing legend who is best known for inventing the tube jig, says that if the tops aren't too far beneath the surface you can often swing a jig past them and catch one crappie after another.

In a clear reservoir, he pinpoints brush that tops out 5 to 12 feet below the surface. In murky water, crappie generally hold in cover closer to the surface.

Polarized glasses make it easy to see shallow wood, weed clumps and large rocks, which can

quickly be checked with a couple of test casts. Probe deep cover with your sonar unit.

"Sometimes if there's only one fish down there it may be hard to catch," Garland explains. "But it's an entirely different story when you have several fish in a group. All you have to do is get a lure into the middle of the pack and one of them will grab it, for fear that another one might beat him to it."

When you find a good piece of cover with fish on it, mark it with a buoy, or take note of objects along the shoreline. If the cover is fairly close to the surface, you've probably made the fish jittery and may have to leave the place alone for several minutes. Come back and fish it later, after the crappie have had a chance to calm down. In the meantime, look for other potential hotspots.

When Garland begins working a piece of cover, he focuses on the shallowest section first.

"I generally approach a brush pile with a little ⅓₂- or ¹⁄₁₆-ounce jig, throw it out over the brush and slowly reel it back to the boat."

Not Too Light

A 6- or 6½-foot, medium-action rod helps him squeeze the most casting distance possible out of the ultra-light lures he prefers. Four-pound-test monofilament is great for many situations, but he

Wood—whether standing timber, blowdowns, brush or stump fields—attracts fall crappie. Look for visual clues above the surface, and watch your sonar for submerged timber.

goes heavier when there's lots of wood.

"I generally fish 6-pound-test line because it's easier to free up jigs when they get snagged. Sometimes I can pull the hook loose just by applying a little pressure.

"And I catch a lot of good bass when I'm fishing for crappie—sometimes more bass than crappie. I can get a pretty good fish out of cover with 6-pound line, whereas 4-pound test might stretch far enough for the fish to get into the brush and break off."

"Learn the reservoir's common fall forage."

Best Baits

You can further solve the puzzle of how to catch more autumn slabs by learning what the reservoir's most common forage is during the fall. Then, match it as closely as possible with your jig or live bait.

Local fisheries biologists can tell you about the forage base, or you can dissect some of the crappie you have caught. Baitfish are a staple in crappies' year-round diet. In many reservoirs, young-of-the-year shad—both gizzard and threadfin—are the crappie's main course. They'll eat a variety of other minnows, too.

Garland uses tube jigs to match small baitfish. His latest favorite is one called a Skirt & Dagger, which tapers to a thin tail and has a tentacled neck. One of his hottest early-fall colors for clear water is pearl white with silver flake, a good minnow/shad imitator. He also likes smoke with a silver/blue/black flake; bluish gray; and chartreuse with a silver flake.

Garland prefers the chartreuse or a dark color on dark days, as well as for deep-water fishing later in the fall.

"Another thing a lot of people don't realize," Garland says, "is that crappie may feed heavily on small crayfish in some impoundments.

"When I used to fish Gunlock Reservoir in Utah, one of the best colors was pumpkinseed. That crayfish color was probably one of my most productive patterns day-in and day-out. The connection?

DEADSTICKIN' AND FLIPPIN'

Bobby Garland's subtle jig stroke is deadly on fall crappie, but it's far from the only game in town. Legendary Weiss Lake, Alabama, guide Sam Heaton has perfected a deadsticking method that's equally lethal.

"When the water starts to cool down in early fall, crappie move from the main basin into stumps and standing timber along the edges of creek channels, maybe 15 to 20 feet deep," Heaton says. "I find the fish with my sonar and get right on top of 'em."

Using a bow-mount electric trolling motor to stay above the fish, Heaton drops a trio of lines over the side. Three rigs see the most action: a ⅟₁₆-

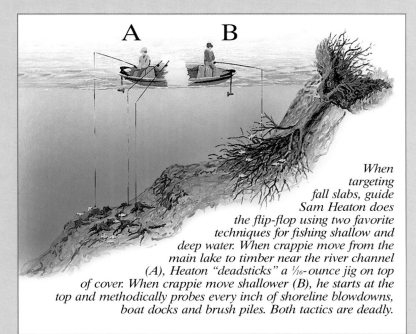

When targeting fall slabs, guide Sam Heaton does the flip-flop using two favorite techniques for fishing shallow and deep water. When crappie move from the main lake to timber near the river channel (A), Heaton "deadsticks" a ⅟₁₆- ounce jig on top of cover. When crappie move shallower (B), he starts at the top and methodically probes every inch of shoreline blowdowns, boat docks and brush piles. Both tactics are deadly.

ounce tube jig; ⅟₁₆-ounce hair jig tipped with a live minnow; and plain 1/0 to 2/0 light-wire hook with an eye-hooked minnow.

Heaton uses 9-, 10- and 11-foot crappie poles he designed himself (the B&M Sam Heaton Signature Series IMX).

"I put the bait right on the top of the cover, lay the poles down (he may hold one) and let everything sit as still as possible," he explains, noting that a low-stretch superline telegraphs light strikes better than mono. "I use 2-10 SpiderWire for this situation."

That's as deadly as it gets. Only after the crappie move into shallow brush as fall progresses does Heaton abandon his deadsticking technique and begin flippin' a tube jig into visible cover.

"It could be a blowdown, a brush pile or a boat dock," he says. "I flip a ⅟₁₆-ounce jig on a long pole, and drop it down about six inches at a time until I catch a fish or hit bottom. If I hit bottom, I move to the next corner of the cover and try again. The key is to work every piece of cover—and all depths—thoroughly before moving on."

This is a clear-water reservoir...and it's chock-full of crawdads."

In murky reservoirs, Garland's most productive color in shallow water is pearl white, followed by chartreuse. For deep water, he opts for chartreuse or black.

Sometimes crappie like a tiny jig, though that's more the case in late winter and spring, when the

slabs are feeding on insect larvae. For fall fishing, Garland usually ties on a 1½- to 2-inch jig.

"I use a ⅟₃₂-ounce leadhead a lot of the time," he explains. "It just kind of floats along and doesn't fall as fast, which gives the crappie time to react. Other times they'll eat a 4-inch bait. A big crappie can get a pretty good size shad into its mouth."

Goin' Down

If Garland's jig produces nothing in the shallows, or if the fishing slows, he will switch tactics—fishing the same wood, just deeper, from about 12 to 20 feet in clear water, or 5 to 10 feet deep when it's dingy.

"If the shallow bite dies off, I concentrate on the medium depth of the brush pile and try to work vertically, jigging the bait straight up and down," says Garland, who uses a 5½- or 6-foot, light- to medium-action rod now for better feel and more control.

"When you're vertical jigging, you can control the speed you work the lure, and most of the time, mid-depth crappie want it just about as slowly as you can work it."

"Success hinges upon a gentle, methodical jig stroke."

"When the crappie are shallow, they're a little more active, and you can get away with swimming the jig toward you. But, in this deeper water, if you toss it out and let it swing toward you, you're swimming it a little too fast for most of the fish."

The success of Garland's mid-depth jigging technique hinges upon a gentle, methodical jig stroke that triggers crappie when faster presentations fall flat. "I simply lift the rodtip up a little bit, then lower it and let it settle a few feet—just a real slow 'pump,'" he says.

Late-Fall Strategies

Garland contends that his early fall, shallow-brush pattern ends on most impoundments when the first prolonged spells of major cold weather arrive, dropping the water temperature down into the low 50s. When the lake turns over and the fishing temporarily becomes very tough, it marks the start of the second half of the autumn crappie season—late fall.

Conditions dictate a different game plan, as do the fish themselves. In late fall, crappie schools often scatter. Why? Because they can. After the warm summer months have beefed up the forage supply, fall's cool temperatures and the turnover eliminate temperature and oxygen barriers for the crappie. The specks can now follow their forage into water they couldn't enter earlier.

Some of the forage, and crappie, might hover just a foot beneath the surface at a murky-reservoir boatdock, or they might swim 50 feet down to the edge of a main channel in the gin-clear water of a mountain reservoir. But these are extremes, Garland says. For the heaviest crappie and most consistent late-fall fishing, channel your efforts toward more moderate depths.

In the final month or so before the onslaught of winter, big crappie abandon their posts at the tops of shallow brush piles and move down into the deeper treetops, Garland says. On a typical clear-water reservoir like Arkansas' and Missouri's Bull Shoals Lake, the best depth range is often the 20- to 40-foot water, where crappie feed on threadfin shad.

Weather changes, however, can greatly affect the crappie's depth from day to day. Anglers, too, must adapt or go fishless.

"One time on Arizona's Lake Mohave, which is a very clear lake, we caught 54 crappie that weighed a total of 112 pounds at depths running from 5 to 12 feet. I was using a Mini Jig and the conditions were perfect—it was an overcast, warm day and the fish had come up."

"Conditions dictate a different game plan in late fall."

"I went back the next day—which happened to be clear and bright—and caught crappie in 40 to 70 feet of water in the same area!"

During periods of warm weather, Garland often experiments with his favorite early-fall methods for taking shallow fish, but usually ends up heading for the deeper brush and trees. There, he vertically jigs in a fashion similar to the technique he used in early fall—with a few slight modifications.

Most of the time, Garland fishes along the edges of brush piles that are located on or near drop-offs in moderately deep water. "I find a brush pile with my depthfinder," he says. "Then I drop the jig straight down 'til the line goes slack. I bring the jig up and keep it up near the top of the brush pile,

maybe down in the limbs a little bit. Sometimes, however, the fish will be suspended over the brush—you never know until you look. Depending on their location, I'll bring the jig back up anywhere from two to six cranks of the reel handle."

To fish the deep cover, Garland often stays with the same size jigs as in early fall, but he adds a split shot to his line—the shot's size depends on the depth he needs to reach, as well as other factors, such as wind. A good rule of thumb is to use enough weight to reach the cover quickly, and keep the line vertical, but not so much that your sensitivity is deadened.

The same principles apply in murky water, except you're fishing a little shallower.

"If the water's very murky, you're not going to catch a lot of fish very deep. They may be deeper than normal for that particular impoundment, but you won't catch 'em in the 30- to 40-foot depths. Most will be somewhere in the 10-, 12- or 15-foot range. Keep in mind, when the water is less than 20 feet deep, you generally don't need to use any split shot—a $\frac{1}{16}$-ounce jig is enough to do the trick."

Deep or shallow, Garland uses the same vertical, slow-pumping motion that's so effective in early fall.

Cold Fronts

The most difficult late-fall fishing comes after a cold front, a pattern-blower occurrence that becomes increasingly common as winter approaches. Severe fronts and the storms that often accompany them can cause major changes in a body of water. You'll know it's happened when the water in the ends of the cove is filled with suspended particles that came from the bottom. Cold rains can also put a damper on the action.

When a big front passes, your best bet is to fish the deeper water in the lower reaches of a creek arm, or even the main lake itself.

"Any time you get a long period of cold weather, the fish are going to react," Garland cautions. "The fish may stay where they were before the front hit, but they usually turn off for a while. In some cases, the weather drives them on out to deep water."

Garland and I encountered those conditions on an Arkansas reservoir. Still, we managed to reel in about 15 good-sized slabs, plus as many bonus bass, by jigging vertically around some deep-water trees and brush.

Garland would locate a deep brush pile with his sonar, mark some fish on it, and position his boat right over the top of it. Then, with a split shot a foot or so above the jig, we'd very slowly pump the bait up and down.

"Vertical fishing is something very few people do in the deep brush," says Garland, "but with this technique, as long as you keep the line absolutely vertical, you can usually get the lure through the thickest tangles of limbs and branches—and that's where I get big crappie most of the time.

Each of Garland's tactics, applied under the right conditions, could do likewise for you in the fall. Give 'em a try when the hills are ablaze with fall color—and the reservoirs alive with hungry slab crappie.

Autumn harvest: Hungry slabs, concentrated in easy-to-find areas—often in the shallows. Can fishing get any better?

Icing Slab Crappie

by Gary Korsgaden

We are in the midst of the "ice fishing revolution."
No longer do we sit on buckets for hours and wait for fish to come.
Here's one expert's plan for hunting out big crappie.

Fritz Kellar and I slowly closed in on our fishing spot with visions of the hand-size crappie we knew were waiting for us. The walk seemed endless because we had to thoroughly prod the four inches of clear, new ice with our ice chisels to test its strength before continuing on. My motto is: Safety first, fishing second.

Behind us, we toted a sled loaded with a bucket of minnows, several rods and a couple depthfinders as we followed the course laid out by our hand-held Global Positioning System (GPS) unit. The route would lead us to a crappie hotspot we had fished just the week before—from a boat!

This was first ice, the situation we had long been waiting for. Crappie swimming beneath new ice are very active, and if you're among the first to fish them, the action can be unbelievable.

Our trek ended over a submerged rim where stumps and cabbage weeds surrounded a 34-foot hole. Our GPS unit led us to the general area, but we'd have to pinpoint the fish with our sonar units by chopping and fishing several holes.

Cover All The Angles

Early-ice crappie are spooky critters, so get all the hole punching done before lowering the first line.

My series of holes started just inside the submerged cover and meandered along the rim before turning back inside again. Fritz zig-zagged his string from the deep-water edge across the open basin. We had all the depths and structure covered and were confident we'd be icing nice crappie in short order. As it turned out, we were right.

I chose a hole over 28 feet of water near a corner formed along the stump edge. An ⅛-ounce chartreuse jigging spoon dangled from the end of my 4-pound mono. But before dropping it into the water, I tipped

the spoon with the head of a fathead minnow.

As the jigging spoon fell through the water, my sonar unit picked it up and tracked its descent on

the screen. I stopped the spoon a foot off the bottom. After pausing for a moment, I lifted the rodtip 6 inches and let it drop. With this jigging motion, I fished the water column all the way to the surface without a strike. That doesn't usually happen if first-ice crappie are nearby.

As I sat there pondering whether to move to another hole, I noticed a wide flash on the sonar dial at 14 feet. I quickly released the spoon, again watching its narrow echo on the sonar screen. I tightened up the line when the lure reached 13 feet. The crappie immediately rose and took the bait. I set the hook.

"What depth did it come from?" Fritz yelled as I slid the slab onto the ice. "Make room, I'm joining you," he said without waiting for my answer.

And just like that, the hunt was over. We had caught our first crappie. All we had to do was fine-tune our presentations and enjoy the action to follow.

I've spent more time catching crappie through the ice than I care to admit. And my fishing logs leave little doubt that the first few weeks of hard-water fishing are always the most productive. NAFC members who live in the part of crappie country where the lakes freeze can experience similar success. If, that is, you follow some basic guidelines.

Scout The Waters

Crappie populations in a particular lake can fluctuate. Waters where anglers have been catching big crappie for several winters may suddenly turn off and finding fish can be difficult.

The highs and lows are determined by factors such as predator numbers and spawning success, so it's important to identify the bodies of water that have the best populations of bigger fish.

Examining the data from your state fish and game department's survey nettings is one reliable method. These reports offer information on both numbers and size of fish.

Check with local bait and tackle outlets, too. Shop owners are more than willing to share information that will help you pinpoint crappie hotspots.

But there's another good source of information I use, and it's one that I don't think many ice fishermen consider. I keep track of local crappie fishing action during the summer. Bodies of water that frequently produce large crappie during the open-water season are at the top of my list when winter arrives.

Winter crappie often turn on during low-light conditions. Preparing yourself to fish after dark can pay big dividends.

Location Keys

During the first couple of weeks after ice has formed, you'll find crappie in the same spots they used during the late-fall period. The tip of a long point extending out to the soft-bottomed main basin, a bottleneck formed by two points, a deep-water pocket surrounded by timber or vegetation and shallow bays, all fall into my "early-ice" hotspot category. Especially bays, because they generally freeze first and provide some of the best early crappie action.

Cover that's near deep water, or even near the main lake basin, is a requirement for every good location. The reason is that such spots provide food in the shallows and security in deep water.

Basins are typically open pockets with soft bottoms where baitfish gather to feed upon insects and other organisms. Depending on state or local regulations, fishermen can further enhance the edge with man-made structure like bundles of discarded Christmas trees, wooden cribs or stumps.

Search For Active Fish

My approach to catching early-ice crappie is one of quickness and stealth. The presentations I use grab the attention of active biters. I don't wait around for crappie to come to me. If a hole doesn't produce

SAFETY FIRST

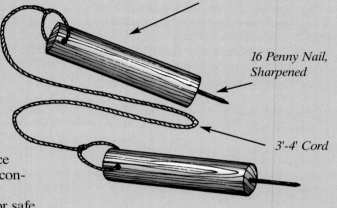

1½" Wooden Dowel

16 Penny Nail, Sharpened

3'-4' Cord

Without fail, the hottest crappie action of the winter occurs within the first weeks after freeze-up. What's not predictable, though, is the condition of the year's first ice.

Ideally, a long spell of extremely cold weather will precede any appreciable snowfall, and a clear layer of ice will form. But typically, the lakes are covered with a blanket of snow as they begin to freeze, slowing further ice formation. Venturing out under these conditions requires extreme caution.

Here are some recommendations for safe travel on the ice.

For anglers traveling afoot, the ice should be at least four inches thick. Five inches of ice is required for snowmobiles and all-terrain vehicles. Automobiles and small pickups need 8 to 12 inches, and a full-size pickup requires 12 to 15 inches.

"It's important to remember that these are rough guidelines," says Tim Smalley, Water Safety Specialist with the Minnesota Department of Natural Resources, "and they apply only to new, clear ice."

It's also critical to remember that a lake's surface does not freeze to a uniform thickness. A foot of ice may be within a few steps of a spot that's covered with only an inch or two. Your best bet is to prod the new ice thoroughly with an ice chisel or similar object every step of the way.

As a final safeguard, it's a good idea to wear a personal flotation device under your outer clothing.

If you do break through the ice, it's important that you stay calm. Panic only worsens the danger.

To climb out, turn toward the direction from which you came, place your hands and arms on the solid ice and kick your feet to push yourself up. If the ice breaks, maintain position and slide forward again.

A pair of ice claws will make it much easier to extract yourself from the water. Use them to get a firm grip on the ice as you slide onto the surface. Ice claws (pictured above) are short wooden dowels, about an inch and a half in diameter, with a 16-penny nail driven into one end. The nail heads are removed and the shanks sharpened to bite into the ice.

Make them yourself, or buy a pair from an icefishing gear supplier.

After you're atop the ice, do not stand up. Instead, roll away from the hole until you're on solid ice.

in 15 minutes, move on to the next.

Consequently, I prefer a lure and bait combination that allows me to quickly fish the entire water column with a lift-and-drop technique. The faster I can eliminate unproductive water, the better. In my opinion, a jigging spoon is the perfect lure.

Small jigs in the 1/32- to 1/8-ounce range are also good. They can be clad in feathers, hair or a plastic grub body.

In clear water, I stick with silver and gold; off-colored or murky waters call for bright colors such as chartreuse, orange or any of the glow-in-the-dark varieties.

A bit of meat almost always means more action, so I tip the spoon with either a minnow head, three or four waxworms or a small chunk of a white Berkley Power Grub, which has built-in scent and flavor attractants.

It's also sensible to focus your efforts during the prime fishing times. The hours around sunrise and the last few hours before dark are usually best. However, fishing after nightfall can also be good.

When you locate an active school, slowly work the spoon or jig up and down, allowing it to drop through the active fish zone.

"If a hole doesn't produce in 15 minutes, move on to the next."

Crappie seem to lose interest if you don't keep a lure in front of them at all times. This explains why one particular hole sometimes seems to get hotter and hotter, producing more fish than other holes nearby. The action triggers the feeding instinct of the other crappie in the school.

If there's a break in the action because of a tangled or broken line, for example, the fish's mood can change and the school may move.

Suspended Crappie

As winter wears on, and the ice thickens and more angling pressure is applied, the active feeding forays of crappie become shorter in duration. When there's nine or more inches of ice, I start looking for crappie suspended over no-man's-land—the deep-water basins.

Locating these fish can mean a lot of searching, but for starters, concentrate on areas where a hard sand or rock bottom meets soft mud. You'll most likely have to drill many holes to find the transition zone.

Basically, drill a string of holes at 20-foot intervals and probe the bottom with a flasher unit through each hole. A bright, wide flash on the dial indicates a hard bottom. Soft bottoms absorb some of the sound energy, so the signal is narrower and dimmer.

When you pinpoint a change in bottom content, check the sonar screen for signs of baitfish. If they're there, start fishing, but you'll have to be patient.

Successful anglers sit and wait out mid-winter crappie because "neutral" fish like to eyeball an offering before they strike. That means a natural-looking bait like a live minnow on a plain light-wire hook suspended below a bobber should be your first choice, though other baits will also work.

Finesse Gear

During the mid-winter period, when the crappie's activity level is more subdued, it's time to break out the finesse gear—light ice flies, small bobbers and tiny split shot.

Among my favorite ice flies, which are basically small hooks with bits of brightly painted lead molded on the shank, are Northland Tackle's Glow Ants and Hackle Ants, with a size 8 hook. Fluorescent orange or yellow are good for daytime angling; use glow-in-the-dark versions after nightfall.

I use bobbers that can barely float a couple of BB-size split shot placed 18 to 24 inches above the ice fly and bait.

As for rods and reels, I prefer a short, medium-light action graphite spinning rod made specifically for ice fishing. Select a reel that makes for a balanced combination. There are many small spinning reels on the market that will do the job. Monofilament can be from 2- to 6-pound test. Four-pound is best for all-around action.

A quality flasher makes your fishing efforts more fun and more productive.

Winter crappie fishing is more than just chopping a hole and dropping a bait. During the early season, go on the hunt when the action stalls, constantly exploring and searching with your sonar and lures.

Then, slow down and use finesse tactics as winter wears on and crappie become more apprehensive. With these tips, you'll enjoy consistent fishing all season long.

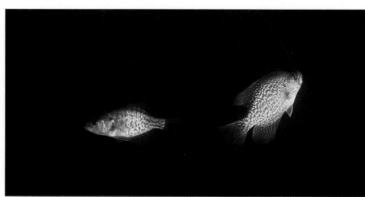

Crappie are *active under the ice. You just have to hunt them down.*

Chapter 5

Catfish

Every year, more and more anglers discover the catfish, and with that discovery comes the need for solid catfishing information. Catfishing isn't just throwing out a gob of stinkbait, propping your oldest rod in a forked stick and plopping down to wait for a bite. There's nothing wrong with that method—it has put plenty of catfish steaks and fillets on the table over the years. But there are many more frontiers to explore.

So here we talk to today's catfisherman—the guy or gal out for a tackle-busting blue, channel or flathead catfish…the kind of fish that, when you set the hook and feel the throb that won't budge, makes you say, "Uh oh."

Those Dam Cats

by Dan Gapen Sr.

Many hot fishing areas below dams receive little or no intelligent fishing pressure for catfish. Here's how to cash in on this bonanza.

High on the red clay bank a scarlet cardinal whistled a bright note of encouragement. Downstream a sad-eyed coon hound bawled about being tied with a scratchy, inch-thick rope. River waters boiled and reddish-brown currents rolled past the muddy boat landing. Upriver, the Tallahoochee bridge groaned a loud protest as heavily loaded semi-trailer trucks rumbled across her trestles. It was an ideal day for catfishing the muddy Alabama River.

The first sighting of this clay-banked river and its churning mass of silt, tree limbs and vegetation repulsed me. I was used to fishing the cool, clear

waters of the North Country. But the dirty water didn't affect the old river rat with whom I was about to share a day of fishing in an ancient, sun-bleached johnboat.

Roy Larson, a bearded catfishing expert of sorts, had fished the Alabama for years, and rumor had it he was the best jugger within a hundred miles. He had enough equipment! His johnboat was nearly filled with more than six dozen jugs.

Roy pushed off. Water rose to within four inches of the gunwale. Along the starboard seat, water sprayed in each time Roy shifted weight on the oars. It would be necessary to bail before long.

Within minutes of leaving the muddy boat landing, we began dropping jugs overboard. Each was fitted with 18 to 30 inches of stout cord and a rusty hook baited with a mixture of chicken guts, liver or gizzard shad, all fresh. Roy saw to it that 15 to 20 feet separated the jugs as they were strung across the river. He wanted to cover the entire river with one setting. That system would prove exhausting to his companion once the fish began to hit.

Ten minutes after laying the pattern of floating jugs, a jug some 100 feet off the far bank went skittering crazily upstream, then disappeared completely.

"Fish on!" exclaimed my jubilant teacher while instructing me to row like mad to reach the jug.

"Hurry up, son. That can won't wait," Roy added loudly.

"Dear Lord," I thought, "This might end up being one of those days."

Suddenly another jug dipped under the surface and started away from us. It was closer, so I immediately changed course.

"Dear Lord," I thought, "This might end up being one of those days."

"No!" came a sharp command. "First one first."

So it went for the balance of the day. In the end I rowed to 43 dancing jugs. In all, we landed 35 cats that day including blues, flatheads and channels. Our biggest was a 17-pound blue.

Thus began my pursuit of North America's favorite table fish. It also began a catfish love affair that lasts till this day.

Since then, I have pursued catfish across the

width and depth of North America. I've even chased them across Canada's prairie provinces. Each area brings new challenges and yields new techniques. Baits vary in as many ways as areas fished. Chicken liver, snails, sucker meat, clams, mulberries, shad and gizzard shad, crawdads, night-crawlers, catalpa worms, minnows (live or dead), leeches, frogs, shrimp and even anchovies are used. In some areas anglers swear by artificials.

Catfish vary in size from the 1-pounders taken from farm ponds to 100-pounders wrenched to the surface below TVA dams in Tennessee.

Catfish species also vary in each water structure fished, with channel cats, flatheads and blues predominating. Of the three, channel cats make up 70 percent of American anglers' catches.

Tailwaters are natural staging and feeding points for cats. Catfish find these structures an impasse to their upstream migrations. Being a somewhat lazy species, they are content to lie downstream from dams.

Areas below dam structures on any river system have much in common. Most have a deep "digout" directly downstream from the gates, rollers or turbine outlets. Each of these digouts will have a "hump" directly downstream from it, and stone riprap usually lines both downstream banks. Some dams have cement "lips" beneath the waterline directly downstream from the dam face. All have "current cuts" and "hardpan" rock and gravel bottoms. Each of these structures will hold catfish (see diagram).

Roller dams, such as those found on the Ohio and Mississippi rivers, create huge, wide sections of turbulent boiling waters. Anglers observing their first "roller" are generally intimidated by its enormity. Waves often reach eight feet in height below these structures. Obviously such an area is not safe to fish; even the catfish tend to avoid areas that are excessively turbulent. Successful anglers have found the best place to fish cats is in the waters along current breaks, on either side of the race area and downstream near displaced bottom piles (the "hump").

A roller dam can be fished from shore, but it is best done from a boat. Boats with rather deep bows, high transoms and better-than-average widths are ideal. Motors should have enough horsepower to get an angler out of trouble. This means an outboard in excess of 10 horsepower; 20 horsepower or more is even better. Don't forget to take along a

Big cats are pure power, and pure fun to catch.

eight feet and drop off to as much as 40 feet on either side. Don't fish on top of the hump. Work the up and down stream edges carefully. Position your boat so your bait rests in the right areas.

Big catfish also congregate in the area below the hump (area D on the diagram). Water depths reach as much as 20 to 55 feet in this area. Flatheads are prominent here, but large channels will also hold at this point.

Another good area is the bank across the river from the locks. Most often the fish here will be channel cats.

The first place to look is along the high cement wall near the dam. A number of cats stay here, mostly close to the bottom, but some suspend. These fish are best worked from the wall itself, but some walls have tie-offs for boats. Tying a couple throwable seat cushions or dock bumpers to the boat's side will prevent damage from it bumping into the wall.

Farther downstream a series of rotating eddies circulates along riprap, which in turn has current cuts forming along its outer edges between eddy and mainstream current. Most of the fish will hold directly along the inner edge of eddy current and mainstream flow. However, cats may wander into the pools themselves at night or during the spawn.

You will also find a number of cats near the locks. Most of the fish along the gate lock wall itself will be larger in size, while those found below the locks will tend to be smaller.

Although various species of catfish can be found along the gate lock wall and high cement wall just about any time, these close-to-the-dam positions are red hot in May and June during the catfish spawning runs. All river fish make an upstream migration in spring/early summer, and catfish are no different. Look for the channels to move into these areas first, with the big flatheads peaking as late as early- to mid-June in more northern waters. The best fishing

couple of good anchors — something that will hold you in a heavy current.

As the diagram indicates, smaller cats hold in different areas from larger flatheads and blues. Directly below the open gates, a place that is nearly impossible to work because of strong current, lie some of the largest flatheads. Fish upwards of 40 pounds will hold at this point. To catch these fish while the rollers are open, an angler must use an extremely heavy lead sinker, heavy rod and reel, and excessively strong line. It is best to fish these areas by casting to the roller gate's tailrace from positions A and B in the diagram. The bait is then left to lie on the bottom, awaiting a big flathead's approach.

Boat positioning is critical when fishing the hordes of small channels and blues that hang along edges of the hump. Some humps are as shallow as

often occurs after dark or when rains stain the water.

Channel cats, like no other cat, generally feed into the current, working a pattern upstream and returning downstream to digest their food. Point G on the diagram marks an excellent staging area for channel catfish.

Channel cats prefer live or fresh bait, and they find it in abundance every time a barge or sport-fishing boat moves through the locks. Periods of fast feeding lasting about 10 minutes occur each time the lock is opened.

Bigger cats, particularly flatheads and big blues, hold tight under dam faces. Food, in the form of chopped-up fish, garbage and carrion run through a power plant's turbine tubes, is extruded below the dam face and settles to the bottom...directly on top of the waiting cats. There is little need for these huge fish to move; food is continuously served to them.

NAFC members need only to properly place their offerings to catch these fish. Water depth at the dam face varies but often exceeds 100 feet. Average depth here is close to 40 feet.

Directly downstream from the dam face where the flatheads hold, anglers will find most of the blue catfish population. This is especially true if the blues are large fish. Blues seem to avoid larger flat-heads but they aren't far away. Smaller blue cats are scattered in and out among the channel catfish-holding structure. At exiting mid-channel (position D), schools of rather large blues may be found.

Channel catfish generally hold in two areas below concrete structures.

The "corner" regions near the dam are best. Most of the time these areas must be fished by a boat, but bank anglers can get in on the action too.

"Various species of catfish can be found along the gate lock wall and high cement wall just about any time."

The deep-water area in front of the hump is also an excellent place to catch channel cats but may be extremely difficult to fish. Water pressure makes boat and bait control tough. Downstream "straightlining" is the only way to fish this structure. I'll explain this technique in a bit.

When fishing below dams, don't forget to work rip-rap shoreline. Such structure is not only good catfish habitat, but also produces walleyes, sauger and bass.

My favorite channel catfish bait is frozen chicken liver. Some will disagree, but if given only one choice and an unknown destination, that's what I would use. Frozen chicken liver stays on the hook three times longer than fresh liver, and its scent is much stronger.

"Freezing and thawing a liver releases a surge of scents from the amino acids that attract channel catfish."

A biologist once told me that freezing and thaw-ing a liver releases a surge of scents from the amino acids that attract channel catfish. I'm not sure of that, but I do know frozen liver works much better than fresh liver.

I use large, short-shanked, beak-style hooks (2/0 to 4/0) with turned-up eyes. Many anglers prefer trebles, but I lose more large catfish on trebles than I do on single hooks.

Flathead cats are live bait feeders, and large, live bluegills (where legal) head the list. Trophy flatheads can't resist the temptation of a floundering 'gill. Next to bluegills would be a 6- to 8-inch bullhead, spines clipped, hooked through its nose from under the jaw. This is done to prevent the hook from snagging on the river bottom. My third choice would be a pound-size live sucker hooked in a similar fashion.

When selecting bait for blue cats, just about any-thing that's decayed or rotten will work. Ripe chick-en guts or some concoction that smells bad will do the job. Blues tend to scavenge more than channels and flatheads.

"Straightlining" is a technique used during the summer months when cats become finicky. If you've had the disheartening loss of bait after continuous

There are several distinct catfish-holding areas beneath dam structures. Knowing how to locate and fish each one effectively will improve your catfishing success. Areas A and B are excellent positions to work big flatheads in the deep digout below the roller gates, as well as the small channels along the cement highwalls. Area C is best for big flatheads, which lie close to the gates. Big blues are generally found near, but below, the flatheads. Area D is also an excellent spot for big cats, especially flatheads and channels. You'll find channels frequenting the eddies in areas E, F and G.

Catfish often suspend upcurrent of the hump (area C) as shown on this illustration. To avoid fishing beneath them, chart the area with your sonar before anchoring.

"tap taps" at rod's end, and no amount of setting the hook or waiting helps, you'll appreciate this technique.

All equipment used remains the same with one exception. Instead of using a lead weight, such as an egg sinker, try a wire-sinker rig such as a Bait-Walker or an L-armed shaped bottom bouncer sinker. Don't go too light. Most straightliners use 1½- to 3½-ounce rigs.

To implement the straightline technique, you must first anchor upstream from the target area. Behind your sinker, attach a 24-inch dropback and a 2/0 short-shanked hook. The sinker's upper wire arm will hold the dropback and the bait slightly off bottom as the current forces it out and downstream.

Cast directly downstream to the targeted area.

Once the rig rests on the bottom in proper position, reel slack line up. This snugs up the line and creates a direct line between the rodtip and bait. Any movement of bait or sinker will be telegraphed instantly. Current shifts will lessen and increase pressure on the rodtip at times. The angler must keep constant pressure evenly distributed between rodtip and bait. This is done by lifting and lowering the rodtip as pressure decreases and increases. With gear ready and rig placed, wait for a cat to take the bait.

> *"It is at that moment the cat is more susceptible to being hooked, as its jaws are firmly locked on the bait."*

Having fished this method for years, I can tell when a catfish is mouthing a bait. Maybe it's their barbels working over the chicken liver or the cut shad that tips me off. Whatever it is, the feeling is immediately followed by a slackening of pressure against the rodtip and a dipping of outstretched line. If this happens, drop your rodtip 18 inches…then set hard!

At that moment a cat is crushing your bait. If the fish hasn't closed its mouth completely on the bait, dropping the rodtip back will entice it to do so. If you wait for the fish to begin backing off the bait, its mouth will again open, and setting the hook when your rodtip tightens up again might pull the hook out of its mouth.

You won't feel any "tap tap" until the cat backs down to the point where it first picked up your offering. Here, the fish will turn, then move downstream to its original resting site. It is on the turn that most anglers feel the "tap tap," which tells them to either set the hook or let the cat run. Often, setting will result only in an empty hook.

You should set the hook when the line slacks off the rodtip, which indicates a fish is working the bait. It is at that moment the cat is more susceptible to being hooked, as its jaws are firmly locked on the bait. Only sinkers with a fulcrum such as the Bait-Walker or bottom-bouncer types will telegraph the forward walk and crush of a cat. Traditional catfish sinkers like the egg sinker won't be of any help in straightlining, but are fine working across currents.

Catfishing is a sport in which anyone can participate and catch fish. Not all catmen smell bad, sprout beards and wear bib overalls. Many a corporate executive finds delight in the surge of power a huge cat can bring.

As for me, I'll still wear faded blue jeans and run a battered old johnboat with its worn 9.8 motor.

Chasin' Cats

by Jeff Samsel

Top catfishermen reveal their strategy for staying on the move to find feeding catfish.

Neither anchors nor rod holders figure into the fishing equation when Glen Stubblefield targets catfish. A master catfish guide on Kentucky Lake, he opts for the active approach, assigning one rod per angler (always in hand) while he continuously runs his trolling motor.

With patient persistence, Stubblefield picks his way along stump-laden ridges washed by strong main-lake currents, plucking fish from the murky breaklines beneath the hull of his boat.

Keith McCoy and Joe Rodgers don't hang around waiting for cats to come to them, either. Tournament-champion catmen from Fremont, Nebraska, McCoy and Rodgers prospect for catfish by drifting across vast, open waters, bouncing blood baits along the bottom.

As McCoy proudly proclaims, "We go after them."

The two enterprising Nebraskans stunned the catfish establishment on South Carolina's Santee-Cooper last fall when they used their drift-fishing tactics to win the National Championship Catfish Tournament. They boated 235.5 pounds of catfish, including a hefty blue that weighed 70.5 pounds and took big-fish honors in the tournament.

Such active approaches to catfish fishing come close to heresy in a sport ruled by still fishing. Indeed, generations of catmen have heeded the doctrine, "If you fish the right spot long enough, they will come." And they often do.

But pioneers like Stubblefield, McCoy and Rodgers have proved that catfish fishing need not be a waiting game. In fact, their active approaches are often far superior to traditional still-fishing techniques. And the best part is, you can put these tactics to work for you.

Different Yet Deadly

Glen Stubblefield's favorite strategy allows him to thoroughly work an entire piece of prime structure, instead of just concentrating on one single spot. It also keeps the minnows he favors as bait just off the bottom, where catfish are most apt to find them.

> *"Heavy currents call for constant attention to the trolling motor and depthfinder."*

It's a demanding task. Heavy currents in the areas he fishes call for constant attention to the trolling motor and depthfinder, while ever-changing bottom contours demand that lines be continually raised and lowered.

Then there's McCoy and Rodgers, who spread their lines over whatever type of bottom happens to be beneath their boat—as long as they're marking catfish and bait on their electronics—and let the wind dictate the direction of their drift.

The active approaches these anglers take are geared for two totally different situations. Stubblefield works very specific areas, while the boys from Nebraska simply want to cover water. Let's take a closer look at each.

Veteran Kentucky Lake guide Glenn Stubblefield prefers an aggressive, tight-line approach to passive cat tactics.

Tight Lines

Glen Stubblefield begins with a large playing field, earning his living on Kentucky Lake, an expanse of water that stretches over 184 miles and covers more than 163,000 surface acres in Tennessee and Kentucky.

He quickly narrows his search, however, by fishing only the lower third of the lake, sticking to the main Tennessee River portion. He looks for the ideal combination of structure, cover and current.

"You see a lot of water out here," he says, his arm tracing an imaginary arc both up- and downstream. "But you won't see me fish very much of it."

Major bends in the old river channel, points that stretch out toward a channel drop, and noteworthy humps rising from an otherwise flat bottom provide the kind of structure that Stubblefield seeks. Prime cover comes in the form of stump fields or flooded old homesteads.

Current flows in the main lake whenever water is being run through the dams, creating another key element in Stubblefield's catfish system—moving water.

During periods of slack water, Stubblefield is forced to work the upstream side of islands, narrow cuts and inside various necked down areas that cause "rips" of stronger current.

Why The Attraction To Current?

"The catfish are much more active in flowing water—and the stronger the current the better," he

TIGHT LINE FEVER

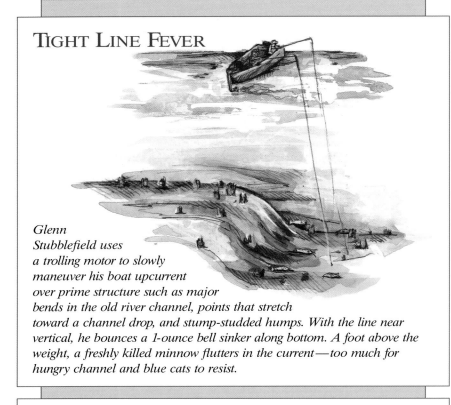

Glenn Stubblefield uses a trolling motor to slowly maneuver his boat upcurrent over prime structure such as major bends in the old river channel, points that stretch toward a channel drop, and stump-studded humps. With the line near vertical, he bounces a 1-ounce bell sinker along bottom. A foot above the weight, a freshly killed minnow flutters in the current—too much for hungry channel and blue cats to resist.

DRIFTIN' THE BLOOD

Drift fishing is a great way to cover a lot of water. On a controlled drift over flats, humps and other likely structure, McCoy and Rodgers' blood baits leave a trail of fresh scent along the bottom, attracting blue and channel cats. Except when it's very windy, or they're fishing deep water, they add no weight to the rig. Just motor upwind of the target drift zone and lower baits to bottom. Use sea anchors to control speed and direction (your trolling motor will push you back on course, too). At the end of the drift, hold your position for 5 or 10 minutes to allow blood-trailing cats to catch up to the baits.

explains. "Sometimes when they turn on the water at one of the dams, it's just like flipping a switch. The catfish start feeding like crazy."

Stubblefield's active approach allows him to work his way through areas that offer a combination of fish-attracting features. Contrast this to the stationary cat-man, who must be satisfied with only one spot—often a happy medium of cover and current, but seldom the best combination all day, every day.

For example, a creek's confluence with the Tennessee River channel near a stump-studded bend in the channel would be great, but such an area would be even better if there was a hole from an old pond nearby. Add a major island downstream to split and strengthen the river's flow and you're in cat heaven. By slow-trolling, Stubblefield can cover all of these important bases.

He uses a tight-line rig, with a 1-ounce bell sinker at the end and a size 1 hook tied to a 6-inch dropper a foot or so above the weight. A fresh minnow is threaded onto the hook through the mouth, so its body is bent slightly by the curve of the hook. This usually kills the minnow, but the angle of its body causes the dead bait to flutter in the current.

The line is kept tight, with the weight touching bottom, but not dragging across it. "You should barely bump the bottom with the bell sinker," Stubblefield advises. "Otherwise, snags eat up more lines than catfish."

With each angler holding a rod, reeling in or releasing line as needed, Stubblefield uses the trolling motor to slowly crawl upcurrent. Often, he follows the edge of a drop or trolls across a stump-laden hump, never taking his eye off the depthfinder as he follows each crease and wrinkle.

While he normally works an area very thoroughly—especially if the cats are cooperative—Stubblefield won't stay long in an area if the fish aren't biting. There are just too many other good spots on

Kentucky Lake to waste time waiting for a particular bunch of catfish to turn on.

Snag City

Newcomers to Stubblefield's style of fishing tend to hook a lot of stumps. It's understandable—with the boat moving, current flowing and adrenaline pumping, the stumps do feel a lot like strikes—and the hook usually gets set pretty hard.

Tight-lining vets, however, recognize the stumps for what they are and finesse the bait over the tops, then prepare for a strike. For some reason, the rig sliding off the upcurrent side of a stump often triggers a hit.

The relationship between cats and wood is so strong that even when one of his clients gets snagged, Stubblefield looks for a strike on another line. He's not often disappointed.

Strikes, especially from big fish, typically feel like nothing more than extra weight on the line—only a subtle difference in the apparent weight of the rig separates fish from snag.

For example, Stubblefield had just bumped his sinker against a stump last summer when his own rodtip began to dip. "Big fish never hit the bait hard," he muses, "they just start moving off, pulling the rod down slowly as they go." True to form, that stump-hugging blue weighed close to 50 pounds.

Blues comprise the bulk of Stubblefield's catch, with channel cats next in line and flatheads showing up only on occasion. He surmises that the reason it works better for channels and blues is because both species typically jump on a bait pretty fast if it looks and smells appealing.

A moody flathead, on the other hand, will often stare at a bait before deciding to grab it.

The catman has caught blues weighing up to 65 pounds, but fish ranging in size from 5 to 15 pounds are his bread and butter. Even these "smaller" cats put up a tremendous battle on his standard tight-line outfit, an Ambassadeur 5500, strung with 20-pound test, and a medium-action rod.

The guide believes that tight-line catfish fishing requires well-defined structural features—as well as steady current, to hold the bait off bottom and make the cats aggressive.

Although he concentrates on the impounded waters of Kentucky Lake, this method also works on big rivers. Use your electronics to slowly work the channel edge, drop-offs and other well-defined, cat-holding breaklines.

High Plains Drifters

McCoy and Rodgers aren't so "civilized" when it comes to bait—they rely on stomach-turning cubes of coagulated cow blood to entice big cats.

"The blood is both a bait and an attractant," McCoy explains. "We bring the bait to the catfish, but as we drift along, the blood also leaves a scent trail. Any fish that crosses this trail can follow it right to our baits."

After the proper aging, the blood forms a coagulated, gelatin-like mass that is easily threaded onto a leader and held in place on a treble hook. As the bait drifts along, the blood slowly dissolves in the water, leaving a path of scent particles that hungry cats can't pass up.

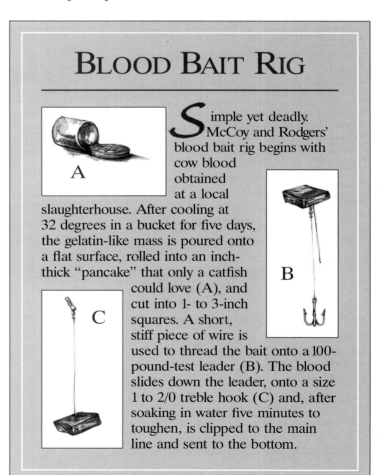

BLOOD BAIT RIG

Simple yet deadly. McCoy and Rodgers' blood bait rig begins with cow blood obtained at a local slaughterhouse. After cooling at 32 degrees in a bucket for five days, the gelatin-like mass is poured onto a flat surface, rolled into an inch-thick "pancake" that only a catfish could love (A), and cut into 1- to 3-inch squares. A short, stiff piece of wire is used to thread the bait onto a 100-pound-test leader (B). The blood slides down the leader, onto a size 1 to 2/0 treble hook (C) and, after soaking in water five minutes to toughen, is clipped to the main line and sent to the bottom.

The blood-bait drifting technique developed by Keith McCoy and partner Joe Rodgers is lethal on monster blues and channel cats alike.

The process actually begins with all lines still in the boat, especially on unfamiliar waters. McCoy uses his depthfinder to study the lake bottom. He looks for catfish and baitfish scattered across large flats or holding on sunken islands and other structure, and marks the depths at which each is holding.

McCoy also searches for areas where shallow and deep water are close to one another, offering catfish easy access to various depths. Such a situation also gives the men the opportunity to place baits in a range of depths in a single drift.

Although finding the right depth is critical, McCoy notes, there is no magic number for every drift. That can change from day to day, and lake to lake.

"It may take a couple of hours to find the fish some days," he says. "But once you discover the

right depth for the bigger cats, you can figure on finding more at the same level."

If McCoy catches small catfish, or marks them with his sonar, he shifts to different depths, having learned from experience that little catfish typically give the big boys a wide berth.

When McCoy and Rodgers find what looks like a potentially productive section of water, they motor well upwind, then set their lines for a drift. Dragging one or more sea anchors to control boat speed and direction, they drop their baits to the bottom and begin a slow pass that will commonly last about an hour.

Often, they begin a drift over open water, pass over the structure, and keep drifting all the way into shore. When the boat comes to rest, they leave their lines in the water for another 10 minutes or so before reeling in to try the process again.

"Sometimes catfish will follow the blood for a long time, but they won't take it until it stops and settles onto the bottom," McCoy explains.

Making Blood Bait

Over the years, McCoy and Rodgers have perfected a unique method for preparing the coagulated blood for the water.

From the slaughterhouse, the blood is cooled in a bucket for five days at 32 degrees, after which it forms an unappetizing mass with about the same consistency as gelatin. The blood is then poured onto a hard, level surface, flattened into a pancake shape about an inch thick, and cut into squares that vary in size from about 1 to 3 inches across.

"McCoy and Rodgers have perfected a unique method for preparing the coagulated blood."

"We typically use smaller pieces of blood bait early in the season, when the fish are a little more tentative," says McCoy.

When it's time to fish, the bait is strung onto a leader—a foot-long section of 100-pound braided Dacron that is not yet attached to the main line. To

TARGETING TROPHY FISH

The number of new world line-class and state catfish records established during the past 20 years suggests that catfish populations are improving in many large rivers and reservoirs.

Or maybe catfish anglers are just getting better.

The current world-record blue catfish (111 pounds, Wheeler Reservoir Alabama) was caught

Member Daniel Cole, Springfield, Vermont, 37-inch channel cat, Lake Champlain.

in 1996; the world-record flathead (123 pounds, Elk City Reservoir, Kansas) was caught in 1998; and a giant, 50-pound-plus Mississippi channel cat taken in 1997 nearly toppled the world record for that species as well.

When you think about it, this shouldn't surprise anyone. Large catfish were once common in North America. Reports from the late 1800s document blue cats weighing up to 315 pounds.

But why the resurgence? Credit improving habitat in some large rivers and reservoirs, as well as changing attitudes in catfish management, and growing popularity among anglers. And don't forget, by nature, catfish are hardly a diminutive clan.

Catfish habitat, once outstanding in medium and large rivers in North America, has been severely degraded by channelization, dredging and water pollution over the past 100 years. Blue cats in particular have suffered in the northern reaches of their range.

Channelization shortens a river and increases water velocity, reducing the amount of preferred living space for large catfish. It also alters catfish spawning areas and rearing areas for small cats, and reduces the food base.

However, habitat seems to be improving in some large rivers. Jack Robinson, fisheries research biologist for the Missouri Department of Conservation, has studied catfish populations in big rivers for more than 30 years. He says the Missouri River is clearing, as upstream dams trap silt and sand—improving water quality and catfish living conditions.

Tailwaters downstream from major dams provide a bonanza of food, especially shad, and optimum living conditions for large blues and channels. Large reservoirs upstream from the dams offer a haven for flathead catfish.

Arguably, the most important reason for the improved catfish fishing has been management officials' realization that populations can be over harvested.

Attempting to predict where anglers might catch gigantic catfish is risky at best. Rather than listing specific waters, let's define habitats which provide the best opportunity.

Flatheads are currently expanding their range, and trophies have been taken on large rivers and reservoirs from Florida to California. Unaltered stretches of large rivers—with lots of woody debris—are good, but it's hard to beat the chow-rich, slack water of a big reservoir.

Blue cats are also creatures of big rivers and reservoirs—though they prefer cleaner, faster flowing water than flatheads. Fish tailwaters below dams, and deep

Member Dennis Flom, Harwood, North Dakota, 35½-inch channel cat, Red River.

Continued on next page...

Targeting Trophy Fish continued …

ledges in unimpounded sections of large rivers. A number of reservoirs are hotspots for big blues, too.

Channel catfish can be found throughout North America. Your best shot at a trophy may be the Red River along the Minnesota/ North Dakota border, and below Lockport Dam in Manitoba. In the South, small, lightly fished lakes and ponds often produce big channels.

Member Ryan Wassink, Hall, Iowa, 43-inch flathead, Minnesota River.

Mississippi's Lake Tom Bailey, which recently produced a state-record 51¾-pound channel cat, is another good bet. Biologists are confident that there are even larger fish in the lake.

—Spencer Turner

Member Chuck Doucot, Costa Mesa, California, 55-inch blue cat, Irvine Lake.

get the blood onto the leader, McCoy and Rodgers use a 6-inch piece of thin, stiff wire. When pressed against the barrel swivel at the top of the leader, the wire acts like a needle, helping thread the blood onto the line.

The chunk of blood bait slips down the leader onto a treble hook (from 1 to 2/0, depending on the size of the bait). The leader is then attached to a snap tied on the end of the main line and the bait is dipped in the water for a few minutes—for toughening—before being dropped to the bottom.

McCoy and Rodgers seldom use sinkers to take the blood to the bottom. Except in heavy wind, current or deep water, the blood is heavy enough to stay on the bottom without additional weight.

Their terminal tackle varies little wherever they fish, but the rods, reels and main line they use may change from lake to lake, depending on the size of the catfish they expect to encounter.

Channel catfish up to 20 pounds dominate the fisheries in the lakes McCoy and Rodgers typically target around home, and they proved at Santee-Cooper that drifting blood also works great for trophy-size blues.

The tactic is less effective for flatheads, which prefer live bait over following a blood trail along the bottom.

Drifting works well on unfamiliar waters. That's a plus for the pair because it allows them to cover a lot of territory when looking for catfish.

McCoy says that no matter where they roam, they always start with the same basic system, then let current conditions dictate the specifics.

"You have to pay attention to wind strength and direction, water depth, bottom structure, baitfish, the mood of the cats—and make adjustments as you go," he says.

Cold Water, Cold Cuts, Cold Cats

by Keith Sutton

While most anglers are just thinking about catching catfish, many knowledgeable anglers are pulling in lots of cats, including plenty of monsters.

February. The Arkansas River churns below Murray Dam at Little Rock, Arkansas. The temperature is 45 degrees but a stiff breeze knocks the wind chill below freezing.

A month from now, the riverbanks will be lined with anglers after white bass and saugers. But today, only two fishermen brave the frigid air.

"Fish biting?" I ask the other guy when I arrive.

"See for yourself," he says, nodding toward a stringer stretched out in the water.

I grab the nylon cord and pull it up. A 10-pound blue cat and four 3- to 5-pound channel cats thrash the water.

"Reckon they are," I say. "Hittin' cut bait, I suppose."

"Yep. Looks like there's been a pretty good shad die-off somewhere upriver. The cats are stacked up in here pickin' off what's left of 'em after they come through the dam."

A few throws of my cast net, and a dozen shad crowd my bait bucket. I cut one in three pieces—head, body and tail—thread the midsection on my hook, and cast toward the dam.

Catfishing can be a waiting

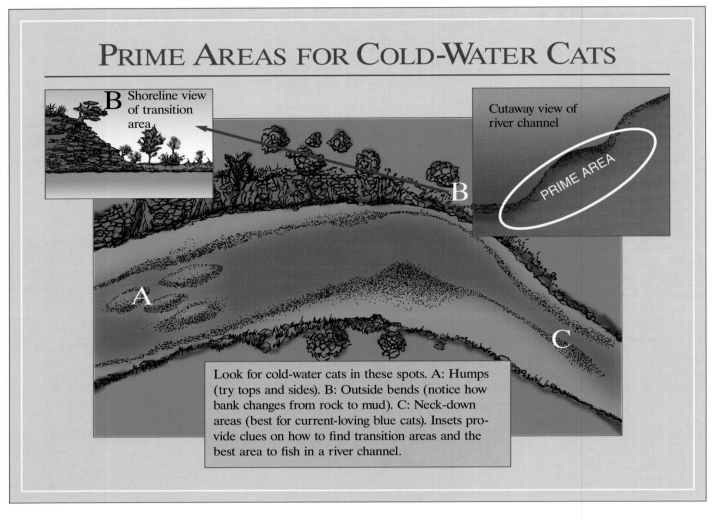

PRIME AREAS FOR COLD-WATER CATS

B Shoreline view of transition area

Cutaway view of river channel

PRIME AREA

B

A

C

Look for cold-water cats in these spots. A: Humps (try tops and sides). B: Outside bends (notice how bank changes from rock to mud). C: Neck-down areas (best for current-loving blue cats). Insets provide clues on how to find transition areas and the best area to fish in a river channel.

game, but not when icy water causes a shad dieoff. On this day, the tailwater cats are in a shark-like feeding frenzy. As soon as my line swings tight in the current, a nice cat nails the bait and is landed.

On the second cast, I lose a sizeable fish. The third and fourth casts produce two more catfish— a 6-pound blue and a 7-pound flathead.

In the same time span, the elderly gentleman seated next to me catches three more blues, including one pushing the 20-pound mark.

"I caught a blue last February that weighed 57 pounds," the elderly catter says. "And the year before that, I caught two that weighed over 40. Folks who think summer catfishing is good should try it now."

The long-standing notion that catfishing is best during summer's heat is folklore. Granted, summer is a blue-ribbon season for busting big cats, but it's not necessarily the best time to catch them. Most catters who fish year-round agree that the winter/early spring period is tops in terms of catfish numbers and size.

World-record listings are one indication of the potential for catching monster cats this time of year. The National Fresh Water Fishing Hall of Fame lists five world line-class-record cats caught in February (1 blue, 2 channels, 2 flathead) and 9 caught in March (3 blues, 1 channel, 3 flatheads, 3 whites).

A catfish's metabolism does slow when water gets cold, but they do feed year-round. The key to winter angling success is knowing what to use for bait, and where to put it.

Cruising For A Bruiser

NAFC member Jim Moyer of Clarksville, Tennessee, is a big cat specialist who has caught hundreds of monster kitties, most of them in the past five years. Unlike most anglers, he avoids tailwater areas ("too many small fish") and warm water discharges ("too many fishermen"), and focus his efforts along the edge of the main river channel anywhere from two to 50 miles below a dam.

The pattern Jim has developed was honed on the Cumberland River near his home, but has definite applications in other waters.

Basically, Jim looks for areas that feature a combination of increased current, sharp break near shore and a mud bank. Incidentally, these areas are often favored by shad.

Jim believes that mud banks warm better than other areas during the winter, which draws shad and cats, especially big blues. During the summer months, he concentrates on rocky banks, since these areas tend to be cooler.

Precise boat control is necessary to keep your baits in the strike zone. Jim uses a 35-pound hunk of railroad track to pin his Stratos on the breakline, then casts his lines on top of the break, along the break itself and as close to the bottom edge as possible. Most cats come on the deep line, but enough hit the others to make it worthwhile. If multiple lines are permitted in your area, fish all three.

Cats tend to congregate near channel features that are different from the norm—brush piles, points jutting into the drop-off, adjacent humps, stump fields, dead snags, and pockets cutting into the bank.

Big cats seem to prefer deeper water, anywhere from 15 to 50 feet, depending on the body of water.

Other good spots include the outside turns of channel bends, near junctions of two or more channels, and on deep channel edges in or near dam tailwaters (better for numbers of small fish).

Tailwaters can produce extraordinary numbers of winter catfish after severe cold snaps, which can cause massive shad die-offs. Dead fish are sucked through the turbines, and cats below the dam feast on the leftovers.

Humps on stream and lake bottoms are also hotspots for winter catfish. The tops of humps attract schools of shad and other baitfish, which offer hungry cats a quick meal a short swim from their deep-water haunts nearby.

OVERDUE IDEA— RELEASE YOUR TROPHY CATS!

Many catfish anglers believe it's impossible to hurt a catfish population with hook and line. They're wrong. Heavy angling pressure can have a dramatic effect on catfish populations if it's not tempered by conservation. Big catfish are especially vulnerable, because once these ancients are removed, it takes many, many years to replace them.

Be selective about your harvest. The tips provided here will put you on monsters. Now do your part. Shoot a photo for memory's sake, then carefully remove the hook and release the fish. If you're fish-hungry, keep a few small cats to eat.

Voluntary catch-and-release fishing will not only protect trophy catfishing opportunities, it will enhance them.

When a bite is on, fishing a hump in winter can produce catfishing action far better than anything you ever imagined.

If an electrical power plant is adjacent to the body of water you're fishing, be sure to look for catfish in the vicinity.

These facilities are hotspots in the literal sense of the term. Lake or river water is used to cool internal machinery, and when the water is returned from where it came, it's usually several degrees warmer than the surrounding lake or stream.

Baitfish congregate in these warm environs, and catfish, stripers and other gamefish move in to feed on them.

Deep channels beneath bridges, deep-water chutes around river islands, long timbered points jutting into deep water, potholes adjacent to the deep end

of river wing-dams, lock-wall edges and tributary mouths—these, too, are among the many areas winter catfish hold.

Wherever you fish, move if the spot doesn't produce after a half hour or so. Active fish will find your offering, so there is no reason to wait for inactive fish to turn on. Keep moving until you find active fish.

Loaded For Bear

If you're fishing from shore, an 8- to 13-foot medium/heavy- to heavy-action spinning rod like those used for surf fishing is best. Such a rig will allow you to cast long distances, and still have the power to muscle even monster cats to shore.

My favorite rig is a Shimano Triton 6500 Bait Runner reel paired with a 13-foot Abu Garcia graphite rod (model SS130-4h). Abrasion-resistant mono—30- to 80-pound test—is best because big cats will destroy anything less.

Fairly long rods are also a good idea when fishing from a boat because short, stiff rods can't load or unload as fast as you'll need them to when fighting big fish, and the results can be disastrous—

pulled hooks, busted lines and shattered rods.

Top anglers rely on 7- to 8-foot rods, preferably outfitted with a long, trigger-grip handle for double-handed fish fighting. Medium-fast action blanks with light tips will help you detect light biters.

Sensitivity and lightness aren't necessarily important attributes of a good cat rod. You want something with strength and durability—something you find in models built with E- and S-glass.

Some anglers have turned to saltwater model rods because many freshwater rods don't have the backbone to stand up to big cats. Ask Moyer—he's broken more than four dozen flippin' sticks over the years fighting big cats. One company that helped solve this problem is South Bend. Their "Catfish Special" series is extremely tough and has exceptional lifting power. Three casting and two spinning rods are in the series. Lengths are 6½ to 8 feet and they feature a glow tip for night or low-light fishing.

Selecting the right reel is a bit easier. Look for models that hold at least 200 yards of 20-pound test, have a good drag system, and gears beefy enough to stand up to fish in the 50- to 100-pound class.

Several of Abu Garcia's reels are popular among

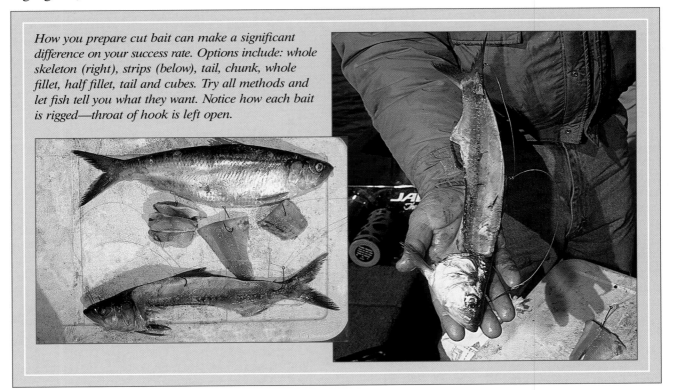

How you prepare cut bait can make a significant difference on your success rate. Options include: whole skeleton (right), strips (below), tail, chunk, whole fillet, half fillet, tail and cubes. Try all methods and let fish tell you what they want. Notice how each bait is rigged—throat of hook is left open.

serious anglers, but models from companies like Mitchell, Daiwa, Shimano and Quantum work equally well. Reels with lower gear ratios are great for powering in big cats.

Lines testing 20- to 30-pound test are fine for most catfishing situations, but go to 40- or 50-pound test if the waters you fish have monster cats.

A good abrasion resistant monofilament like Stren Super Tough or Berkley Big Game will fit the bill. The new super braids also have their fans.

"Folks who think summer catfishing is good should try catfishing in winter and early spring."

The Business End

It's rare to find a rig more effective for cats than a basic three-way set rig. To make one, tie your main line to one eye of a size 1 or 2 three-way swivel and tie drop-lines 12 and 24 inches long to the other two eyes. Tie a needle-sharp, heavy-wire hook on the longer drop and a bell or pyramid sinker to the shorter line. Use lighter line to weight so if you hang, the whole rig won't break off. Putting a snap in front of the weight will allow you to quickly change weights to cope with various depths, wind or current.

Another option is running your main line through a 1- to 5-ounce egg sinker, and tying off on a 1/0 swivel. Below the swivel, run a 2- to 4-foot leader down to your hook. Use the shorter leader in less current; the longer one in faster water. These leader lengths maximize bait movement under various conditions.

Most top cat anglers are turning toward the Kahle-style hooks because their large throats make it easy to bury the barb, even when the hook is loaded with chunks of cut bait.

Depending on the baits used and the size of fish being targeted, hook sizes from 1/0 to 6/0 are best. The sinker should be heavy enough to carry the bait straight to the bottom.

Cold Cuts For Cold Cats

Cut bait is best for winter cats, but what you use and how you cut it can make a huge difference in your success.

According to Moyer, nothing beats a skipjack herring, though he will go with gizzard shad or other baitfish if necessary.

But what's unique is how he prepares the bait. While most catfishermen will steak a bait, Moyer cuts his baits four different ways and uses them all until the fish tell him what they want.

Sometimes, he'll use a whole skipjack fillet, half a fillet or the tail section of the fish. Most likely, though, he will cube the fillet into 1-inch strips and thread four or five of them onto his hook.

Moyer says the strip bait not only gives off more scent than a fillet, it will not spin in the current.

Cut bait works because it leaves a trail of blood and oil that catfish find irresistible. Fresh bait has more of what the cats are looking for, so change baits often.

"Cut bait works because it leaves a trail of blood and oil that catfish find irresistible."

Hot Fishing In Cold Weather

If you're still not convinced that prime time to chase kitties is in winter and early spring, consider this: three of the four all-tackle world records listed by the National Fresh Water Fishing Hall of Fame were early-bird cats.

South Carolina's Cooper River produced a mammoth 109-pound, 4-ounce blue on March 14, 1991, and Toledo Bend Lake kicked out a 92-pound flathead on February 25, 1995. And the world record white cat was a March fish.

Perhaps you won't land a world record catfish. Then again, maybe you will. Moyer caught and released an 87-pound, 3-ounce blue, and lost another that was noticeably bigger.

Cold water, cold cuts, cold cats — a cool recipe for hot fishing.

Chapter 6

Walleye

To fish walleyes is to know frustration. These fish can be tough to find — and moody — but they will open their finicky mouths when you find the most productive pattern of depth-bait-presentation-speed-etc. for the day. And then, suddenly, all the effort is worth it as you hold that beautiful, golden-flanked, marble-eyed creature in your wet hands. Get your line back in the water — fast!

To help you experience that thrill more often, we've pulled together *North American Fisherman's* best walleye (and sauger) insights, and our ideas on what you can do to catch more of these fish more consistently.

After Hours 'Eyes

by Kurt Beckstrom

*Three generations of trophy walleye anglers have helped develop
this system that has accounted for thousands of giant fish!*

Walleye fishing during the day is a safe, sane, wholesome sport, superbly suited to polite society. Under the bright light, anglers pluck tasty 2 pounders from reefs, breaklines, points and other typical walleye haunts.

Sure, an occasional 8 or 9 pounder shows up, stirring the blood of even the most staid fisherman, but daytime double-digit fish are elusive, residing mainly in the dreams of most anglers.

It's at night, they say, that things go bump—and if you'd like to bump into more monster 'eyes, then join the nocturnal nomads like NAFC member Mark Martin, who focuses his efforts after dark simply because it's the best time to catch the biggest fish.

Trophy walleyes become killer fish with attitudes after dark, cruising the same structures that sensible anglers abandoned just hours before.

They use the darkness to shed their low-key, Dr. Jekyll personalities and become the Mr. Hydes of the underwater world—unbridled predators searching for unsuspecting prey.

How good can the fishing be? Well, Martin has more than 1,000 10-pound-plus walleyes to his credit, and most of them were taken at night.

In The Blood

During normal business hours, Martin seems like an average guy. It would be difficult to pick him out of a crowd. But with the setting sun, this Twin Lakes, Michigan, angler becomes as predatory as a hungry walleye.

That's because Martin isn't just somebody who happened to develop a special niche in the world of walleye fishing. Rather, he was born into it. It's his heritage.

Even before he learned to walk, father Bob and Grandpa Smitty would wrap little Mark in blankets and lay him down in the old aluminum rig. The rhythmic creaking of the oarlocks, intermingled with the men's hushed conversation, lulled him to sleep better than any bedtime story, he recalls.

And that wasn't even the beginning. In Grandpa Smitty's diary, Martin says the first mention of nightfishing is on a page dated 1929. With blood lines like that, how could he become anything but a nightfisherman?

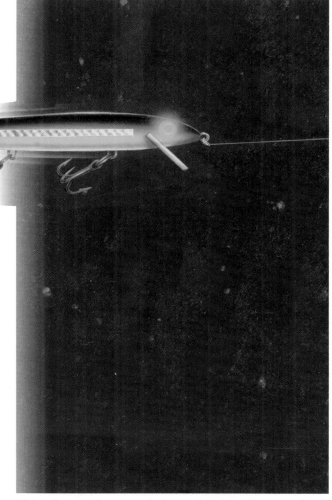

Using these nighttime techniques, it's virtually a sure thing that you'll have a run-in with a big walleye.

Now, Martin earns most of his livelihood by leading other anglers to trophy 'eyes. And he gets so much satisfaction from it, he's willing to share his

"With blood lines like that, how could he become anything but a nightfisherman?"

time-forged techniques with his fellow NAFC members across walleye country.

Nocturnal predator Mark Martin. His system for catching oversize walleye will work for you, too.

If you're searching for a double-digit 'eye — something in the class of Martin's 13.56-pound personal best, or even the family record 14.11 pounder caught by his dad when Mark was 12 years old — then, read on....

The Martin Method

With Martin's approach, locating a hotspot isn't as critical to success as using the proper technique once you start fishing.

"In mid-season, you can generally catch big fish on all the same spots you'd typically find walleyes during the day—weedlines, breaklines, riprap shorelines, submerged islands," he explains, "but to be 98-percent successful, you have to follow some rules."

On any given summer evening, a breakline (edge) is a good place to start. Chances are, the action will continue, but with much larger fish after dark. And if the breakline isn't producing, try other structure. The fish could just as easily be scattered over a shoreline flat.

"At that time of year, the walleyes can wander 300 yards or more from the nearest drop-off," says Martin, "so be prepared to cover a lot of water."

During the fall, Martin turns his attention toward structure that tapers quickly into deep water. Big walleyes prefer the more vertical contour because it allows them to move up or down to a comfortable or forage-filled temperature zone without having to travel a long way.

"They won't be far from the breakline in the fall," he explains. "Concentrate on that first major drop-off and you'll catch fish."

As for Martin's rules, they may seem like nit-picking to some. But then, he's the one with all the trophies under his belt.

"First, I don't even start fishing during the mid-season until 11 p.m. I want to give the lake and the fish plenty of time to settle down after the other anglers and pleasure boaters have gone home. In the fall, you can start much earlier, depending on length of day and the amount of traffic that had been on the lake."

Once on the water, the key is to move slowly and quietly as you troll. "You can motor to your fishing spot, but shut off the gas engine and drop the electric well—before you get there."

Martin prefers a bow-mount electric motor, which he says is easier to control when following a tricky breakline or similar piece of structure. He perches in the bow chair, usually with one client half-way back on the port side and another on the starboard stern.

His eyes are glued to the sonar screen as he searches for irregularities on the bottom and twists and turns in the breakline. "I troll the contour line as closely as possible because I want the lures to run about 1 to 2½ feet off the bottom. If you're fishing a weedline, you can occasionally allow them to tick the weed tops. But don't stray too far from this edge or you'll be fishing either too deep or too shallow.

"If you suddenly come upon a hump like a rock pile, all you have to do is stand up and lift your arm. The lure will rise over it. Be alert, though, because a lot of strikes come as the lure passes over the hump."

Another option is to jack up the motor speed. The extra burst makes the short-lipped balsa

stickbaits he generally uses rise in the water column, avoiding potential snags on the bottom.

"Whenever possible, I troll with the wind to maximize battery power and eliminate wave-slap on the hull, which can spook fish," he says. "And I don't move very fast, usually about 1 mph, never more than 1½ mph."

"The boat is simply a tool for getting lures into the right area."

To Martin, the boat is simply a presentation platform—a tool for getting his lures into the right area. Triggering strikes is the angler's responsibility, and Martin has developed a whole system that incorporates modified lures and a special twitch/pause technique to entice fish.

"Another thing NAFC members should remember, especially those who are targeting trophies instead of numbers of fish: The biggest walleyes on any particular spot almost always come on the first or second pass. After that, the chances of catching a trophy fish drop off dramatically. So make first passes count."

Night Gear

Of all the new developments since Grandpa Smitty's time, the electric trolling motor, and especially sonar, did more than anything else to make nightfishing more fun and efficient.

When Martin was a kid, his dad and grandpa would throw a dozen or so empty bleach bottles overboard in deep water. A brick was attached to each one with a 15-foot cord. As the buoys drifted toward shore, they'd anchor themselves at the 15-foot level and thus create a path the anglers could follow.

Nowadays, Martin has an Ultra III LCD on the bow, plus an Eagle Accura GPS unit on the bow and another on the console. With this equipment, he can simultaneously plot a trolling course, monitor boat speed and track the bottom.

His trolling arsenal consists of three different rods, all medium-action trigger models that are basically interchangeable when it comes to

application. The first is the Gary Roach Signature Series GR50-7-10SL in Berkley's Select line. But he often gives clients his second rod, a GR50-6-8 model, which is a bit shorter and a little easier to handle. The third is Berkley's Series One, model B50-6-6M.

Each rod is paired with a Mitchell Count Master 40 line-counter reel. "I really like the Count Masters because they're tough, yet lightweight; you can hold on to them all night without your hand, wrist or arm getting tired."

Martin sets the drag a bit more loosely than most anglers. "Loose enough so the drag slips on the hookset," he says. "Oh, yes, you should pump the fish in instead of pulling it, too."

The reason: You want the equipment to be just a bit forgiving. Corralling a thrashing 10-pound-plus 'eye can be tough when your hands are shaking and your heartbeat is in the red.

The biggest change in Martin's equipment lineup has been in the line he fishes. Up to a couple of seasons ago, it was strictly 10-pound Berkley XT. Now he uses FireLine, Berkley's new low-stretch, thermo-fused fiber line.

NIGHT FIGHTER BASIC TRAINING

Battling a double-digit walleye during daylight hours is one thing, but going hand-to-hand after dark is something entirely different.

"Although it's tempting to use a flashlight when netting a fish—don't!" says Martin. "They'll go bonkers at boatside. It's like somebody flipping on your bedroom light at 3 a.m. It's pure panic, and the fish can move faster than you can react."

Another tip is to turn the boat broadside to a hooked fish. It gives you more room to move, and there won't be any props in the way during that last critical second when you attempt to net the fish.

The rod man should keep the tip high to avoid reeling down too close to the fish. Plus, according to Martin, the net man can look at the rodtip and see exactly where the walleye is at all times.

THE MARTIN TOUCH

Mark Martin's trolling techniques are strictly hands-on. No rod holders or trolling boards in this scenario.

It's up to the angler to impart fish-attracting movement to the lure. And Martin does it using a technique he's developed over years of nightfishing. (See the box at far right.)

"It's a pull-then-pause kind of a motion. You sweep the rodtip forward, but not too far or you won't be able to make the hook-set. Your hand should move only a couple of feet or so. Let it drop back, pause for a two-count, then do it again."

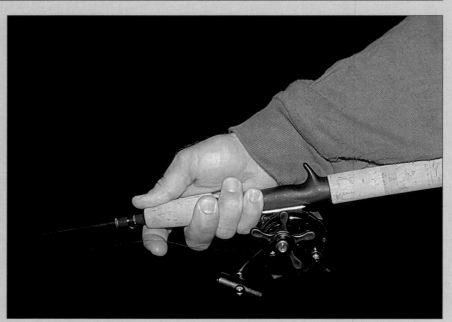

Martin's "spinning rod" grip on his levelwind outfit allows him to feel strikes better. It's also very comfortable.

Both the forward pull and the drop back are done at a moderate speed. When fishing a short-lipped stickbait, the lure rises a bit because its small diving lip can't overpower the extra resistance of the water on the line.

A diving lure will dig in and run slightly deeper on the rod sweep. "With a deep diver, slow your trolling speed until you can't feel it wobble. Then, on the forward pull, you'll be able to detect a telltale thump. Vary the length of the sweep—maybe start with three thumps, then go to four or five—until you determine what the fish want.

"After the sweep, just ease it back on a semi-tight line. If it's too tight, lure action is inhibited, and if there's too much slack the action dies completely. Plus, you won't feel a strike on the let-back."

Martin maintains control and a positive touch by holding his levelwind rig upside down, with the reel hanging below the rod and the line draped across his index finger.

"It's a much more comfortable position, and you can feel even the slightest bump on the lure," he explains. "And when you do, set the hook!"

"Twenty-pound FireLine has about the same diameter as 8-pound mono, and it allows you to feel the fish, plus get a good hookset. In fact, since I've switched to a low-stretch line, not one client has ever questioned a strike. When a fish hits, they know it."

Martin's bread-and-butter lure, the one that he runs 80 percent of the time, is the No. 13 Original Floating Rapala. During the fall, though, it pays to jump to the larger No. 18, he says.

"You won't get as many hits, but any fish you

catch will definitely be a trophy. If you're strictly after monster 'eyes, you have to have a lot of patience and be satisfied with getting, maybe, three hits in an entire night."

No matter which lure he uses, Martin always adds a few of his own special touches before it goes into the water.

"I doctor every bait by dabbing glow-in-the-dark paint on each eye and painting a small ring around the tail," he says. "I also place prism tape on each side. It all makes the lure more visible.

"Martin's bread-and-butter lure: the No. 13 Original Floating Rapala."

"To increase hooksetting potential, I widen the gap on each of the three trebles by bending the points slightly outward, then hone the points to razor sharpness. That way they'll stick at the slightest bump and give you that extra tenth of a second to bury the barb."

Martin also created his own quick-change trolling rig that makes it easier to swap lures in the dark.

"Basically, it's a 2- to 3-foot length of FireLine with one end tied directly to the lure and the other attached to a ball-bearing swivel. A cross-lock snap goes on the end of the main line.

"If a lure is damaged or I want to swap colors, I just have to open the snap and change the entire rig instead of trying to tie knots while holding a penlight in my mouth. I keep dozens of the pre-rigged lures ready to go at all times."

Just ahead of the snap, on the main line, Martin pinches on three size 7 split shot. This gives him the precise depth control he needs with his system—line, letback, trolling speed. But he says others may have to modify a bit.

"Every NAFC member will have to do his or her own homework because everyone fishes differently," he explains. "With my system, I have to let out about 75 to 80 feet of the FireLine to make the No. 13 run at about 10½ feet; 120 feet of letback puts the lure at 12 to 12½ feet.

MASTERING THE MARTIN TOUCH

Lure action is critical to Martin's presentation. During the pause stage, the lure runs straight and at a constant speed.

The forward motion is a moderately paced sweep (not a jerk), which causes the lure to move faster and with an accentuated wobble.

Short-lipped baits rise a bit while divers dig in toward the bottom.

After the sweep, move the rodtip back to the starting position while keeping the line semi-tight.

A quick backward motion puts too much slack in the line and kills the lure's action. Many strikes occur on the letback, so be ready.

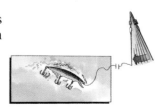

A battle-scarred veteran and a new recruit. Tooth marks, shredded prism tape and a bent split ring loop (middle) illustrate what the brand new Shad Rap might look like after just seven nights of fishing.

"But remember, the amount of line you let out isn't really important. It's the lure's running depth. Most of the time you want it in that strike zone that's a foot to two and a half feet from the bottom.

"If you need more depth, let out more line, or pinch on a couple more split shot just in front of the snap. It will add weight without affecting the lure's action, and you can run the lure closer to the boat."

When Martin probes deeper waters, he'll tie on a diving lure like a Shad Rap, Bomber, Rebel or a Storm Deep ThunderStick. Divers, however, are clipped to the snap on the main line because tying directly to the lure kills some of the action, he says. If he needs to run deeper, he switches to a lure with an even larger lip.

The exception to the strike zone rule comes into play during late fall or early winter on lakes with a shad forage base.

"Shad often hold as little as two to four feet from the surface in 10 to 15 feet of water. Then, you'll have to fish the baitfish as if they were structure."

Lure color is important when it comes to offering the walleyes something they can see. Martin doesn't try to match the forage, but rather chooses color according to weather and water conditions.

"On a clear to partly-cloudy night, with the water being clear to stained, and calm to a slight ripple, I go with the standard silver-and-black, gold-and-black or silver-and-blue patterns. Sometimes perch or rainbow patterns work a bit better.

"Water color being the same, flashier colors like fluorescent orange-and-gold or chartreuse are more productive if cloud cover is thick, or it's raining and there's a bit more wind.

"Any type of rattling lure is the choice when the wind is strong enough to put at least a two-foot chop on the surface. All that commotion drowns out the rattle. It doesn't sound like a freight train; it just catches their attention."

Noisy lures, he adds, are also the choice in stained to muddy waters where the walleyes' visibility is somewhat limited.

Lunar Connection

Much has been written about the moon's influence on fish activity. And many anglers say the best fishing occurs during the full moon phase. Martin isn't one of them. In fact, he'd just as soon fish under a canopy of clouds.

"I've experienced good fishing under all moon phases, but I'd say most of my really big fish have come before, during or just after a half-moon.

"A lot of guys swear by the full moon, but I'd rather have thick clouds or a big chop to cut down on light penetration.

"The one thing experience has taught me is that the best fishing of the night will occur during the moon rise or moon set. I don't know why that is; it's just something I learned from my grandpa. But if fishing is tough, and I mean if you're not hooking a fish at least every 15 minutes, hang on until the moon sets.

"Make sure you're on your most productive spot

when the moon has to travel about the last quarter of its arc to reach the horizon, and it's virtually a sure thing that you'll have a run-in with a big walleye."

There won't be a moon rise every night, Martin

"I prefer thick clouds or a big chop to cut down light penetration."

adds. It depends on the time of year and where the moon is in the sky when it gets dark. But it's something to tuck into your mental bank of fishing knowledge so you can pull it out when you need it.

Fishing after dark may not be every angler's choice. But if you're one who feels the predatory juices begin to flow as twilight gives way to night, you might as well take advantage of Mark Martin's system. After all, it's the combined knowledge of three generations of trophy walleye hunters.

ACCENTUATE THE POSITIVE

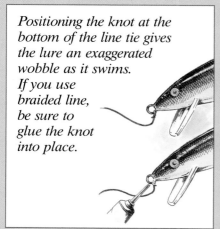

Positioning the knot at the bottom of the line tie gives the lure an exaggerated wobble as it swims. If you use braided line, be sure to glue the knot into place.

When Martin builds one of his "quick-change" rigs, he forgoes the classic loop knot and ties directly to the lure's line tie with an improved clinch.

But instead of leaving it at the center of the eye, he pushes the knot to the bottom and all the way back to the balsa. In this position, the knot accentuates the lure's wobble, he says, which helps catch the fish's eye.

One caution, however. Though monofilament will stay put while trolling, you'll have to "re-cock" the knot back into position after every strike or snag.

Low-stretch superlines, on the other hand, are too slippery and the knot must be welded in place with a drop of Stren's Lok-Knot or Super Glue.

River Review

by Jim Saric

Here's how to catch walleyes and saugers out of different types of rivers, plus a review of the techniques that have been most effective the last decade.

Sunshine pierced the clouds as I eased off the throttle and idled up to the dock. More than satisfied with the morning's results—a mixed bag of river walleyes and sauger—I smiled as another angler knelt to catch the bow of my craft.

A forced grin on the man's face couldn't hide his frustration. "Tough morning?" I asked, hoping I'd read the guy wrong and he'd report success similar to mine.

Two Thumbs Down

"Tried everything I could think of up and down the river, just couldn't connect," he lamented. "You?"

I gently broke the news, explaining where and how I'd gotten my fish. The man shook his head. "Guess I didn't try everything after all. That's what I get for fishing a big river like this. Ought to stick to the small ones, without channels, wing dams and all that other crap."

Sad to say, even though the guy had a great boat, a ton of tackle and looked like he knew what he was doing, his situation didn't surprise me. A lot of knowledgeable walleye and sauger anglers face tough times when they switch from natural to channelized rivers, or vice-versa.

Fortunately, it doesn't have to be that way. Both types of rivers can produce a ton of fish—if you know how to approach them.

Breaking It Down

Walleyes and sauger are the same wherever you go, but their location can vary dramatically from one river to the next. You'll catch more fish if you learn to read the waters you're on—and adjust your techniques accordingly.

While this requires some thought, it's not exactly brain surgery.

Let's start at the beginning—identifying different kinds of rivers. I divide 'em into two very broad categories: natural and channelized.

Natural rivers flow freely across most of North America. Dams exist on many of them, but for the most part, the natural channels are undisturbed. As the river meanders along, the channel switches from bank to bank, creating a ton of potential fish-holding habitat, with an equally mind-boggling amount of fishless water.

Major channelized rivers have been altered to fit the needs of society—dredged to accommodate barge traffic and other forms of transportation, or to control water levels. Such rivers are characterized by a distinct channel running down the center, and straightened bends.

Major channelized rivers include the Columbia, Illinois, Monongahela, Ohio, St. Lawrence and portions of the Mississippi. Many smaller rivers, characterized as canals due to channelization and straightening, hold lots of fish, too. Also throw in tamed waterways such as the Tennessee River—a series of reservoirs and tailwater stretches which offer a ton of saugers and some walleyes.

Natural rivers are more common, and include the Delaware, Saginaw, Wisconsin, St. Joseph, Maumee, St. Croix, Missouri, Youghiogheny, portions of the Mississippi, and a host of smaller rivers across walleye country.

> *"walleye and sauger location can vary dramatically from one river to the next."*

Both natural and channelized rivers have similar areas that hold fish, yet certain spots are unique to each. And some seem to produce better on one or the other. To further complicate matters, some rivers have sections that could be considered natural, while other portions are channelized. Mix and match tactics to conditions if you want to score consistently.

By learning to identify and understand the two basic river types, NAFC members can locate key fish-holding areas and apply the right techniques to catch mind-numbing numbers of walleyes and saugers—even while other river rats are scratching their heads.

Understanding Natural Rivers

Several key areas hold walleyes and saugers on natural rivers. And, since channelized rivers originate as natural rivers, these areas are worth checking out on dredged rivers, too.

CHANNELIZED RIVERS

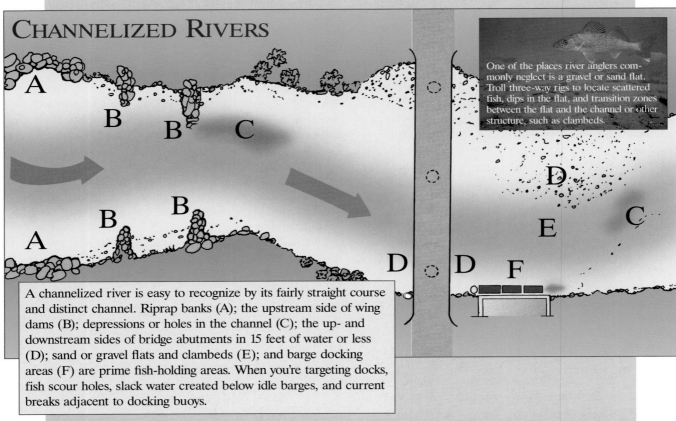

One of the places river anglers commonly neglect is a gravel or sand flat. Troll three-way rigs to locate scattered fish, dips in the flat, and transition zones between the flat and the channel or other structure, such as clambeds.

A channelized river is easy to recognize by its fairly straight course and distinct channel. Riprap banks (A); the upstream side of wing dams (B); depressions or holes in the channel (C); the up- and downstream sides of bridge abutments in 15 feet of water or less (D); sand or gravel flats and clambeds (E); and barge docking areas (F) are prime fish-holding areas. When you're targeting docks, fish scour holes, slack water created below idle barges, and current breaks adjacent to docking buoys.

NATURAL RIVERS

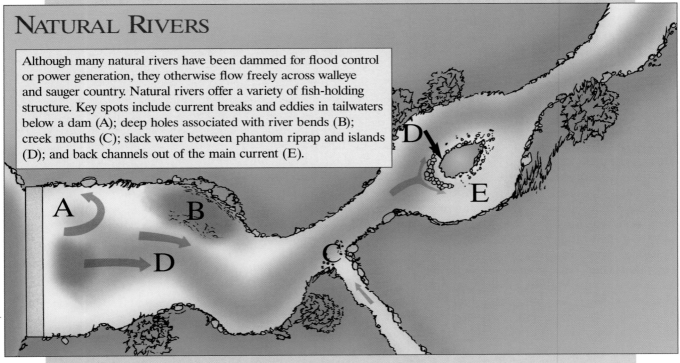

Although many natural rivers have been dammed for flood control or power generation, they otherwise flow freely across walleye and sauger country. Natural rivers offer a variety of fish-holding structure. Key spots include current breaks and eddies in tailwaters below a dam (A); deep holes associated with river bends (B); creek mouths (C); slack water between phantom riprap and islands (D); and back channels out of the main current (E).

The Ultimate Fishing Book: Strategies for Success

Holes—Holes associated with bends are found in both categories, but they're most common in natural rivers. Depending on their depth and location from the dam, holes can hold walleyes and saugers from pre-spawn throughout the rest of the season.

The steepest break generally lies near shore—against the river bend—where current is strongest. The opposite side is characterized by a gradually sloping bottom of rock, sand or gravel. Fish often move up on the gradual break to feed, then drop back into deep water.

Walleyes and saugers often slide into deep holes

"A small rock hump in the center of a back channel can be a gold mine for both walleyes and saugers."

during cold fronts, so don't forget to check the hole immediately downstream from a shallow area that was kicking out mega catches before the weather soured. Light jigs, stinger hooks and subtle jig strokes are a must.

Tributaries—Feeder creeks are excellent fishing areas, especially during spawning migrations and whenever conditions in the main river are inhospitable. Tributaries are also dynamite anytime baitfish are moving out of a creek and into the main river, or migrating back upstream.

You'll find them on all rivers, but in general, tributaries seem to be a bigger factor on smaller, natural rivers.

Fish mudlines, temperature breaks, islands and humps at the creek mouth. Then move into the tributary and target downed timber, holes in creek bends, flooded brush and any natural current breaks.

Feeder creeks that connect backwaters to the main channel can produce awesome fishing, especially when baitfish are migrating in or out.

Back Channels—The area between an island and the main bank—back channel—is dynamite whenever the main river is high. Also, the humps, holes and eddies that go with them are good when conditions are normal. A small rock hump in the

center of a back channel can be a gold mine for both walleyes and saugers. The same goes for current breaks around bends, islands, bars and other structure.

Some partially channelized rivers have back channels, too. For example, certain areas on the Mississippi are loaded with 'em, and man, do they hold walleyes!

Don't overlook the area where the back channel meets the main river channel. Any type of current break here will concentrate baitfish migrating in and out of the back channel, thus attracting hungry predators.

Channelized Rivers

In addition to areas similar to those found in natural rivers, you'll find that channelized rivers have their own set of unique options.

Riprap—Riprap is a great spot for walleyes and saugers, especially when it's located near a dam or tailwater area. These chunks of rock or concrete are commonly used in channelized rivers to prevent

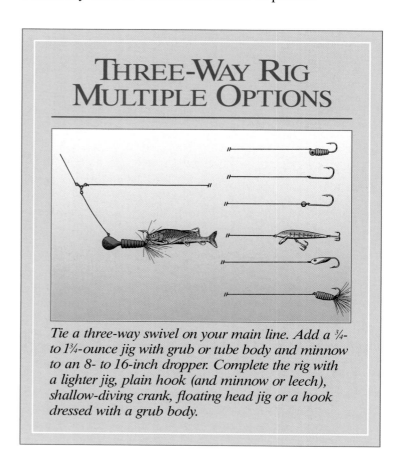

THREE-WAY RIG MULTIPLE OPTIONS

Tie a three-way swivel on your main line. Add a ¾- to 1¾-ounce jig with grub or tube body and minnow to an 8- to 16-inch dropper. Complete the rig with a lighter jig, plain hook (and minnow or leech), shallow-diving crank, floating head jig or a hook dressed with a grub body.

TELLING THEM APART

SAUGER

- Generally smaller than walleyes
- More blotchy coloration
- Spotted dorsal fin
- No white patch on tail
- Prefer slack current, holes on big, slow-moving rivers
- Occupy muddier rivers than walleyes
- Often prefer deeper water than walleyes
- NAFC member and veteran pro John Campbell caught this one

WALLEYE

- Uniform color pattern; gold, green or white, depending on water fished
- Generally larger than saugers
- White patch on lower tip of tail
- Prefer moderate current
- Found in faster current than saugers
- Hold in sharp current breaks, seams
- Less tolerant of poor water quality
- This one was caught by the author, NAFC member Jim Saric

generally weaker right next to the rocks, too, so always pitch a jig tight against them.

One of the hottest areas on any river is "phantom" riprap. It occurs when the upstream shoreline of an island erodes away behind its riprap shield, leaving a gap of slack water between the submerged line of old riprap and the existing bank. Walleyes and sauger stack up in this current break, feeding heavily on forage washed over the top and along the edges.

Pockets—Depressions in the main channel are a hotspot for walleyes and saugers in channelized rivers, especially during low-flow conditions. Depressions come in all shapes and sizes, ranging from large holes to small pockets and subtle dips.

Here's a common scenario: You run up the river more than a mile and never see the channel exceed 15 feet. Then, for no apparent reason, the bottom drops to 20 feet and boom—there's a bunch of fish. In fact, as you follow the hole a quarter-mile upstream, you mark fish the whole way!

In other cases, the channel looks like a large flat, pock-marked with hundreds of 2- to 3-foot depressions. Each one acts as a mini-current break, and each may hold fish. These smaller depressions are tougher to find than large holes, but they're definitely worth looking for. In fact, several big-fish spots on my favorite rivers are nothing more than small dips on a big flat.

Here's a tip: On an unfamiliar river, look for areas where the flow widens. This commonly indicates shallow areas associated with flats and depressions. Conversely, a sudden narrowing of the channel usually signals a large hole.

The real key to locating channel holes big and small, of course, is watching your electronics.

Hold That Barge—Barge docking, loading and unloading areas are unique to channelized rivers, and they can be hotbeds of walleye and sauger activity. The reason? As tugboats struggle to maneuver their mammoth charges into position at the docks, they scour holes in the river bottom, thereby creating fish-holding current breaks. I've caught a ton of fish in them.

Again, use your electronics to locate such areas. Another tip on docks: Loaded barges touching the river bottom act as current breaks and hold fish, too.

Wing Dams—A channelized river just wouldn't be complete without wing dams—manmade rock

bank erosion and funnel current to maintain channel depth.

Not all riprap is created equal, however—at least not in the eyes of sauger and walleyes. Avoid riprap with strong current rushing past. As a general rule, if you can't hold a boat or slowly slip downstream with your trolling motor along a riprap bank, the current is too fast.

Target subtle cuts, points and other irregularities, which act as natural current breaks. Current is

bars that jut out from shore. They deflect the current and help keep the channel deep and clear. Although their main purpose in life is aiding barge traffic, wing dams perform another useful service: they're key walleye feeding areas.

Some rivers have hundreds of wing dams, so you have to know what to look for. I target wing dams that are at least four feet under the surface. In addition, wing dams on outside bends, the mouths of side channels, and those with bends or cuts in them are usually the best producers.

Wing dams in a section of river with large concentrations of fish are the hottest, day in and day out. As water levels change, however, so do the fish, so be versatile and don't fish yesterday's memories. If a wing dam fails to produce, move to another.

Also, be aware that the walleye's position on the wing dam may change. In low-flow situations, the channel side or tip of the wing dam may be best, whereas in higher water, the shoreline side may be best. In general, fish the upstream side of a wing dam.

Common Ground

A couple of key areas are fairly common in both types of rivers. Look for them no matter what kind of river you're fishing.

Abutments—Bridge abutments and pilings are must-fish structures found wherever a highway crosses the river. Abutments do a couple of things. They create current breaks, and may also increase or create turbulence—producing a small scour hole immediately up- and downstream of the abutment. Fish will hold in both the breaks and holes.

A word of warning: In some channelized rivers, abutments are located in water too deep—or with current too strong—to hold fish. As you select prime abutments and pilings in channelized rivers, focus on those in less than 15 feet of water—typically the abutments closest to shore.

In natural rivers, bridge abutments hold fish almost anytime. In fact, I've taken a limit of fish off a single abutment quite a few times.

Flats—Sand and gravel flats are natural spawning and feeding areas, often associated with islands or river bank deposits. Spawning walleyes prefer rock/rubble and gravel, while saugers tend to favor sand and gravel flats. Fish may be scattered across them anytime, however.

Bends and turns in flats hold small schools of walleyes and sauger, but your odds of locating a major concentration of fish skyrocket if the flat is adjacent to a deep hole, current break or incoming creek. Concentrate on these edges, then move onto the main flat.

Tailwaters—Current breaks in tailwater areas are one of the most common places to find walleyes and sauger. Fish may shift position as current breaks change with water-level fluctuations (as well as the opening and closing of dams), but rest assured, they'll be there somewhere.

The relationship between tailwater current breaks and a deep scour hole immediately below a dam can be critical. Scour holes are sauger magnets—better still is a combination of tailwater current breaks and scour holes.

In walleye-dominated tailwaters, look for large fish along sharply-defined current breaks, and where the current splits in multiple directions. Slack water and deep holes below the dam usually contain small walleyes and sauger.

Presentation "Triad"

Many presentations will catch river walleyes and sauger, but three are effective almost anytime: vertical jigging or slipping; quarter pitching; and trolling 3-way rigs.

Slipping—Vertical jigging is probably the most talked about, yet underutilized river fishing method. That's because many anglers anchor and fight the current with heavy jigs and bowed line.

Enter the slipping technique, which allows you to fish light jigs on a tight line. It's great anytime, but clearly the method of choice for finicky fish.

Point the boat upstream and use the electric trolling motor to slip slowly down-current. Drop a jig-and-minnow to the bottom. I prefer a ¼-ounce Fuzz-E-Grub or a 3-inch Kalin grub tipped with a lip-hooked minnow. A size 8 or 10 stinger treble in the minnow's back will hook most short strikers. For finicky fish, switch to ⅛-ounce or lighter jigs. Conversely, big jigs—up to 1½ ounces—will often trigger big fish even during a tough bite, so don't be afraid to tie on a magnum-size leadhead.

Raise and lower the rodtip to create a subtle lift/drop presentation. Most strikes occur on the drop, so watch your line.

THREE PRESENTATIONS FOR RIVER WALLEYE

SLIPPING

QUARTER
PITCHING

THREE-WAY
TROLLING

How: Vertically jig ¹⁄₁₆- to ¾-ounce leadhead tipped with grub body and lip-hooked minnow. Use your electric motor to "slip" downstream with the current, keeping the line tight and vertical to bottom (A). If the line angles upstream (B), increase motor speed; if it tilts downstream (C), back off on the juice. Practice makes perfect.

Where: Works almost anywhere. Best slipping areas are current breaks, deep holes, breaklines, flats and bridge abutments.

How: Cast an ⅛-ounce leadhead jig, tipped with minnow, upstream about 45 degrees off the bow. Keep the rodtip high as jig falls to bottom. Begin slow, hopping retrieve, allowing jig to roll and bounce downstream with current.

Where: Anytime water is 8 feet deep or less. Use it to target specific structure such as riprap, bridge abutments, shallow flats and slight depressions in bottom.

How: Tie three-way swivel to main line. Attach a ¾- to 1½-ounce leadhead jig, tipped with grub body and minnow, on 8- to 16-inch dropper line. Run crankbait or plain hook tipped with grub or tube body on second line; vary length from 3 to 5 feet. Troll upstream at a "slow walk," periodically sweeping the rodtip forward.

Where: Anytime fish are scattered or have refused slipping and quarter-pitching. Also on large sand or gravel flats, side channels, wing dams and the edges of holes. A great "search" technique for locating active fish.

Keep your line vertical as you slip down-current. If the line starts angling upstream, you're drifting too fast—increase motor speed. Back off if the line tilts downstream.

Thin-diameter, 6-pound mono helps me both see and feel bottom. Yes, "see." The line remains vertical on the drop, but it bows when the jig lands. This is the key to visually detecting bottom. A sensitive rod will help you feel bottom and detect

strikes. There are a number of rod-and-reel combos that will do the job. Whether you see or feel a hit—set the hook immediately.

Where legal, fish two rods. You'll cut in half the time it takes to determine hot colors for the weather and water conditions. Experiment with leadhead and grub body colors, always looking for contrast. Pink/white and blue/chartreuse are solid choices.

Fish a bright color combination on one rod, a

darker, more subtle pattern on the other. When you catch a couple of fish on a particular combination, switch both jigs to the hot colors until the bite dies.

Vertical jigging works in almost any river situation: around current breaks; deep holes; along breaklines at creek mouths; sand and gravel flats; barge docking areas; and bridge abutments.

Quarter-pitching—This is another proven method for river walleyes and saugers. Like vertical jigging, it requires the use of a trolling motor to slip with the current. The difference is that you can target specific fish-holding areas.

Cast a jig-and-minnow 45 degrees upstream, keeping the rodtip high as the jig falls to bottom. Then, lift the rod and begin a slow retrieve, allowing the jig to roll and bounce over the bottom as it drifts downstream.

"Quarter-pitching presents the bait in a natural fashion, and works well in many areas."

I use an ⅛-ounce jig tipped with a minnow, on 6-pound mono. The rod should be slightly longer than one used for vertical jigging, and sensitive, but with a strong butt section for hooksetting power.

Quarter-pitching presents the bait in a natural fashion, and works well in many areas. Try it around current breaks in tailwater areas, riprap, wing dams, bridge abutments and shallow rock, sand and gravel flats. Although vertical jigging works in many of the same areas, quarter-pitching is the way to go in 8 feet of water or less.

Three-Way Rig—If you want to cover lots of water and catch lots of fish, troll a three-way rig against the current.

The three-way setup I use has two variations, both of which begin with a three-way swivel and a short drop line. It consists of 8 to 16 inches of 6-pound mono, attached to a ¾-ounce or heavier jig. The large jig is necessary to maintain bottom contact when moving slowly up-current, and consistently takes large walleyes and sauger.

Tie an 8-pound mono trailer, ranging from 3 to 5 feet in length, to the other swivel eye. Now you've got several options: a plain hook with a grub body and lip-hooked minnow; minnow-imitating stickbait or spinner rig with a 'crawler, or a number of others.

A heavier rod and reel combination is necessary to handle bone-jarring strikes and deal with frequent snags. I use a medium-heavy baitcasting outfit, spooled with 10-pound mono, or 10-pound FireLine.

Baitcasting rigs are great for double-trolling. Thumbar spool releases make it easy to let out line from each reel as you follow a dropping bottom contour into deep water.

Troll upstream with your electric motor, using only enough power to move at the pace of a slow walk along shore. Let out line until the jig hits bottom. Slowly sweep the rod about a foot ahead, then lower the rig back toward bottom until you feel the jig land.

You'll know when a walleye or sauger hits a three-way rig—they smack it. Most fish hook themselves, but set the hook anyway and maintain steady pressure.

A three-way rig presents multiple attractions. Sometimes fish prefer the pounding of a big jig or they want the subtle action of a grub body/minnow combination. Sometimes, they want nothing but the crankbait. The key is varying dropper and trailer line lengths until you get it right.

If it's legal to fish two rods, do it. Each angler is presenting four offerings to the fish, and it really gets exciting when you and a partner hit a school of active fish.

Key areas for three-way trolling are slight depressions in the river channel, sand and gravel flats, side channels, breaklines along holes and wing dams. Actually, it's ideal anytime fish are scattered and you need to cover a lot of water. Also, fish that strike this rig are more aggressive and may ignore a vertical jigging presentation, so it pays to try a three-way rig in areas where slipping jigs failed.

In Conclusion

Rivers are dynamic environments. Fluctuating water levels, current and other challenges are the rule. Areas and methods that produced yesterday might not do squat today. But it's worth the effort to figure it all out. By understanding the differences between natural and channelized rivers, you're more than halfway there.

Bar Hopping

by Greg Bohn

*Does this system work? The author guided 12-year-old
Marcus Steigerwaldt to a 15-pound, 13-ounce giant by crankbaiting the rock bars.
It was the largest walleye caught in Wisconsin in decades!*

*I*magine knowing, as you point the boat away from shore, that your chances of catching a monster walleye—one that you've fought and landed at least a hundred times in your dreams—are better than good. In fact, they're excellent.

Now imagine knowing that you could return again and again with the same valid expectation. Too good to be true? Not really.

The secret is to fish at night, but steer clear of the traditional shallow-water flats and rock piles where most after-dark anglers go.

Sure, it's fun to flirt with dozens of 2 to 4 pounders in the skinny water. But those walleye are no more than a diversion compared to the big and bold fish of your dreams.

Instead, head for the bars at night, deep bars, where real trophy-class walleye—fish that start at 8 pounds—are waiting for you.

If you think you're up to this kind of action, be prepared to fish water as deep as 35 feet. Different, yes. Difficult, no, because most techniques are the same ones you've been using for years.

The majority of large walleye come to the shallows only to spawn. The rest of the time they spend their days holding over deep water in the main lake basin. And while suspended walleye are catchable, they also tend to roam with the baitfish, which can make them difficult to locate. Therefore, the best and most consistent action occurs when they're on an after-dark feeding spree.

The techniques we'll discuss work best from late June through early September, with peak action in July and August. Nighttime target areas are deep rock bars and submerged points topped with rock, gravel and boulders.

The Right Waters

These spots consistently hold the largest walleye in lakes with the right forage base and proper bottom composition. Learn to identify these types of lakes, and you're more than halfway to cashing in on the trophy night bite.

Several factors will help pinpoint lakes likely to produce good nightfishing for oversize walleye. Generally, these lakes have clear water with plenty of 60- to 100-foot depths. Lake size is not critical, however. Big fish can be caught in little, 300- to 400-acre lakes as long as these waters have the right characteristics.

Forage base is an important factor. Nutrient-rich baitfish like ciscoes, smelt and whitefish allow walleye to reach their maximum size potential. Consequently, lakes where your sonar readings show huge clouds of forage fish suspended far off the bottom are the best choices for this technique.

Finally, the lake must have an abundance of rock bars or rocky underwater points. The best ones top out at about 12 to 35 feet and fall off into water 50 to 70 feet deep. Weed growth on top of the bar or point is not a welcome addition. What you're looking for is a mixture of rocks, ranging from gravel to boulders. Boulders are particularly important—big fish like big rocks!

"Those walleye... weighed from 12 to more than 14 pounds."

After you've pinpointed a few likely spots on a lake map, it's best to do some scouting before the night's fishing begins. The best way is to circle a number of bars and search for suspended baitfish with your sonar. In most cases, you'll find an average depth at which the forage fish are holding. Then, concentrate on nearby bars that top out at that approximate depth.

Weather conditions, seasonal water clarity and water temperatures will influence how deep baitfish suspend from day to day. But the one constant is that, on any particular day, most forage fish will hold at nearly the same depth all over the lake. If you find forage fish near a bar that tops out at about that depth, you can be certain the forage will move up on that bar sometime after dark.

To make your target areas easier to find in the dark, punch their locations into your GPS unit (if you have one). Otherwise, you can anchor a white plastic bleach bottle on top of each bar. Later on, when you're ready to fish, take another slow cruise around the bars, this time scanning for forage fish traveling toward the structure. When baitfish arrive at the bar, expect the walleye action to start almost immediately!

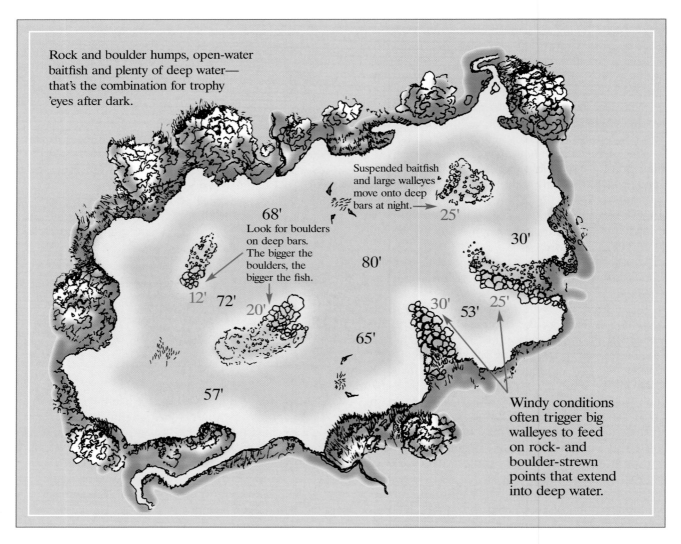

Rock and boulder humps, open-water baitfish and plenty of deep water—that's the combination for trophy 'eyes after dark.

Suspended baitfish and large walleyes move onto deep bars at night.

68'

Look for boulders on deep bars. The bigger the boulders, the bigger the fish.

25'

30'

80'

12' 72' 20'

65'

30' 53' 25'

57'

Windy conditions often trigger big walleyes to feed on rock- and boulder-strewn points that extend into deep water.

I'm a professional fishing guide and have often amazed my clients by being able to predict exactly when a bite would start just by monitoring baitfish movement toward the bar we were fishing.

My sonar unit, a Bottom Line Tournament Master with sidefinding capabilities, allows me to see schools of forage that are away from the boat. I can't emphasize enough the great advantage this type of sonar offers. It's one of the keys to success when fishing the bars at night.

Realistically, a strong movement of baitfish toward a bar, and the subsequent walleye bite, can start at dusk. Many times, in fact, the first two hours after sunset are my most productive times. This may be due in part, however, to the fact that anglers—myself included—are always more alert at

the beginning of a trip. We pay more attention and we fish more effectively when we are fresh. But even if the bite does start at dusk, you can always count on the action increasing after dark.

Follow The Signs

Bright, clear days that put a damper on daytime walleye angling are the nightfisherman's dream. It usually indicates an active night bite because the larger fish rarely feed under bright conditions. Consequently, the fish make up for the lack of daytime foraging opportunities by becoming more aggressive at night.

Clear nights with strong moonlight are especially good. The added advantage is that it's easier for you

to see what you're doing.

Cloudy days, on the other hand, usually mean you'll see less action at night. I suspect some daytime feeding in the shallows takes place under the cloud cover, slowing the night bite somewhat.

Wind can give nightfishermen a tremendous advantage, too, especially when fishing shallower bars. The breeze helps generate current that triggers stronger feeding activity and also camouflages boat noise that can spook fish.

Incidentally, when the wind blows, rocky shoreline points surrounded by deep water are also good places to fish.

Another signal to watch for is condensation that forms on boat seats, tackle boxes, windshields and other surfaces. I've noticed that on nights like this, I find walleye in deeper water. So, when you see condensation forming in the boat, it's a sign to move off a shallow bar and onto a deeper one.

Another indication that you're at the right spot at the right time comes from the forage species. Every once in a while, as you approach a bar, the water's

> *"Bright, clear days that put a damper on daytime walleye angling are the nightfisherman's dream."*

Author Greg Bohn's nighttime trophy technique departs from traditional shallow-water wisdom. But look at the results! Big walleye fight harder than most anglers realize. Keep a firm grip on the rod and loosen the drag.

surface will suddenly erupt with baitfish. What it should tell you is that walleye are below the forage and are feeding heavily.

In other instances, when fishing before it gets totally dark, you may see surfacing baitfish some distance away. It's well worth your time to get over there. Remember, however, that you don't have to actually see the baitfish. Seagulls or other birds diving into the water are another indicator that small fish are being forced to the surface by larger predators.

Tackle And Techniques

Tackle for trophy nighttime walleye includes live bait rigs, medium-sized crankbaits and large,

muskie-type crankbaits. A closer examination of this tackle will also help explain the simple, but productive, techniques involved with this type of fishing.

• **Live bait rigs:** My version of the popular live bait rig consists of a light walking sinker, a very long snell and a large nightcrawler on a double-hook harness. Set up a 7- to 7½-foot medium-action spinning rod with 6- to 10-pound monofilament line.

Pass the line through an ⅛ -ounce walking sinker and tie on a barrel swivel as a stopper. On the free end of the swivel, tie a 5- to 7-foot, 6-pound leader.

The terminal end of the leader is rigged with a double-hook quick snell consisting of two size 8 Eagle Claw No. 089A bronze hooks. To make this rig, tie on the first hook with either a quick snell

The Lunar Effect

Without a doubt, the best time to catch trophy-size walleye is during a full moon phase, including the three nights before and three nights afterward. In particular, the full moon periods in July, August and September offer outstanding fishing opportunities.

Another observation I've made is that when a full moon shines in a cloudless sky, big walleye seem to face toward the bright disk, just as they turn their noses into wind-swept current. I believe walleye look toward the light source because baitfish passing overhead are silhouetted and thus more easily seen.

knot or a common clinch knot and leave about a foot of tag line. Attach the second hook about 6 to 8 inches from the first hook. The 089A hook is a heavy-duty model that even a very large walleye can't straighten.

Dig out the largest nightcrawler you can find and place the lead hook in the tip of its snout. The trailing hook goes closer to the tail, but leave some slack between the hooks because it allows the 'crawler freedom to wriggle more naturally. And be sure to inject the bait with air so it rides well off bottom. Big nighttime walleye hold just above the rocks and look upward to find forage.

To get the bait into the strike zone, lower the sinker until it hits the rocks, then raise it slightly. Backtroll or drift slowly over the bar, allowing the bait to leave a tantalizing scent trail in its wake.

Trophy 'eyes almost never hit lightly at night, so leave the reel bail open, holding the line with your index finger. When a fish hits, release the line. With the double-hook harness, you should have to wait no longer than 10 seconds before setting the hook firmly.

• **Do-nothing rig:** This is an extra rod (where fishing more than one rod is legal) set in a holder

that boosts the odds of connecting with a walleye. Use a 7½-foot casting rod and a good levelwind reel spooled with 10-pound line for this rig. A bait clicker feature on the reel helps greatly, since you have to watch and listen for a strike with this outfit.

The bait rig is usually another double-hook 'crawler harness, but instead of a light walking sinker, use a ½- to ¾-ounce egg sinker to keep the bait directly under the boat. You can also swap the 'crawler with a large minnow like a 6- to 10-inch chub. If you do, go with just one hook of the same make and model, but in size 2 or 4.

• **Deep-diving crankbaits:** Rig a 6-foot casting rod with 10-pound line to run 6- or 7-inch deep-diving cranks.

Among my favorite cranking lures are the Shad Rap and Super Shad Rap from Normark, and Storm's Deep Thunder-Stick and Big Mac. An important feature when fishing a lure of this size is its ability to dive at a steep angle and reach maximum running depth quickly.

The basic approach to working these lures is to cast and reel the lure down until it bumps bottom. Then, use a slow and steady retrieve that allows the lure to "tick" the rocks occasionally. If the lure doesn't dive deeply enough to touch bottom, add a rubber-core sinker to the line. Sinker weights can run from ¼ to 1 ounce or more depending on lure size and the depth of the bar.

Two-tone baits such as silver-and-black patterns, or lures with a scale or prism finish, are good choices when fishing on clear nights. Under cloud cover, try solid colors such as orange, chartreuse or gold.

"Use a slow and steady retrieve that allows the lure to 'tick' the rocks occasionally."

Most anglers have no idea how hard big walleye hit at night. These fish can easily engulf a lure and cut the line. You might try a thin steel leader or one of the super-strong braided lines to avoid the problem.

• **Muskie crankbaits:** The walleye I target weigh 8-pounds and larger, and according to what many

especially the new sinking model. Bright glitter or prism patterns, as well as the more standard fire tiger colors (orange, green, red, yellow), are proven choices.

Muskie-size baits are also a good last-resort lure after you've fished a bar using other methods. Before leaving a spot, fancast the area with one of these huge lures. You could connect with a walleye that wasn't interested in chasing your smaller offerings.

In other cases, start casting these baits when a sudden flurry of activity shows that monster walleye are present. Always keep at least one rod rigged with the biggest crankbait you've got. My experience shows it won't be too large for the walleye you are trying to catch.

Break Rules, Catch Fish

Need proof? Still wondering if these techniques take big walleye? Consider this: While working on late-season patterns one fall, my clients caught five walleye that ranged from 31 inches to $33^1/2$ inches in length, and weighed from 12 to more than 14 pounds. Four of them were released.

Most of the fish were suspended 15 feet below the surface over 50 feet or more of water while feeding on smelt. We also released close to 100 other large walleye while catching these fish.

The point is, if you do a little scouting to find the right lake, and dare to break the rules of nightfishing by heading for deep structure instead of shallow flats, you too, might catch the walleye of your dreams.

When Marcus Steigerwaldt hooked this monster while fishing with his dad and guide Greg Bohn, they thought he had a musky or big pike on. But when the fish was the trio sat in stunned silence. This giant walleye, caught out of Lake Tomahawk in Oneida County on a Storm Thunderstick, was then quickly rushed into shore to be officially weighed.

of them have regurgitated after being netted, they eat baitfish measuring up to a foot in length. This means you don't have to worry about using a lure that's too big. Trophy walleye can handle anything.

Standard muskie tackle, a 6- to 7-foot casting rod, with matching reel and 40- to 50-pound-test line, is the best combination when slinging big baits. Be sure to use a steel, braided or heavy monofilament leader with this rig, as well.

Lures include large minnow imitators like a Slammer, Cisco Kid or a Bucher DepthRaider,

CONSERVE THE RESOURCE

*E*very angler is entitled to put a trophy on the wall. But the days of mounting a stringer of 8- to 10-pound walleye are long gone (or should be). If you become adept at this type of fishing, you will catch trophy 'eyes regularly, but remember your responsibility to the resource. Catch-and-release is the name of the game when targeting numbers of big fish.

Bait & Switch, Part I

by Dick Sternberg

It's been known for years that leeches and crawlers are the hot bait for warm-weather walleyes. But these baits and their presentations can be fine-tuned to give you even greater success.

Little things mean a lot when you're walleye fishing. Replacing a ¼-ounce jig with an ⅛-ounce model, or swapping an orange spinner blade for a green one can make all the difference. So can switching to a slightly different kind or size of live bait.

But while changing the size or color of your lure is relatively simple, making the right bait selection is a much greater challenge.

First, most bait shops don't carry a wide assortment of baits, and even if they do, there is little consistency in the names of baits, so it's hard to know exactly what you're getting. What one bait shop calls "fatheads," another may call "crappie minnows," while still others refer to the same bait as "tuffies" or "mud minnows."

Another complication in live bait selection: A bait that works magic in one body of water may not be worth a hoot in the next. And even in the same body of water, a bait that is dynamite in spring may be worthless during the late fall.

What's a walleye fisherman to do?

Well, there are no hard-and-fast rules in choosing live bait, but in a lifetime of walleye fishing, I've fine-tuned the bait selection process and assembled a bag of bait fishing tricks that I'm sure will greatly improve your success.

Ribbon Leech *(Nephelopsis obscura)*

Everyone knows that the ribbon leech (the standard variety available at most bait shops across walleye country) is a first-rate live bait. And it's especially effective at water temperatures above 50 degrees.

The reason leeches work better in warmer water is that's when they're more active. They wiggle and squirm like crazy, which is exactly what it takes to tempt a stubborn walleye. At colder tem-

The Ultimate Fishing Book: Strategies for Success

peratures, they often roll up into a ball and refuse to swim or, if they do swim, they barely move.

Ribbon leeches come in a variety of colors, from light brown to brown-and-black, spotted to pure black. The latest craze is picking out only the black ones. In fact, some bait shops will do it for you— for an extra $5 a pound.

My advice: save the five bucks, but make sure you have fresh, lively leeches. Examine them closely and if they seem lethargic or some of them are covered with white fungus, try another bait shop.

As much as you hear about jumbo leeches, or "mud flaps," you'd think they're the only ones a walleye will eat. Bait shops love to sell them because they can charge upwards of $3 more per dozen than what they get for smaller varieties. But in most cases, you'll catch as many, or even more, walleyes on large leeches.

By large, I mean leeches about 1½ to 2 inches long when relaxed and maybe 3 to 4 when stretched out. A jumbo leech may stretch out to 6 inches, which means that you'll get more short strikes and miss more fish. Early in the season, or whenever the fish are fussy, you'll get more bites on medium-sized leeches.

Noted walleye guide, Dick "The Griz" Grzywinski, takes leech selection a step further.

I was fishing with him a while back on Minnesota's Lake Winnibigoshish, his favorite summertime walleye hole. We were slow-trolling mid-lake bars with slip-sinker rigs and leeches. Yet, even though our rigs were identical—same size hook, same size sinker and same length leader—he was catching most of the fish.

> "A jumbo leech may stretch out to 6 inches, which means that you'll get more short strikes and miss more fish."

It was starting to bother me a little when I noticed him carefully sorting through the leeches. "Okay, whattaya lookin' for in there?" I asked.

"Tryin' to find a good swimmer," he replied, reluctantly divulging his secret. "Some of these leeches swim all over the bucket—ya can't hardly catch 'em. Others just lie there like a blob; I want the lively ones."

> "The straight hook shank gives me a better hookset than the turned-up eye used on many bait hooks."

To Hook A Leech

How you hook your leech also affects its swimming action. Normally, I hook my leeches just ahead of the sucker on the fat tail end, from the bottom up. This way, you're pulling the leech backward and forcing it to swim.

But when bait-stealing panfish are a problem, I sometimes hook the leech just behind the narrow head where the flesh is much tougher. The leech won't swim as actively, but the pesky panfish will have a harder time ripping it off the hook.

I don't do a lot of bobber fishing, but when I do, I usually hook the leech through the middle, from the bottom up. Hooked this way, it will undulate wildly on the hook, even when the bobber isn't moving.

For all of these hooking methods, I prefer a very sharp, size 4 VMC National Round hook with a short, straight shank. This lightweight hook doesn't restrict the leech's action, and I believe the straight shank gives me a better hookset than the turned-up eye used on many bait hooks.

A jig tipped with a lively leech is one of the deadliest walleye baits I know, but this combo has failed to gain widespread popularity. It may be because anglers find it harder to fish than a plain leech on a slip-sinker rig.

If you snap the jig too hard, its hook often impales the leech and you have to reel it in and straighten it out. The best way to prevent the problem is to use small leeches, only about 2 inches long, and work the jig with twitches of no more than a few inches.

If bait-stealing panfish are a problem, hook the leech through the neck rather than the sucker, just as you would if using a plain hook.

Most slip-bobber fishermen rely on leeches for bait, but there are times when 'crawlers are more effective.

Keep 'Em Lively

The best way to keep your leeches healthy and thus lively is to keep them cool. I keep my "stash" of leeches, usually a couple of pounds, in a 5-gallon pail in a bait refrigerator in my garage.

I change the water at least once a week, replacing it with cold well water, not chlorinated "city" water. You can use city water, but you must first let it stand a day or two in your refrigerator. Then you'll have the cold, dechlorinated water you need for a water change.

For a day of chasing walleyes, I carry my leeches in an 8x12-inch lunch cooler, the type with the refreezable ice pack in the lid. But even then, the water may warm too much on a hot day, so I usually carry some ice cubes in another cooler, adding a few to my leeches as needed.

What happens if you allow your leeches to get too warm? Temperatures above 55 degrees initiate the spawning process, which accelerates as the water gets warmer. Nothing against procreation, but once ribbon leeches spawn, they die. It won't happen immediately, but they soon hemorrhage, weaken and expire.

If you allow the water to reach about 65 degrees, the process is irreversible. In other words, cooling the water again will not stop the spawning process. You'll lose your leeches regardless what you do.

Ironically, the worst leech container you can buy is a flow-through bucket specifically designed for leeches. They work fine in spring when the water is cool, but they become leech killers in the summer. Of course, if you're not interested in keeping your leeches after the day's fishing, most any container will do.

Ribbon leeches have a two-year life cycle, spawning in their second year. That explains why the larger leeches are the first to die when the water warms. It also explains why the majority of leeches available in fall are small ones. If you want good-sized leeches at your disposal in the autumn months, you'll have to get a supply of them during summer and take good care of them.

> *"Ironically, the worst leech container you can buy is a flow-through bucket specifically designed for leeches."*

Tiger Leech *(Erpobdella punctata)*

Never heard of tiger leeches? Don't feel bad, neither has anyone else. Scientists refer to them as Erpobdella punctata. I made up the term "tiger" because it seemed to fit these super-active leeches, which are easily recognized by the four rows of closely spaced black spots along their backs that look like stripes.

Normally, tiger leeches are only about 2 to 3 inches long, even though the books say they can reach 5 inches. But because they're so lively, tiger

leeches don't have to be big to be extremely effective. If you try to hold one in the palm of your hand, chances are it will jump out.

At this point, you're probably wondering, "Why haven't I seen them and where do I get them?"

> *"Tiger leeches don't have to be big to be extremely effective."*

The answers are, you probably have seen them; you get them at the bait shop, mixed in with the ribbon leeches. If you buy a pound of leeches, you may get four or five tiger leeches, or you may get none. The only way I've been able to find numbers of tiger leeches is by walking the banks of the Mississippi River and turning over flat rocks.

They're worth the effort.

One day, while fishing with NAFC member Dennis Kleve, I found a good-sized tiger leech in the bait bucket.

"Watch this," I said with a confident smirk. "I've got the secret bait." Seconds after dropping the wildly squirming leech to the bottom, I hooked a nice walleye. Kleve shook his head in amazement. "What in the heck did you put on there?" he asked. "We haven't had a bite in half an hour."

There have been many incidents much like that since I discovered tiger leeches. I really believe that their intense action makes them more effective than ribbon leeches. Knowing this, maybe somebody can figure out where to get a supply of them. I'd gladly pay twice the price of ribbon leeches.

Incredible 'Crawlers

It's true, a nightcrawler is a nightcrawler, whether it's imported from Canada or picked up on your local golf course. I get my 'crawlers from the latter source; they are free, and I can select only the biggest and best ones.

Also, I seem to have a tough time finding decent 'crawlers in bait shops. If you buy them by the dozen, you normally get about six that are big enough to make good walleye bait. The other six are usually about the size of a garden worm, so I use them for sunfish bait. When you're paying maybe $2.50 a dozen, that makes each good worm worth about 42 cents—pretty expensive bait.

The best time to pick your own 'crawlers is in early spring.

Wait for a warm, drizzly night, put on your rain gear, grab a flashlight and a plastic bucket and head for the nearest public golf course. But before you go, check to see if they use chemicals to control the 'crawlers (golfers don't like those nightcrawler bumps). If they do, go elsewhere. Private courses are more likely to use chemicals because they have the budgets to do so.

Wait until the 'crawlers are completely out of their holes. If they're halfway in, you may injure them when you try to pull them out.

In a couple hours of picking, I can usually get several hundred good-sized 'crawlers, enough to last me most of the summer. I can store them for an extended period in the same bait refrigerator where I keep my leeches.

The best nightcrawler box I've found is a foam cooler just the right size to fit on a refrigerator shelf. I cut the cooler down to a depth of about 8 inches,

LEECHES THAT DON'T WORK

When I first saw those monster leeches, visions of giant walleye danced in my head. But after dragging them around behind Lindy Rigs for two days on prime big fish spots and not getting a bite, I knew something was wrong. My fears were substantiated when rock bass (who eat anything) visibly spit them out in a blink of an eye after sucking them in. Further investigation proved these large, soft "mud leeches" were worthless as bait. They are considerably larger than a ribbon leech, have soft, mushy bodies and distinctive small ridges running perpendicular to their length. Another type of leech to avoid is one with any red or orange on it. It could be the whole underside, dots, slashes—any red or orange in any form means stay away!

—Spence Petros

A tiger leech is characterized by four rows of closely spaced black spots that look like stripes along its back.

fill it with fairly moist worm bedding and cover them with the cooler's original lid.

Put maybe 200 'crawlers in that box and the rest in the same type of ice-pack coolers you used for leeches. Keep the big box in the fridge and take the smaller coolers in the boat.

Livelier Is Better

Many walleye anglers don't realize that liveliness is just as important in 'crawler fishing as it is in leech fishing. Jack Schneider, who specializes in catching trophy walleyes, likes his 'crawlers fat and sassy—for good reason.

"If a big walleye inhales a 'crawler and it doesn't feel the worm squirming in its mouth, it will proba-

bly spit it out," Schneider contends. "You may get by with a half-dead worm for smaller walleyes, or when the fish are committing suicide, but the big ones are more finicky."

> *"I prefer a nightcrawler that stretches out to a length of 7 or 8 inches, not 12-inch rattlesnakes."*

"Everything's got to be perfect, so if your 'crawler doesn't wiggle around in your hand, or if a perch bites even a quarter-inch off the end, put on a fresh one."

Summertime is 'crawler time, but it's also the toughest time to keep your bait in good condition. The worst thing you can do is carry a big box of 'crawlers in your boat on a hot summer day. Unless you keep your 'crawler box in a separate cooler, or use the ice-pack type, your worms will get too warm and lose their zip, or worse yet, turn into a gob of stinky mush.

Earlier, I mentioned the importance of good-sized 'crawlers, but let me explain what I mean by that. I prefer a nightcrawler that stretches out to a length of 7 or 8 inches, not 12-inch "rattlesnakes."

It's not that the walleyes won't hit big worms, it's just that you'll miss a lot more of them. Most walleye experts will tell you that the fish are harder to hook on 'crawlers than on most other live baits. Using giant worms only compounds the problem.

You're probably thinking, "Why not use a

QUICK "CONDITIONED" CRAWLERS

Plump, lively crawlers are definitely superior bait. Many anglers keep crawlers in bedding and feed them prior to a trip. But a quick way to achieve active, fat crawlers is to put a bunch in a bucket of cold water while fishing. This saves a mess in the boat from dirt or bedding as bait is being used, and the crawlers stay active. Keep the bucket in shade and periodically toss some ice into it.

'crawler harness or one of those worm threaders that strings your line through the 'crawler so you can add a small treble hook to the tail?" It's true that either of these rigs will improve your hooking percentage, but in my experience, the number of strikes will decrease. The reduction is most noticeable when you're talking big walleyes.

Fishing With 'Crawlers

Here's my favorite 'crawler-hooking method. Use the same size 4 VMC National Round hook I described for leech fishing; insert the point at the very tip of the 'crawler's nose, thread it down no more than ⅜ of an inch, then bring it out the side. If the worm isn't centered this way, it may spin when trolled or retrieved and won't look natural.

Schneider recommends using a 4-pound-test monofilament leader for the ultimate natural presentation when fishing 'crawlers.

When slip-sinker fishing, be sure to release line right away when you feel a pickup. There's no definite rule on how long to wait before setting the hook, but I usually wait a little longer with a 'crawler than I would with a leech.

If the fish are really feeding, however, you can set the hook almost immediately. Try a couple of quick sets to see. When the fish are finicky, you may have to wait 30 seconds or longer. But if you wait too long, the fish may sense something it doesn't like and spit the bait.

One common mistake I see people make, not only when fishing 'crawlers, but with all types of live bait, is before setting the hook they slowly reel up the slack and "test" to see if the fish is still there.

Chances are, the walleye will drop the bait during that tightening process, and when the person finally does set the hook, the fish is already gone.

When you think you've waited long enough, instead of testing, start cranking until you feel tension, then immediately set the hook. This way, the fish hasn't got time to spit the bait. Testing accomplishes nothing other than tipping off the walleye.

Although most slip-bobber fishermen rely exclusively on leeches for bait, there are times when 'crawlers are more effective. If leeches aren't working and you think there are walleyes around,

LEECH & CRAWLER RIGGING OPTION

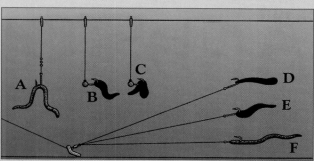

There are a number of ways to hook leeches and night-crawlers for walleye, but you can handle most conditions with these six methods. Below a slip bobber, a 'crawler hooked through the middle (A) so both ends dangle evenly is hard for walleyes to pull off; a leech hooked through the wide tail end (B) is ideal for aggressive walleyes; a leech hooked through the middle—from the bottom up—increases the odds that light-biting fish will inhale the hook and the bait (C). When live bait rigging, vary leader lengths to match conditions. Sternberg recommends 4-pound Trilene XL, but other super-thin monos work fine. Many anglers now swear by Stren's fluorocarbon leader, which virtually disappears under water. Hook leeches through the tougher narrow end (D) if panfish are stealing your bait; however, hooking leeches through the wide tail end (E) forces them to swim as you drift or troll. A nose-hooked 'crawler (F) is always tough to beat.

try switching.

But don't hook the 'crawler as described earlier. Instead, hook it through the middle so both ends dangle evenly. Walleyes find it hard to resist the writhing worm, and with shorter lengths of the 'crawler dangling, you'll hook more fish.

Even though you don't have a great number of choices in selecting different kinds of leeches and 'crawlers, there are plenty of decisions to make regarding how and when to use them. Know how to make those calls and you'll catch more walleyes.

Bait & Switch, Part II

by Dick Sternberg

by Dick Sternberg

In the cooler waters of spring and fall, a fresh baitfish is a top choice…but not all forage fish are created equal. Here's how to make the best selection and presentation for walleye success.

Walleye are opportunists, meaning that they'll eat whatever food nature provides. I've seen their bellies crammed with crayfish, mayfly larvae, bloodworms and a host of other aquatic delicacies. But, day in and day out, by far the most important item in their diet is baitfish. And this preference for baitfish grows stronger as the walleyes grow larger.

Surprisingly, the baitfish that walleye feed on naturally seldom make the best bait. Yellow perch, for instance, are number one on the list of the walleye's most commonly eaten food in many waters, yet perch don't seem to be a particularly effective bait.

Over the years, I've experimented with practically every kind of baitfish you can name, including not only the usual bait shop varieties, but also a hodgepodge of specimens seined in rivers and small streams. Following are my top picks for walleye fishing:

Fathead Minnows

These minnows are a staple in most bait shops. They're also called "tuffies" or "mudminnows," and I've even seen them mistakenly labeled as chubs. Most of the time, any lively fathead makes a good walleye bait. But, believe it or not, there are instances where a fathead's sex makes a big difference. A couple years ago, I was fishing the walleye opener in a northern state with my buddy and fellow NAFC member, Dennis Kleve. The water was very cold (in the low 40s) and the bite was super tough.

I was occasionally graphing what I thought were walleyes on a shallow gravel bar, but got nary a tap on a jig tipped with a fathead minnow.

Most of the fatheads in our bucket were the black, bumpy-headed males, but after digging around awhile, I came up with a plump, silvery female. Almost immediately, a 3-pound walleye inhaled it. After I sorted out three more females and caught three more walleyes, Kleve was beside himself.

"What are you lookin' for in that bucket?" he demanded to know. "Females," I replied, feeling sort of guilty.

"Whattaya mean females? Lemme see one." The results were nearly instantaneous.

Later that evening, we brought a limit of 2- to 3½-pound walleyes into the fish-cleaning shack at the resort. We were surprised to see that the cleaning table hadn't been used. If not for the female fatheads, the table would have remained spotless.

> *"Believe it or not, there are instances where a fathead's sex makes a big difference."*

The female fathead phenomenon is most noticeable in spring. I'm not sure why, but I'd guess it has something to do with scent, possibly from spawning pheromones. The scent of the female could be more appealing than that of the male, or maybe it's just that the silvery females are more visible than the blackish males. Later, when the males lose their spawning bumps and regain their silvery coloration, I don't see much difference in their productivity.

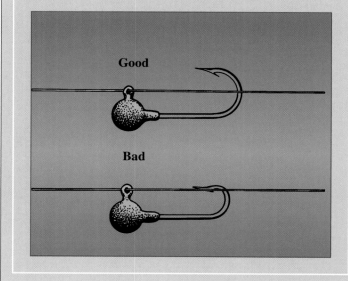

All jigs are not created equal. Select only those with hooks large enough, and gaps wide enough, to offer a good hookset. You can tell if the hook has the proper gap by drawing an imaginary line through the eye to the hook bend. If less than half the gap is open (above the line), you're better off selecting another jig for baitfishing.

Good

Bad

walleye

Fatheads have one big advantage over other available minnow species: they're extremely hardy, especially in cold water. At water temperatures of 50 degrees or below, you can keep as many as you want in an ordinary styrofoam minnow bucket with no risk of losing them from lack of oxygen. They simply come to the surface and gulp in air.

They'll also stay alive better than other minnows in warm water, but you can't keep as many, unless you use a flow-through bucket or aerate them.

On the down side, fatheads tend to run on the small side, which means switching to a different bait if the walleyes are keying on larger forage.

Spottail Shiners

Until recently, I'd never been much of a proponent of any kind of shiner minnow. I just didn't like the idea of paying four bucks a dozen, and finding most of them dead by the time I got my boat in the water. So I was surprised when walleye guru Tom Neustrom strongly recommended that I bring spottail shiners on an early-June trophy-walleye hunt on one of his favorite lakes.

Spottails are easy to identify. As their name suggests, they have a prominent black spot at the base of the tail, and bright silvery sides. Being the stubborn sort, I had to test my usual fare before trying Neustrom's recommendation. But a couple hours of dragging leeches and jigs tipped with fatheads proved fruitless, despite some likely-looking marks on my graph.

Frustrated, I switched to a spottail on a slip-sinker rig. Within a

"If you blindly accept what the bait shop proprietor offers, you're the biggest sucker of all," says author Dick Sternberg, holding the result of careful bait selection.

few minutes, I felt a pickup and set the hook. At first, nothing moved, but then I felt the strong head shakes. Soon, I was admiring a gorgeous 30-inch walleye.

Over the next two days, I boated 13 more walleyes in the 28- to 30-inch class and dozens of smaller ones. Every walleye hit a spottail shiner, despite the fact that I repeatedly tried the other baits. When I ran out of spottails, I bought some "pit" shiners from a local bait shop, but they didn't produce a single bite.

Since that experience, spottails have proven to be a near-magical springtime bait, especially in clear lakes when the water temperature is less than 60 degrees. Don't let anybody talk you into some of the other types of shiners, including golden shiners, grass shiners, sand shiners or pit shiners. They just don't have the same appeal.

"spottails have proven to be a near-magical springtime bait."

If you're going to use spottails, you must know how to keep them alive. They'll do fine in a flow-through bucket, as long as the surface temperature stays below the 60-degree mark. If it gets warmer than that, keep them in a well-insulated, aerated bucket and add ice cubes as needed to keep the water below 60 degrees. If you add too much ice too fast, however, you'll kill the bait.

Emerald Shiners

One of the hottest live baits on the Great Lakes, particularly Lake Erie, emerald shiners are a great option any time you need a bait with plenty of flash.

Emerald shiners are excellent early in the season for both pre- and post-spawn walleyes. These shiners will be fairly small this time of year, however, so use two or three of them on a jig or on a jigging spoon's treble. Hook them through the nose like any other minnow. Emerald shiners are also good fall baits.

To keep them alive, take the same precautions you would with spottails.

Shad

Various species of shad, such as gizzard in the

McClelland's Baitfish Tips

Mike McClelland is no stranger to using live bait for walleyes, and the longtime pro angler and NAFC Walleye Advisory Council member has developed several theories for selecting the right bait for the situation.

"One of the most important factors is convenience," he explains. "If a bait is easy to get, easy to keep alive and easy to use, chances are it will do the job better than baitfish you have to struggle with. This is true as long as the bait matches local forage preferences.

"Size is also a consideration," McClelland adds. "In the spring, for example, some people think you have to use small minnows, but just the opposite is true—all the forage is at least a year old, so the walleyes are used to eating bigger baitfish."

If you can't get your hands on large minnows early in the season, McClelland suggests adding a plastic curlytail grub to the bait to bulk it up.

"Finally, one of the most important considerations deals with learning not only what types of forage walleyes prefer on a given body of water, but also where the baitfish will be found, and their behavior patterns. Find and match the forage, and you'll catch more walleyes, guaranteed."

—Dan Johnson

North and both gizzard and threadfin in the South, are prime forage for walleyes in many large lakes, rivers and reservoirs.

Shad are very delicate, however. They are particularly susceptible to changes in water temperature, which causes major die-offs, particularly in the North. Shad seldom do well on the end of a hook, but they will survive for modest periods of time when impaled through the nose on a light-wire hook. Use a stinger hook if necessary.

Obtaining shad presents another hurdle, since bait shops don't carry them. They're also tough to keep alive for very long in a minnow bucket.

Since it's extremely important to match the available—and preferred—food species, it still makes

---

COMMON WALLEYE BAITFISH

Fathead minnows are excellent baits, but avoid using the bumpy-headed males (background) early in the year. Walleyes seem to reject them in favor of the silvery females.

Excellent early-season baits, spottail shiners are easy to identify by the distinctive black spot at the base of the tail.

A willow cat (foreground) closely resembles the bullhead, but is a far superior bait. Unfortunately, willow cats (also called madtoms) can be difficult to find unless you catch them yourself.

Redtail chubs, or hornyhead chubs, are large, extremely tough baitfish characterized by a reddish tail margin and a lateral band extending from the head to the tail spot. Excellent bait in the fall.

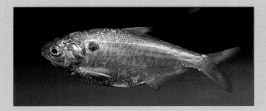

Silvery, wide-bodied gizzard shad are prime forage in many walleye waters. They have a dark spot behind the head and a long ray at the back of the dorsal fin.

Popular among Great Lakes walleye anglers, emerald shiners are identified by their slender bodies and faint band along their sides.

sense to take the time to catch your own, and make the extra effort necessary to keep them alive. In some cases, a handful of rock salt in the baitwell will help accomplish the latter task.

Willow Cats

Under the right circumstances, willow cats have astounding walleye-catching powers. On the Mississippi River, I've seen them produce stringers of big 'eyes in the heat of summer, when veteran anglers using other methods were coming in skunked.

Although willow cats are mainly known as a river-fishing bait, I've talked to anglers who have had good success using them in lakes.

What's a willow cat, you say? Its proper name is the madtom, and it's found mainly in weedy backwaters of large, warm-water rivers, mainly in the Mississippi River watershed but also along most of the East Coast. One of the smallest members of the catfish family, the willow cat looks pretty much like a small bullhead, but its tail is more rounded and it has a potent venom on its pectoral spines.

"Under the right circumstances, willow cats have astounding walleye-catching powers."

For some reason, probably odor, walleyes greatly prefer them over bullheads, although bullheads are a pretty decent bait, too.

If you've ever been "stung" by a bullhead, you know how painful that can be. Well, a madtom's sting is 10 times worse. Once, while pulling into a boat landing, I saw a fishermen lying on the dock, moaning. Some people were kneeling down next to him, so I assumed he'd had a heart attack. Turns out he'd been stung by a willow cat.

If you know how to handle bullheads, you'll have no trouble with willow cats; just grab them with your fingers on either side of the pectoral spine. For bait, the best size is 2½ to 3 inches long. I hook them through both lips using a short-shank, size 4 hook and fish them on a slip-sinker rig.

Although willow cats were once very popular walleye baits and were sold at many riverside bait shops, only a few dealers still sell them, and they're very expensive.

Fortunately, you can catch them yourself, using either of two methods. The easiest is to string a few pop cans together by tying some strong fishing line to the tabs, and sink them in a shallow, weedy river backwater. Just as big catfish like to get inside a barrel, willow cats like to get inside something smaller. You can also catch them with a sturdy dip net.

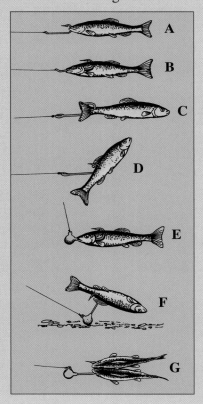

BAITFISH HOOKING OPTIONS

When rigging live bait, try hooking the minnow through the lip or slightly in the head (A), or running the hook through the mouth, out one gill and through the back (B), just be sure to leave enough gap for a good hookset. For tough-bite situations, try reverse-rigging—hook the minnow through the tail (C), or through the back between the tail and dorsal fin (D). With a jig, hook the minnow through the lips or through the gill and back (E), or just behind the dorsal fin (F) for sluggish walleyes. If the fish are very aggressive, prefer larger baits or your minnows are fairly small, hook two baitfish on the same jig—threading them on sideways, just ahead of the eye (G).

Willow cats may not be quite as hardy as bull-heads, but they're among the toughest baitfish. They'll stay alive indefinitely in clean, cool water.

Redtail Chubs

Officially known as the hornyhead chub, the redtail gets its name from the reddish margin on its tail. With its dark lateral band and dark spot at the base of the tail, it resembles the creek chub, but the creek chub does not have the reddish tail.

This distinction is important, because creek chubs are a much inferior walleye bait, yet I've often seen bait shops label them as redtails.

Among the largest of walleye baits, redtails seem to work best in fall. By then, the natural forage has grown much bigger than it was in summer. I normally use redtails from 4 to 5 inches long. For trophy-class walleyes, I may even go with 6 inchers. The reason redtails work better than creek chubs, suckers, big shiners or any of the other large walleye baits is their toughness.

"Redtails seem to work best in fall."

If you tip a jig with a sucker, for instance, it will be stone dead after a few casts. But a redtail will stay alive indefinitely. In fact, when it seems to be slowing down, just take it off the hook and put it back into your bucket to rest up. An hour later, it will be almost as good as new.

Redtails are found mainly in rivers and are excellent river-fishing baits, but they work equally well in lakes, both natural and man-made.

Back in the mid-80s, when North Dakota's Lake Sakakawea (Garrison Reservoir) was routinely kicking out numbers of 8- to 12-pound walleyes, I fished it several times each year.

Once, by casting ⅛-ounce jigs tipped with redtails onto shallow, rocky points, a friend and I caught and released 37 walleyes over 7 pounds, including five over 10 pounds and two over 12, on a three-day trip. Local anglers were catching a few good-size fish on jigs and fatheads, but the difference was astounding.

The toughness of a redtail opens up another fishing option. When slip-sinker fishing, instead of hooking them through the lips or snout as you normally would, try hooking them through the tail. This way, they will struggle to swim against the retrieve, rather than lazily gliding along with it. Walleyes are quick to detect any struggling baitfish, so this hooking method often makes a big difference. If you try hooking most other large baitfish this way, they'll run out of steam within a few minutes and won't swim at all.

Buyer Beware

When buying baitfish, look them over carefully to make sure they're healthy. If you see white fungus on their tails, or if they're cruising around near the top of the tank rather than schooling tightly near the bottom, buy your bait elsewhere.

And make sure you know what you're buying. Sometimes the labeling is not specific enough. You'll see a tank marked "shiners," and it will be up to you to figure out which of the 100-plus species of shiners you're getting.

Worse yet, the tank might not contain what the label says it does. In tanks marked "redtails," for example, I've found stone-rollers, blacknosed dace, creek chubs and even suckers. If you blindly accept whatever the proprietor doles out, and then pay the full price, you're the biggest sucker of all.

Jumbo Jigs

by Jeff Murray

*Since this revolutionary technique was revealed in our magazine
several years ago, it has been accepted by thousands of savvy anglers across
the country who target larger-than-average walleyes and saugers.*

Jigs. I've worked hard trying to refine the best presentations for these universal walleye baits. That usually means ⅟₁₆-, ⅛- or occasional ¼-ounce leadheads fished with light line, sensitive rods and riveted concentration.

You know why—the guy with the lightest leadhead generally outfishes the next guy because walleyes inhale a light offering easier than a heavier one. And during cold-water periods when fish aren't very active, this rule of thumb is even more important.

Right? Not always, say well-known Walleye pros Ted Takasaki and John Campbell.

"We've developed a system that's pretty radical, and it has taken off like wildfire. Thousands of big fish have been caught on the 'jumbos' in recent years, and it's a rare river tournament where some anglers don't score heavily on these rigs," Takasaki stated. "Yeah, it's interesting stuff," agreed Campbell in his usual soft-spoken manner.

The concept these anglers developed is so close to walleye fishing heresy, that if I hadn't witnessed its effectiveness firsthand, I'd dismiss it as a pseudo-refinement with very limited applications.

Get this: Instead of going to lighter jig heads like everyone else, Takasaki and Campbell often go superheavy. We're talking ¾- to 1½-ounce jigs!

And while we're talking heavier-than-normal walleyes, we are also talking numbers of fish, as jumbo jigs can be fished in conjunction with other baits that appeal to walleyes of all sizes.

The Evolution

Every new concept undergoes a trial-and-error process, and Takasaki and Campbell's experiments with jumbo jigs were no exception.

"We fish 3-way rigs quite a bit for river fish," Takasaki began, "and our favorite presentation is a

Ted Takasaki (above) has been using jumbo jigs to take big walleyes in a variety of waters. Mastering the technique is easy.

Not Just Rivers

One day the light bulb flickered. If jumbo jigs worked so well on river fish, why not try them in lakes?

The first test was on Lake Huron's Saginaw Bay, where there's an impressive population of trophy walleyes. Trolling the mud with a modified 3-way "river" rig—again with a jumbo jig serving as weight and bait—produced big walleyes!

"Knowing when and how to make it work will definitely make you a more effective angler."

The guys then applied the concept at Little Bay de Noc on Lake Michigan, this time with a jumbo jig and a shallow-diving crankbait on a 3-way rig.

"I caught most of my fish over 8 pounds on the jig," Takasaki recalled. "I never expected it to out-produce the crankbait."

"Ted and I fished out of different boats that day, and I caught more fish on the crankbait," noted Campbell. "That was the beginning of defining the whens and whys of the presentation. I had been blown around by the wind a bit more than Ted that day, and the extra speed probably sparked more interest in the crankbait. Also, the fish were a bit higher off the bottom where I was fishing."

So, like all walleye tactics, jumbo jigging isn't a panacea. However, knowing when and how to make it work will definitely make you a more effective angler.

Why Jumbo Jig?

Knowing why jumbo jigging works helps you determine where, when and how to use it. By definition, a jumbo jig is a leadhead that's bigger— the rule of thumb is at least twice as big—than what you'd normally need to work the bottom. An arbitrary starting point is ½-ounce, but if you're fishing a shallow (less than 8 feet) hole or drop-off that usually calls for an ⅛-ounce jig, a ¼- or ⅜-ounce jig could be considered a "jumbo" offering.

heavy jig on the dropper dressed with a Fuzz-E-Grub or tube body; plain hook and minnow or crankbait trailing behind on a 2- to 3-foot leader.

"The heavy jig served mainly as a sinker at first, until we began to notice that it was consistently producing some nice fish."

"Jumbo jigging soon became our favorite presentation," added Campbell. "During a tough bite we'd boat, say, 10 fish with eight being keepers. Usually the two biggest would have smacked the big jig. Day after day this pattern held up."

The advantages of jumbo jigging are many. First and foremost is positive bottom contact. Most anglers struggle with distinguishing snags and obstructions from fish when working lightweight jigs; many have a hard time just feeling the bottom.

Not so with jumbo jigs. There's a definite "tunk" on every down-stroke. Toss in wind, waves, current and depth, and solid bottom contact becomes a huge advantage. And this is just the beginning.

"A heavier jig allows you to work a more vertical presentation," Campbell continued. "That means better control, fewer snags and more solid hooksets. You can also use slightly heavier line, which telegraphs the bottom better, stretches less and stands up to more abuse than the thin mono used with ultra-lightweight jig heads."

"A more vertical presentation means better control, fewer snags and more solid hooksets."

"And the larger profile also bangs up the bottom," adds Takasaki. "Its impact on rocks and silt stirs things up down there, which accounts for more reaction-oriented strikes."

"And you can cover more water with jumbo jigs," said Campbell. "If you want to speed-troll, say, a 1¼-ounce jig, no problem. Then, once you locate a pod of fish, slow down and yo-yo the bait. It's versatile."

There's another advantage: walleyes usually pound jumbo jigs! "Most fish take the jig deeply," Takasaki said. "They get the whole bait even when we tip the jigs with a big bait like redtail chubs. It's as if the action makes them mad.

"We theorize that if it's tougher to inhale the jig, then it's also tougher to spit it out. Most strikes occur on the drop where all a walleye has to do is come up and open his mouth. We don't lose many fish on jumbo jigs."

Where To Jumbo Jig

"Big walleyes are used to feeding on large baitfish, so a large-profile jig seems to make a lot of sense," Campbell said. "It's really not that big when

JUMBO JIGS: WHAT TO LOOK FOR

*I*t might not be easy to get your hands on heavy leadheads. Stock up when you find a supplier because jumbo jigs are still considered a specialty item by wholesalers and distributors.

Lindy Little-Joe has come out with a ⅝- and 1-ounce Jumbo Fuzz-E-Grub that is rod hot on the pro circuit. One model has a small propeller that sends out vibration and flash. This is excellent for attracting aggressive walleyes, but we may also use it during adverse conditions when the walleyes aren't chasing. Often it will be "still fished" in current as we hover over a good spot. Walleyes are drawn to the spinning blade, but often hit the trailing rig, which in this instance is usually a plain hook with a colorful bead or two, that's baited with a minnow or crawler.

If need be, make your own jigs. Lead can be obtained from numerous sources and jigs hook of all sizes are available from a number of sources. Molds can be carved out of wood. Just be careful that you work in an area with good air circulation—lead fumes are dangerous.

The best jighead design? In my opinion, one shaped like a tear-drop—streamlined and fairly slim. It cuts through the water easily.

you consider how common 8-inch smelt, herring and alewives are in the diet of 25- to 30-inch fish."

So the Great Lakes, where trophy-size walleyes roam, are ripe for this tactic.

Rivers are also hotspots for jumbo jigging. The pair uses this method to hammer walleyes and overstuffed saugers on various rivers.

Natural lakes in the fall, particularly those with

JUMBO JIGS CAN BE FISHED ALONE...

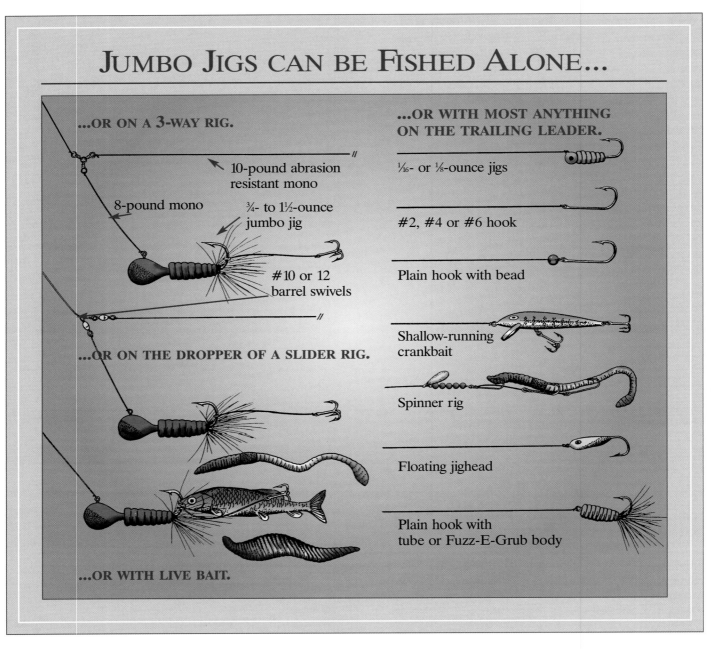

...OR ON A 3-WAY RIG.

10-pound abrasion resistant mono

8-pound mono

¾- to 1½-ounce jumbo jig

#10 or 12 barrel swivels

...OR ON THE DROPPER OF A SLIDER RIG.

...OR WITH LIVE BAIT.

...OR WITH MOST ANYTHING ON THE TRAILING LEADER.

¹⁄₁₆- or ⅛-ounce jigs

#2, #4 or #6 hook

Plain hook with bead

Shallow-running crankbait

Spinner rig

Floating jighead

Plain hook with tube or Fuzz-E-Grub body

deep structure, or mud basins and hard-bottom transitions, are solid bets. Simply stated, a heavy jig is the best way to work over these fish.

And don't overlook erratic deep weed lines that can be jumbo-jigged effectively. A heavy jig quickly gets down to the bottom, so it can be fished on a shorter line. This makes it a lot easier for you to accurately follow a weed edge with lots of points, turns and cuts. Your jig is reaching tough-to-fish

places, and is being worked in a faster, strike-provoking manner than a lighter jig.

Mastering The Technique

If you choose equipment wisely, mastering jumbo jigging is easier than most standard walleye techniques. There are two basic approaches. In rivers, these two anglers run 8- or 10-pound Stren Super

Tough (for abrasion-resistance) on baitcasting reels with a flipping feature. Rods are 6½-foot medium action "rigging rods," with fairly flexible tips.

The 3-way setup previously mentioned, is tough to beat. So is trolling upstream, which goes against the flow of current mainline river theology.

"We catch a lot more fish slow-trolling upcurrent because the walleyes have an easier time zeroing in on the bait," explained Campbell. "Most guys slip downstream slightly slower than the current, reasoning that the fish face up-current, which is true, but the fish only have a split-second to make a move on a bait swept past them. That's why we inch slowly forward, and often hover in one spot. This keeps the jig in the strike zone much longer."

A steady lift-and-drop motion, with the rodtip moving no more than a foot, is the bread-and-butter jig action. Propel the boat forward slowly with a small "kicker" motor or a bowmount electric, and expect most hits to occur on the drop. Some fish smack it, others are "just there."

Stinger hooks (small size 8 to size 12 trebles tied on stiff monofilament line) are used when the fish are striking short.

Wing dams are also consistent producers when rivers are at normal levels. Takasaki and Campbell fish the front edge from an up-current position. But the real sweet spot is the rock/mud transition zone at the base of the wing dam. Jumbo jigs are ideal for telegraphing this critical change in bottom content.

Start by lowering the jig to the bottom, lifting it forward, then dropping it back again. Precisely how you do this is key.

"Every day out is different," Campbell said. "You need to get into the rhythm of the fish's mood." Added Takasaki, "One day it might be lifting on a 1-2-3 count then dropping the jig back. Another time out it could be two- or five-count, then drop. Vary the rodtip sweep from six inches to a foot until you discover the right cadence."

Jigs are unique in that what you do to the bait is what it does underwater. Not so with most other baits that have built-in actions of their own. Don't underestimate the action you impart to a jumbo jig, which is more responsive to rodtip motion than most baits.

On the other hand, don't overwork the jig—

A JUMBO LAKE HOTSPOT

Jumbo jigs are at their best in deep structure that's not too snaggy. Rock ledges, hard pan, gravel bars, pebbles and sandy bottoms are prime candidates. Follow the contours that the most fish are using.

But there's a better bet, if you can find it.

"Mud basins with a hard-bottom transition are always a winner," says Ted Takasaki. "And nothing beats a heavy jig for telegraphing the bottom. If it's soft, the jig will stick. If it's hard, the jig "thunks." Even a beginner can keep track of the transition line.

Walleyes tend to stack up here on the line during early-summer bug hatches and later in the year when large schools of young-of-the-year baitfish roam deep bays. Use your sonar to first define the transition.

You may wish to toss out a few marker buoys or punch in a waypoint if you own a Loran or GPS unit. This will help you stay on top of the fish and structure—something that's tough to do when fishing big water.

many times simply dragging it along the bottom triggers the most fish.

Final Tips

Two more tips on jumbo jigging. Fluorescent colors—chartreuse, hot pink, lime, orange work well in stained or dirty water. Purple and brown are great colors for clear water. Try some two-tone finishes for the best of both worlds.

Finally, tip jigs with meat—minnows, crawlers, leeches, you name it. Add some plastic (grub body, shad tail, salamander) for color and to bulk up the presentation; walleyes inhale the whole offering and you can set the hook immediately.

Lightweight jigs on light tackle will always be a great way to take walleyes, but there are times when jumbo jigs are better. Taking time to learn these basics will help you put more walleyes in the boat.

Stratified 'Eyes

by John Neporadny Jr.

During the summer a narrow band of water attracts and concentrates a high percentage of a reservoir's walleyes. Here's how to find and fish this "hot zone."

Here's a tough one for you: Southern summer walleyes. How tough? Well, by the time summer arrives in the walleye's southern range and the fish have abandoned their shallow springtime haunts, many anglers have simply given up on them until the next spring. But there is no reason to throw in the towel. In fact, it's easy to home in on summer walleyes once you realize that a natural barrier keeps them corralled for the most part. That barrier, the line they can't cross for any length of time, is the thermocline.

The thermocline is the transition zone between the epilimnion, the warm, oxygen-rich upper layer of water and the hypolimnion, the cold, oxygen-poor lower layer.

"Within the thermocline, water temperature drops very rapidly," says Kevin Meneau, a Missouri Department of Conservation fisheries biologist and former walleye specialist for the state of Wisconsin.

In Northern waters, the epilimnion usually remains cool enough for walleyes, but in many Southern lakes and reservoirs the upper portion sometimes gets too warm for comfort.

Consequently, walleyes seek the cooler temperatures near the thermocline. They will occasionally

drop into the hypolimnion, but lower oxygen levels there will drive them back after a period of time. They'll also move higher into the upper layer, but don't remain long because of uncomfortably high water temps. In the evening and at night, surface waters cool somewhat and the fish can enter shallow feeding areas.

"Since the walleye is a cool-water species that requires plenty of oxygen," says Meneau, "they're kind of caught between a rock and a hard place in Southern reservoirs during the summer."

That's good news for walleye fishermen, however, because once you locate the thermocline, the battle is half won.

Electronic Locators

Finding the thermocline—and fish—requires the use of electronic gear such as a good sonar unit and a temperature gauge or oxygen meter. Meneau prefers keying on oxygen and temperature when he fishes, saying that with either device, a 30-foot probe cord is needed to reach the depths.

A chart recorder (paper graph) helps professional fishing guide Guy White of Perry, Missouri, find the thermocline on Mark Twain Lake in northeastern Missouri. Because the water within the thermocline is more dense than the upper layer, it shows up on the paper as a distinct two- to three-foot-wide band. Sometimes he sees schools of forage fish near the thermocline as well.

Walt Reynolds, who spent 12 years guiding

Walleyes don't disappear during the hot summer months. You just have to know where to look for them.

> *"Once you locate the thermocline, the battle is half won."*

anglers to trophy walleyes on Truman Lake in central Missouri before moving to Florida, goes a step further when he's fishing his former home waters. He uses a chart recorder or the temperature probe on his Combo-C-Lector to find the thermocline, then looks for a zone he calls the "pH-cline" with the Combo-C-Lector's pH meter. It usually occurs three to five feet above the thermocline, he says.

Water in and near the thermocline usually has a lower pH (more acidic) because dead microorganisms collect in the dense water of the thermocline and decompose.

Reynolds believes locating the pH-cline is important because that's where the most active fish will be.

"A pH level between 7 and 9 is what I'm looking for," he explains. "I believe that's the pH range in which walleyes absorb and use oxygen most efficiently. When the pH is above 9 or below 7, walleyes aren't as aggressive."

The Structure Factor

Even though the thermocline concentrates walleyes above a certain depth, locating productive structure is still the key to finding fish. Reynolds concentrates his efforts on submerged humps, islands and rocky points that jut above the thermocline.

"It's imperative, though, that you find a spot with deep water close by," he says. "The fish will sometimes go into relatively shallow water (six to eight feet deep), but there's got to be a deep-water access, too."

A favorite feature in any of Reynolds' hotspots is something he calls a "compression zone."

"If there's current, I look for something such as a

ridge that rises out of, say, 40 feet of water and into 10 feet. Baitfish (shad, in most cases) in that 40 feet of water will be 'compressed' into a constricted area of water as they migrate up and over the ridge. Essentially, the density of baitfish is increased by four times on that 10-foot bar, and predator fish stack up behind the ridge where they wait for an easy meal to swim past."

In reservoirs such as Truman and Mark Twain, the thermocline is usually shallower than those in clearer Southern reservoirs. "They push fish to the 12- to 18-foot level on Truman Lake and hold them against breaks above the thermocline." Reynolds says. "The walleyes have nowhere else to go."

On Mark Twain Lake, where Guy White fishes, the thermocline averages 20 to 25 feet deep and he catches a lot of walleyes from mid-June to September in the 15- to 25-foot range. He rates June as the best month because that's when the thermocline is just beginning to develop on his home lake.

Weather also influences walleye fishing greatly

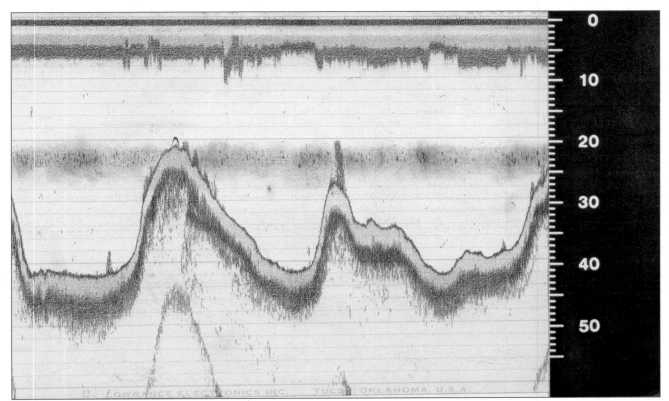

In the above graph, the thermocline shows up as a distinct black band at 21 feet. Notice how the fish relate to the submerged humps, yet remain above the thermocline.

Crankbaits, either casted or trolled, are the best way to coax summer walleyes into hitting.

during the summer. Cloud cover, for instance, often keeps the surface waters cool enough that walleyes can forage in shallow areas for extended periods.

"The worse the weather, the better the shallow water action becomes," explains White.

> "Find a spot with deep water close by."

Reynolds also prefers pursuing walleyes in adverse weather. "I like a typical cold-front day," he says. "In fact, most of my trophy walleye catches have come on cloudy days with a north wind."

Stained water gives the fisherman a similar advantage, according to Reynolds, because it reduces light penetration into the water, which in turn limits the walleye's ability to see.

"They tend to hit baits harder and faster in stained water," he says, "because they don't get a very good look at the lures and must react quickly before they disappear into the murk."

Crankbait Bite

Okay, you now have a good idea on how to find walleyes in Southern reservoirs. So how do you coax them into biting? Most experts agree that crankbaits are the way to go.

For shallow-water fish, Reynolds' top choices include the Bomber Model 6A or 7A, Homer Humphrey's Diving Ace or Peter Allen's Ditto crankbait, preferably in the fire tiger pattern because of its high visibility in stained water.

White uses a chartreuse Cordell Spot with an orange belly when fish are on the mud flats at Mark Twain.

A long cast and a slow retrieve work best for Reynolds. "Walleyes aren't known for chasing a lure, so you need a slow retrieve," he says. "You also need to be right on the fish."

Long casts allow Reynolds to crank the lure to the bottom and keep it in the strike zone. While dredging the bottom, the crankbait bumps through stumps and attracts feeding walleyes.

> *"A long cast and a slow
> retrieve work best."*

Both men use baitcasting equipment when throwing crankbaits. White varies his line diameter depending on water clarity, but never drops below 12-pound test. Reynolds sticks with 15-pound test for his shallow-water cranking.

For fishing near the thermocline, White uses a deep-diving crankbait, such as Bagley's DB3 in the fire tiger pattern. He catches more fish on it and the Cordell Spot than anything else.

Reynolds' favorite tactic for taking thermocline-

THE TROLLING OPTION

*C*asting crankbaits and jigging slab spoons are great methods for catching walleyes on the thermocline, but trolling can often be even more productive, especially when fish are suspended along this break-line—a common occurrence in shad-based lakes.

In the past, leadcore line, weights, Dipsy Divers and jet planers were used to reach the 20-25 foot depths, but these devices are no longer needed. Sharp trollers are using thin diameter no-stretch super lines like 6- or 10-pound test FireLine and line counter reels. A few companies that make these reels are Daiwa, South Bend and Mitchell.

Many modern crankbaits will reach these depths. Some of the best deep-diving walleye crankbaits are RistoRap, Reef Runner Deep Diver, Bomber 24A, 25A and 26A, Cordell Wally Diver, #9 Lindy Shadling, Luhr Jensen ¼ and ½ oz. Hot Lips, Mann's Stretch 15+, Down Deep Rattlin' Fat Raps, and Storm's Magnum Hot 'n' Tot and Deep Thunder Stick. All these lures will dig down at least 18-20 feet with 100-120 feet of 10-pound-test mono out, plus they are proven walleye catchers.

related walleyes is a vertical presentation with a ½-ounce Hogjaw or ¾-ounce C.C. Spoon. He uses a 6-foot, 6-inch medium-heavy action baitcasting rod and a reel spooled with 15- to 20-pound test. The longer rod gives him more hooksetting power, and the heavy line stands up to the wear and tear created by the twisting action of the spoon.

Positioning his boat over the break, Reynolds pitches the spoon up on a ledge and bounces it back down the shelves toward the boat. Then, before he reels in, he slowly jiggles the spoon about a foot off the bottom with a twitch of the rodtip.

"You don't want to make big violent jerks," he explains.

"These summer techniques have paid off many times in fillet dividends."

He drops the rodtip to keep a tight line as the spoon falls. The trick allows him to feel any strike or hesitation in the spoon's descent. He also eyeballs his bow-mounted sonar unit to maintain boat position near the break.

These summer techniques have paid off many times in fillet dividends for the two fishermen. Reynolds' best trip on Truman resulted in 15 walleyes weighing more than 4 pounds each. One summer evening, he and three other anglers landed four limits of four fish each ranging from 3 to 9½ pounds.

Southern reservoirs can produce good summertime walleye fishing for those willing to learn about a lake's thermocline and its influence on walleyes.

chapter 7

Northern Pike

*T*oothy and mean. Handsome and streamlined. Sort of slimy. Ready to whack your bait—live or artificial—to kingdom come and back. That's the pike, and that's why, where available (which is more and more places these days), pike fishing means pure excitement. When you latch onto a pike and then finally get him to the net, you look in those glaring eyes and think, now that's a *fish*. And then he explodes in a thrashing of tail and body ...

Yet, despite their aggressive nature and voracious appetite, pike aren't pushovers. Especially the big boys. Here's *North American Fisherman's* best ideas on finding and catching them regularly.

Trophy Pike!

by Larry Dahlberg

For truly big pike, watch that water temperature and watch your catches soar!

My very first early-season trips to killer pike water was to one of Manitoba's large, pristine lakes that never sees much fishing pressure. My native guide, who was famous among the camp staff for his fishing prowess, liked to troll Five-of-Diamonds spoons.

Unfortunately, we went all the first morning and half the afternoon without seeing a single pike. As an explanation, he said: "Need a north wind to blow pike in from the big lake."

I remember that struck me as odd, but what did I know about pike fishing at the 55th parallel.

As we motored out of a sandy basin, I noticed a narrow channel leading to a small, flooded depression in the grass and tundra bushes. The springtime water was high and some of the flooded vegetation was under two feet of water.

We had just entered the channel, using a paddle as a push pole, when I spotted the head of a midteen pike poking out of a hole in the submerged grass. It spooked and a handful of other pike surged away with it.

When I asked the guide if he knew of any similar spots, only much larger, he obligingly cranked up the 25 Merc and motored around the corner to a huge rocky bay with an acre or more of flooded grass and brush at its back end.

It was just the type of spot I was hoping for, and to our amazement, it was full of pike! I had savage strikes on cast after cast with traditional metal spoons, but seldom actually hooked a fish. One short-striker was a real monster that came from an isolated weedbed. I made a mental note of the location and continued on.

It turns out the guide's "north wind" theory was at least half right. If the north wind had blown (that is, if a cold front had arrived), the fish would have ended up in the basins the guide was intent on fishing. But the fish wouldn't have been blown in from the main lake — the front would have pushed them out of the shallows!

It seems no one had ever fished the flooded depressions before and had no idea the pike were there. The hooking problem occurred because the shallow water and dense cover made any metal spoon difficult for the pike to grab.

We quit fishing about 11 p.m., but the pike were still going wild. Trouble was, they were so far back in the brush, we could only hear them.

The next morning, on a hunch, I broke out my fly rod. We moved toward the isolated clump of weeds where I'd seen the monster the day before and I made a 90-foot cast parallel to the weed edge.

A slow strip of the fly line caused the fur strip diving fly to emit a two-foot gurgling bubble chain. With each strip of the line, the fur and supple flashabou tail undulated liquidly. There was a boil the size of a hot tub, and I reared back on my 9-foot, 7-weight rod. Water and grass blew 10 feet into the air when the fish blasted off.

Turned out to be a 50 incher and nearly 50 percent larger than the existing International Game Fish Association's fly rod world record!

> "Shallow, dark-bottomed waters that warm quickly in early spring are a pike's favorite spawning grounds. Before spawning, fish move into and out of the shallows as the waters warm during the day and cool down at night."

In the years since that trip, armed with every conceivable electronic device, rod, reel and lure, and with almost unlimited access to float planes, I've chased pike on some of the finest waters in the United States, Russia, Ontario, Manitoba, Saskatchewan and the Northwest Territories. I've caught some big pike in the process and at the same time made some discoveries that pike anglers everywhere will find interesting—and useful.

Temperature Is Key

Early-season pike activity is totally temperature driven. The myth, however, is that there is some specific temperature at which pike become active. Sure, water temps from 40 to 45 degrees trigger the spawn, but that's only a few days out of the year. We're talking about a pattern that may last for weeks.

During the spring, it's not some magic temperature that matters; it's the fact the temperature is rising

Spring is one of the best times of the year to catch a trophy!

through a particular range for the first time in many months. For example, a spot where the water temperature has risen from the mid-30s to 50 degrees may be gangbusters one day. But days later, after it had risen to 65 degrees then dropped to 50, you'd get skunked.

In the spring, falling temperatures are bad, rising temps are good, and understanding the temperature game is essential to catching ice-out pike.

Areas That Warm First

Water temperatures in various parts of the lake will rise at different rates. The deep main basin will be in the 30s as the ice breaks up, then quickly rises into the 40s.

During this period, water from about five to 20 feet in the bays will warm up each day and cool down at night, but usually won't reach more than a few degrees higher than the main basin.

Fluctuations here are related to wind and sunlight, but are not nearly as rapid or extreme as in the

shallow areas adjacent to the bay basin.

These flats, which warm quickly in the sunlight, may contain water that's 20 or more degrees higher than that in the main lake basin.

In this light, locating ice-out pike on a regular basis appears easy, but there's more to it than simply heading for the backwaters, especially if you're targeting trophy fish.

Early-Season Hotspots

To maximize your chances of catching oversized pike, choose a lake that's a known trophy producer. Be there at ice-out, or soon after, with a good lake map and a surface temperature gauge on your boat. Most good portable liquid-crystal sonars have one.

Check every bay, every nook, every cranny on the map. Protected areas on the north end of the lake (which gets more exposure to sunlight than other areas) are usually the first to warm. This can serve as a barometer as to what stage the lake is in. A bay with a number of smaller coves at the back end is an ideal spot, especially if it has a dark bottom and is necked down so the warmed water can't escape. Of course, any shallow bay with good spawning habitat can attract pike.

You'll find that most shallows contain at least one hotspot—an area that generates more heat or one that catches more of the warmer water blown in by the wind. This area of the flat will collect fish first.

> *"Be there at ice-out, or soon after, with a good lake map and a surface temperature gauge on your boat."*

In one extreme case super-early in the season, I watched pike concentrate on a little corner of an island. There was no creek, no inflow of water, just a four-degree temperature differential. After a bit of checking, it became clear that the warmer water had been blown from a shallow, dark-bottomed mud saddle at the end of the channel a mile away! In fact, the mud flat is what caused the whole channel to open up.

In the early, early stages of spring, hotspots can be very small, maybe only 40 square feet in a

20-acre bay. When you become better at finding them, you'll also discover why they exist.

Sometimes it's the shape of the bay in relation to the wind direction. Other times it may be warm water from a stream that gets blown into a corner. (Incidentally, it's been my experience that water dribbling from a series of small ponds is likely to be warmer than the water from a large stream or river.)

Dark-bottomed areas that absorb heat from the sun are always a good bet, as are stands of reeds or other vegetation that create temperature breaks.

Make a game plan to locate all potential hotspots. If you have several boats in your party, assign a section to each boat or leapfrog around the lake. Don't forget islands.

The hunting process is both visual and electronic. I like to cruise large expanses of shallow water, visually scanning areas my temp gauge says are the warmest. It's faster than blind casting.

It's okay to move fairly fast, expecting to spook fish. You can always watch them until they settle down, then make your cast. The higher up you can get in the boat, the better you'll be able to see.

Spring Pike Leave Tracks

There's another trick to sight-locating pike that may sound incredible, but I assure you it's true. I discovered it during an extended trip to monster pike waters.

THE CASE FOR NEUTRALLY BUOYANT BAITS

*I*n some instances, Ice-out pike will be aggressive enough to hit a fast-moving lure like a spinnerbait. For belly-to-the-bottom pike, a jig-and-pig is better. But sometimes, even that slow presentation is too much for them to handle.

That's when a neutrally buoyant bait, one that remains at or near the depth it's cranked to, is the best choice.

On one trip to a fishing camp on sprawling Reindeer Lake, which straddles the border between Saskatchewan and Manitoba, a Bagley Magnum Finger Mullet was the lure that saved the day.

The fish were suspended in 15 to 20 feet of water, and not actively feeding. Granted, the Mullet was designed for tarpon, but after the pike had rejected the combined lure stocks of all 39 anglers in camp, it was the only thing left to try— and it worked!

The 4-inch lure is neutrally buoyant and has little or no action of its own, perfect for fussy tarpon, and as it turned out early-season pike, too. I cast and let it sink for several seconds, then slowly pulled it about a foot, paused, pulled again.

I felt something and set the hook. It was a 10-pound pike. Same thing happened on the next cast, and the next and the next. For several hours it was an orgy! I caught pike on every cast.

Most were 6 to 12 pounds, with a few in the high teens. When the other 38 anglers, who had thus far gone fishless, heard about it, they were intensely interested.

That night I volunteered to tune one lure for every angler. After hours of drilling, adding solder, lead or different hooks, then testing buoyancy in a water-filled wastebasket, each fisherman had a neutrally-buoyant lure. They ranged from Rapalas to Redfins to Pikie Minnows.

The next evening every person came back with stories of the pike they'd caught. The largest weighed nearly 25 pounds. Neutrally buoyant lures are so effective because they remain in the strike zone for as long as it takes to trigger a bite.

And, because it's essentially the same "weight" as the water surrounding it, the lure easily flows into the fish's mouth when it does strike.

It's not difficult to make a lure neutrally buoyant. Simply drill holes part way into the bottom of a floating lure (wood lures are easiest) and fill them with enough split shot or lead to offset the lure's natural ability to float. Then seal the holes with epoxy. Lead-bodies, Suspend Dots and SuspenStrips made by Storm Mfg. Co. make this job a lot easier. Just attach as many as needed on the underside of the lure to create neutral buoyancy.

DAILY ACTIVITY CYCLE

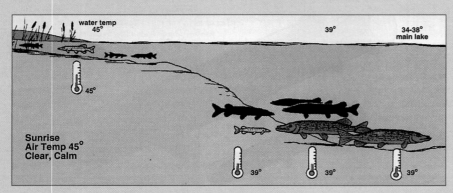

water temp 45°

39°

34-38° main lake

45°

39°   39°   39°

Sunrise
Air Temp 45°
Clear, Calm

1. Sunrise finds the fish scattered, with many smaller pike in the shallows and larger fish in the bay basin. The shallows cool rapidly during the night, pushing most pike, especially the bigger fish, into the more stable waters of the bay basin. Note that we have highlighted four fish of various sizes and the fact that each fish's body temperature is the same as the water surrounding it. Now watch what happens with these individual fish during the course of the day.

2. By noon, three of the four fish in our example have moved into the warming shallows. It's important to note the differences in body temperatures as it relates to water temperature and the size of the fish. Fish number 1, which has been in the shallows all day, is the same temperature as the water. Fish 2 and 3, on the other hand, just moved into the warmer water. Notice that the smaller fish's (2) body temperature is already higher than that of the much larger fish (3). It will become active sooner. The larger fish, with more body mass per square inch of surface area, requires more time to absorb enough heat to become active. Fish 1, 2 and 4 are definitely catchable; fish 3 probably won't feed until its temperature stabilizes.

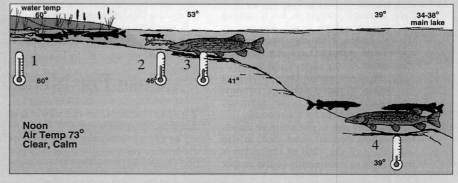

water temp 60°

53°

39°

34-38° main lake

1   60°

2   46°   3   41°

Noon
Air Temp 73°
Clear, Calm

4   39°

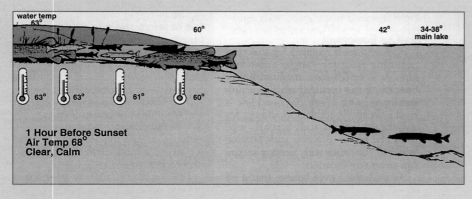

water temp 63°

60°

42°

34-38° main lake

63°   63°   61°   60°

1 Hour Before Sunset
Air Temp 68°
Clear, Calm

3. Shallows continue to warm all day, then cool again as sunset approaches. All fish have been in the shallows long enough to acclimate to the surrounding water and are actively feeding. This is the prime time to be fishing the shallows.

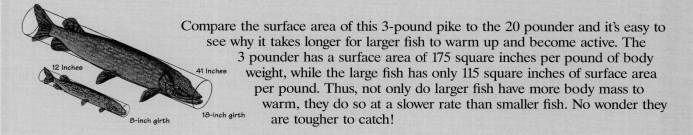

BIG PIKE LITTLE PIKE

Compare the surface area of this 3-pound pike to the 20 pounder and it's easy to see why it takes longer for larger fish to warm up and become active. The 3 pounder has a surface area of 175 square inches per pound of body weight, while the large fish has only 115 square inches of surface area per pound. Thus, not only do larger fish have more body mass to warm, they do so at a slower rate than smaller fish. No wonder they are tougher to catch!

12 Inches

8-inch girth

41 Inches

18-inch girth

All week, I'd noticed round, white deposits on the bottom. Some were only three or four inches in diameter; others were as large as a dinner plate. Out of curiosity, I examined one of these deposits close up—fish scales, lots of fish scales. Based upon this premise, I set out hunting for the biggest white spots (figuring bigger deposits meant bigger fish). In every case, I found them where the warmest water had been the day before. The picture of the pikes' daily cycle then became complete. Early spring morning finds them loosely grouped in the bay basins. Here they are more or less neutral and won't chase a spoon or spinnerbait.

"I was looking at pike scat!"

As the water warms, they move into the rapidly warming shallows, remaining inactive until their bodies warm up. Once warmed, they feed ravenously.

Then they rest in the warm shallows, make their deposit, and bask in the warmth until the chill of night drives them back to the stability of the deeper bay basin.

Some years, water levels are so low that it's impos-sible to get a boat into some fishy areas. Neoprene or Gore-Tex waders are just the ticket for this situation.

If you can float your boat, I guarantee that a push-pole will beat a paddle or motor for moving

around. Buy one before the season starts; you'll be glad you did.

Ice-Out Equipment

Rods and reels required for this type of fishing are a pike angler's standard fare. A 7- or 7½-foot, medium-heavy baitcasting rod outfitted with a quality reel loaded with 17- to 20-pound line is hard to beat. Fly rodders should opt for a 7- to 10-weight rod; actually two would be better. Rig one with floating line and the other with sinking so you can cover any situation.

As for lures, I truly believe that if all ice-out anglers swapped their spoons for a pointed-head, weedless jig rigged with an Uncle Josh Big Daddy pork frog, the number of pike caught during the first three weeks of the season would increase tenfold. It's a killer pike lure. You can cast it anywhere without getting hung up and you can work it shallow or deep, fast or slow. And it catches pike of all sizes. Every serious pike fisherman ought to be using this lure more often.

A weedless plastic spoon like a Moss Boss is great for pike in shallow vegetation like grass. I'll often replace the original hook with a larger 7/0 to 8/0 hook and use a pork frog for more bulk and casting weight. Johnson Silver Minnows also work well.

Pike also love topwater lures that create a steady surface disturbance, like a double-buzzer. It's super effective in reeds and when fish are very aggressive.

For the pure thrill of a kamikaze surface strike, I'll throw a Zara Spook, but normally avoid lures with multiple treble hooks. Even barbless trebles beat up the fish more than single hooks do.

LOCATING ICE-OUT PIKE

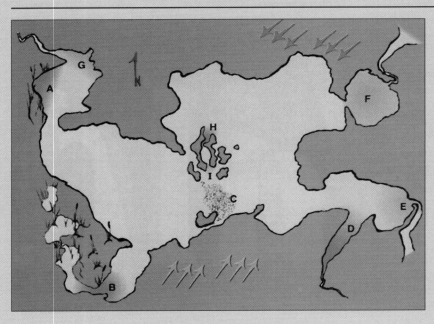

Locating ice-out pike often depends on the direction of the wind. While sunlight heats water in a particular area, the wind may blow that warm water to another location, often stacking it along a shoreline.

On the lake in the example, spots in red represent warm-water areas created by the strong spring sun, then pushed somewhere else by a wind from the northeast. Those in orange are created by a southwest wind.

A northeast wind would push water warmed in the shallow bay against the shoreline marked A. Likewise, it would push water that had been warmed by the shallow flat, C, into the southwest bay, B. Warmer water would also come from the series of shallow ponds that drain into the bay. Bay D is shallow and would be filled with warm water.

When the wind blows from the southwest, areas E, F and G become the hotspots, particularly F. On a calm day, the necked-down area traps warm water already inside the bay. The wind simply helps hold the water inside.

Islands also create warm-water hotspots. The middle island contains a small pond that warms quickly and drains rainwater both to the north and south. A wind from the northeast would hold the warm water in the small bay, H, while a southwest wind would do the same thing in the bay marked I.

Sometimes, as when pike are suspended, you have to let them tell you what they'll strike. That means varying your lures and retrieves. If a fast retrieve doesn't produce, try an erratic retrieve or a twitch-and-pause or a slow sweeping retrieve.

Spinnerbaits are my day-in and day-out favorite for covering a lot of water and searching for pike in water with some cover. I use mostly large Hildebrandt willowleaf blades from sizes 4½ to 7 on ⅜- to ⅝-ounce heads. I like the closed line loop on spinnerbaits. With the open, "R-type" loop, the steel leader constantly slides out and interferes with the spinning blades. In bays with very little or no cover, a straight shaft spinnerbait will allow you to cover a lot of water and will hook a higher percentage of pike than a safety-pin-style spinnerbait. A steady retrieve that keeps the lure running near bottom is usually best. A number 5 Mepps, Blue Fox and Panther Martin are a few choices.

Pike love plastics but can chew up pounds in a day's fishing. A great lure to toss back at following pike is a 6-inch Slug-Go-type jerkworm. Rig it on a light (18- to 30-pound-test) wire leader. A longer leader adds weight that kills the action. Toss it to the side of the fish, let it sink, and twitch it off the bottom. Watching a 20 pounder suck one down in clear, shallow water is quite a thrill.

When fly fishing I use either a Dahlberg Diver or a jigging fly. That is all you need to catch every pike under any circumstance.

Stealth Is Required

Once you spot a fish and begin your presentation, it's vital that you don't spook it. Where you cast and the angle you choose to present the lure can make all the difference in the world.

If you swim the lure toward the fish, it could be interpreted as an attack. As implausible as it sounds, a 3-inch bait can frighten a 3-foot pike.

It's best to cast past the fish, being careful that the line's shadow doesn't fall over its body. If you are using a jig, let it settle to the bottom, then move it in front of the pike at an angle going slightly away. Use a stop-and-go retrieve until it's one or two inches in front of the fish's nose. "Shake" the jig slightly with tiny movements of the rodtip until the fish moves. It shouldn't be a violent shake, but rather a quick and subtle movement that simply tightens, then puts slack into the line.

Allowing the lure to sit there, forcing the fish to look at it, is as good a way to trigger a strike as I know. Stay with a fish until it seems scared. If you're careful, that can be along time. Just remember, you can't catch a fish that knows you're after it.

Trophies Take Longer

It's important to note that a pike's, especially a big pike's activity level depends on the length of time it's been exposed to warm water. This point stood out during one enlightening experience as I watched pike slowly filter into a shallow spot in a sandy bay.

"A big pike's activity level depends on the length of time it has been exposed to warm water."

Wanting to get the best view possible for my observation, I had rigged a 10-foot step ladder in the boat by using a couple of 1x6 boards across the floor as a base. Two 2x4 boards were strung across the gunwales and the whole thing was wired into place. Standing midway up, it was comfortable to lean on the top platform which was at my waist.

Perched on the ladder, I saw pike swimming in singles, doubles and pods of a half-dozen. Some were near the surface, others at the bottom. After watching for a while, their behavior became predictable. They used particular routes and parked in certain spots before resuming their journey. Most importantly, their behavior toward a lure seemed to change dramatically as they moved shallower over the course of the day.

I could fish in eight to 15 feet of water in the basin and catch almost every pike I saw on a jig-and-pig. Likewise, the small and midsize fish laying in the warm shallows were easy to catch, hammering anything I threw.

But the large fish that were just moving up wouldn't hit anything until they'd been there for a while. Conversely, small pike would move into the shallows and begin feeding right away.

While trying to entice one of the largest fish, I accidentally snagged it. Before releasing it, I took its rectal temperature with my stream thermometer. The mystery was immediately solved.

The pike's body temperature was a full five degrees lower than the water she had just entered. She was in thermal shock and not about to feed! Smaller fish became active right away because they had less body mass and thus adjusted to the temperatures around them much faster. (See sidebar on page 203.)

Experience Comes With Practice

The better you get at recognizing features that cause water temperatures to rise, the better you'll be at locating ice-out pike. You'll also find that the hardest, firmest rules aren't always reliable and that while hunting monster pike, the only real truth is what you actually see with your own eyes.

Most good pike waters hold so many fish that once you get into the main schools you can catch and release up to a hundred fish or more in a day. The size will range from a few pounds to who knows what.

You may run out of time before connecting with the fish you want, but rest assured, your trophy is there waiting for you. All you have to do is put together the right strategy.

The Soft-Plastic Advantage

by Spence Petros

"Accidental" catches of big pike and muskie on jigs in the early 1970s evolved into a system that every angler who chases these fish should know.

They're my aces-in-the-hole—my secret weapons, and believe me, they're deadly on big pike and muskies. I'm talking about plastics, and if you're not using 'em, you're missing out on some fantastic action. Plastics take shallow-water fish when no other lures can, and will turn following pike and muskies into biters better than other baits.

I also use plastics to work erratic weed edges and slot-like corners that can't be fished effectively with any standard crankbait, spinner, jerkbait or spoon presentation. They're also dynamite for rooting fish out of thick weed clumps during bright or calm conditions, and are deadly below the 10- to 15-foot range that most conventional lure presentations are designed to work.

Soft plastics found a home in my big pike/ muskie tackle box almost 25 years ago, and every year I learn more about how and when to use these deadly lures.

Here are the deadliest patterns for taking big pike and muskies on plastics.

Early Spring

Feeling confidence that bordered on cockiness, I loaded the boat one cool spring morning. I knew exactly where the pike would be, as well as the best method to catch them. Now that the ice had gone out, the fish would be laying in a couple of shallow bays, soaking up the warm spring sun. They'd be suckers for Slug-Gos, too, a bait I've used successfully on spring pike for years.

"Plastics will turn following pike and muskies into biters better than other baits."

As we began a slow, gentle drift through the first bay we fished, I stood high in the boat, scanning the shallows. Polarized glasses, combined with a long-billed hat to cut the glare, enabled me to easily see the sandy bottom up to 50 yards away. Within seconds, I began to see pike. Some moved

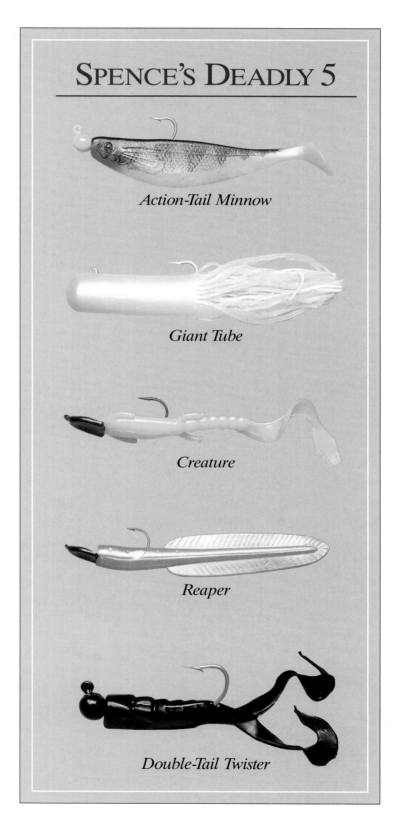

SPENCE'S DEADLY 5

Action-Tail Minnow

Giant Tube

Creature

Reaper

Double-Tail Twister

This 48-inch pike twice followed a bucktail to the boat, but it took a plastic lure on a flat, swimming head jig to convince her to open her mouth.

slowly off, while others held in an almost trance-like manner.

My 6-inch Slug-Go landed a few feet from a 12 pounder and slowly settled to the bottom. I let it lay about five seconds, then gave it a slight twitch, stirring up a small puff of sand and silt. I readied

for a hookset that was never needed. The fish ignored my bait. The scenario repeated itself numerous times over the next few hours. I was dumbfounded. This tactic had never failed me under these conditions!

Experienced pike anglers know a slow-falling, near weightless lure will catch early spring pike that ignore the standard spoon and spinner presentations. Some anglers opt for large streamer flies, while others favor various unweighted plastics. My favorite is a 6-inch Slug-Go-type jerkworm, but lizards or even large bass-type worms will also produce well. Steve Pennaz showed me a large, nearly neutrally-buoyant plastic worm/hair skirt combo he uses effectively on shallow-water pike.

> *"Success came by simply slowing things down a little more."*

I wondered if my drop speed was a bit too fast, so I shortened my wire leader to reduce weight. My success improved slightly, so I took it one step further and removed the leader completely, opting instead for a large split shot clamped on the line 18 inches above the jerkworm.

This gave me plenty of weight to cast, and once the weight touched bottom, the lure would glide downward slowly. Pike after pike inhaled the slow-falling lure. Success came by simply slowing things down a little more.

The negative side of the leaderless rig was cut-offs. I've since learned how to keep them to a minimum—about one per six to seven pike—by using 50-pound-test Berkley Gorilla Braid and a well-sharpened hook. The hookset is merely a sweep of the rod, not a strong jolt, and I play the fish gingerly.

Most of the time, however, a jerkworm used behind a short wire leader is all that's needed. Cast it past and in front of a pike, and work the lure toward the fish with short jerks and long pauses that allow the lure to touch bottom.

Because the muskie season is not open during the ice-out period on waters I fish, I have never tried this tactic on spring muskies. But anglers I know in states where spring fishing is legal, such as Ohio

and Illinois, have had excellent success with it on muskies that ignore other presentations.

Following Fish

One of the deadliest uses for plastics on pike and muskies is taking fish that follow another lure to the boat, but won't hit. Sometimes a figure-8 at boatside will take these fish, but I turn to plastics when the fish drops out of sight or turns to leave. I've found that about 60 to 70 percent of the pike and about 25 percent of the muskies that follow can be caught with plastics. Here's how I do it.

I rig the plastic on a swimming head jig and fish it on spinning gear, which allows me to quickly and accurately flip the bait in front of the fish.

A major key to catching fish that follow is to act fast. My jig rod sits next to me all day long so I can quickly grab it. The jig isn't hooked on a hook holder or line guide either, to save time. I open the bail and cast as I pick up the rod.

If a muskie or pike suddenly turns away from a lure and disappears from sight, make a fairly long cast with the jig in the direction from which the fish came. Retrieve the jig quickly with three to four bursts of the reel handle, followed by a three- to four-second pause, then another burst of speed.

Don't try to maintain bottom contact with the jig. Retrieving it about half to two-thirds of the way down toward the bottom works best, because the fish that followed the lure up to the boat is usually holding fairly high in the water column.

The exception is when you're fishing early-season pike in water under 6 feet deep. In this situation, allow the jig to touch bottom between each forward motion.

Jigs also work great on fish that stay near the boat after a follow. A fish that is being worked on a figure-8 maneuver at boatside will often dart away to hit a jig pumped up and down five to 10 feet away.

But remember, if you try to tempt a fish that your partner is working with a figure 8, don't toss your jig into the area where he or she is fishing. Nothing is worse than a big, hot muskie or pike briefly looking at tangled lines, then swimming away.

Use a flat, swimming-type jig head on following fish. This head allows you to easily keep the lure off bottom, or hold it in a small area while pumping it up and down for a fish milling around the boat. Also, its slower fall rate is easy for fish to zero in on.

In late fall, or for deeper waters and faster

JERKWORM RIGS

These are the soft-plastic jerkbait rigs I use most of the time. The Standard Rig (A) features a fairly short wire leader and small swivel. Too much weight hurts the lure's side-to-side movement.

The Reverse Rig (B) runs deeper and has less darting action. It catches fish and gets more use out of a chewed up lure. Break ½ inch off the end before attempting to rig this so you'll have enough plastic to hold the hook.

Mid-lure rigging (C) works best when sight fishing non-moving pike over a clean bottom. Dance the bait a few feet in front of the fish. The Split Shot Rig (D) saved us last year on some very lethargic pike. The leaderless worm fell slowly and gentle pulls caused a slow side-to-side movement. Just what the fish wanted right after ice-out.

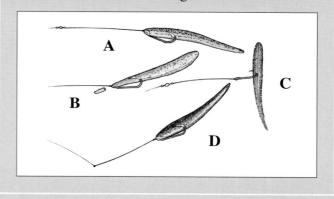

retrieves, I use a more compact, ball-shaped jig head.

Hard-To-Fish Spots

Small, isolated features are often tailor-made for fishing with plastic. One of my favorite spots for a jig-n-plastic rig is a tight "inside turn" or corner along a drop-off. These slot-like areas in a weed bed are productive in summer through early fall. In mid- to late-fall, deep, fast-breaking, hard-bottomed drop-offs that cut toward shore are great, especially if baitfish are in the area and the wind is blowing into the slot.

Most of these areas can't be trolled or worked

KEY SPOTS TO JIG

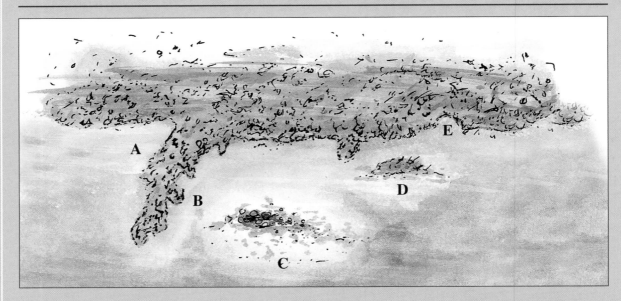

An ideal spot to toss a jig-n-plastic combo is an inside turn (A). Pike and muskies love to hang in corners, and most anglers bypass these slots. A lot of fish-holding nooks and crannies along an edge (B) are also prime jigging areas. Fish holding along an edge like this generally won't move up or out for a more conventional lure presentation, but a jig can root them out. Deep-water structure (C) is easy to fish with a heavy jig, as are small, isolated weed humps (D). Isolated spots (E) are great places to toss a jig. If a fish is there you'll find out quickly, and if it hits, a jig will land a higher percentage of strikes than any other lure.

correctly with a bucktail, crankbait, jerkbait or top-water presentation, yet a good jig fisherman can live off them.

Years ago I fished western Pennsylvania's Conneaut Lake in late October. In three days, four of us caught and released 22 muskies, most of which went 10 to 18 pounds. Almost all those fish were caught trolling deep-diving crankbaits just outside the weedline in 15 to 20 feet of water. While fish numbers were great, their average size was disappointing, considering this lake has produced several fish well-over 40 pounds.

Two weeks later, I was back on Conneaut. The first morning there, I caught two muskies weighing about 15 pounds each, while trolling off the weedline. Obviously, trolling the deep edges was not the answer for catching larger fish.

My contour map was a good one that showed bottom consistency, along with depth changes. I studied the map and found four sharp drop-offs with shale or rock bottoms that cut in sharply toward the shoreline.

I immediately reached for my jig box. The first drop-off we fished with jigs produced a large walleye and a nice pike, then a 31-pound muskie. We had trolled past that sharp corner numerous times and had caught one small muskie off a nearby projection, but no monsters. Jigging allowed us to reach many of the bigger fish the trollers missed.

The harder a corner or turn is to fish with conventional lures, the better that jigs will work. A jig gets into narrow spots, can be hopped down steep drop-offs and will penetrate weed edges. Tough conditions? Not for a jig-and-plastic combination.

Other Weedbeds, Too

Certain areas, such as an erratic weed edge, can create presentation problems for most pike or muskie anglers. If the fish are aggressive, a lure trolled across the projections can trigger strikes, and fish may even come up for a lure worked above their heads. But when fish are tucked into corners or pockets, or are just holding tight to shaded cover, it's jig time.

I've seen jigs root muskies and pike out of hard-to-fish areas that other anglers fished with cranks or bucktails to no avail.

Jig and plastic combos are also deadly in depths beyond the range of standard lure presentations. A 1-ounce or heavier jig head will easily drag a plastic minnow, large swirltail or "creature" down 15 feet or more, allowing you to work a deep finger off a point, sunken hump, bluff bank, large, scattered, deep rocks or other deep structure. A round jig head that sinks fast is best suited for deeper waters.

Jigs also allow you to get into a small weedy area without ripping it up. A jig-n-plastic rig can usually be worked with precision over the tops or along the edges of clingy weeds, or even right down into crispy, easy-to-tear weeds like cabbage.

Non-Aggressive Fish

When bass fishing is tough, what has been a popular tactic the experts have gone to in recent years? Flippin' and pitchin'—basically short casts into cover using a slower, more up-and-down presentation. You know what? These same short casts also work great for muskies and pike. Often, these brutes tuck up in a pocket, slide into a slot between a couple pieces of cover, or move into a thicker clump of weeds, and there is no better way to root them out than with a jig.

These fish may not be hungry. Calm, bright conditions may have caused them to "hole up," or a cold front could have slowed them down. But the up-and-down action of a smaller lure presented right into their lair often tempts them into gulping it in.

After many years of tossing plastics for muskies and pike, I can honestly say these baits provide me with 10 to 50 percent more fishing time in any given day. Instead of having just three to four hours when fish are active and catchable on standard presentations, jigging extends the bite because it reaches places other lures can't, and catches fish that shun faster-moving presentations.

SINKING JIGS

*A*nglers using a round jig head in the customary lift/drop fashion often miss a strike, then bring in a leader with a big curl in it. This hap-pens when the fish pins a vertically falling lure against the leader. To avoid this problem, turn the reel handle one-half to one full turn as the lure heads downward between lifts, pumps or rips. The turning of the reel handle separates the leader from the lure and eliminates most curled leaders and missed fish.

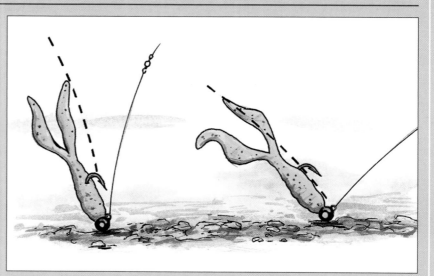

I designed a quality IM-6 graphite rod for South Bend (Spence Petros System 9 model) that is ideal for ½- to 1-ounce jigs.

I also use baitcasting gear, especially when working a dark water lake that offers thick vegetation.

I make short casts or pitches to the weed edge, and set the hook hard, with enough leverage to move the fish that bite quickly away from cover. Big flippin'-type rods with longer handles work best in this situation.

I make my own wire leaders using single-strand wire in the 27- to 44-pound test range. A haywire twist is used to connect one end of the leader to a quality ball-bearing swivel, another one to attach the jig. The finished leader should be about 14 inches long.

"A variety of plastic dressings work well."

A variety of plastic dressings, such as action tail minnows, lizards, swirltails, Reapers and assorted "creatures" work well, especially those in the 6- to 9-inch range.

Two styles of jig heads work best. Use flat, swimming-type jig heads from the deep weedline to the shallows, when tossing back to a following fish, and when using an off-bottom presentation to target suspended fish.

The eye tie on the swimming style head is right on the tip of the jig, making it much less likely to hang up in the weeds. Its wide, flat body also pushes the weeds aside to create less weed-hook contact.

Ball-shaped jig heads sink the fastest and are more suited for deeper water, especially when faster retrieves are desired. If trying to get the maximum depth range out of a certain weight jig, use a ball head with a plastic dressing that has minimum drag, such as a big double-tailed twister, plastic lizard or Reaper. Action-tail minnow-shaped plastics send out maximum underwater vibrations, and are best for stained water conditions.

Plastics deserve a place in your tackle box. I know I won't fish pike or muskies without 'em.

NAFC Life Member Barry Glosniak took this 40-inch muskie on a jig-n-plastic rig while working a deep weed edge.

Tackle Tip

In the past, I fished plastics with stiff spinning rods rated for lines in the 10- to 20-pound range, matched up with light saltwater or heavy-duty freshwater reels. These bigger reels had larger spools to handle the necessary 14-pound test or heavier mono. This is still a great combination, but today's superlines, such as FireLine or Fusion, enable you to pack enough line on a standard size reel to comfortably—and effectively—fish plastics. Put 10–15 yards of mono on the reel first to prevent slippage.

My favorite combination for most conditions is a spinning reel with a long-cast spool filled with 30-pound-test FireLine (diameter of 12-pound-test mono), matched with a gutsy 6½-foot spinning rod.

Pike Fever

by Otis "Toad" Smith

*In many areas, the biggest pike of the year are caught through the ice.
Here's a game plan that works!*

*W*ater wolf, gator, slough shark, toothy critter—call the northern pike what you like—this sleek predator provides ice anglers some of the hottest fishing action Mother Nature has to offer.

Add to this the fact that there's a real chance of catching a true trophy— 17, 20 or even 25 pounds— and it's clear why pike are among the most sought-after "hard-water" gamefish.

Ice fishing has come a long way in recent years. With the advent of light-weight, insulated clothing, portable heaters, portable sonar units, refined tackle and power ice augers, ice fishermen have become increasingly productive and stay more comfortable while they catch fish.

The most popular methods for taking big pike through the ice are jigging, and tip-ups rigged with dead or live bait. Most of the big pike I've caught, including several weighing more than 20 pounds, have come on dead bait and quick-set rigs dangled below a tip-up.

Dead-Bait Temptation

Warm-water pike offerings range from flashy spoons to gaudy-colored spinnerbaits to violently-wobbling crankbaits, but when fishing under the ice, your speed should be slow to "dead still."

The reason is that while pike must eat regardless of the season, their wintertime metabolism rate is as slow as 90-weight oil on Christmas morning.

Consequently, they want a meal that's easy to catch, even if it is dead. Pike are scavengers, and it's not uncommon for big gators to cruise the lake picking up every dead fish they find.

Naturally, then, a large, dead bait suspended below a tip-up is often the right ticket. And when I say large, I mean it. An 8-inch sucker is about as small as I'll go.

I'm also very particular about the tip-ups I use. There's an army of pike hunters who rely on inexpensive wooden tip-ups—you know, the ones that come with two cross-pieces and a plastic spool. There's nothing wrong with them, but I prefer the new generation of hard plastic, low-profile tip-ups. My favorite is the Polar.

Polar tip-ups feature a unique design: a horizontally mounted spool attached to a spindle encased in a metal tube. This design keeps the mechanism from freezing up. It can be set to go off with the lightest of strikes, or it can be adjusted so that a very large, lively bait won't trigger a flag. When a fish does take the bait, the reel turns, which causes the T-top spindle to turn, releasing the flag.

If there's a drawback to the Polar tip-up as a trophy pike rig. It's the spool's line capacity. You just can't get enough line on the small spool to handle a hard-charging pike.

Polar manufacturers remedied the situation, however, by offering a larger spool that can be easily installed on existing tip-ups. I recommend investing in the bigger spools.

Tip-Up Tips

The type of line that you use is very important. Some monofilament lines tend to coil when they're cold, keeping them from flowing freely when a fish makes its run.

Dacron line is popular among ice anglers, but I dislike it because it absorbs water. When you retrieve the line to land a fish or rebait the hook,

it freezes on the ice. The resulting tangles can boggle the mind.

I prefer to use a good-quality fly line. That's right, fly line, one that's equivalent to about 80-pound test mono. Fly line doesn't absorb water, flows freely from the spool and will not easily coil or tangle. It also offers a good grip when cold, wet fingers attempt to set the hook.

To the terminal end I tie a sturdy snap, followed by a wire leader. Wire leaders are essential for big, toothy pike that can shred monofilament line in seconds.

One other item you'll find useful is a common button. Threaded through two holes onto the fly line, it becomes an inexpensive but very effective depth marker.

Position the button right at the spool after you set your bait at the depth you intend to fish. When a pike strikes, it's a simple matter to reset the new bait at the exact same depth.

> *"I prefer using good-quality fly line with my tip-up. That's right, fly line."*

Another innovation in tip-up technology is the wind-powered, jigging tip-up. I like the Windlass tip-up from H.T. Enterprises. It consists of a plastic base, stand and rocker arm. The arm has a spool at one end and a metal blade at the other. When the Windlass model is rigged properly, the metal blade catches the wind, causing the arm to rock up and down. This motion, in turn, continually jigs the bait.

When pike feed aggressively, the jigged bait is often too tempting to resist. Since all the working parts remain above the ice, exposed to the elements, this is strictly a mild-weather tip-up, however.

One other modification that I like to make on tip-ups is to increase the size of the strike-indicating flag. The small flags provided can be difficult to see, especially if the sun is in your eyes. I also like to add a black flag alongside the red one. Sometimes because of the snow or cloud cover, black is more visible than red.

Quick-Set Rigs

European anglers were the first to recognize the

fish-catching abilities of a quick-set rig. They also discovered that these rigs cause less injury to the pike because you can set the hook before the fish swallows the bait—a valuable aspect, considering the importance of releasing trophy fish in good condition.

Quick-set rigs are simple in design. They consist of a wire leader and two treble or partridge hooks in sizes 6, 4 or 2, depending on bait size and the size of the pike you're after.

Partridge hooks have a smaller hook attached to the shank. The small hook is embedded in the bait, leaving the large hook exposed.

Whether you use partridge or treble hooks, attach one to the end of the leader while the other slides up or down the wire. The adjustable hook allows the angler to custom fit the hooks to the size of the bait. The beauty of a quick-set rig is that 99 percent of the fish you catch will be hooked in the mouth, because you can set the hook as soon as the fish strikes.

In the event that a pike is hooked deep, cut the wire as close to the hook as possible and release the fish with the hook intact.

Pike Hotspots

Pike basically prefer bays and submerged points, whether they're in lakes, reservoirs or rivers. Bays are true hotspots in most lakes because they offer weeds where baitfish like to hide and big pike like to hunt. Bays in reservoirs and rivers often hold submerged or drowned timber, also very attractive to baitfish.

Points tend to hold baitfish as well, but they also act as funnels, concentrating cruising pike into a small area near the end of the point.

When you've found a likely looking bay, use a calculated approach. Fish the back end of the bay, setting your tip-ups in openings between the weedbeds, or you can set up along the weedline. If you are fishing in submerged timber, place the tip-ups alongside the trees, or between groups of trees. Always pick spots that funnel cruising pike through narrow corridors of travel.

You may want to fish deeper waters in the bay itself. Pike often hold in 20 to 40 feet of water between feeding periods. Deep-water pike can be scattered, however, and less inclined to feed.

A general rule of thumb is to start fishing shallow at the early-ice stage, and move deeper as the season progresses.

There is one all-important key to success with

QUICK-SET RIG

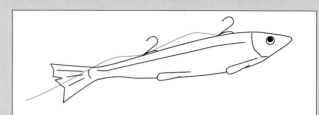

Place hooks near head and dorsal fin of baitfish (top) so that baitfish swims away from the rigging. This way you can set the hook immediately, hooking the pike in the mouth and greatly decreasing the chance of deeply hooking her (bottom).

this type of fishing—mobility. Ice anglers sometimes forget that it's critical to keep trying new spots until they've connected with fish. Often it's because they don't want to drill new holes.

The fact remains, however, that you wouldn't anchor your boat in one spot all day if you weren't catching fish. The same logic holds for ice fishing. In fact, there's no excuse for fishing a single hole these days. With today's power augers, portable depthfinders that read through the ice, and light-weight shelters, an ice fisherman can scout an entire bay in a very short time.

On the other hand, moving at random is nearly as worthless as staying put. Smart pike hunters follow a plan of attack when working a bay. I like the leapfrog method best. By leapfrogging, a group of anglers can efficiently search an entire bay.

Leapfrog Fishing

Say that you've chosen a big bay, for example, that's a mile or more across and filled with submerged timber. You want to fish the shallow back areas—spots where pike are likely to feed.

Start by drilling two rows of 10-inch holes in key locations at the edges of brush piles or between areas of standing timber along one side of the bay. Begin in shallow water near shore and continue drilling holes out into deeper water—down to 10 or 12 feet.

As you drill, your partners should follow behind,

setting the tip-ups. If an hour goes by without a strike, drill a new series of holes in front of the furthermost tip-ups, and "leapfrog" the rear ones into the new holes.

Every hour or so, leapfrog the rear tip-ups to new holes in front of the spread. Continue the pattern until you start catching fish, then move the other tip-ups to key spots near the hot hole.

When set up, the spread of tip-ups resembles a mine field waiting for a school of hungry pike to arrive. There have been many days while fishing in eastern South Dakota that four or five of us caught and released 100 pike while leapfrogging tip-ups.

Jigging For Pike

Jigging for pike can mean some exciting action. It's quite a thrill to have a short jigging rod almost ripped from your hand when a bruiser pike smashes the lure.

Many anglers jig in conjunction with fishing a tip-up. The combination works well; you can test new waters with the jigging rod while setting the tip-up in a prime spot.

Jigging equipment must be stout to handle pike. Even an 8- or 10-pounder can make a pretzel of the heaviest rods, and test the strength of any line.

Your reel should be a spinning or baitcasting type with a high-quality drag, and outfitted with 10- to 12-pound line. Again, don't forget the leader.

My jigging rig consists of a stiff rod with a Garcia 5500 baitcasting reel. I like the reel because its freespool feature allows the lure to drop quickly and smoothly, and the drag system won't fail, even in the coldest weather.

It's important to use a limp line when jigging. If it's stiff or coils badly during cold conditions, you simply cannot get the proper lure action or make a strong hookset.

Several high-quality wire leaders are on the market, but you can also make your own. All you need is a spool of uncoated leader wire, leader sleeves, leader sleeve pliers, a pair of scissors and some swivels. It only takes a couple of minutes to attach a lure using a leader sleeve. Best of all, you can make the leader as long as you want.

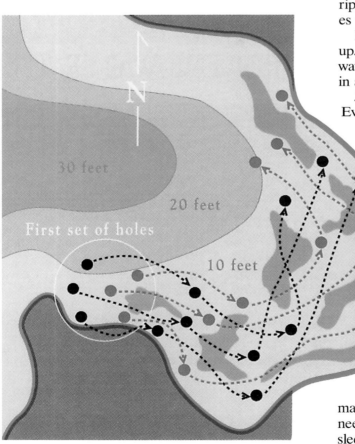

Leapfrogging allows you to methodically work an entire bay. In this example, six holes were drilled in the southwest corner, then leapfrogged through all potentially productive water.

Do Gas Augers Spook Fish?

I have always been curious about the effect that ice augers have on fish—so curious, in fact, that I conducted a series of tests on 10 inches of ice on a farm pond. Diver and videographer Merlyn Hilmoe swam to the bottom in eight feet of water. He was equipped with a Sony underwater video camera and measured the sounds produced when we punched holes in the ice with three commonly used tools: an ice chisel, a Jiffy hand auger and a Jiffy Model 30 gas-powered auger.

There was little, if any, difference between the noise levels produced by the hand and gas powered augers. Both were very quiet, making soft, whirring sounds that increased slightly when the blades finally penetrated the ice. The sound of the gasoline engine simply wasn't heard.

The power auger, however, cut the holes much more quickly, which means the noise was also of a shorter duration.

The ice chisel? It was much louder than the augers, but we didn't know about the worst part of it.

Hilmoe told us about it when he surfaced.

"That ice chisel is unbelievable," he said. "It's terribly noisy, and you can't believe the shock waves it sends through the water. I could feel them in every fiber of my body. I felt like a soldier in a bunker with bombs going off above me."

I recalled the many times I caught fish while a partner was drilling holes with a power auger. Perch, bluegills, largemouth bass and even those notoriously spooky walleye were among the fish that bit while my buddy cut away. Yet, until these tests, in spite of my actual fishing experience, I believed that power augers spooked fish.

Now I know better.

The next time that latecomer arrives and starts cutting holes, I won't worry—unless he's punching them with an ice chisel!

—*by Tony Dean*

Tony Dean's tests show that both hand and power augers hardly make a sound that can be heard underwater.

Kastmasters, Jigging Rapalas, Rocker Minnows, Walleye Hawgers or any type of flashy jigging lure will catch pike, but it often pays to tip the lure with a piece of meat. Sometimes a whole fathead minnow hooked through the lips works best, other times tipping the lure with just a minnow's head is more productive. Some days a simple perch eye on the hook is all it takes.

Pike usually hit the lure as it falls, or just as it stops its descent. Let the lure fall on a tight line, and be ready for action. Aggressive pike will slam the lure, but just as often all you'll feel is a slight "thump" and sometimes it will simply feel like extra weight.

The pike you catch while jigging will most likely be smaller than those that come on dead bait and tip-ups. Large female pike normally aren't aggressive enough to take a fast-moving jig.

Granted, ice fishing is synonymous with numb fingers, chilled toes and a wind-burned face. But there's nothing like seeing the head of a trophy northern pike fill a 10-inch hole in the ice. Give it a try and I promise that any negative thoughts you may have about winter fishing will quickly melt away.

chapter 8

Muskie

A true muskie hunter is a fanatic—
a loner who goes his own way, happy
in the focused pursuit of a single, formi-
dable, humbling and beautiful fish. As far
as personalities go, a muskie isn't that
much different—a real loner just minding
his own business, which is laying low and
engulfing some good meals when the
time is right. Fisherman and fish
come together only rarely,
and even then usually for
only a few fleeting
moments.

Muskies are worth
the time, and the effort.
Here's our best advice
on how to make those
waits between muskies a
little shorter.

Payback Time

by Spence Petros

*It happens just like clockwork. Every year just before the fall turnover,
big muskie and pike charge into the weeds on a heavy feeding binge.
Here's how to cash in on the action!*

Revenge can be sweet. It's like getting back at a bully or telling your boss what you really think. For instance, how would you like to get some payback for all the "beatings" you've taken on those deep, clear, so-called trophy pike and muskie lakes?

High-powered boats, water-skiers, limited daytime fish activity, deep fish, suspended fish—yes, these waters can be tough, but they can be conquered.

My philosophy has always been to stay on the peaks and avoid the valleys as much as possible. And one sure way to get stuck in a valley is to fish during the warm summer months using the pike and muskie tactics your grandfather taught your dad.

Oh sure, there are more modern techniques that can ease the pain. If you have enough confidence, or maybe it's determination, you can troll feature-less open water for suspended fish—and maybe even catch a few. A skilled motor troller could bump fast-moving, diving crankbaits over

deep structure to try to trigger strikes. Or, if you don't have a day job, nightfishing can pay off, particularly for muskies.

But there's an easier way to conquer these waters, and all you have to do is wait until the fish activity heats up and the competition for lake space from recreational boaters dies down.

The pre-fall peak period is when big pike and muskie leave their deep-water haunts to prowl the weedflats in search of an easy meal. They begin to fatten up for the winter, become less cautious and thus very available to knowledgeable anglers. Moreover, it's a time when fishermen have the water to themselves.

Matter Of Timing

"The weather seems just about right," I told my partner Mike Nielson, as we slowly motored away from the launch on one of my favorite pike lakes.

Though it holds sizable pike in good numbers, it's tough to fish during the summer because of its location. Planted midway between two sprawling metropolitan areas, it draws all manner of water sport enthusiasts— sailors, pleasure boaters, water-skiers and more.

On this day, however, the skies were dark, there was a healthy chop on the water, and a few days earlier a severe cold front had sent the water temperature plummeting—perfect conditions for this

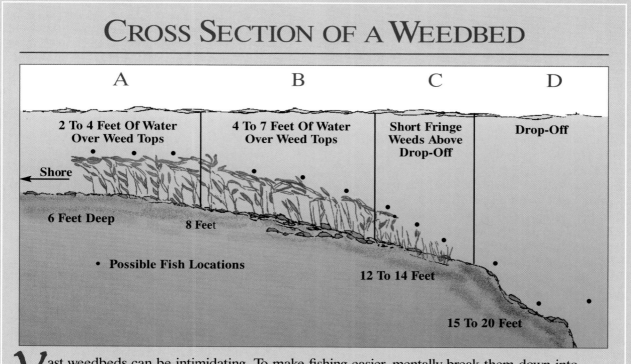

CROSS SECTION OF A WEEDBED

A — 2 To 4 Feet Of Water Over Weed Tops

B — 4 To 7 Feet Of Water Over Weed Tops

C — Short Fringe Weeds Above Drop-Off

D — Drop-Off

Shore

6 Feet Deep

8 Feet

• Possible Fish Locations

12 To 14 Feet

15 To 20 Feet

Vast weedbeds can be intimidating. To make fishing easier, mentally break them down into manageable sections.

Zone A, the shallow zone, has a depth of about six to eight feet, with two to four feet of open water over the weed tops. Pike and muskies in this zone will be active.

Normally, the greatest number of fish come from Zone B. It runs from about 8 to 14 feet deep, with 4 to 7 feet of water over the top. Use cranks, spinnerbaits or other lures that skim over the weed tops.

In Zone C, the deep weed edge and short fringe weeds, you'll catch pike and muskies on their way out of the main weedbed.

Zone D is the drop-off into deep water. It's not a major spot during the pre-fall bite, but you can troll up a few extra fish as they begin leaving the weedbed.

Big baits work best on autumn pike and muskie.

beds. Second, panfish such as perch and bluegills bunch up in and around the weedbeds.

As cold weather takes its toll on the weeds, they'll slump over more and more, eliminating a lot of existing cover and providing better feeding opportunities for pike and muskies.

Weed-oriented bluegills will cluster together, trying to hide behind each other, while yellow perch will move en masse into the weeds from deep-water positions.

Seeing schools of panfish in and around the weeds on your sonar screen is a major clue that the fall feeding frenzy is close at hand. The panfish can also help you zero in on specific areas in a sprawling weedbed where the predators are most likely to hold.

As a rule, September is the prime month throughout much of muskie and pike territory. But it doesn't happen at the same time everywhere. I've seen the peak start in late August in Canada. In Pennsylvania, northern Illinois and other areas on roughly the same latitude, it may occur as late as early October.

Deep Water, Big Beds

Anglers who cash in on this pre-fall activity usually target deep, clear lakes that have a population of suspended, open-water forage such as ciscoes, whitefish, tullibees, herring or shad. And when I say deep, I mean it. Maximum depths in these waters run anywhere from 50 to more than 100 feet.

"Have deep, clear lakes got you licked in the summer? Get revenge come fall."

late-September day.

Before heading to a massive weedbed along the southeast shore, I decided to check a couple of smaller beds located near deep water. Five to 10 casts in each area would tell me whether the pike had moved out of the depths.

If a pike of at least 4 or 5 pounds didn't come out of one of these "test" areas, our time would be more wisely spent chasing walleyes or bass on this 5,000-acre aquatic playground.

We quickly caught several medium-size pike, though, then motored to the sprawling weedbed.

A day and a half of fishing produced 33 pike up to 13 pounds, along with a few bonus bass that went to 4 pounds. Not bad for one of the toughest lakes to fish I've ever encountered. It was mostly a matter of timing.

The pre-fall peak occurs just before the turnover when the cool, heavy surface water sinks through and mixes with the warmer, deeper water.

It usually coincides with the second severe cold snap of the season—a time when nighttime temperatures plummet, and you just know that winter is on its way.

When this happens, two things begin to occur: mature weedbeds that grew near or to the surface get knocked down, creating open water above the

I like to concentrate my efforts around the biggest weedbeds that border deep water. They don't, however, have to be adjacent to the very deepest spot in the lake. Often a lake has more than one deep-water basin. In one area, the deepest available water may be 90 feet, while in another the maximum depth could be 60 feet. Yet, a third section of the lake may be only 35 feet deep.

But I wouldn't fish weedbeds in these deep, clear lakes during the pre-fall peak unless they were adjacent to a basin that's at least 40 to 50 feet deep. The vegetation near shallower maximum depths may be great during late spring or early summer, but the odds of getting into big fish at these locations later on are considerably less.

The worst fishing condition, when you're looking for pre-fall pike and muskies, is sunny, calm weather. Conversely, the best fishing takes place under heavy, dark skies, especially if there's a good chop on the surface.

This is one time of the year when a cold front with a harsh north/northwest wind can aid your efforts. As long as the skies stay cloudy, a brisk north wind and a drop in air temperature may actually turn the fish on.

When picking out weedbeds, concentrate on the ones that are being battered by the wind. You're far better off using the wind than trying to avoid it by fishing lee-side shorelines.

Zero In On Zones

Pure and simple, nothing beats trolling when it comes to catching big, pre-fall pike and muskies. You can cover a lot of weeds, which means less time between strikes.

If you live where trolling is illegal, then fire up your sonar unit and search for schools of panfish. Mark the spots and make long casts and fast retrieves.

There are four potential areas to probe for weed-related pike and muskies. The first is the shallow zone, waters in the six- to eight-foot range that have two to four feet of open water above them.

Big spinnerbaits, bucktails, glider-type jerkbaits with a lot of side-to-side movement, and shallow-running crankbaits are my favorite lures. Fish in this zone are generally very active. About 25 percent of the pre-fall pike and muskies I catch come from the shallow zone.

The second zone to consider is where the depth runs from about eight feet to the deep weed edge. The deep edge generally ends at about 12 to 14 feet, and approximately half the fish I catch come from this key area. It's usually where I start fishing.

I present lures a little deeper in this zone since the weeds often top out four to seven feet under the surface. Heavier spinnerbaits, jerkbaits and shallow-running crankbaits, fished with slightly more

Spence Petros' tactics for fishing deep, clear lakes will put you in the middle of the action.

letback when trolling, are also good choices in this depth range.

If fish are active in the 8- to 12-foot depths, check out the shallower zone, too. Those fish may be really hot. But if the action starts slowing down, probe the deeper weeds. They're often my "barometer" that helps me stay on the fish.

The deep weed edge, and short grass just outside the edge, provide a holding area for the fish after they quit cruising the vegetation. I've never caught pike or muskies in this zone before they moved shallower, but have followed them out to this area as they retreated toward deeper water. About 15 percent of my fish have come off the deep weed edge, mostly on trolled deep-diving crankbaits and weighted jerkbaits. I fish a little more slowly than I do over the weeds.

Big pike and muskie in deep, clear lakes go on a feeding tear in the early fall.

The final zone is the main drop-off into deep water. Pike and muskies will pause here when vacating the weeds and are susceptible to trolled cranks. It isn't a major spot, but you can count on picking up an extra fish or two. Generally, they make up about 10 percent of my total pre-fall catch.

Guide To Gear

Monster pike and muskies require tough tackle, rods rated for at least 14- to 17-pound test and running 6½ feet long or longer. Where trolling multiple lines is legal, the two outside rods should stretch to 8 or 9 feet to prevent the lines from tangling. In all cases, it's best that the rod has at least 10 inches of handle behind the reel seat for added leverage during the fight.

When it comes to reels, the most important

feature is a drag system that operates smoothly. The strength of these fish is incredible, and a sticky drag will just cause disappointment. They should hold at least 150 yards of line, and offer a retrieve rate of 4.3:1 to 5.1:1. I've been using the faster reels for two years and am very satisfied.

Low-stretch superlines, like Berkley's FireLine in 50-pound test, have added a new and improved dimension to pike and muskie fishing. Their strength and toughness put more of these big fish in the boat.

A tough wire leader is also mandatory when calling on these toothsome fish. You can find high-quality leaders in any tackle shop in pike country, but I've been making my own for some time and have yet to lose a fish because something broke.

When fishing crankbaits or spinners, I use 50- to 70-pound, single-strand wire; jerkbaits require 80-pound. I attach top-of-the-line ball-bearing snaps and swivels with a Haywire twist.

As for lures, a ½-ounce or heavier bass-size spinner-bait, bulked up with a pork or 5- to 6-inch plastic lizard is dynamite for pike in the shallow weeds. Beef up to a ¾- to 1-ounce spinnerbait such as a tandem-blade Lindy Big Fin for muskies. In-line spinners such as a size 700 Buchertail, Lindy Musky Roller, size 5 Mepps and others work well, too.

Shallow-running crankbaits such as the Shallow-Raider, Jake, size 9 Shallow Shadling, Red Fin and Bomber Long A are my favorites for skimming over the weed tops.

A wide variety of jerkbaits can be trolled or cast over the weeds and along the edge. For pike, go with 6- to 7-inch models, 8 to 9 inchers for muskies.

When trolling, point the rodtip at a 45-degree angle toward the stern, and pump the lure to add action. Don't end up with the rod pointing toward the bow or you won't get a good hookset.

Just about any high-quality crank that's 5 inches or longer and has a tight wiggle will work when fishing deeper water. The lure should tick the weed tops or run close to the bottom. Silver, pearl or shad patterns are the choices when the sun is shining. Fire-tiger, fluorescent orange or chartreuse are best under darker skies.

Yes, deep, clear lakes can be a nightmare to fish during the busy summer season. Put these tactics to use in the pre-fall peak period, however, and you'll know how good it feels to get even.

A Deadly 1-2 Punch For Fall Muskies

by Joe Bucher

The weather can be cold but these deadly systems have been hot as they have accounted for hundreds of muskies in the last few years!

The weather had finally broken! High winds, driving sleet and frigid temperatures had ruined four potential guide trips for me already. The muskies might have been biting, we just couldn't fish for them in those conditions. But the bad weather had finally subsided.

This morning we woke up to light winds and bluebird skies—somewhat rare conditions for mid-November in northern Wisconsin. We weren't about to miss being on the water today—muskies or not. It was a beautiful day.

Once on the water, the wind leveled off to a slight breeze barely pushing us on a slow drift. My sonar unit lit up with baitfish activity along the entire weedline. All systems were go.

I had set up on a drift covering the same deep weed edge and hard-bottom area that had been productive all fall. I was hoping today would be no different.

DO-IT-YOURSELF QUICK STRIKE RIG

The "Herbie Rig"—a great quick-strike setup—was developed by top muskie guide Steve Herbeck (Andy Myers Resort, Eagle Lake, Ontario). He hooks about 90% of all strikes and the fish are easy to release unharmed. Suckers are dragged behind the boat, free-lined or fished below a float. Use good hooks such as Mustad or VMC. Follow these steps to create your own quick-strike rigs.

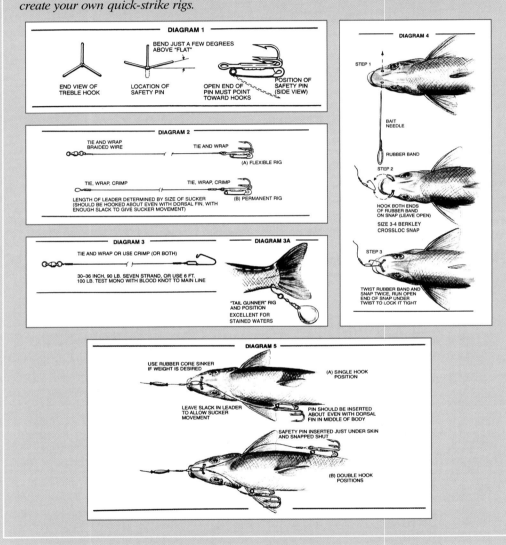

much bigger fish. After some quick photos, I released it.

Suddenly one of the live bait outfits sounded off. My partner quickly grabbed the rod, cranked up the slack and set the hook firmly.

This fish was definitely larger than the first. It stayed deep, making long, drag-burning runs in a seesaw battle that lasted more than 15 minutes. Eventually, my partner wore the lunker down and was able to boat it. The hefty 42-incher weighed 21 pounds.

We had five more strikes that day and were able to land two more muskies before the sun set that evening. Not bad, even for the muskie-rich waters of northern Wisconsin.

Odd as it may seem to some, muskie action like this occurs rather frequently in the fall if the right methods are employed. Practitioners of the old adage that muskies are "the fish of 10,000 casts" would have a hard time believing such a claim, but it is true if you master fall muskie tactics.

We set out three big, lively sucker minnows to drift behind the boat while we probed the weedline casting muskie jigs.

Astonishingly, a muskie pounded my jig as it fluttered toward the bottom on the third cast! A long, hard fight ensued. I was surprised by the size of the fish when it eventually surfaced at boatside. It was "only" a 35-inch male. This muskie fought like a

In my book there are two techniques that stand out, especially when the air and water temperatures fall below the 40-degree mark. They are: live bait, or sucker fishing; and jigging, something Midwestern muskie veterans commonly call "creature fishing." Combining both of these techniques into a 1-2 punch system has proved deadly not only for me, but also for other full-time muskie guides.

"Two techniques stand out when
the air and water temperatures fall
below the 40-degree mark: sucker
fishing and jigging."

Sucker Fishing

Sucker fishing for muskies is one of the oldest traditions in sportfishing. It was highly productive for lunkers in the early 1900s and takes as many big fish today. The secret, of course, is that suckers are the real thing. Suckers are a natural food for muskies in most, if not all, lakes, rivers and reservoirs. Muskies love these soft-finned, slow-moving meals.

Big muskies feed on big suckers. In fact, my biggest fish, a 44½-pounder, came on a 22-inch sucker! That's about 3 pounds of meat! And I've taken smaller muskies on even larger baits!

Any size sucker can catch a muskie. Smaller bait has taken some big fish but your odds for a lunker 'lunge definitely improve when you select larger specimens. Most top fall trophy hunters agree that no sucker is too large. When you consider that one of the largest walleyes I caught last year, a 30-incher, had 8-inch bite marks on its side, obviously made by a huge muskie, no bait is too big.

"Quick strike rigs feature treble hooks
anchored throughout the sucker's body,
which allow for an immediate hookset."

Suckers can be rigged in a variety of ways. Some anglers prefer to rig them on a large, single hook attached to a 3- to 4-foot wire leader. The big, single hook is most effective when anchored through the sucker's upper lip. When a muskie strikes this setup, ample time must be given to let the fish swallow its prize. The long wire leader prevents a bite-off after the bait is consumed.

How much time is needed before setting the hook is an arguable point. Anglers who favor the single-hook rig have done everything from waiting a specific length of time, usually 15 to 45 minutes, to smoking a cigarette or two.

By watching the line closely and staying near the fish, it's usually pretty easy to know when to bust 'em. Commonly, when the fish rises toward the surface and takes off on a dead run, it's hookset time! This may take anywhere from a few minutes to an hour.

In recent years, many anglers have switched to various "quick strike" rigs. These rigs feature treble hooks anchored throughout the sucker's body, which allow for an immediate hookset. This makes it easier to release muskies unharmed because the fish is hooked in the lip, not in the throat. It may also allow you to hook an extra fish or two during a short feeding period.

Our company, Bucher Tackle, has developed two "Quick Strike" rigs. The standard rig features 2 1/0 trebles and a 10/0 sneck (goes in the sucker's head) hook. The magnum model sports 3/0 trebles and a 12/0 sneck hook. Several other companies make excellent quick strike rigs.

Large capacity baitcasting reels outfitted with a free spool and live bait clicker are used when fishing live suckers. These reels are put in the free-spool mode with the clicker on. When a muskie strikes, the line pulls freely off the reel, and the loud clicking lets the angler know something is happening. I generally spool up my reels with heavy test mono (30- to 50-pound) such as Stren's High Impact or Magna Thin. Some anglers are also having excellent success with the new "superlines" in the 50- to 80-pound-test range.

Suckers are usually best fished deeper in the fall over hard-bottom areas and along weed edges and holes. Suckers are not particularly hardy so a very slow drift-like presentation is required. Otherwise, these rather sensitive, lively minnows die rendering them ineffective as muskie attractors.

Most of the highly regarded late-fall muskie guides work one very small area with their sucker presentations in the cold-water period. They know that muskies are in the area and simply wait them out.

Muskie Jiggin'

Many huge muskies are taken each year "accidentally" by anglers fishing jigs for walleyes or bass. Some years the number of outsized lunkers caught

on jigs far outnumber those caught by all other methods. Plainly put, the jig is an excellent muskie weapon. It not only takes numbers of muskies but also big fish.

Recently, a jig fishing fraternity has evolved. Perhaps the best-known members of the group hail from Rockford, Illinois. The "Rockford boys," as they are called throughout the Midwest, have refined a method of jigging for muskies that has grown immensely popular. It's locally referred to as "creature fishing," because most of these jig fanatics originally made their own large plastic-bodied "creatures" to fit on various jigs.

> *"What is a muskie jig? Basically it's an oversized bass jig."*

During the last decade, many excellent larger-size, soft-plastic lures have been developed that work on the ¾- to 1-ounce jig heads that are generally used. The original flap-tailed Reaper is still a favorite, along with 7- to 9-inch lizards, action-tail minnows such as the Sassy Shad, even giant tubes. Your choices are many, but you'll develop favorites with success.

The more popular outfits for muskie jigging are 6½- to 7-foot spinning rods and 7- to 7½-foot bait-casting rods. Stiff enough spinning rods are a little tough to find and you might want to look at one designed by my good friend Spence Petros for South Bend. Flipping stick actions are great on baitcasting gear. Use 14- to 20-pound-test low stretch mono such as Stren Sensor, or the non-stretch superlines (FireLine, Spider Wire, etc.) in the 20- to 30-pound-test range.

One Milwaukee company, Jack's Jigs, has developed an entire line of muskie jigs and plastic creatures to boot.

The best color choice for jigs might vary somewhat among veteran jig fishermen, but most prefer black in warmer waters and silver when the water temperature is less than 43 degrees. The reason is not clear, but it might have something to do with the muskies' forage preference at that time. Ciscoes,

silvery cold-water baitfish, come into the shallows to spawn right before ice-up, and there's probably a connection between the two.

So what is a muskie jig? Well, basically it's an over-sized bass jig. The primary modification is hook size. A good muskie jig needs a big, thin, tempered bronze wire hook. The thinner wire hook allows easy hook penetration when setting with light tackle, a prerequisite for muskie jigging. Jigs do not perform well on standard heavy-duty muskie rod-and-reel outfits.

A very light-gauge wire leader, 18- to 38-pound-test, bronze-coated 7-strand or something comparable, should be attached directly to the jig to prevent bite-offs. Muskies commonly engulf the entire jig, and their sharp teeth will cut an unprotected line.

Leaders shouldn't be too short. Most pros prefer a longer leader, 18 inches or more, so they can cut and retie it after a fish is caught.

Most important, however, is that the wire leader is attached directly to the jig. This means no snaps. A bulky muskie snap hanging off the front end of a jig ruins the action and appeal. Of course, this also means that you'll have to make your own jig leader. Pick up a 30-foot roll of 7-strand wire and a few wire-making components at a local sporting goods dealer or through a mail-order catalog. Making homemade wire leaders is very simple.

Muskie jigging is fairly basic, but it does require some finesse and concentration. Cast the jig, engage the reel and watch the line as the jig sinks. When the line suddenly bows slack, the jig has hit bottom. Point the rodtip toward the jig and quickly swim it off the bottom with three to five quick turns of the reel. Then let it drop back to the bottom. A strike will nearly always occur as the jig is dropping back. Be alert. Muskies don't usually hit a jig much harder than a bass or pike. If you feel a peck, set the hook immediately!

There are occasions when muskies will follow a jig up to the boat. You can convert many of the follows into strikes by circling the jig at boatside.

So there you have it! If you're looking for a big muskie this fall, try the 1-2 punch. It's worked well for me and a score of other muskie guides. There's no doubt it will work for you, too!

Muskies Out In The Open

by Joe Bucher

Savvy muskie anglers now know these brutes commonly suspend.
Here's how to fish and catch them!

The insistent beeping of my sonar's fish alarm urged me to quickly finish rigging my clients' rods and get on with business. The unit was noisily reacting to the heavy clouds of baitfish that hung from 12 to 22 feet below the boat. Almost everything seemed perfect for trolling for big muskies on this dark, overcast summer day. Everything, that is, except the sound of distant thunder and a few rain drops that dimpled the otherwise calm waters. I began to wonder whether our trip would be cut short.

I was determined to make the most of whatever time we had to fish, so upon placing the sixth rod in its holder, we began to troll in earnest.

A sudden shift in the wind from east to north made me subconsciously turn the boat into the waves, while the rain started to come down hard. A frantic scramble for rain gear, coupled with the wind and wave noise, let the tug-of-war taking place between the outside "board rod" and a 41-inch muskie go almost unnoticed. The reel's screaming drag finally captured our attention.

With his rain gear bibs only half assembled, one of my fishermen wrestled the straining rod from the holder and leaned into the battling brute. With the boat moving slowly into the wind, the other angler and I watched the war intently, eager to lend a hand where needed.

Suddenly, a second rod bowed heavily in its holder, telegraphing the impact of another violent muskie hit. This time a lure on a "deep-set" line was the target. In no time, this deep striker became a high-powered missile launching itself completely out of the water!

Now, general consensus claims getting one muskie to strike in a single day is an accomplishment, yet we now had a double going. This in itself was surely

MUSKIE FORAGE

Smelt

Cisco

Shiner

Perch

Wnen forage fish like smelt, ciscoes and minnows suspend in open water, hungry muskies
will be nearby. Likewise, when gamefish such as
walleyes or crappies suspend. Yellow perch and other
weed-oriented species normally don't draw muskies
into the open.

a great accomplishment, but considering that it happened again later the same day meant we were
doing something really special.

It took more than 15 minutes to boat and release
that pair of muskies, and at least that long on the
second double. When the storm finally forced us off
the lake we had boated and released seven muskies
from 33 to 44 inches long.

This kind of score card is impressive in most
muskie circles, but in truth, it's the kind of day I
almost expect when trolling for suspended muskies.

A Pack Of Wolves

Until recently, anglers — and biologists —believed
that muskies were not school oriented, but loners which,
once in a chosen spot, chased other predators away.

While it's true that a muskie in shallower water
will occasionally hold on a particular spot for several
days, it is unlikely that it is guarding anything or
chasing other muskies away. In reality, this seemingly
territorial behavior is nothing more than a dominant
fish holding in a given area containing food. When
the food is gone, so is the dominant muskie.

Usually several muskies will hang out near a
dominant fish in a loosely formed group-what I like
to call a "wolf pack."

*"When the storm finally forced us off the
lake, we had boated and released seven
muskies from 33 to 44 inches long."*

This relationship is important to understand, since
it answers lots of questions about muskie behavior no
matter what the situation. I have found that, unless
there are very low populations of muskies in a body
of water, communal wolf packs are common.

Mid-Water Muskies

Muskies suspend in open water a great deal more
than most anglers realize. What's more, they do it in
all types of lakes and reservoirs.

Several years ago, an increasing number of "accidental" muskie catches by anglers trolling mid-lake
water for other species, along with telemetry studies
by fisheries biologists, confirmed this phenomenon.
Still, a lot of muskie anglers continue to thrash
shallow waters, even when they're not enjoying any
action. They never even consider trying to fish open
water where "no self-respecting muskie would dare
to venture."

The fact is, muskies do suspend in open water, and
for a very good reason—to be near their forage.
Muskies in any body of water, shallow or deep, that
contains any type of minnow, panfish or small gamefish that suspends over open water, can, and usually

will, suspend right alongside them. Whether they're ciscoes, whitefish, shad, walleyes, crappies or any other forage species, muskies will be holding nearby.

Look for small, deep-water holes in shallow lakes. Always key on baitfish presence first. On large, open-water lakes, a necked down area of deep water can be hot. So can a deep flat with a series of humps on it. When fishing on lakes with excessively deep water, key on areas frequented by trout species. In natural lakes, anytime you locate a group of suspended crappies in the summer or fall, it's a potential muskie gold mine.

Again, remember the wolf-pack behavior. Scoring on a single muskie is likely just the tip of the iceberg. Continued trolling passes could result in several more fish.

Finding Suspended Muskies

The biggest problem with suspended muskies is finding them. Since you have no visible clues like weedbeds, fallen trees or large rocks to guide you, you must rely on covering as much water as quickly as possible. This doesn't, however, mean you should troll haphazardly around the lake.

As I've said, muskies don't aimlessly suspend in open water. They are there for a reason—to eat. The troller's job is to locate forage fish. Look for any sign of suspended fish (gamefish and baitfish) on your sonar screen. They could be ciscoes, whitefish or

---

"Muskies are likely to suspend in any body of water."

---

lake trout holding over a 75-foot basin, or crappies holding over a 15-foot flat. The bottom line is that muskies are likely to suspend in any body of water.

They're also just as likely to suspend at any time of the year. While it's true that more muskies suspend during the heat of the summer when the thermocline is distinct and boat traffic is at its peak, muskies in many waters head for open water during the spring and fall.

One February evening a while ago, Tom Gelb, a muskie fishing friend and I were discussing where early-season muskies could be found in deep, clear, featureless lakes. Since these types of lakes have

little of either classic shallow-water structure or new weedbeds for the fish to relate to, we theorized that they must be suspending.

Tom tested the theory the following May and caught and released an incredible 21 muskies during his first four trips. The biggest was a 47 incher. All of them had been suspended from 12 to 22 feet down over a 40-foot basin.

Likewise, I've caught many big muskies during the fall while trolling open water. In years past, I ran a two-day trophy muskie fishing school in October in Wisconsin. During one of our last sessions, the weather (wind, rain and snow) made fishing very tough. All the muskies caught the first day and a half came on big sucker minnows slow-trolled along deep breaklines.

I decided to be the guinea pig and started trolling a 30-foot basin that contained scattered schools of suspended crappies and walleyes. It took several hours, but one of my three rods finally doubled over as a muskie hit the crankbait that had been running about 18 feet down. After a 20-minute battle, I eventually boated and released a 51½-inch giant. Better still, several anglers attending the program also caught trophy muskies before the weekend was over.

High-Tech Trolling

When trolling, the idea is to cover as much water as possible. This is best done by running a selection of crankbaits at various depths and using planer boards to spread them out away from the boat.

DepthRaiders, Cisco Kids, Magnum Rapalas, Hookers, Believers, Bagley Bang-O-Bs and Jakes are all good crankbait choice. I prefer perch-type patterns in warmer months and cisco/shad patterns during the fall or whenever the water is very clear.

Running them off planer boards on both sides of the boat can increase a typical trolling swath from 10 to 100 feet or more *(see illustration)*. This concept alone really increases the angler's chances of scoring on suspended fish.

There are two basic planer board styles, the ski-type and in-line planers. Ski-type planers are much larger than the latter and are anchored by a stout cord to a central mast in the boat. A number of fishing lines can be attached to this cord at various positions. They break free of the cord after a strike. Ski-type planers require a big-water trolling boat, and therefore, are most commonly used by salmon

and trout trollers on the Great Lakes.

In-line planers, on the other hand, can be used by anyone in any size rig. In-lines attach directly to the fishing line much like a snap-on bobber. Most can be rigged in a variety of ways, but ardent muskie trollers have their preferred method. Among the most popular in-line planer boards are the Yellow Bird, SideLiner, Rover and OffShore. While many salmon trollers like to rig them to break away from the line on the strike, muskie anglers prefer to tighten them down so there is little loss in hooksetting power. On the downside, the board must be removed from the line while battling the fish.

Trolling rods and reels must be as tough as the quarry. Longer, tough bait-casting rods in the 7½- to 9-foot range are ideal, as they offer plenty of leverage to quickly tire out a big fish. Expensive graphics are unnecessary. Rods can be composites or fiberglass. "Dipsy Diver" style rods are ideal. Reels should have smooth drags and plenty of line capacity, enough to hold at least 150 yards of 30- to 50-pound-test mono.

As for trolling speed, during the warm months almost any speed will work. Most of my muskies caught on DepthRaiders, however, come when lure speed is no more than 5 mph. Once the water really gets cold, below 45 degrees, the slowest possible trolling speed when the lure still has a good wiggle is usually the way to go, but not always. It is surprising how these fish will continue to bust a fast-moving plug, even in very cold water.

Trolling Variables

Line diameter, lead weights and letback (the amount of line let out) can all greatly affect how deep a lure runs. Basically, the more letback, the deeper a lure will dive (within boundaries); thinner diameter lines also increase running depths; and adding sinkers to your line also adds diving capability to your lures.

While some fishermen aren't overly concerned about how deep their lures dive, more fish are

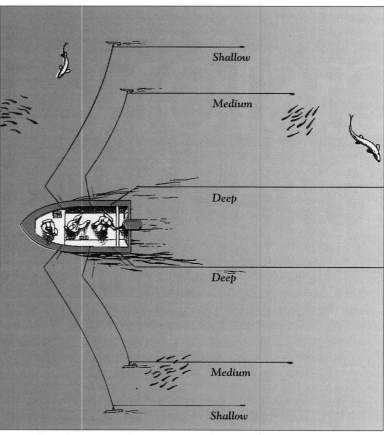

Planer boards increase the area covered on each trolling pass, increasing your odds of presenting the lures to suspended fish. Lead-core line and lead sinkers (for precise depth control) and a good selection of crankbaits are all part of the author's high-tech trolling method. Begin with lures that run at various depths, and when a pattern emerges, change your set accordingly.

caught by anglers who know precisely where their lures are running. It pays to know the variables. Take the time to develop a depth chart of your

> *"Take the time to develop a depth chart of your favorite lures and laminate it for in-boat use."*

favorite lures and laminate it for in-boat use. It will become an invaluable tool.

In recent years, line counter reels have become

very popular when trolling. They tell you exactly how much line you have out, and when a strike occurs, you can quickly return to the exact same depth. Excellent line counter reels are made by companies such as South Bend, Daiwa, Penn and Marado.

Downriggers are another way to get crankbaits deep, and a small handful of trollers use them successfully. While this seems like a foolproof technique, downriggers have many drawbacks for inland lake trolling. For one, they are good only on deep, open flats with a consistent bottom. Areas with a lot of humps, bars and ridges make trolling downriggers difficult since the heavy cannonball is likely to get hung up.

When using downriggers, you also lose some rod tip sensitivity, making it more difficult to tell if your lure is running weed free. This, of course, is also a drawback to the planer board. A flatline (no planers or weights of any kind), on the other hand, shows a distinct rod tip vibration transmitted directly from the lure.

Many deep-water muskie trollers have turned to lead-core or wire line for additional depth control. Both lead-core and wire line double the attainable depths achieved with mono of similar test weight.

Attaching 2 to 3 ounces of lead 24 to 36 inches above the lure on a lead-core or wire line system, really adds depth to the presentation. This combina-tion is perfect for deep-set lures with a short letback.

Combining both planer boards and lead-core or wire line into one trolling system is the ideal way to maximize the potential of any trolling run. The board rigs can then be utilized to cover shallow to mid-depth ranges, while the wire/lead-core lines probe the deepest depths.

The number of lines that can be legally fished by one person varies from state to state and Canada. Make sure you check this out beforehand. In areas where I do most of my trolling, three lines per person are allowed. This provides a great deal of room for experimenting. Many states and provinces, however, limit the angler to a single line, making experimentation with depth and lure size, action, shape and color more difficult.

Last Words

High-tech trolling for suspended muskies is a specialized tactic that surely has its place and time. It works on nearly all muskie waters under the right circumstances. If you become frustrated with a lag of productivity from casting to the same old weed-bed, or if you would just like to try something that's completely different, start trolling open water. Once you connect, you'll know that the shallows aren't the only place big muskies call home.

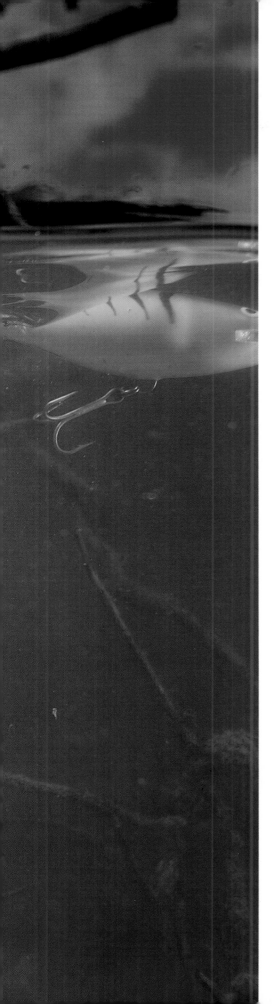

Chapter 9

Striped Bass

*A*long our coasts and across America's middle and southern tiers of states, stripers draw anglers to big rivers and freshwater reservoirs. Few fishing moments are as exciting as feeling a freight train clobber your bait and then take off down the underwater tracks at full throttle…and then you get to do it all again if you've located a good school of stripers.

To find and catch these saltwater transplants consistently, it takes some real strategy and then considerable muscle. We provide the strategy here … you add the muscle. And rest up your arms before you go.

In Search Of Trophy Hybrids

by Randy Vance

*Hybrid stripers are one of the hot fish on the angling scene.
Once you engage one in combat, you'll be a fan for life.*

*W*hile guiding anglers on Lake of the Ozarks in Missouri, I must keep my hands free to tend to my clients. That's usually not a problem; I simply wedge my spinning rod between the seat and the six-gallon fuel tank in the back of the boat. When a white bass or other fish strikes, the rod bends over the back of the seat and I take care of it when I can. The ¾- to 2½-pound white bass we generally target aren't strong enough to do much, if any, damage.

Recently, something happened that forced me to rethink my method. The fishing had been good, and wanting to make sure my clients wouldn't surpass their limit, I looked in the livewell and started counting fish. Moments later, I heard the fuel tank shift. I turned around just in time to see my new rod flying out of the boat. Whatever was dragging it was moving so fast that the rod skipped on the surface for a while before sinking from view.

I sat there dumbfounded, trying to figure out what stole my rod.

Later that day, I called a few of the other guides around the lake and discovered that at least a dozen hybrid stripers had been caught that morning. Most of them weighed 6 to 8 pounds, but one 15-pound brute was reported. I believed the story. I had to. It was just such a fish that levered the heavy fuel tank off the floor and stole my rod.

What Is A Hybrid Striper?

What is this fish called hybrid by most anglers, and striper by those who don't know any better? That's a good question, and if you're not catching them, it's one you likely have the time and energy to ask.

The truth is, fisheries biologists aren't always sure

what a hybrid is either. They know where the fish comes from, and how to hatch and rear it for stocking. But catch one in the wild and even they may have to take it to a geneticist for positive I.D.

Striped bass are the biggest lugs of the sea bass family. They roam in fresh and saltwater pretty much nationwide. Coastal anglers, east and west, make a religion of fishing them in their local waters. Stripers live long and grow big.

Then there is the white bass, a freshwater panfish that grows into table fare in about two years—one year if you aren't too choosy. At three years, they can weigh 2 or 3 pounds. Natural mortality usually takes them to the happy hunting grounds at five years.

Telling a striper from white bass isn't too difficult. Stripers are longer and more torpedo shaped. White bass have a flatter, deeper profile.

Both fish can be raised in hatcheries, but white bass are more resilient as fry and don't mind the handling as much. Stripers, both wild and hatchery varieties, don't grow as fast, but live much longer and reach weights exceeding 75 pounds in saltwater and more than 50 pounds in fresh.

It was only a matter of time before some enterprising biologist tried to combine the striper's size potential with the rapid growth and resilience of the white bass. The result is—hybrids!

There's nothing new about hybrids. Whites and stripers run together at times, and hybrids are sometimes the product of natural reproduction.

"Hybrids grow fast, are challenging to catch and fight hard. Better still, they are plentiful."

What is new in the '90s is that 20-pound-plus hybrids are regularly showing up around the country, and more anglers are targeting them specifically. So much so, in fact, that hybrid hysteria is a growing phenomenon. And why not. These fish grow fast, are challenging to catch and fight hard. Better still, they are plentiful enough that it's a good bet you can catch big hybrids within a few hours of your home.

Stocking programs were initiated in Southern lakes and impoundments in the early '80s. Virtually every state south of the Mason Dixon line has waters with a

Hybrids are the result of mating striped bass with fast-growing white bass. The result is a hard-fighting fish that quickly reaches trophy size.

fishable population of hybrids. The surprise to many anglers, however, is that hybrids are not just Southern fish. Illinois, for example, has been stocking hybrids long enough in more than a dozen popular angling lakes on which 15- and 16-pound fish are caught on a frequent basis.

In most waters where they exist, catching a 15-pound hybrid is within reasonable expectations. Six pounders are common and a stringer of 15 white bass probably holds a number of small hybrids that the angler takes for whites. These look-alike fish have been a problem for many state fish and game agencies. How do you manage a fish species that no one can differentiate from its parent species?

When hybrids are large, distinguishing them from stripers is not difficult. Normally, they have a deeper, broader body, like that of a white bass. And no one will mistake a 10-pound hybrid for a white bass. White's just don't get that large.

A 5- or 6-pound fish is another story. More than one excited angler has thought he's caught a record

Hybrid stripers (fish on right) don't grow as large as striped bass (left), but they grow fast. Hybrids in the 20-pound class are available in waters across the country.

white bass when he's actually got a modest hybrid.

Missouri officials attacked that problem in a unique manner by lumping all three species of bass together. Anglers are allowed to keep 15 fish per day. Only four, however, can exceed 18 inches in length. Blue Springs and Montrose lakes, where there are no white bass, are the exceptions. The daily bag limit is four fish that are 20 or more inches long.

The plan eliminated the problem of species identification. It also eliminated an enforcement problem and kept greedy anglers from excessively harvesting the larger, more valuable hybrids.

Hybrids have been popular among anglers and biologists largely because they thrive without competing with other species. They roam the broad, open stretches of lakes and rivers, leaving the snags, deadfalls and shore-lines to large- and smallmouth bass, and crappies. Bottom-hugging walleyes don't suffer from their encroachment either.

In Illinois, Alabama, Georgia, Missouri, Texas, South Carolina and everywhere else these inland sea bass swim, there is one common link—shad. If gizzard shad exist in a body of water, then so can hybrids.

To Catch A Hybrid

Like most species, stripers and white bass spawn in the spring. Hybrid stripers follow this instinct, too, even though they are normally sterile.

They move upstream to gravel bars just as their fullblood cousins do.

Dams are a barrier to this migration, and while that may be frustrating to the fish, it's great for anglers.

Tailwater fishing is perhaps the most exciting way to pursue hybrids because they become concentrated

in these waters. Much of the action occurs on the surface. If the fish go deep, crankbaits, spoons and jigs will fool them. The action can be hot and continuous for anglers who are flexible—and prepared.

The ability to make long casts is essential when fishing topwater. Hybrids may only surface briefly and most likely will do so at the extreme edge of your casting range.

Spinning reels with wide, tapered spools are helpful in reaching distant fish, but some anglers prefer baitcasters and heavy-action rods which give them more confidence in handling bigger fish. If you choose a baitcasting rig, be sure to keep the reel clean and well oiled to maximize casting distance.

Lures should be heavy and compact, for long-distance casts. Near Nuthin's by Cordell are excellent for surface fishing. Heave it toward the breaking school and retrieve it on the surface with a rapid, irregular rhythm. Jigging spoons like the Hopkins or Bomber Slab Spoon are also excellent if fished with high-speed reels to keep them near the top.

Another popular topwater rig is a jig-and-chugger plug combination. A Big Pop-R or Hula Popper with a jig trailed about 18 inches from the tail hook is deadly. Cast this rig and bring it back with a pop-rest-pop-rest retrieve. Two or more anglers doing this together can often draw fish up to the surface.

Nearly all your strikes will come on the trailing jig, but if a fish takes the plug, a second is apt to hit the jig.

When the surface action subsides, use a jig or spoon and bring it back with a pump-reel retrieve.

Hybrids are true schooling fish. Though bass and crappies are found in large schools, it's often because they are simply sharing space near structure. Hybrids and their parent species, however, travel in tight schools because they feed more efficiently in that manner.

Like packs of wolves, hybrids will pounce on a school of shad, slashing, snapping and devouring everything in their path. After scattering the baitfish, they swim below the carnage, capturing injured and disoriented shad as they settle to the bottom.

An attack like this may last only moments. Often, by the time you can start the outboard and charge to the school, the action is over and the fish are on the hunt again.

For that reason, the ideal craft is light and capable of getting on plane quickly. The ideal engine is one that idles smoothly and quietly while you wait out the fish. Big outboards won't take that kind of operation for long. Midsize engines in the 45- to 90-horsepower

range are the ticket.

When the spawning run is over, usually in late April, hybrids turn downstream and focus on eating full time. Young shad fry begin to appear in May and the hybrids home in on them.

My favorite lures at this time are Rooster Tail and Shyster spinners, jigging spoons, blade baits like the Gay Blade and curlytail grubs. Most anglers use ¼-ounce lures and medium-weight spinning tackle. This is open-water fishing so there is plenty of room to fight feisty hybrids. Light line in the 6- to 8-pound category works fine.

I like to keep things simple and usually opt for plastic grubs. The 3-inch version on a ¼-ounce leadhead is my favorite. However, when the shad are very small,

---

"Hybrids will pounce on a school of shad, slashing, snapping and devouring everything in their path."

I use a 2-inch grub on an ⅛-ounce jig head. If more casting distance is needed, switch to an ⅛-ounce jig.

Cast the jigs or spinners and retrieve them at a steady rate. Trolling a flatline is also very effective. Keep the lure relatively close to the boat. I usually let the lure out just past the prop wash, which is about 50 feet behind the boat.

Finding Hybrids

The easiest way to find fish is to ask anglers or tackle shop owners. Hybrids may work an area for days, even weeks at a time. On Lake of the Ozarks, where I generally fish, the surface bite doesn't last much past 8 or 9 a.m. Its length depends on sunlight intensity.

On clear days, it normally ends abruptly about an hour after it begins. When it's overcast, the action lasts an hour, sometimes two, longer.

When it's over, I fish main lake flats and points where they drop into the primary river channel. White bass, hybrids and stripers tend to work these areas later in the morning, perhaps returning to pick up shad that were injured during an earlier attack.

This is when trolling is the best method. Downriggers are excellent for catching hybrids on large, open

impoundments, when they are holding around submerged trees or drop-offs. The risk of losing expensive gear, however, can outweigh the pleasure of catching fish.

One inexpensive way to "downrig" lures for hybrids is to attach jigs to deep-diving crankbaits. It takes a true-running crankbait to maké this rig perform.

Effective deep-trolling crankbaits are Storm's Deep ThunderStick, Luhr-Jensen's Hot Lips, Poe's 400 Series, Magnum Hellbender, Bomber Model-A (9A) and B25 Long A. Others will work if they dive deep, wiggle hard and track well at faster speeds.

Troll the rig along points, sweeping turns in the river channel and the edges of flats. During the summer, when the water is warmer and the days are brighter, trolling is the best way, very often the only way, to catch hybrids.

A hot trolling tactic for hybrids in the heat of summer is a troll that jams big-lipped divers into the sides of sunken humps and points at fast speeds. The lures bash and bump bottom, bouncing wildly up one side of the structure, across its top, and down the other side. Needless to say, strikes are jarring. This is often the best tactic for triggering strikes when the water temperatures are at or near their summer peaks.

As autumn approaches, hybrids begin to feed on the surface again. This activity tends to center on points and drop-offs. Action is best under low-light conditions.

Wind direction is a big factor in locating hybrids anytime, but it becomes particularly important during the fall. Shad go wherever surface currents take them, so if the wind blows heavily from the west, it's a cinch you'll find them along the eastern shore.

Ripping Rat-L-Traps and other rattle baits is a great way to catch hybrids along wind-blown banks. A fast retrieve entices strikes and enables you to cover a lot of water.

One final word of advice—hang on to your rod! I learned my lesson. By the way, if you catch one pulling a graphite rod and Shimano reel, would you give me a call?

The Ultimate Fishing Book: Strategies for Success

Hybrids On Top

by Don Wirth

Certain conditions trigger surface feeding frenzies from these explosive predators. Here's what to look for, and how to take advantage of the action.

One moment there was serene smoothness on the lake's surface, the next a shower of shad erupted like sparks from a welding rod. Hundreds of hungry hybrids rose from the depths and began blasting baitfish on top, churning the water into foam. Gulls sensed the carnage and dove into the melee to snatch wounded shad. The school of bait regrouped and fled directly under my boat.

It was the moment I'd been waiting for since daybreak, and yet I never made a single cast. All I could do was watch and marvel at this awesome display of predatory savagery.

The hybrid (a.k.a. wiper, whiterock or sunshine bass) is much like a pit bull terrier. It's been bred to be a killer. Picture the look on the face of the first biologist who successfully crossed a white bass with a landlocked striper. Like Dr. Frankenstein, chances are he realized he'd created a monster.

Hybrids have been called the fish of the future for good reason. They've become the darling of many state fisheries agencies because of their fast growth rates and ability to adapt to a wide array of conditions. In fact, most states east of the Rocky Mountains include hybrids in their record books.

Fishermen like them because their savage nature makes them

suckers for both live bait and artificial lure presentations. And whether you're a fan of this critter or not, few would deny that nothing in the world of freshwater fishing can outfight a big hybrid.

Heck, if hybrids grew as large as muskies, you'd have to nail your shoes to the boat deck to keep 'em from jerking you overboard.

Pack Attack

Of all the ways you can latch onto a hybrid, nothing compares to topwater fishing. If you've seen either white bass or stripers feeding on the surface, you'll begin to get some idea of the rush of excitement a hybrid surface bite can provide.

I'd rank hybrids as major league surface feeders in both spring and fall. Like both white bass and stripers, hybrids travel in large packs, hunting down roaming schools of baitfish.

They'll locate a school of shad, alewives, blueback herring or whatever the prevailing forage species happens to be, swim beneath it, then gradually push it toward the surface. At that terrible and wonderful moment when the baitfish realize there's no place left to go but out of the water, hybrids swipe and pop and boil and swirl in what is truly a feeding frenzy.

Fishing hybrids is a recent phenomenon. These fish are the new kids in town, and knowledge of their seasonal movements has not yet penetrated the psyche of the angling public.

Everybody knows that largemouth bass move shallow in the spring, but relatively few anglers have a clue where hybrids hang out at any given time of year.

Because hybrids relate more to baitfish than structure, they seem elusive, even evasive. Anglers who are used to chunking lures against the shoreline will have an especially difficult time figuring out the nomadic tendencies of this fish.

For now, trust me. I've fished with some of the best hybrid guides in the nation, guys who virtually live on the water and monitor daily the movements of this exciting fish. Together, we'll put you on one of the most fantastic topwater bites you'll ever experience!

Spring Topwater Patterns

As the water temperature approaches 60°F in the spring, you'll find scattered groups of hybrids off main-lake points, in deep coves with a channel access and on flats with a mud bottom. This is the time when bass fishermen most often connect with a hybrid or two while casting crankbaits or grubs.

In the highland reservoirs (those created in steeper terrain) where I have done a lot of hybrid fishing, this pre-topwater period typically falls in mid-April. Battling a 12-pound hybrid on a light spinning rod is an experience you'll long remember.

But a dramatic shift occurs when the surface temperature bumps 65°F. Those isolated pockets of hybrids begin merging into bigger and bigger schools.

> *"For exciting fishing action, nothing can compare with taking hybrid stripers on surface baits."*

These large schools gravitate to areas where massive concentrations of baitfish are found—long, tapering points on the main lake that eventually cascade into a deep river channel. Baitfish use these points as migration routes, sliding shallower or deeper as conditions dictate. It's on these points where spring topwater action usually begins.

As the water continues to warm, the megaschools of hybrids often break into smaller "squadrons" of unusually aggressive fish. These packs, often numbering 10 to 20 fish, fan out to cover points, offshore humps, islands and flats. Flats action will normally be in water from about 15 to 30 feet deep.

This is when fishermen can experience outstanding topwater action all day simply by watching for birds working fractured schools of bait, or the baitfish themselves swimming near the surface around these spots. Water that's 72°F is usually perfect for this scenario.

Summer Slump

By the time the water has warmed to 80°F, day-long surface feeding has halted, replaced by a dawn-and-dusk bite. High-percentage areas now

Keep a strong grip on your rod, because few freshwater species can outfight a big hybrid. Any number of lures will take surface-bustin' hybrids. A good selection includes (see inset): top row—slab spoon, A.C. Shiner 450; second row—Rebel Pop-R, Slug-Go; third row—Topwater Bass Bug, A.C. Shiner 403; fourth row—Heddon Zara Spooks.

"If hybrids grew as large as muskies, you'd have to nail your shoes to the boat deck to keep 'em from jerking you overboard!"

include the mouths of the largest coves that have a deep channel access, islands and humps surrounded by deep water, and yes, those long channel points. Continued warming sends the fish increasingly deeper and makes the likelihood of any surface activity slim.

Back On Top

Hybrids can tolerate warmer water than can land-locked stripers (one reason they're being stocked more than stripers in many lakes nationwide), but not as warm as white bass can handle. In the hottest part of the summer, some will utilize deep channel structure; others will move to the cooler headwaters of the reservoir or river system.

As the water cools down into the upper 70s in the early fall, look for surface feeding to pick up again as these fish begin to gravitate to long points. Key on the upper half of the lake at this time.

You'll first notice topwater activity at daybreak and dark, gradually increasing in duration as the water temperature drops to around 70°F. Schools grow larger, and fish begin a slow, deliberate migration

down lake. They roam increasingly farther from points, humps and other structure, often chasing baitfish into open water.

The topwater angler must now watch for bait, not structure, on his sonar screen. The telltale presence of a cloud of shad wadded just under the surface in a tight ball tells me there's gonna be some hybrids busting the surface soon!

Large creek mouths are fall schooling hotspots that are often overlooked. Most anglers religiously fish main-lake points but ignore the mouths of larger down-lake tributaries. Again, watch for massive schools of suspended baitfish in these areas and expect hybrids to push the forage fish to the surface.

Hybrids will gradually move into the creek arms as the water cools to 60°F, but there's a brief period beforehand when scattered groups will hang around mid-depth main-lake flats with a mud bottom. The fish that adhere to this pattern are often trophy-sized, and may be tempted with a topwater presentation. A fishing partner nailed a 19 pounder on this pattern last fall. The monster ate a Heddon Zara Spook and the strike sounded like a toilet flushing.

Wide Range Of Lures

Hybrids aren't picky. As long as your lure looks and moves like a baitfish, it's a potential meal.

But a couple of factors should be considered when selecting topwater plugs. First, a hybrid, even a trophy-class fish, has a smaller mouth than a striper and tends to prefer smaller forage.

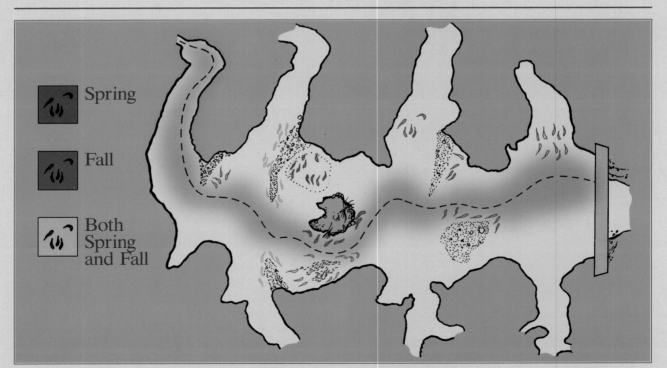

FINDING STRIPERS

Spring

Fall

Both Spring and Fall

During the spring, look for hybrids to congregate on long points, in large coves, over mud flats and along the river channel near islands and submerged humps. In the fall, concentrate on long points in the upper half of the reservoir, creek mouths and on schools of baitfish roaming open water.

When I'm guiding for big rockfish, I prefer big topwater lures like the Cordell C10 Red Fin and Ozark Mountain Big Game Woodchopper, as well as some muskie plugs. These same lures will assuredly draw strikes from hybrids, particularly when they're at their most aggressive in extra-large schools. But for most hybrid situations, I feel more confident with smaller lures, often the same topwater lures I might choose for largemouth bass.

Another factor to consider is the length of the cast required to reach surfacing hybrids. You often need a bait heavy enough to be chucked long distances. This rules out smaller topwaters favored by some bass anglers.

This gamefish is one tough dude when it comes to pulling power. Choose a topwater bait with strong, sharp hooks and good-quality split rings. It's common for hybrids to straighten these components!

You should enter the battle with these weapons in your tackle box:

• **Zara Spook**—It's perhaps the greatest of all hybrid topwater lures, but one of the more difficult to fish. "Walking the dog" is by far the most effective retrieve with this stickbait, but it requires some practice.

I'll fish a ¾-ounce Spook whenever I sense that hybrids are likely to feed on top, both in spring and fall.

• **Prop Baits**—Lures with propellers on one or both ends are unusually effective on hybrids during periods of low light, in the rain and when a light breeze ripples the surface.

Their loud gurgling helps the fish pinpoint the lure when visibility is limited. Try the Cordell Boy Howdy (C41), A.C. Shiner (403) and Smithwick Devil's Horse (F-200).

• **Poppers**—I like surface poppers more for hybrids than I do for stripers. Try Rebel's P65 Magnum Pop-R.

• **Metal Spoons**—When is a sinking spoon a topwater lure? When you reel it like crazy so it skips over the surface! Spoons like the ⅛-ounce Hopkins are perfect for long-distance casting and are capable of reaching a fast-moving school of hybrids.

• **Minnow Lures**—Use a floating minnow at the cold-water extremes of the topwater bite in early spring and late fall. My favorite is A.C. Shiner's No. 450.

• **Soft Plastics**—The standard is the 6-inch Slug-Go soft plastic jerkbait. Zia Bait Company's Topwater Bass Bug, a floating tube bait, is perhaps the ultimate finesse topwater for hybrids. When they're very reluctant to surface, use this one to draw 'em to the top!

Topwater Tackle

For all-around hybrid-bustin' with topwaters, choose a 6- to 6½-foot, medium-action baitcasting rod outfitted with a medium-speed reel and 14-pound mono. Avoid the new super-strong braided lines when fishing hybrids on top; their lack of stretch may result in a hard-pulling hybrid either ripping the hooks from your lure or shattering your rod.

For smaller, lighter minnow lures and soft plastics, spinning gear may be needed. Use a 6½-foot, medium-action rod with 8- to 10-pound mono.

You haven't experienced everything this exciting gamefish has to offer until you've popped one on top. Key on the high-percentage areas. Watch for baitfish. And whatever you do—keep that drag loose!

LURE COLORS

Many hybrid fans stick to chrome-finish topwater plugs, figuring they look like shad or other reflective baitfish. They do—under sunlit skies.

But a chrome lure tends to disappear when it's cloudy or when you're fishing early or late in the day. The chrome simply reflects the overall grayness and doesn't flash. I like bone white better than chrome under most conditions. Hybrids are also suckers for outrageous colors like fire tiger or orange.

Here's a trick to greatly increase your strikes. If a hybrid boils on your topwater lure but fails to eat it, immediately cast a sinking lure like a grub, hair jig or metal spoon to the strike site. It'll usually get devoured on the way down.

Soft On Stripers

by Don Wirth

Most anglers don't associate the word finesse with giant striped bass.
But you'd be surprised how a big slice of soft plastic can turn them on!

uge striped bass had been active for two days. The best we'd taken weighed close to 40 pounds and one went to 33. Both took big top-water plugs. Naturally, I felt confident this damp, foggy morning would produce several explosive strikes. After an hour of casting, however, neither my client nor I had raised a fish. Worse yet, the wind began blowing the fog off the river, revealing a burning midsummer sun. I knew we had to find the fish quickly because big stripers and direct sunlight don't mix very well.

We spent another unsuccessful hour probing deeper holes I knew held big fish before the sun began shooting its rays into the clear water.

"Looks like we'll have to get some bait and park over a hole," I advised my fisherman, who was

The Ultimate Fishing Book: Strategies for Success

clearly disappointed that he hadn't experienced a trophy striper's awesome topwater strike.

A couple tosses of the cast net yielded a half-dozen big gizzard shad, a favorite forage of river stripers. While my client soaked shad beneath floats, I rummaged through my tackle box looking for something that would bring a reluctant striper to life.

At the very bottom, I found a 6-inch Slug-Go. This soft jerkbait had worked well for me on large-mouth bass, but it was the first time I'd thought seriously about trying one on stripers.

While our live shad danced beneath floats, I tied the stoutest worm hook I could find to the 30-pound line and rigged the jerkbait. A looping cast toward a sunken tree made the squiggly lure land with a soft plop.

The jerkbait was almost out of sight when a huge striper shot out of its woody lair and sucked it in. I lowered the rodtip, silently counted to three and set the hook as hard as I could.

> *"I lowered the rodtip, silently counted to three and set the hook as hard as I could."*

The violent thrashing of the monster literally rocked my aluminum boat. My client spun around in his chair, eyes wide and jaws agape. "Put down your rod and get this fish," I grunted, passing him the bucking rod. He held on as the big fish blasted downriver, fouling the two live-bait lines in the process. "Whadda I do now!" he hollered as mono melted from the reel.

"Hang on," I yelled. I knew the fish was big and too much pressure would break the line or straighten the hook.

I quickly cut the entangled lines, then gunned the motor and followed the striper downriver. It cut toward the bank, looking for cover. Just before it reached a tangle of stumps and trees that would have snapped the heavy mono, it rose to the surface where it thrashed and rolled and shot gallons of water skyward. Its tail looked as wide as a pushbroom.

This fish was over 50 pounds!

The striper then ran toward the opposite bank, but didn't make it. The line snagged under a tree

limb resting on the bottom and parted. My client was crushed.

We ended the day catching two nice stripers both around 25 pounds, but the monster fish that ate the Slug-Go stayed on my mind for months. I began experimenting with soft jerkbaits for these land-locked giants and have come to the conclusion that few artificials are better for catching trophy stripers.

Perfect Imitations

Soft jerkbaits have been the lure sensation of the '90s. Herb Reed, a graphic artist and avid bass fish-erman from Connecticut invented the genre with the introduction of his Slug-Go in the late '80s. Today virtually every manufacturer of soft plastic artificials makes a version of these effective bass catchers.

The genius of the soft jerkbait lies in its simplicity. Most models lack "action tails" or similar appendages. They're simply long, featureless globs of plastic with a keel-like belly, and when properly rigged, fall almost horizontally. A slight jerk of the rodtip sends the lure darting this way and that, a totally realistic simulation of an injured baitfish. Properly presented, soft jerkbaits imitate shad and herring and readily fool stripers. For these big fish, I stick with the 6- to 9-inch varieties.

Soft jerkbaits do have their limitations, though. I don't like to fish them in stained, murky or muddy water. They're also notorious line twisters, although rigging the hook dead-straight in the body can off-set this problem to some degree. They're also easily overfished—too much rodtip action is probably worse than not enough. And though they draw lots of strikes, it can be maddeningly difficult to actually hook a fish.

Rigging For Stripers

Most problems anglers have stem from improper rigging. You need to rig these lures for stripers, not largemouths, which means super-strong hooks and some off-the-wall rigging tricks.

For bass, soft jerkbaits are traditionally rigged with a single worm hook passed through the head, then stuck back into the belly so that the hook point lies exposed on top of the body. Many models have a depression in the back, allowing the hook point to ride exposed but still protected from hang-ups. Stripers in reservoirs are usually open-water feeders,

Soft plastic baits and some finesse can equal big striper rewards!

so a weedless rigging isn't necessary.

I use the worm hook merely as a device from which to hang a stinger hook. Simply thread the treble over the worm hook's point before pushing it up through the belly. The treble can either dangle or you can bury one of the barbs in the lure.

When stripers attack a surface lure, they usually deliver a violent strike in an attempt to kill the bait. A soft jerkbait rigged with a single worm hook won't often hook the fish on the initial wallop, but the treble hook usually connects.

Another trick I use is to push a small piece of a plastic coffee can lid or old inner tube past the worm hook's barb after rigging the jerkbait. This acts as a stopper, preventing the hook from sliding back into

the worm, yet it doesn't seem to decrease hooking percentages.

Big hooks often tear holes in these soft lures. Plan to go through a lot of baits or use a battery-operated soldering gun or worm repairing device to seal up rips and tears in the plastic.

Adding insert weights is another deadly trick, especially when stripers are deep, as is often the case in reservoirs. By changing the location of the weight within the jerkbait's body, you can make it sink in different ways.

Another weighting trick is to attach a rubbercore sinker to the single worm hook. Take out the rubber and slide the sinker on the hook's shank. Bend the "dog-eared" ends down to clamp it on the hook. This works best when a trailing treble hook is used.

Carolina-rigging is another method that's highly productive for reservoir stripers. A long rod rigged with a 1-ounce egg sinker, red plastic bead, heavy swivel and soft jerkbait on a 2-foot section of 20-pound leader is the best bet for probing points, bars and humps. With this rig you can cover a lot of acreage quickly. Just crank it back slowly and steadily. The heavy sinker roots along the bottom while the jerkbait darts and settles behind it.

Trolling soft jerkbaits on downriggers is the latest wrinkle in reservoir striper hunting.

Impale the lure on one or two treble hooks, and add a swivel about a foot above the bait. Slow-troll the rig off points and other likely reservoir hotspots at the depth most baitfish appear on your sonar display.

Big-Water Stripers

In deep reservoirs, big stripers often prowl open water where they intercept baitfish schools near points, humps, bluffs and other types of structure.

What most anglers hope to see is a school of these big predators attacking a ball of baitfish on the surface. They normally throw large topwater lures like the Cordell Redfin and Heddon Zara Spook, but soft jerkbaits work as well and are an exciting alternative.

They're especially good when stripers flash at, but won't strike, a hard bait. When this happens, I cast a 6- or 9-inch jerkbait with an exposed treble stinger past the last surface boil and skip it across the top like an escaping shad. Then, I'll stop and allow the lure to sink slowly. Most strikes come as the lure falls.

Another presentation, one that produces violent strikes, is to hold the rodtip high and retrieve the lure at medium speed. The lure stays on the surface, producing a V-wake, simulating a shad swimming close to the surface. When the strike comes, it will be explosive! Drop the rodtip immediately and wait for the fish to pull the line tight. Very often the initial strike is meant to kill or stun the prey. If you set the hook too soon, you can pull the lure right out of the fish's mouth. I've had countless stripers blow up on a jerkbait only to swim in a wide circle before returning to eat the lure.

Few anglers use soft jerkbaits on stripers holding deep, say below a school of baitfish, but it's an avenue worth pursuing. When faced with this situation, rig a jerkbait with insert weights and allow it to drop slowly through the baitfish. Stripers target weak or injured baitfish, and a jerkbait falling into their territory represents an easy meal. With practice you can put the lure at the proper depth using the count-down method.

Reservoir stripers often lurk near submerged standing timber. In one reservoir I fish, there are trees standing in 90 feet of water with their tops only 20 feet below the surface. In this case, I rig the treble hook stinger so that two barbs are embedded in the lure to reduce hang-ups. One or two insert weights make the lure sink horizontally into the treetops. Warning: deep standing timber often holds monster fish, and your strike-to-catch ratio can be low due to the high probability that the fish will break the line in the trees.

Using Jerkbaits In Rivers

Although reservoirs are great, I do most of my striper fishing in the cool, clear rivers and tailwaters of Tennessee and Kentucky. Stripers in these waters grow to legendary size and I've found soft jerkbaits to be unusually effective on them.

My favorite striper waters are quite clear and very cold. During the spring and fall, the fish run into these areas in droves and readily attack all sorts of big lures, including Red Fins, Zara Spooks, and large prop baits like the Woodchopper. But sometimes you have to finesse these fish into striking, and that's where soft jerkbaits come in.

As a rule, I'll reach for a jerkbait when the sun is high and stripers are holding around submerged objects. One of the revelations I discovered when first fishing for river stripers was the startling propens-

ity these bruisers have for holding near submerged or standing timber. Many rivers are choked with sunken trees that wash in during floods. Stripers hold in these areas, both when actively feeding and when they're inactive during midday. Live bait is one way to draw them out, but a soft jerkbait is just as, and sometimes more, effective.

When high water floods shoreline trees, even super-shallow water can hold big stripers. My top choice then is a 9-inch Slug-Go or Fin-S-Fish rigged with a massive worm hook and a stout treble stinger. I cast the lure as far back into the trees as possible and keep the rodtip high on the retrieve. The lure coasts along the surface like a fleeing shad. Once the bait is in open water, I quicken the retrieve. Very often, a huge wake tells me that a striper has rolled out of the trees and is zeroing in on the lure. I drop

SOFT PLASTIC ALTERNATIVES

We've only seen the tip of the iceberg in soft plastic lures suitable for striper fishing. Many of the most productive offerings are saltwater creations which have been effective on both river and reservoir stripers, either fished as is or with modifications.

Perhaps, the most exciting alternative is the Tora Tube, a giant tube body manufactured by Canyon Plastics of Kingman, Arizona. This 7½ incher was developed for saltwater use, but has gained a following among California's big-bass anglers. I fish it on a leadhead jig around sunken trees or across deeper river bars. To convert the Tora Tube into a tremendous topwater lure, stretch it over a wooden dowel with a hole drilled down its length. Run the line through the hole after fitting the tube over the dowel. Attach a strong saltwater snap swivel to the line and add a treble hook. With practice, you can make it walk-the-dog.

Another highly effective soft plastic alternative is the Big'n Grub from the Kalin Co. of Brawley, California. This giant curlytail grub measures a full 10 inches, and is great for stripers when the water is murky. I fish it on a 1-ounce leadhead and a strong hook, casting to shallow coves where I've seen baitfish on the surface. Fishing it near the bottom or buzzing it over the surface produces strikes.

RIGGING JERKBAITS

Jerkbaits, such as the Slug-Go-style (shown) or Lunker City's Fin-S-Fish, can be rigged in various ways for striper fishing. The author uses an 8/0 worm hook when fishing the 9-inch varieties and a 5/0 or larger single or treble hook stinger, which can be imbedded in the lure or left to dangle free if the bottom is relatively clean. Note the plastic disk which is punched from a coffee can lid and pushed over the hook barb. It prevents the hook from sliding back into the body and tearing a hole in the soft plastic, yet it doesn't interfere with hooking ability.

the rodtip slightly so the lure sinks, and set the hook hard when the line goes taut.

"Properly rigged and presented, a soft jerkbait will fool the biggest stripers in any water."

Another technique, one that requires a bit more patience, is to fish deeper submerged trees. "Deeper" is a relative term. In some of the rivers where I guide, "deep water" may be only 10 to 12 feet. I'll cast the lure past the tree, skip it along the surface,

then stop when it's directly over the tree. The lure sinks slowly with the current.

This tactic often pulls a striper out for a look-see; if the fish refuses to take, I make another cast and let the lure wash deeper into the tree. A jerkbait presented in a striper's face is an offer most fish can't refuse.

River bars are another hotspot, especially during low-light periods. Stripers push baitfish schools onto these bars and the feeding activity is violent. No artificial lure looks more like a stunned baitfish than a soft jerkbait. Just cast it onto the bar and reel it quickly along the surface. Then, stop and twitch the rodtip while the bait sinks.

When you can't find them near trees or on bars, look for river stripers around craggy bluffs with deep, undercut crevices. One of my fishing companions, a man who has caught several river stripers exceeding 50 pounds and certainly knows big fish, once hooked a striper he estimated at 80 pounds from a deep river bluff.

When fishing these areas, I use the biggest jerkbait I can find, rigged with a treble stinger embedded in the lure. Facing the bluff, I cast upstream and let the unweighted jerkbait tumble tight to the rock wall with the current.

Tough Tackle

Because the fish I'm likely to encounter in rivers are big and the obstructions are many, I use extremely heavy tackle—as heavy as I can get away with and still be able to cast a soft jerkbait a good distance.

I've fished soft plastics on several different type lines. First it was mono in the 30- to 40-pound range, then I went to the no-stretch "superlines" in the 50- to 75-pound-test range. They hooked fish well but there wasn't much room for error because of virtually no stretch. Currently, 40- to 50-pound-test mono is my choice.

For river stripers, the stuff is absolutely awesome because it's extremely abrasion-resistant. It may require going to a slightly softer rod, however, to compensate for the almost total lack of line stretch. If you don't, your graphite striper rod may just explode in your hands on the hookset.

Properly rigged and presented, a soft jerkbait will fool the biggest stripers in any water. Next time you're planning a striper trip, toss some jerkbaits in with your plugs. You may find that your hard lures never get wet.

Giant Baits
For Giant Stripers

by Don Wirth

It's war! Bring out the heavy artillery. Giant stripers feed regularly on super-size baitfish. Moral: Give them what they want—a big bait!

*U*sually I'm pretty accurate judging the size of a striped bass by the intensity of its surface explosion. A big fish easily detonates an area as big as the hood of a pickup. Anything less is likely to be a "Timmy," my term for an undersized fish.

But one fish I'll never forget fooled me. More importantly, it taught me some lessons about the lures I'd been using.

The sun had just dropped below the tree line on the river I was fishing, and a fog was already forming on the surface. The bewitching hour was about to begin.

Using a bass-size topwater stickbait in a clear minnow pattern, one of my favorites for stripers when there is still plenty of light on the water, I cast toward shore. As I dog-walked the lure at the edge of a hole, it suddenly disappeared in a swirl.

"Small fish," I told my angler as my rod bowed. "Go ahead and work the same area. There's got to be a bigger one close by."

On the cast, silver flashed beneath his Red Fin and the surface erupted. From the size of its tail, which threw buckets of water, I put the fish at around 35 pounds.

My plan was to boat Timmy quickly and help out with the trophy. But I discovered Timmy's real name was Brutus.

"This fish is a lot bigger than I thought!" I grunted, as the 40-pound mono melted from my spool.

The striper headed downstream toward a bluff hole, where it stopped and did a vicious head shake. I put more pressure on the fish, hoping to gain some line. I knew that if the striper reached the tangle of sunken limbs on the opposite side of the hole, it would be history.

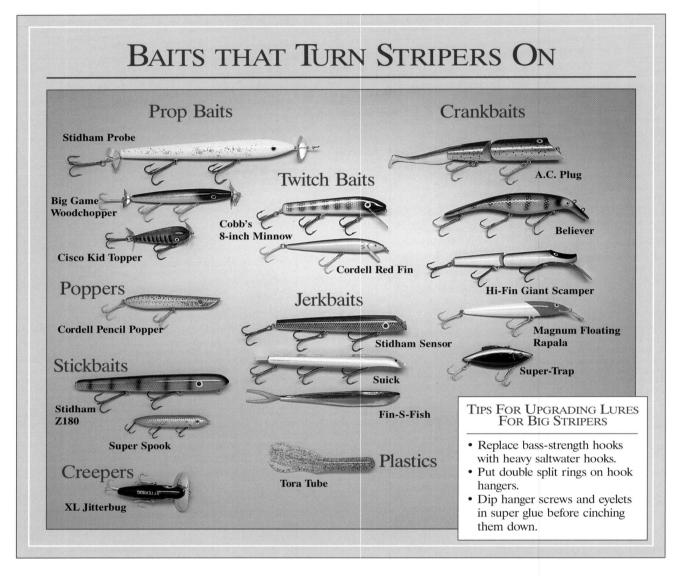

BAITS THAT TURN STRIPERS ON

Prop Baits

Stidham Probe

Big Game Woodchopper

Cisco Kid Topper

Poppers

Cordell Pencil Popper

Stickbaits

Stidham Z180

Super Spook

Creepers

XL Jitterbug

Twitch Baits

Cobb's 8-inch Minnow

Cordell Red Fin

Jerkbaits

Stidham Sensor

Suick

Fin-S-Fish

Tora Tube

Plastics

Crankbaits

A.C. Plug

Believer

Hi-Fin Giant Scamper

Magnum Floating Rapala

Super-Trap

TIPS FOR UPGRADING LURES FOR BIG STRIPERS

- Replace bass-strength hooks with heavy saltwater hooks.
- Put double split rings on hook hangers.
- Dip hanger screws and eyelets in super glue before cinching them down.

The battle ended seconds later as the line went slack. I was sure the fish had popped it. But as I reeled in, I saw the end of my line—and the head of the lure—skipping across the surface.

The lure's lifeless yellow eyes laughed at me as I turned the mangled piece of plastic in my fingers. The fish hadn't broken the line. It hadn't even straightened the hooks. The brute striper actually pulled the bait apart!

Yes, my client boated his striper, a 36-pound, 2-ounce beauty, and he was one happy camper. He was sure he'd caught the biggest fish in the river, but his bubble would have burst if he'd gotten a look at Brutus. My fish could have eaten his for lunch.

Today, the severed head of that lure dangles from my boat's key ring, a silent reminder that when you're dealing with monster stripers, you can't go into battle undergunned.

Heavy-Duty Lures

Like most striper junkies, the first landlocked fish I caught were on bass lures—stickbaits and prop plugs, metal blades, even 1/4-ounce leadheads. These were adequate for handling small fish, even good ones when there was plenty of water beneath the boat. After all, in waters where there aren't obstructions to deal with, all it takes to land a 30-pound striper

is 20 minutes and a loose drag. Eventually, they'll tire themselves out.

When I started actually targeting the big bruisers, though, I realized I had to upgrade my arsenal. I found that even some of the most popular striper plugs needed upgrading if they were going to hold giant fish. I began replacing bass-strength hooks on some plugs with heavy-duty saltwater hooks, and put double split rings on the hook hangers. For added measure, I dipped the hanger screws and eyelets in Super Glue before cinching them down.

I also started toying with muskie lures. I'd wager that eight out of 10 striper nuts in my part of the country have never seen a Believer, Swim Whizz or Stidham Probe, let alone fished one. When a local river rat saw me tying a giant Probe on my line, he exclaimed, "Son, are you gonna fish that thing or fillet it for supper?"

But trust me, big lures aren't a joke if you're serious about catching a wallhanger striper. In fact, you can't get too big as far as the fish are concerned. The Tennessee state record, a striper that topped 60 pounds, was caught on a live 22-inch skipjack.

"Son, are you gonna fish that thing or fillet it for supper?"

Often the sturdy construction of a monster muskie lure will tip the scales in your favor. For example, many of them have a wire running through the body to which the hooks are attached. This is a super idea, one I wish the manufacturers of popular plastic striper lures would employ.

Godzilla Topwaters

One of the most exciting moments in fishing occurs when a huge striper detonates on a topwater lure. And in the waters I fish, a topwater presentation is a great way to attract a big landlocked.

Prop baits work great at first light and at dusk. I started using the Stidham Probe last summer and was truly impressed. This noisy prop lure comes in 8- and 13^1/$_2$-inch versions and features through-the-lure wire construction. A client and I caught three fish weighing more than 30 pounds apiece

When the battle's done and the pictures finished, nothing tops the feeling of watching a trophy striper swim away. Catch and release does work, and ensures future action.

on 8-inch models one rainy morning.

Luhr-Jensen's Ozark Big Game Woodchopper is one of my longtime favorite prop baits, as is the Big Game Chugger. Both produce a surface disturbance that stripers find irresistible.

The Cisco Kid Topper is another fine prop bait. Although it's relatively small, it's just as noisy as the other two baits and extremely well constructed.

Poppers are popular among saltwater anglers, and they work on landlocked stripers, too. Several are sturdy enough to stand up to big striped bass, and among them, two of my favorites are the Cordell Pencil Popper and the Atom Striper Swiper. I like to fish poppers in fast, churning water, especially

the boils right below a dam.

The Arbogast Jitterbug is a classic topwater lure, and the big XL Jitterbug is in a class all its own. At night, in calm, shallow water, this is an awesomely effective striper lure.

Big stickbaits are another class of muskie topwaters that are simply super for stripers. Stidham's Z180, a 10 incher, retrieves in a wide Z-pattern. It can put a hex on big stripers.

STRIPERMAN'S TACKLE CHOICES

Big artificials demand heavy tackle, but don't go overboard. Rods that are too stiff, too long and too heavy will wear you out before the day's fishing is over. I like a 7-foot rod with a fairly soft tip for stripers. You have to corral a big fish, sure, but more importantly, you need some shock absorption to keep from jerking the hooks from your lure.

For topwaters, crankbaits and twitch baits, I like All Star's SJ1 Special Jiggin' Rod, Quantum's Tour Edition TC707FJ heavy pitching stick, and Cabela's model GC704 rod.

For you custom-rod nuts, Thorne Bros. Pro Series "muskie" rods are as tough as they are beautiful. The 7-foot Bucktail Rod is perfect for fishing the 10-inch Fin-S-Fish. They also offer three stiff jerkbait rods built on Sage 569 blanks.

For big stripers, always use a wide-spool baitcasting reel like Abu Garcia's Ambassadeur 6500 series, Ultra Cast UC 6500C or the new C3 series (6500 C3). Several other companies also make wide spool reels.

I spool up with 30- to 50-pound mono line, avoiding the braided lines. They're too visible in clear water, and their lack of stretch will break your rod or rip the hooks from your plug if you aren't careful.

Braided lines, however, do make fishing muskie-style jerkbaits a lot easier. Consider a mono leader when fishing them.

—Don Wirth

Twitch Baits

Big minnow-imitating plugs are probably the most versatile of the giant striper lures. They can be twitched on top, reeled across the surface, cranked steadily below the surface or simply trolled.

Cordell's Red Fin is easily the most popular of all striper lures. The classic retrieve is to swim it slowly over the top so it throws a telltale wake. If a striper boils on the lure, but doesn't commit, stop reeling and jerk the lure two or three times so it emits a series of loud pops.

I modify my Red Fins when gunning for big stripers. I install two heavy-duty split rings on each hook hanger, then remove the tail hook and replace it with one that's a size or two larger. The extra weight sinks the tail a bit, allowing me to crank the lure faster when swimming it across the surface— highly effective in clear water.

"You can't go into battle undergunned!"

There are several excellent twitch baits on the market that striper anglers should check out, including the Jake, A.C. Shiner, Hi-Fin Twitchin' Minnow, Bagley's Bang-O-B and Top Gun, jointed Amma Bamma, Cobb's 8-inch Minnow and the Slammer.

Monster Crankbaits

Many striper fishermen use bass-sized crankbaits, but for serious lunker hunting, try something that's more appealing to a trophy-size striper. The Bill Lewis Super-Trap will snare some big stripers, but you'll have to eat your Wheaties and do some weight training if you intend to crank this baby all day long.

I'm a big fan of Drifter's Believer and Best Tackle's Swim Whizz, two monster crankbaits that have caught record-class muskies and are just as deadly on stripers.

Other jumbo crankbaits that will work for big stripers include Cobb's Shad, Mac's Big Crank, Gries' Esox Minnow, the Magnum Floating Rapala, Hi-Fin's Giant Scamper and the A.C. Plug.

Hard and Soft Crankbaits

Muskie addicts love jerkbaits—magnum hunks of wood or plastic that are repeatedly jerked in a gliding motion, which really triggers the trophies. Surprise—they work great on stripers, too. The Suick and Stidham Sensor are amazingly effective on big river stripers lurking in submerged timber.

Other jerkbaits that should work for striper hunters include the Fudally Reef Hawg, Bagley B-Flat Shiner, Bobbie Bait, Smity Large Jerk, Eddie Bait and the Burt Jerkbait.

The secret to fishing these big jerkbaits is to use a short, stiff rod and braided line. The rod allows you to easily make the sharp downward snap required to impart the right action to the bait, and the line's low stretch gives the lure extra zip with less effort.

Soft plastics like the oversized Tora Tube and Lunker City's 9-inch Slug-Go are potent striper medicine. Lunker City's 10-inch Fin-S-Fish, which I just started using, is outstanding. I landed two fish weighing more than 40 pounds each on my first two trips using this lure. It's one of the most convincing striper artificials on the market—perfect for clear water. I fish it on 50-pound mono and add a stinger treble hook.

"I landed two fish weighing more than 40 pounds each on my first two trips."

Get Serious

If you're serious about connecting with a giant striper, magnum baits are the hot ticket.

I prefer large striper lures in white, chrome, shad, perch and trout patterns; chartreuse works well in murky water, and black is best for nightfishing.

Of course, there's a certain stigma that comes with using a monster lure. Your fishing partners may chuckle when you tie on one of these foot-long monsters, but you can bet they'll quit laughing when the water suddenly boils and Brutus begins peeling line from your reel.

Stout tackle is needed to land huge stripers—and to fish large baits. But don't overdo it. A 7-foot rod with a soft tip and some backbone will serve you well.

Chapter 10

Trout

"**F**inesse" describes the trout: brookie, brown, rainbow or cutthroat…each are incredibly lovely in their own way, finessing together wonderful colors, delicate but strong bodies and wary ways into a challenging fishing package. "Finesse" also describes fishing for trout, most of the time…coming up with just the right offering and presentation, at just the right time, in just the right manner and at just the right depth… you get the drift.

So here's how to finesse a few more trout this year, out there in the great places that trout call home.

Deadly Little Secrets

by Don Wirth

Stocked trout, wild trout, small trout, big trout...these lures will catch them all.
Now here's what you have to know to make these tiny jigs produce.

*W*hen I got a good look at the brown trout that had just swallowed the tiny marabou jig on the end of my line, I knew how David must have felt when he faced Goliath. The brown swam lazily toward a sunken tree, not even realizing it was hooked. My ultra-light spinning rod bent crazily; only when it loaded up completely did the spotted monster shake its head in protest. The trout powered along the gravel bottom, then disappeared into the tangle of limbs, parting my line with a loud pop.

It was the biggest brown I'd ever tangled with—easily weighing 15 pounds. Yet, it had eaten that little ball of lint without hesitation. Here's the deal: Use a micro marabou or tube jig for trout and you'll outfish every other angler using any other lure in the same water 3-to-1.

Sound like baloney? Trust me—microjigs are so effective on rainbows, browns and other trout species, it's downright scary!

Like the stone in David's sling, a microjig is tiny, but lethal. The ones I use in streams, tailwaters and lakes range from $1/32$ to $1/100$ ounce, the latter being the size of an underdeveloped gnat. They'll catch a ton of pan-size trout, but the welcomed bonus is the occasional lunker you'll land when fishing them.

NAFC Member Rip Collins knew about microjigs. The late

Heber Springs, Arkansas angler spent hundreds of hours wading the nearby Little Red River, pitching these tiny lures into every snag, logjam, riffle and mossbed he could find. On May 9, 1992, his ⅟₆₄-ounce piece of fluff was devoured by a true behemoth—the world record 40-pound, 4-ounce brown. This catch put Collins in the IGFA record book, and gave trout anglers nationwide the incentive to try microjigs.

Staunch Following

For years, microjigs have enjoyed an almost cult-like following among trout anglers. These fishermen have quietly developed subtle techniques for using them that have resulted in incredible numbers of 'bows and browns.

One true believer is Arden Von Haeger. He learned how to fish microjigs for stream trout while living in Missouri, and has refined his expertise in Tennessee's frigid tailwaters. He ties his own micro-jigs in weights from ⅟₃₂ to ⅟₁₀₀ ounce.

"Use a micro marabou or tube jig for trout and you'll outfish every other angler using any other lure in the same water 3-to-1."

Why do trout crave microjigs? "Probably because they match the general look of the small living organisms they're used to feeding on," says Von Haeger. "But then, some microjig anglers believe that trout think they're hatchery pellets! Whatever the reason, microjigs will work when other artificials haul water."

Many anglers refuse to believe a lure this small and simple will catch fish, according to Von Haeger. "They're used to using spinners, spoons or small creature-imitators like plastic crawfish or minnow

CURRENT TACTICS

Shoals And Rapids

In fast water, pop the rodtip as you take up slack. The jig should hit bottom occasionally.

Eddies

In an eddy, let the jig fall on a semi-slack line.

Deep Holes

Deep holes with slow-moving water require a vertical jigging presentation.

Mid-Depth Runs

Allow the microjig to sweep through or around trees in mid-depth runs.

STILL-WATER MICROJIGGING

Backs Of Flowing Creeks

Alternately pop the rodtip and crank the reel during the retrieve. A great cold-weather pattern.

Mossbeds

Allow the microjig to drop into holes and along the edge of the moss.

Intermingled sunlight and shadow camouflages trout perfectly. Pitch your jig toward the bank and swim it quickly through the dappled light.

lures—something bigger, shinier and more gimmicky."

"Trout will hit these types of baits, but often a more subtle approach is required—and that's when a microjig really shines."

Marabou and tubes are used interchangeably by some microjig fishermen; others develop a strong preference for one over the other. The only way to know which works best on your waters is to try them both. The tips presented in this story will work with either marabou jigs or tubes.

While you're at it, stock up on a good variety of weights and colors—these lures are incredibly cheap. A card of 12 Prolite jigs will set you back just a few dollars.

An Ultra-Light Touch

It takes a light or ultra-light spinning outfit to fish a microjig effectively. Soft-action rods in the 6-foot range are best for casting these light offerings. They are also more forgiving when you're playing a big fish on light line.

"A subtle approach is required."

Match line weight to potential trout size as well as conditions. For most fishing situations in moving water, a soft 4-pound mono is ideal. Switch to 2-pound in crystal-clear streams, or where the fish run small.

I'll move up to 6-pound mono in lakes or rivers with a lot of submerged brush and a reputation for good-size fish.

Oh, and remember to keep that drag loose! It may take you 15 minutes to play and land a big trout hooked on a microjig.

Current Tactics

Over the years, I've found that nothing beats microjigs when fishing a clear-water stream or highly-pressured tailwater. So I mean it when I say that learning to fish these little lures will be the single most important step you can take if you want to catch more trout!

The first step is casting. You don't want to put too much snap into it. Trying to coax a few extra feet from your cast will invariably result in line loops and messy tangles. Besides, long casts are often unnecessary with microjigs. Many anglers (myself included) use short underhand pitches, merely flipping the jig gently into cover.

This causes fewer line problems and allows you to get the lure into tight spots where overhead cover would prevent a traditional cast.

And whether you're fishing from the bank, wading or casting from a boat, there are a few more simple tricks that will help you tackle a stream or river:

• Shoals And Rapids—In fast water, cast or pitch the jig upstream at a 45-degree angle. Slowly take up slack and pop the rodtip repeatedly as the jig washes downstream.

FISHING MICROJIGS

*H*ere are some tricks the microjig cult uses to catch more and bigger trout:

• Fish 'em fast—Beginners usually fish microjigs too slowly. In the clear, shallow water typical of many streams and tailwaters, trout learn to shoot out and nail fast-moving prey. If you aren't seeing fish behind your jig, or if following fish refuse to strike, you're fishing the lure too slowly. Allow the jig to drop less than a foot, then reel very rapidly so the jig shoots at least six feet before slowing down or stopping the retrieve. The sudden burst of speed mimics fleeing prey and often triggers a savage strike.

• Shake 'em deep—In slack water, trout often hold on the bottom in deep holes during periods of bright sunlight. Position your boat over a hole, lower the jig to the bottom and squeeze the rod handle repeatedly. This subtle action will make the jig dance in place on the bottom, often drawing a strike.

• Fish dappled light—Trout are camouflaged by the dappled light along stream banks caused by shadows cast from trees, brush and grass. Pitch your jig against the bank and swim it quickly through the dappled light until you see a fish follow. Stop reeling and get ready for a strike.

• Vary weights and colors—Micro-jigs are the cheapest of all trout lures. It pays to have a good selection of weights and colors with you at all times. In murky water, use bright colors like chartreuse or fluorescent red. In clear water, try more natural colors like brown, black, silver or olive-green. Start with heavy jigs, if you can call $\frac{1}{32}$ ounce "heavy," and switch to lighter lures if the fish aren't cooperating.

• Trim 'em—Scissors are a must when fishing marabou microjigs which are often tied with far too much fuzz. Wet the hair, draw it back and snip it off behind the hook bend (below). Otherwise you may be pestered by short-strikers.

WHY THEY WORK

Big, Bad Browns

by Gary Borger

Many waters harbor populations of big brown trout that are near uncatchable during warmer weather. But come fall these wary and often cannibalistic trout throw caution to the wind and will succumb to the tactics outlined here.

Brown trout are the wariest of the salmonids. Therefore, when you catch a *big* brown, it's a real trophy. For anglers intent on catching such a fish, the search continues year-round, but reaches a frenzied peak in the fall. It's at this time that brown trout prepare for spawning and become as aggres-sive as they are elusive during the other seasons.

This period of the big, bad browns begins as early as August, when the shorter days trigger the fish's sexual urge. It culminates with the actual spawning event, which takes place sometime between October and December. In the southern

hemisphere, spawning is also a late-fall event, but autumn there occurs in April, May and June.

In August, the big fish become restless, feeding more heavily than normal and shifting about the big pools impatiently. This fidgeting soon turns to single-minded purpose, as the trout begin moving upriver, following ancestral trails to the spawning grounds. Some fish start early and move slowly, while others wait, making a mad dash upstream at the last moment.

But browns are browns, and they don't totally throw caution to the current. Their upstream migration is mostly done at night or in the twilight of dawn or dusk. During the day, they seclude themselves in deep holes or back under a cut bank. In Europe, the browns often swim out to sea to feed, returning to the rivers to spawn. Fishing for these returning "sea trout" is a uniquely nighttime affair.

In the Great Lakes states, big browns move up into the rivers almost exclusively at night. Reservoir-bound fish also migrate after hours.

Not only does the shortening of the autumn days cause the fish to begin moving upriver, but it makes them especially aggressive as well. Browns, particularly the males, display territorial urges, at first just shoving and bumping each other. Eventually, outright fighting occurs.

This is where the angler comes in. As big, aggressive fish move up from huge pools of the lower river, or forsake the lake or reservoir for the stream, they become susceptible to standard sportfishing methods. The fish are concentrated, and with more trout per acre of water, catching gets easier.

My first real introduction to the great angling potential offered by the browns of autumn came when I was an undergraduate student at Penn State University. Fisherman's Paradise was catch-and-release and open year-round. And what a paradise it was. I fished it every chance I got (and some chances when I should have been studying). In the fall, while other students cheered the Penn State football machine, I stalked the big browns on the Paradise waters of Spring Creek.

By October, the fish had begun to establish terri-

Fall is the brown trout's spawning season. Action can be hot and heavy, but remember to practice catch-and-release to protect the fishery.

tories, and every gravel bar held several highly aggressive males. These big, brilliantly colored browns fiercely defended their selected holding sites. I would hook two large marabou streamers together (one through the eye of the other) and sneak quietly along the stream, carefully presenting the big double rig to the holding fish.

The resulting strikes were terrific! I'd often catch and release more than 20 big, hook-jawed males, each more than 20 inches long. Every trip was another lesson in fish behavior and fishing technique.

Oversized Baits

Big streamers have remained my favorites for the browns of autumn. Trout aggressively take these large flies for two reasons. First, they represent the substantial mouthful of food that big browns want this time of year. Second, large flies represent a territorial threat, causing the defensive instinct of the brown to take over. Big browns will slash and bite at smaller intruders.

By big, I mean big. Most anglers think of 2- to 3-inch trout flies and lures as being large, and under most circumstances, they are. But for the browns of autumn, "big" starts at 3 inches and goes up from there.

As a fly fisher, I favor patterns such as the Strip Leech, various muddler imitations, Wooly Bugger and big bucktail patterns in the 3- to 6-inch lengths. Lefty's Deceiver, a great saltwater fly, is a sure bet

Big, hungry browns dine heavily in the fall. Fish a substantial fly or lure if you want to battle a trophy like this.

Wyoming's Fontenelle, Arkansas' Bull Shoals and many others, contain excellent populations of truly large browns. The rivers and streams that feed such reservoirs are surefire places to find big browns in the fall.

As a unit, the Great Lakes are the world's largest producer of big browns. All five support enormous populations of browns that reach substantial sizes. Fish in the 6- to 10-pound class are common, and many browns over 10 pounds are taken each year.

In the fall, the feeder streams can be filled with these huge trout. Some spawning gravels are closed to fishing to protect the highly vulnerable fish, but the lower stretches are open to anglers.

On rivers such as Arkansas' White, Wyoming's North Platte, Montana's Missouri and others where there are a series of dams, the browns from one reservoir are confined to the pools below the upstream dam. Fishing in such places can be truly phenomenal. And on these rivers, as well as on rivers where there are no dams, the fish will move up feeder streams in search of spawning gravels. Don't overlook the mouths of these streams, where the fish may stack up before running upriver.

Rules For Nightfishing

The heavy tackle used for big nighttime browns is very different from the lightweight gear used under normal daytime fishing conditions. Many anglers feel over-gunned or intimidated by the robust size of both

---

"Concentrate nighttime efforts on shoals where big fish congregate."

---

the rod and the lures. Taking a bit of time to practice casting and manipulating the heavier gear before fishing can pay off when the nighttime strike does come.

for big fall-run browns.

Anglers who use spinning or baitcasting equipment should step up to magnum-sized Rapalas, large Mepps or Panther Martin spinners. Trophy brown trout take these and similar lures very aggressively, so I recommend replacing the trebles with single hooks — preferably barbless ones. The fish can then be released more easily and usually with less injury.

While big, streamer-style flies are my first choice, fall's browns can also be duped with other large imitations — large stonefly nymphs, sizable Wooly Worms, chunky dragonfly nymphs and big attractor dry flies like the Royal Wulff and Humpy. And while most hatches of aquatic insects have long since ceased, or are diminutive in size, the heavy fall hatches of the giant orange sedge of the Pacific Northwest can provide some significant fishing action for large browns.

In addition, if the weather stays warm, grass hoppers will still be around, and they can tempt even the largest trophy brown trout into striking.

The first criterion for finding the big browns of autumn is to find big water— or at least small water that feeds big water. That's where browns grow to substantial size. Lakes and reservoirs are prime big-fish locations. Reservoirs like Montana's Hebgen Lake, Oregon's Wickiup, Utah's Flaming Gorge,

Likewise, big waters that are intimidating during daytime hours can be positively frightening at night. The first rule of wading at night is to stay out of waters you don't know. The second rule is to remember the first rule. If you plan to fish new waters, go during the day and explore them carefully. Then be extra cautious at night.

I hardly ever use a wading staff during the day because I don't like to wade where the water is so deep or swift that I need one. But at night, a wading staff is essential. I use it to feel my way around, locating deep-water edges, big rocks or other obstructions. It can also help you get out of places that you shouldn't have gotten into in the first place. Many anglers who fish big, swift waters at night also wear some sort of flotation gear. It's a good idea. In the same vein, a wader belt is an essential piece of gear. Pull it tight so that if you do take a dunking, your waders will not immediately fill with water.

Shallow Versus Deep

Nighttime anglers should concentrate their efforts on shoals where the big fish congregate — the tailouts and top ends of pools are especially good areas. Reaches of smooth, even-flowing water can be good as well. Below dams, areas of turbulent flow over big rocks can also produce some exciting fishing.

Anglers fishing by day should look to deeper water and places where browns like to hide. On big rivers, trout shift to the depths of big pools or tuck themselves in close to boulders or sunken logs. Getting a fly or lure down to these secluded fish is half your battle.

For the fly fisher, leadcore tips or high-density, uniform-sink lines and heavily weighted flies are necessary. Spinfishermen should add split shot ahead of the spinners or use lures that run deep, such as metal spoons, jigs or plugs that dive right down to the bottom. If you don't occasionally get snagged on the bottom, your lure's not running deep enough.

Perfect Water Conditions

Fall is prime time for fishing the big Western rivers by day. Not only are the browns gearing up for their annual nuptials, but the water is in great condition. Unlike spring and summer, when excessive runoff disperses the fish, fall waters are usually low and clear, and trout are concentrated in the pools.

Anglers usually drift the rivers, searching with their big flies, or they stop and wade, fishing the particularly good stretches.

Even fall's sometimes foul weather can be a boon to the big-river angler. On these overcast, low-light days, seemingly more fit for ducks than anglers, the big browns shift out of deep water and prowl around as they do at night, hunting the shallows for food.

In smaller streams, look for browns not only in deep holes but beneath undercut banks and under in-stream piles of brush and logs. The fish will search out these places and can hide there most effectively. During late November, my fishing partner John Beth and I were prowling along a stream in search of coho salmon. I was shooting video footage as John fished for the aggressive salmon. As he worked down a stretch of good-looking water, he spotted a small jumble of logs and debris. He drifted his fly back into the dark recesses of the pile and suddenly had a very nice fish.

"It's a small coho," he yelled, then suddenly his voice rose in pitch. "No, it's a nice brown!" The 6-pound hen fish fought well, and John had a smile of satisfaction on his face when he released her.

The season of the brown has just begun. Don't put away your fishing tackle and miss the best time of year to take a trophy.

Fall makes for great water conditions ... and great trout fishing.

Fishing The Hidden Calm

by Sam Curtis

Once you know what to look for it's almost like fishing virgin waters; small out-of-the-way spots that harbor husky trout.

Most trout anglers would admit to finding some measure of beauty in a stream. The sparkle and bubble of riffles, the chop and swirl of runs, the placid mystery of deep pools—all beguile us into casting our bait, lures or flies for rainbows and brookies, cutthroats and browns.

But trout are much less romantic about their stream habitat. They're interested in territory. Top territory means an easy meal, plus good resting and hiding cover. When fish find these qualities in a stretch of water, they lay claim to it. And defend it.

Big trout, especially, seek out areas where they can find the most food by expending the least amount of energy. They are efficient feeders, holding in slow water so they don't have to fight current, yet tapping into food that sweeps through nearby swift currents.

Slow water next to fast water—it's perhaps the most beautiful of all trout water, because that's where most fish are found.

Now, the majority of NAFC members who fish trout know enough to fish eddies and backwaters, and the heads and tails of pools where riffles enter and leave. These are places where we can see fast water and slow water side by side.

But any moderately flowing trout stream also has pockets of "hidden" calm water that are camouflaged by fast water swirling around them. These hidden calms are key areas for catching trout—fish most anglers never know are there.

Uncovering Hidden Calms

Obstructions in the stream flow, such as exposed boulders or shallow-to-deep water transitions,

account for many untapped hidden calms.

But even a hypothetical trout stream with a slick bottom and smooth banks would contain hidden calm areas because of a phenomenon called "laminar flow." On straight runs, laminar flow causes water flowing closest to stream banks and bottom to move more slowly than midstream water because of the friction produced by the water moving over the streambed.

In fact, a trout lying on the bottom may be in water moving seven to eight times slower than water directly overhead or near the surface. That's the reason why trout hold tight to banks and bottoms, and the reason why you need to get your lure or fly close to those spots to catch fish.

But let's get even more specific. Where in a stream's riffles, runs and pools do hidden calms exist and how can you identify them?

Getting Straight On Riffles

Within stream riffles, there may be a few larger rocks that provide shelter for fish. But on the whole, the choppy water of a riffle generally doesn't point to any specific trout-holding areas. You'll have to fish these stream sections systematically, casting in patterns that cover the entire riffle.

That doesn't mean, however, that hidden calms don't exist in riffles. One of the best and easiest to find is the triangle of quiet water wedged between the fast riffle water and any inside bend of the streambank. At the very tip of these wedges, which are found both before and after the bend, a trout has its nose within inches of fast, food-filled water and yet is resting in water that is almost dead calm. These spots are prime trout stations where fish can conserve energy and still find an easy meal, but few anglers fish them because the areas tend to be small.

Fish downstream of the calm water with lures and streamers; fish upstream and down to it with nymphs and dry flies. In either case, keep your lure or fly right on the edge of the fast water—within easy reach of the calm water lie.

For years, I ignored this spot. Then one day on the Yellowstone River a nice brown barrelled into a hopper I'd inadvertently let coast down past a calm riffle wedge. Now, I get "buck fever" every time I cast to such a spot because they have been so productive for me.

CHEATING DRAG

Successful fly fishing depends on presenting your fly in a way that looks natural. With dry flies this means a drag-free drift on top of the water; with nymphs it means a drag-free tumble below the surface. Even streamers, which to a certain extent depend on drag for action, must be fished with a controlled drift to look natural.

Drag occurs when the current puts a belly in your line, causing your fly and leader to "drag" behind the bowed fly line. Trout will refuse the unnatural looking fly as it drags. Fishing hidden calms complicates the job of maintaining a drag-free drift because the fast water/slow water transitions will play havoc with your line.

The first defense against drag is to use a long rod. Defense number two is to make short casts— 25 to 30 foot casts are plenty in most situations.

Also, when fishing upstream with dry flies, throw an arc in your line so you've got a little slack on the water for conflicting currents to play with. And don't be shy about using an upstream mend to keep the line out of quick currents.

To mend your line, lift your rod tip up at the same time you roll your wrist upstream.

For fishing a dry fly downstream, a stop cast— where you prematurely stop the forward motion of the line by pulling back on the rod tip—gives you slack line on the water and provides a drag-free drift.

With nymphing, the rule is to fish the fly on a dead drift, using short upstream casts. Remember to keep your rod tip high and strip in the slack line. However, the nymph should tumble and bounce downstream naturally, without any pull from your line.

Finally, when it comes to streamers, you want the drag effect to come at the right depth and in front of the fish so that the fly looks alive. It won't be natural if a streamer rooster tails along the surface. Adding weight can keep the fly down and solve this problem. In addition, when using a cross-current cast, throw some arc in your line; it will give you slack to work with when the fly lands.

Hidden calms are efficient feeding stations for trout and efficient catching stations for anglers.

Running Into Trout

As good as riffles are, most bigger fish are found elsewhere. One prime area to look is a run.

A run begins where the stream flow eases up at the bottom of a riffle. Bigger rocks and boulders get pushed downstream from the riffle and form a hodgepodge of hidden calms that appeal to big fish.

Start fishing at the head of a run where fast, light-colored riffle water abruptly changes pace into the slower boils and swirls of darker, deeper water. Here, trout vie for position within the calm water.

Surprisingly, right at the transition line between riffle and run—where the water color deepens and the water appears frothy and agitated—fish find pockets of calm created by the conflicting current directions. In this spot, invertebrates spill into the head of the run and trout hold there to pick them off.

Fish this transition zone thoroughly and patiently. The trout are there. Because the water is agitated you should use a stiffer leader and tippet, or a weighted fly; it will give you more control over your lure.

Most insects are washed underwater through this part of the stream, so don't use high-floating dry flies. A weighted nymph fished on a 5X leader with short casts can get you down where big fish hang out. With conventional spinners or other lures, you'll want to add a little extra weight, too.

Let's drop farther downstream, to where larger rocks break the surface of a run. Most anglers cast behind a rock to the obvious slack water there. But fish also hold in the hidden calm in front of a rock, and to its sides.

On the upstream side, flowing water "piles up" to form a pocket of quiet water where trout lie and feed on passing insects. Big rainbows seem especially fond of these hidden boulder pockets.

Rocks that lie slightly below the surface and betray themselves with a "V" of water that points to their location, also have hidden calms—but not where most anglers think. The tendency is to cast between the arms of the V where you may in fact pick up a fish. But a hidden calm lies upstream from that point and fish hold there, too.

If a rock is fully submerged, you'll see a slight hump or boil on the surface. Fish these spots with weighted line or heavy lures to get down where the fish are.

These types of upstream lies should be fished from above and to the side. Let your fly or lure swing down and across current, just in front of the rock.

Prospecting Pools

At the head of a pool, where fast, shallow water in a run suddenly drops into slower, deeper water, trout hold against the drop, where a hidden calm creates a holding spot within the turbulence. This is the best place in a pool for fish to take advantage of insects drifting and swirling through the back eddies.

Invertebrates, however, are not always what big pool-dwelling trout are searching for. Big fish are more apt to feed on larger foods—crayfish, minnows and leeches. This is why riffle fishing is usually productive for numbers of smaller fish, whereas pools provide fewer but larger trout.

Although you can't see it, the calmest part of a pool is in the deepest water, right at the bottom. Generally, spin fishermen have the easiest and most productive fishing in pools, because they can get

FINDING AND READING THE HIDDEN CALMS

RIFFLES offer a hidden calm at a stream bend. Look for the triangle of calm water before and after the bend.

DEEP POOLS are prime feeding stations for big trout. Fish lures or streamers right on the bottom.

RUNS provide pockets of calm water where trout will lie. Try the upstream side of exposed or submerged boulders.

SEAMS are created at the edges of the main current where shallow bank areas create "helical flow."

When reading a trout stream, the place to start is where slow water flows next to fast currents. Trout will hold at these transitional areas, resting in the calm water while waiting for an easy meal to be swept past in the nearby quick current. Hidden calms exist at the spots highlighted above.

lures deep and avoid obstacles. Fly casters will want to bring out the "chuck and duck" tackle—large streamers fished on a sinking line.

This is a good area for sculpin-type flies like Muddler Minnows, and leech imitations like Woolly Buggers. If you aren't using a sinking line, you'll want to use a weighted fly or add some weight to your leader. Vary your retrieve, starting with a fast strip that suggests a fleeing baitfish.

Separating Seams

Anywhere in a stream where slower currents run next to faster currents, or where the current eddies, you'll find what's called a seam. Sometimes a seam is fairly obvious, but often the calm water is camouflaged.

Seams occur at either side of a main current where shallow bank areas produce more friction and create a phenomenon called "helical flow." This is a slower, spiraling current of water that moves parallel to the main current, sweeping along the bottom toward the bank and pushing out toward the main current at the surface. A seam of calm water exists between the helical flow and the main current.

The edge of the main current next to this seam, where you'll see miniature whirlpools if you

look carefully, is a prime spot for trout. It's an especially great place to fish dry flies because the outward thrust of the helical flow at the surface tends to keep a fly in the main current with the natural insect drift.

"Seams are prime trout spots."

You'll also find seams at the confluence of two streams, or where channels meet at the downstream point of an island. In the latter areas, trout hold in the slowest current and intercept food flowing in from either channel.

Dealing With Currents

Now you know how to find the hidden calms and the trout they hold. But successful fishing depends on presenting your fly or lure in a way that looks natural to the fish.

With dry flies this means a drag-free drift on top of the water; with nymphs it means a drag-free tumble below the surface. Even streamers, which to a certain extent depend on drag for action, must be fished with a controlled drift to look natural.

Drag occurs when the current puts a belly in your line, causing your fly and leader to "drag" behind the bowed fly line. Trout refuse an unnatural looking fly as it drags. Fishing hidden calms complicates the job of maintaining a drag-free drift because the fast water/slow water transitions play havoc with fly line.

Lures and monofilament line won't be as affected by current, but spin anglers must still retrieve their lures so fish identify the offerings as food. Remember: trout rarely, if ever, see bait traveling against a heavy current, so make your presentation in a cross-current or downstream manner.

When fly fishing, the first defense against drag is to use a long rod. Defense number two is to make short casts—25- to 30-foot casts are plenty in most situations.

Also, when fishing upstream with dry flies, throw an arc in your line or make "S" shapes with it, so you've got a little slack on the water for conflicting currents to play with. And don't be shy about using an upstream mend to keep heavy, thick fly line out

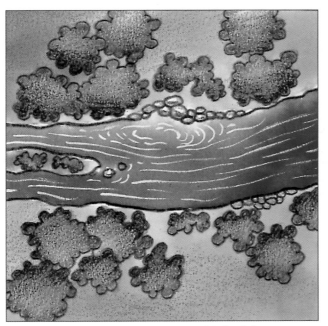

Shallow bank areas create seams and helical flow.

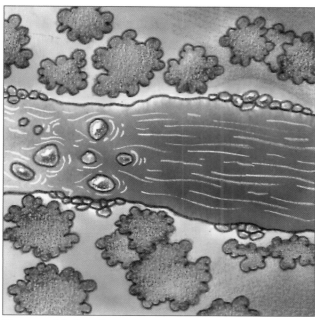

Deep pool below those rocks … prime feeding station.

so that the fly looks alive. It won't be natural if a streamer rooster tails along the surface.

Adding weight can keep a fly down and solve this problem. In addition, when using a cross-current cast, throw some arc in your line or make "S" shapes with it, to give slack to work with when the fly lands.

Your fly will bounce along naturally, so you don't have to work as hard at controlling the drift. And that way, you can fully concentrate on feeling that electric jolt when a trout darts from its hidden holding spot and nails your fly!

of quick currents.

To mend your line, lift your rod tip up at the same time you roll your wrist upstream. This maneuver flips line upstream, eliminating drag.

"Imperative: Drag-free drifts."

For fishing a dry fly downstream, a stop cast—where you prematurely stop the forward motion of the line by pulling back on the rod tip—gives you slack line on the water and provides a drag-free drift.

With nymphing, the rule is to fish the fly on a dead drift, using short upstream casts. Remember to strip in slack line. However, the nymph should tumble and bounce downstream naturally, without any pull from your line.

When it comes to streamers, you want the drag effect to come at the right depth and in front of fish

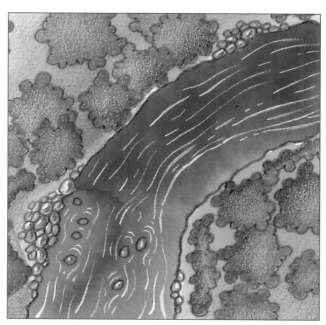

Inside bends can create calm-water holding spots.

Fishing The Long Flies

by Gary Borger

Many anglers believe in the "big bait equals big fish" theory. And you know what? It even works when fly fishing.

*O*ne of the unique and great advantages of fly fishing is the ability to create and fish imitations that vary from the sublime to the ridiculous—from the most delicate of insects to relatively large critters like baitfish, leeches, crayfish, crabs, eels and others.

And while I love to take big, selective trout or salmon that are feeding on tiny flies, opportunities to do so are few in any single season. So, when I target big fish, I usually go with long flies—imitations like the strip leech series, woolly bugger, muddler minnow and fleeing crayfish. These creations offer built-in movement and bulk to push water, and the vibrations they send out pull fish in from long distances. Powerful strikes are common.

The tactic most often used with a long fly is to rifle it out and retrieve it with quick strips, trying to make the imitation look like rapidly fleeing prey. This simple tactic works so

well that most fly casters never progress beyond it, which is unfortunate because there are other methods that are often much more productive.

One of them, a variation of the basic cast-and-strip technique that I call "Baitfish From L," is a tactic for fishing the edges of relatively shallow, medium- to swift-flowing waters. It uses the current in riffles and rapids to create drag that replaces the angler's need to strip. Because this water is thin, I normally use an 8- to 10-foot leader and a floating line, but a sink-tip works, too.

Wade some 10 to 20 feet from the bank and downstream (this is why it's a tactic for relatively shallow water). Cast about 30 feet down-current and tight to the bank—I mean within inches of the edge. Sometimes I'll even toss the fly up onto the bank so the pull of the current will drag it into the water.

"This trigger often causes big fish to nearly turn themselves inside-out while trying to grab the fly."

Aim the cast four or five feet over the water and add an in-the-air parachute mend at the end of the forward cast. Overcast the target by four or five feet, and as the line extends over the water, simply draw the rodtip back up toward vertical.

This not only pulls the fly back so it drops on the desired spot, but also provides controllable slack. As soon as the fly touches down, drop the rodtip and allow the slack to run down-current.

Because the angler is standing in swift water and the fly is landing in very slow water, the difference in speed causes the added slack from the parachute mend to be pulled into an L shape, with the end of the foot next to shore.

As current pulls against the line, it draws the fly straight out from the bank toward midstream. This movement shows the imitation in full side silhouette to any fish holding in the near-shore shallows.

As the imitation moves away from the bank, the increasing drag causes it to accelerate, making it look like a fleeing baitfish. This trigger often causes big fish to nearly turn themselves inside-out while

Borger has taken long-fly techniques far beyond the standard cast-and-strip used by most anglers. His results speak for themselves.

trying to grab the fly.

A few up-and-down jigging movements with the rodtip give long flies the look of a wounded natural, another strong triggering characteristic.

When the fly has moved out from the bank and swings around to face upstream, curious fish often follow. This is another moment when savage strikes frequently occur, because the fly appears to be making an evasive move (as natural prey would do) and the predatory instinct of the trailing fish kicks in.

Even after the fly has swung fully around, there's still a chance for a strike. Strip the line a couple of feet, and jig the rodtip up and down before lifting to make the next cast. I've even had fish nail the fly as I lifted the rod to make the backcast, so be ready. If you drop your guard, that's when the biggest fish of the day will decide to hit.

BAITFISH FROM L

Great technique for taking fish holding tight to shore in shallow, medium- to swift-flowing water! Overcast your target by four or five feet, then parachute mend to drop the fly at the edge of the bank and put slack in the line. As current catches the line, it pulls the fly cross-stream away from the bank, perfectly imitating a fleeing baitfish.

Expanding The L Tactic

The L tactic proved so successful in shallow, moving water that I had to develop a way to use it when casting into deep mid-currents, slower moving stretches and still waters. In these areas, instead of using the current, simply create the L shape with a curve cast.

Because of their heavy weight, long flies curve around very nicely. To make a curve, tip the rod out to the side at a 45-degree angle and stop just a bit more abruptly than normal at the end of the forward stroke. Aim the cast four or five feet above the surface so the fly has time to flip around and the line can curve before it hits the water.

When fishing deep water, choose a floating line, sink-tip or full sinking line to hold the fly at whatever level produces the most strikes.

In fast water, once the cast is made, allow the flow to swing the fly and pull it cross-current.

In slow-water areas, once the fly is in, drop the rodtip right to within a few inches of the surface and strip the line in an accelerating fashion. The fly will travel cross-current in response to your stripping. Add rodtip twitches if you think the extra action is needed. The fish will respond to this "fleeing baitfish" with as much gusto as they do in fast water.

The L is a wonderful tactic when fishing along the edge of a weedbed in still waters, whether from shore or from the lake side. Throw the curve so the base of the L drops close to, and parallel with, the weed edge. Keep the rodtip close to the surface as you strip line and jiggle the rodtip. The fly will follow the line's curved pathway perfectly.

Strikes may come as the fly moves along the weed edge, but most often they occur just as the imitation turns the corner and heads away from the weeds.

Drag And Drop

Another highly effective variation is the drag-and-drop technique. It can be used from any position in a stream or lake, and it's my favorite method for fishing visible trout.

When fishing toward the bank in moving water, make the same cast and parachute mend as for the L tactic, but this time, keep the rodtip high after the fly lands.

Hold the rod in this vertical position and allow line drag to pull the fly toward midstream. After it's travelled a foot or two, drop the rodtip a couple of feet. The fly will immediately halt its movement and drop both downstream and toward bottom.

Hold the rodtip stationary while the fly is dropping. As the current continues to pull on the line, the fly will suddenly come to life again and resume moving away from the bank.

"Drop the rod and allow the fly to tumble right into the fish's face."

After it has made a foot or two more progress, drop the rodtip a bit more and allow the fly to dead drift again. Repeat these drag-and-drop movements until the cast has been worked through. Then, in case a reluctant fish has followed, tease it by stripping the line upstream for a few feet before lifting to recast.

This is a wonderful way to accurately place a fly in a fish's feeding lane, and I use it regularly when salmon fishing. Cast so the fly lands upstream of the fish and several feet beyond its lane. Let drag pull the fly into the fish's pathway, then drop the rod and

FACT: Long flies take big fish. It's the classic case of monster fish wanting a substantial meal—in this case, a strip leech.

allow the fly to tumble right into the fish's face. Big kings are often reluctant to chase a rapidly moving fly, but they take tumbling imitations quite well.

When fishing without the benefit of knowing whether a fish is present, simply make the "drop" portions of the tactic so the fly tumbles through those areas that are most likely to harbor fish.

In still waters, fish the imitation on a floating line to cause the fly to rise to the surface during the drag, and fall toward bottom during the drop.

The drag-and-drop strategy can also be used in a straight-line fashion. In streams, fish the fly directly downstream with a parachute mend. Again, hold the rod stationary and allow the moving water to swing the fly toward the surface. Lower the rodtip, and the imitation moves straight down-current, sinking as it goes.

This tactic is highly productive in places where currents run back under banks or overhanging vegetation because it lowers the fly directly into the fish's feeding lie.

The straight-line variation of the drag-and-drop is also highly effective when fishing a lake. Because

the fly should rise and fall on the retrieve, the angler should use a full floating line or sink-tip.

Make the cast, allow time for the fly to sink, then give a single, long strip on the line. The floating line causes the imitation to rise toward the surface. Wait for the fly to fall back toward the bottom, and repeat until the cast is fished out.

Drifting Long Flies

When my son, Jason, and I were shooting a video on fishing with crustaceans and snails, I wanted a nice fish for the final sequence. We were exploring a lake that was new to us, but one we knew held some quality trout.

Our friend Garry McCutcheon was fishing with us and pointed out some particularly good spots, but the trout were deep. Tying on a fleeing crayfish, I kicked out to the designated areas and let the float tube drift in the wind.

Pitching the line about 50 feet, I waited for the fly to get down. The wind drift was just right, so I didn't have to retrieve, just troll. Every 10 seconds,

THE LONG FLY ADVANTAGE

The advantages of long flies are many. First and foremost, they have enough bulk to displace water as they are being retrieved, just like a natural forage item does as it swims or crawls. The resulting vibrations are readily detected by the lateral line mechanisms of trout or salmon, exciting their predatory instincts.

The motion of long flies is another advantage. Real prey moves, but not in a straight line. Body parts wave, pulsate, flare and quiver, and long flies mimic these characteristics. At night, especially, fish hunt by sound and feed by sight, so a big bulky fly that moves water and has plenty of built-in action is much more likely to take fish.

These are the two primary reasons why imitations such as the muddler minnow, strip leech, woolly bugger and others are so effective.

Size

Fly size is important. When targeting big fish during non-hatch periods, I want a fly that's large enough to grab attention; one that's tough to lift with a 3-weight rod. I normally use size 2 or 4 leech style imitations that are 3 to 4 inches long, with plenty of bulk, when trying to attract the big boys.

Color

Color is another consideration. I normally stick to natural colors: black, brown, olive, silver and gold.

That's not to say that a bit of flash can't be built into the fly. I like to add flash to the silver and gold versions by building the body of tinsel or crystal chenilles. These materials suggest the natural flash of a minnow's scales, and are a real turn-on to the big predators.

Occasionally, however, more garish colors can be even better. I especially like yellow, red and purple/blue. Sometimes exotically colored long flies trigger the most savage attacks, especially from salmon.

—*Gary Borger*

Gold strip leech

Muddler minnow

Marabou streamer

I'd lift the rod high to pull the fly up and create slack so the imitation could drop unhindered.

As my tube neared the end of the drift, the fly snagged some weeds and I tried to jerk it free. Suddenly, the "weeds" tore off across the lake, snapping the rodtip down sharply. It was a nice, 7-pound rainbow that we taped excitedly. Several minutes later, that one was followed by an 8-pound fish. We filmed that one with even more excitement. It made a great ending for the video.

Dead-drifting long flies can also be highly effective. Joe Brooks' Broadside Float tactic is well worth learning. His idea is to dead-drift the fly in a way that keeps it continually oriented sideways in the current so the imitation's full silhouette is always visible to fish facing current.

This technique is ideal with a cross-stream delivery on a floating line. The only trick is keeping the fly facing across the stream.

As long as the line runs straight across, the fly will, too. Position the line by mending, flopping the belly of the line either upstream or downstream as currents and the fly drift dictate.

There's one more dead-drift technique that all fishers of long flies should know. It's really a nymphing tactic, in which the leader is key to making the long fly go where you want it to go. Start with a body of 4 feet of .020 Maxima Chameleon, followed by 1 foot of .013 Maxima Chameleon. The tippet consists of 4 feet of .011 tippet material (0X, use your favorite brand) followed by 8 to 10 inches of 1X, 2X or 3X, depending on fly size.

Pinch one or two split shot on the tippet just above the knot connecting the 4-foot piece to the 8- to 10-inch piece. Stick a strike indicator on the .013 piece.

Now, fish the long fly just like a nymph. Cast up or up-and-across, and just let the fly tumble and work in the current. I've caught so many fish this way that I'd have to say it's a favorite tactic.

During the non-hatch times, the old axiom "big fly, big fish" was never more true. These steroid-charged hulks are a real turn-on for huge fish looking to eat something of substance. Develop your skills with the long flies and join in on the wrestling match.

DRAG AND DROP

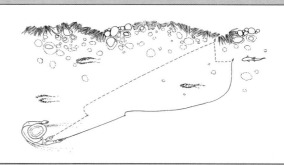

Nearly the same as the Baitfish From L, this technique gives you the flexibility to drop the fly back to a fish in its feeding lane—a temptation that fish can't resist. Keep your rodtip high after the cast and hold it there as the current sweeps the fly away from the shoreline. When the fly reaches the feeding lane of the fish you're targeting, drop the rodtip to introduce slack, thereby allowing the fly to dead-drift to the fish.

STILL-WATER CAST

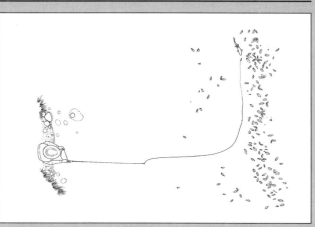

In still-water situations, make a curve cast so the base of the L lands along a weed edge. Stripping brings the fly parallel to the edge, then turns the fly abruptly. Most strikes come as the imitation turns and heads away from the weeds.

In The Film

by Gary Borger

Not being able to catch feeding trout isn't because the fish are "smart;" the problem is that the fly fisher isn't observant enough. Here's how to open your eyes to detail.

Surface film is a tough, rubbery layer of water that is neither on the surface, nor below it. The film concentrates food organisms into a broad, thin sheet of edible items, making it a prime trout feeding location. The film is strong enough to support relatively large insects like water skippers, mayflies, caddises and stoneflies, or even an errant beetle, inchworm or ant. Its elastic nature also traps aquatic insects that must push through it during metamorphosis from immature to adult stages.

During a hatch, trout respond to this smorgasbord by moving to feeding lies and turning their attention toward the film. The surface rings of rising fish are everywhere.

Exciting, yes, but this is also where the fly fisher usually goes wrong. Seeing the rings, many anglers immediately reach for dry flies, tying on one high-floating imitation after another, then watching as they float over the "wise and noble" fish without a single take.

Fishless after the feeding has ceased, the angler stumbles ashore, muttering and shaking the confusion from a befuddled brain, perplexed at the obvious intelligence of even the small trout. But trout are not smart. Not even close. Their pea-size brains are largely devoted to hearing and vision. And their feeding is genetically dictated, not intelligently thought out.

The problem isn't that trout are too smart, it's that the fly fisher isn't observant enough. Rings on the water do not necessarily mean you should fish a dry fly. In fact, more often than not, those rings signify trout feeding in the film.

Trapped In The Film

During a hatch of aquatic insects, the nymphs or pupae migrate to the surface and pause there to push the backs of their thoraxes through the film so the adults can emerge. Trapped in the elastic, watery film, the hatching insects are immobile. They can neither swim nor fly away—easy pickings for any feeding fish.

"Take a few moments to observe a feeding fish."

DECIPHERING RISES

Rise forms can fool you if you're not careful. A fish's nose poking through the surface (above) can indicate feeding in the film, as well as from the surface. A ring that expands from a bulge on the surface (below) is caused by a fish feeding below the film.

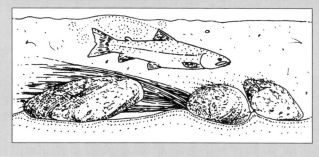

Under these conditions, it's easy to see how the fly fisher could be confused. Adult insects cover the water and the rings of rising fish appear regularly. So how do you know whether the trout are feeding on adults or emergers in the film? Just watch.

Take a few moments to observe a feeding fish. If an adult insect floats over its position and the trout doesn't rise, then get suspicious. If the fish rises and seems to miss a nearby adult, then get even more suspicious. If the trout rises when there are no nearby adults, you can be sure they're feeding in the film.

Don't be fooled by the fish's snout. You will see its nose poke out of the water, which will make you think it's feeding on the surface. But it has to get its upper jaw above the surface in order to get the insect out of the film.

TOP FLIES FOR THE FILM

Parachute floating nymph

Wet/dry fly

Twinkle wing mayfly spinners

Sparkle caddis pupa

Devil bug

Three groups of aquatic insects hatch in numbers that can trigger film feeding—mayflies, caddises and midges. When the hatch is on, adults of all groups will be floating on or flying above the water. Here's a list of the flies I like to use:

• **Parachute floating nymph**—This is an excellent imitation to represent mayfly nymphs in the hatching process. The ball of fur dubbing at its front represents the unfurling wings of the adult.

• **Wet/dry fly**—The best imitation for the immature adult. It may be tied with or without a short tail of sparkle yarn fibers (to represent the partially cast nymphal shuck). The soft hackle at the head imitates the partially unfolded wings and legs.

• **Spinner designs**—Those that consistently take fish mimic the natural's mired profile. Keep the bodies thin so the weight of the hook pulls them into the film, and dress the wings across the top of the hook so they ride like those of the natural. Fish these imitations in the same dead-drifting fashion as the emergers.

• **Sparkle caddis pupa**—For caddis emergers, a sparkle caddis pupa fished in the film can be highly successful.

• **Devil bug**—This fly was designed to mimic an emerging caddis. Its low profile and unhackled body that rides low in the film are keys to its outstanding success.

• **Poly caddis**—This imitation represents a newly emerged adult and can be tied with or without a short shuck of sparkle fibers.

Both the devil bug and poly caddis are excellent in-the-film imitations to suggest a female that has returned to the surface after laying her eggs. The devil bug does better in the riffles, the poly caddis in the quieter water.

• **Griffith's gnat**—Midge emergers are wonderfully imitated by the Griffith's gnat trimmed on the bottom. Sometimes when the fish are being extra picky, they can be fooled by trimming both the top and the bottom of the fly.

• **Sparkle midge pupa**—Another pattern that works wonders is the sparkle midge pupa. Although originated to imitate the insect several inches below the surface, it still works extremely well in the film.

• **Para ant**—The best ant and beetle imitations are not full-hackled, high-floating dries. Instead they are film flies, dressed to partially sink like their natural counterparts. The para ant is tied with a ball of dubbing placed both fore and aft on top of the hook shank. A hackle is parachuted one or two turns around the fore ball of dubbing. The weight of the hook causes this fly to have a deep draw, and it sits well down in the film.

• **Foam beetle**—These imitations are great. The body need be

nothing more than the tying thread. A couple of turns of hackle trimmed top and bottom represent the legs. The back is a piece of closed-cell foam tied in at the rear of the hook, drawn tight over the top of the shank, and tied in at the head. The imitation rides down in the water with the foam just above the surface.

•**Snail fly**—Yes, they can be extremely important in lake systems. Some species actually are air breathers and climb plants and other emergent objects from time to time to get air.

Washed off by waves, they float in the film. And they can be dense enough to cause heavy feeding. Other snails get forced to the surface by rough waves during storms.

A fat body of peacock herl or dark olive crystal chenilles with two to three turns of dry fly hackle fore and aft makes a fine imitation. Keep the hackle sparse so the fly will ride in the film, not on it.

—Gary Borger

Poly caddis

Griffith's gnat

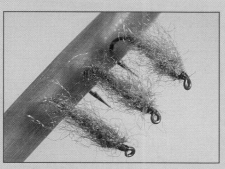

Sparkle midge pupa

Para ant

Foam beetle

Snail fly

How about the times trout are feeding on nymphs or pupae drifting below the surface? Again, careful observation will yield the clues you need. Rings on the surface appear to indicate rises, but if you watch closely, you won't see snouts poking out of the water. The ring of a sub-surface feeder starts as a bulge caused by the fish's afterwash as it turns downward at the end of its rise.

During a heavy hatch, when trout snouts are everywhere, I'm so confident that most of the fish are feeding on emergers, I try those imitations first. And 99 percent of the time, I'm right. In a light to modest hatch, the fish may be feeding on any stage of the hatching insect, and a dry will be successful, but then, so will the emerger.

Two Types Of Flies

Two types of imitations match emergent aquatic insects. First are patterns that suggest the immature stage, with the adult partly out of the husk. These are the floating nymph and suspender-pupa designs. Dressed sparsely, they ride awash in the film with the hookpoint pulling the rear of the fly down, while the wispy hackle or other flotant materials at the head hold the front of the fly just above the film.

"careful observation will yield the clues you need."

The second style is the immature adult; an imitation of the newly hatched insect with crumpled wings and tail, possibly with the immature husk still clinging to the rear of the abdomen.

Both types are exceedingly effective. I usually try the floating nymph or suspender pupa first unless I see ample evidence that the immature adult would be more effective. For instance, during a hatch of the tiny, blue-winged olive mayflies, the floating nymph is deadly. But during a hatch of the pale morning dun mayflies, there are often many cripples and partly emerged adults awash in the film. In this case, the immature adult is my fly of choice.

Even during a heavy hatch like this one, an emerger often outproduces a dry fly.

Conquering Drag

Fishing these flies can be frustrating because the patterns ride so low in the film that they're hard to see, making it difficult to detect drag.

Remember, these are dead-drifting flies, so use slack-producing casts, mends and line-handling tactics to keep as much controllable slack in the line as possible.

How do you know which type of cast or mend is right for the situation? First, make a straight cast to the fish's position. Watch how the currents distort line and leader as drag sets in. The drag-eliminating cast/mend will be the mirror image of this shape.

For example, if you cast straight across a central current tongue, the fast water pulls the middle of the line downstream while the slow waters in front of you and the fish hold the line back. The line assumes a broad U shape with the bottom of the U pointing downstream in mid-current. To prevent drag, make an upstream curve mend with the bottom of the U falling up on the center of the current tongue.

Add to the casts and mends a slack-producing leader design. These George Harvey-style leaders have a long butt of thin material, and a long tippet. They turn over, but just barely, dropping to the surface in S curves that nullify the drag-inducing effects of small variations in surface currents.

A typical leader for size 12 and 14 flies would consist of 4 feet of .014 Maxima Chameleon leader material, 1 foot of .010 tippet material (1X, your favorite brand), and 4 feet of .007 (4X). For size 16 and 18 flies, add a foot of .005 (6X) to the end of the 4X leader.

After the leader and fly are in place, add a tiny yarn or commercial bead strike indicator to the tippet, about 18 inches above the fly. Simply tie an overhand knot in the tippet, insert the yarn into the knot and pull it tight. The knot won't weaken the tippet because the yarn prevents it from tightening down. Trim the indicator to a tiny tuft about the size of a 16 or 18 dry fly, and treat it well with flotant so it rides high and dry.

For best visibility, use a strand of black yarn and a strand of any bright color you like. On a dark surface, the bright yarn will leap out at you. On a surface shining with glare, the black yarn will stand out in strong relief.

The indicator serves several purposes, the most

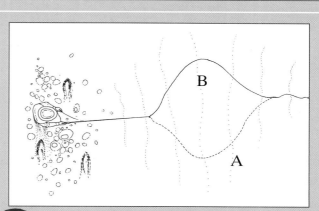

*D*etermine the mend or cast you need by first casting straight across the current, then using the technique that neutralizes the type of drag you're facing. In the initial cast (A), the middle of the line was pulled downstream. An upstream curve mend (B) solves the drag problem.

important being an indication of drag. If the indicator shows drag, you can be sure the fly is dragging. Adjust your casts, mends, line-handling tactics or leader segments to eliminate the problem.

The indicator also serves as a marker to help you locate the general position of the fly. If a fish rises nearby, set the hook. Sometimes you won't see the take, even with the indicator in place. If the indicator snaps around and moves upstream, obviously, this is a good time to tighten up on the line.

"How do you know which type of cast or mend is right for the situation?"

There are times on very smooth water when a yarn indicator isn't necessary if the angler uses a greased leader. Dress the leader with a paste-type flotant to within a few inches of the fly. The leader will float high and dry, leaving a visible track that leads directly to the fly.

the surface. If the spinners are falling in the riffles, anglers plying the downstream pool may not know a spinner fall is occurring and be confounded by the subtle rise forms. As always, check the surface when confusion reigns.

Splashy rises at the film usually mean the fish are feeding on caddises, which lay their eggs on the bottom. The female crawls or dives to the bottom, carrying an air bubble trapped around her body by numerous hairs. After depositing her eggs, she floats back up to the surface. When the bubble bursts at the film, the adult flies away.

> *"I'm so confident that most of the trout are feeding on emergers, I try those imitations first."*

This looks like a hatch, but it's not. Many times what anglers see is really post egg-laying activity, rather than an actual hatch. To tell the difference, look for the pupal skins that designate a hatch floating in the film.

To suggest the egg-laying females returning to the surface, fish the dry, adult imitation, but pull it under so it catches an air bubble as it dives below the surface. When fish are splash-rising in riffles, cast down and across and allow the dry to be pulled under the choppy surface by current drag. In slower waters, pinch a micro-shot a foot or so ahead of the fly. This will cause the imitation to dive when you give the line a short, quick strip. After the strip, allow the fly to rise back to the film and hang there as it drifts over the fish's position.

Beetles, even large ones, and ants are the two low-rider terrestrials that are most commonly caught in the film. Their dense, compact bodies force them down where they often go unnoticed by the fly fisher. Once, while fishing the Yellowstone River, I located a particularly nice cutthroat feeding in the current seam just downstream from a large boulder. Excited by the regular rises, I figured it would be easy to fool the fish. It wasn't. Fly after fly drifted over the trout without even the briefest nod.

I was starting to get upset until I did what I

Captured in film! Borger says targeting the surface layer is much more productive than fishing above or below.

Special Situations

During egg-laying, spent mayfly spinners ride awash on the surface, with some legs and often their tails poking below the film, their bodies partly submerged, and their outstretched wings hugging

Emergers and even low-riding terrestrials pluck trout out of the film.

should have done in the first place—stop assuming and look. A check of the surface with a small bit of screening revealed ants coming downstream. They were impossible to see with just a glance at the water.

On the next drift, the big cutthroat came slowly up through the waters and gently plucked my para-ant out of the film.

"Fishing the film is often the solution to seemingly unsolvable rises."

On another day, Bob Pelzl and I were fishing the high country of the Vermejo Ranch in New Mexico, and encountered a lake dotted with rings. We rowed out and began casting midges, damselfly nymphs and more of our favorites. Nothing worked.

Suddenly, a powerful gust of wind shook the lakeside trees, and tiny, black bark beetles rained into the boat and onto the water. Didn't take us long to figure that one out.

Lake anglers plying the film should be every bit as careful in their tactics as stream anglers. At first glance, this seems like a bit of overkill, but remember, lakes have currents, too. Whenever the wind blows, the surface moves with it—and so do the bugs trapped in the film. Don't leave your drag-

eliminating casts and Harvey-style leaders on the stream bank. You'll find they are just as important on the lake.

Fishing Number One Lake on the Vermejo Ranch one gusty morning, we encountered a heavy midge hatch. Clouds of the small flies were being blown to and fro just above the water. I knotted an emerger to the long tippet and cast it downwind from the boat. I stopped the rod high and drew it back before the fly landed (a parachute mend), in order to give me plenty of slack. As the tiny imitation rode the waves, sliding slowly away from the boat on the slack line, a nose poked out and gently took it in. It was the first strong fish of a memorable morning.

Emergers are often the secret of the hatch, and fishing the film is often the solution to seemingly unsolvable rises. Don't neglect this very important molecule-thin layer of water, for it can hold a great depth of fly fishing satisfaction.

PRESENTATION IS EVERYTHING

*C*atching flies in the surface film is delicate, usually ultra-clear and low-water fishing, so proper fly presentation is essential. When possible, it's a good idea to have as much fly line as possible off the water, with ideally only the wispy leader tippet resting on the film. This isn't possible on most lakes and ponds, or large rivers. But on small trout creeks it's not difficult, especially when long rods are employed (9 1/2-footers are great). By "reaching out" with the rod and guiding flies in the surface film with a long rod, there's little or no drag, which proceeds in a perfect, life-like presentation.

Also, in such clear-water fishing, be sure to keep a low profile, as trout rising to take flies from the film easily spot a waving rod or a high-standing angler on a stream bank. A low, crouching, careful approach is best, and don't be afraid to use streamside boulders, trees and brush to help conceal your fishing approach.

Trolling For Trout

by John Pirkkala

Here's a systematic approach that allows you to eliminate lots of water while straining different depths to uncover the trout. These are high-percentage strategies for rainbows, browns, cutthroats and lake trout.

*I*magine trout fishing, and what images flash in your mind first? Crystal-clear streams? Delicate flies? Chest waders? Typical, but the truth is, lakes and reservoirs offer some of the best trout fishing action you'll ever find.

Even if you're not a master of the long rod, you can enjoy the thrill of catching big 'bows, browns, cutthroat and more. All you have to know is how to troll 'em up.

Trout in lakes are often scattered, moody and unpredictable, and catching them requires an approach that covers a lot of water.

Successful trolling takes a solid understanding of your quarry and your options—and you have many of them available.

Trout And Lakes

The availability of food and preferred water conditions are the most critical keys to locating fish.

Rainbows feed mainly on insects such as damselflies, but will also dine on plankton, small fish and crustaceans. Rainbows often feed at or near the surface. Water temperatures from 55 to 60 degrees are ideal, as long as there's plenty of oxygen available.

Brown trout are more structure-oriented than rainbows, often relating to areas with uneven jumbles of rocks, boulders and debris along the bottom.

"The availability of food and preferred water conditions are the most critical keys to locating fish."

Browns can also tolerate warmer, more turbid water than rainbows and other trout—up to 75 degrees. Still, they thrive in clear water and prefer temps in the 60- to 65-degree range.

The main forage of small to midsize brown trout is usually insects—and fish in pursuit of such delicacies are a common sight near the surface. Large brown trout often switch to a diet of crayfish, chubs and other forage fish, including their own young.

Cutthroat trout prefer insects and small fish, but they also eat crustaceans, freshwater shrimp, frogs and the eggs of other trout. Generally considered

DODGERS, FLASHERS AND TROLLS

*T*rolling spoons, spinners and plugs is an effective way to target trout in lakes. At times, running flashers and trolls (cowbells) ahead of your baits helps trout home in on your lure from greater distances, effectively increasing the swathe your lures cut through the water. Dodgers and flashers also give baits more action, causing them to dart erratically through the water.

Here are a few basic tips:

Dodgers And Flashers—Both produce plenty of flash and vibration. The main difference between the two is how they run underwater. Dodgers have a side-to-side swaying action, while flashers rotate 360 degrees.

Dodgers work best with minnow plugs, spoons, flies and squids. Flashers, which tend to run better at faster speeds, are paired with flies and spoons.

You can rig dodgers and flashers behind a keel sinker, diver, three-way swivel and lead ball, or a downrigger. Use at least a 4-foot monofilament or wire leader between the weight and the dodger or flasher. Anything less will greatly reduce bait action.

When you're using a diver or a keel sinker, keep 12 to 18 inches of space between the dodger or flasher and the lure. A little more breathing room is necessary for larger baits behind lead-ball sinkers and downriggers.

Lake Trolls—Most effective in deep, murky water and on overcast days, trolls, or cowbells, consist of a rudder to prevent line twist, followed by a series of free-swinging blades. A 12- to 18-inch leader separates the troll from the lure.

Trolls work well with many baits, particularly small spoons and plugs.

Blade options are many. Styles range from standard Colorado and willow-leaf varieties to the "Ford Fender" and "Beer Can."

In general, a blade's shape determines how fast it will rotate, as well as the type of vibration and amount of flash it will produce. Narrow blades are best for fast trolling; rounder shapes swing slow and wide. Large blades are best for deep, dark water. Use fewer and smaller blades in clear, shallow water.

COVER THE SPECTRUM

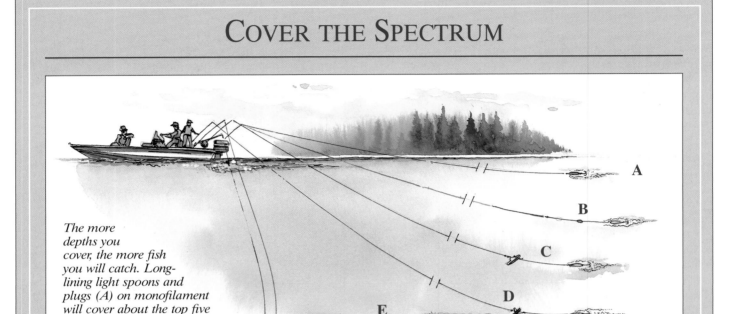

The more depths you cover, the more fish you will catch. Long-lining light spoons and plugs (A) on monofilament will cover about the top five feet. Add a rubber-core sinker just ahead of your lure and you'll get six feet of depth for every color of lead-core (B). Dipsy Divers (C) take baits down to about 60 feet, while a size 2 Deep Six (D) will dive to 90 feet. For ultra-deep fish, or when you're trolling over rapidly changing bottom contours, a down-rigger (E) is the way to go.

among the most willing biters of the trout clan, "cutts" are common along shoreline areas that hold abundant forage and cover.

Lake trout prefer deep, well-oxygenated water between 48 and 52 degrees. Trollers using downriggers often take lakers in depths of 60 to 100 feet or more during summer. Fall through spring, when water temperatures are cool, lakers can be found much shallower. They feed almost exclusively on other fish, such as whitefish, sculpin, herring, smelt and kokanee salmon.

Where To Fish

A few key areas will hold more trout on any lake or reservoir you fish.

One of the best areas to fish year-round is the mouth of an inlet. Inflowing rivers, streams and creeks deliver cool water and plenty of food. Inlets often deposit silt, gravel, sand and other sediments,

forming bars and deltas. While the tops may be too shallow to hold fish except after dark, trout will hang in deep water near the edges waiting for morsels to wash down to them.

"A few key areas will hold more trout on any lake or reservoir you fish."

Current from a large inflow may extend up to a mile into the lake, though with most smaller streams, the distance is more like a few hundred feet. As long as there is an indication of current—seams or ripples—you can bet that trout will be in the area.

The shoreline also speaks volumes about fish location. For example, long stretches of smooth,

The Ultimate Fishing Book: Strategies for Success

shallow rock shelves or sandy bottom are among the least attractive to trout. They lack aquatic plants, rocks and structure that nurture the food chain.

Conversely, a shoreline strewn with boulders and/or rock rubble that extends well into the water is a haven for aquatic life, including trout. Banks lined with trees and brush, including downed logs and limbs lying in the water, are also potential hotspots. They offer trout both food and cover from other predators.

> *"A shoreline strewn with boulders is a haven for aquatic life."*

During the day, trout also hold in deep water along points and steep drop-offs, then move shallow during low-light periods and at night. During daylight hours, troll the edges to cover the entire water column.

Winds blowing across a point concentrate fish on the lee side. Wind and waves knock forage loose from shallow rocks, attracting trout.

Other must-fish areas include reefs, islands, weedbeds and well-defined, protected bays.

Trout often suspend above structure as well as in nearby open water. Begin your search by trolling near a shallow structural element, then working your way out until you connect.

Trolling Options

Depending on the lake and the season, trout can hold at nearly any depth. Sonar is an essential part of finding them, but by using a combination of flatlines, in-line planer boards, lead-core, diving planers and downriggers, you can scour virtually every inch of the water column.

Even in very large lakes, trout often hold relatively close to shore. Consequently, I normally begin trolling just 20 to 30 yards from the bank.

Spool the inside rod, closest to shore, with 8- to 10-pound monofilament and rig with a ³⁄₈-ounce spoon. Run it 100 to 150 feet behind the boat.

A lead-core rig goes in the outside rod holder. Each 10-yard stretch of lead-core is marked by a

different color. You can usually assume that three colors (90 feet) of 15- to 20-pound lead-core between the main line and leader will take a light lure to about 15 feet. If you add a 1½-ounce rubber-core sinker to the leader about three feet ahead of the spoon, figure about 6 extra feet of depth per color.

On my first shoreline pass, I typically start with three colors and a 30-foot mono leader of 6- to 8-pound test. I tie on a Super Wedding Ring spinner tipped with a nightcrawler and set the trolling speed at about 1.5 mph.

To cover water, and to scope the underwater scene, troll in a zig-zag pattern, making lazy S-curves down the shoreline. Keep one eye glued to the sonar screen.

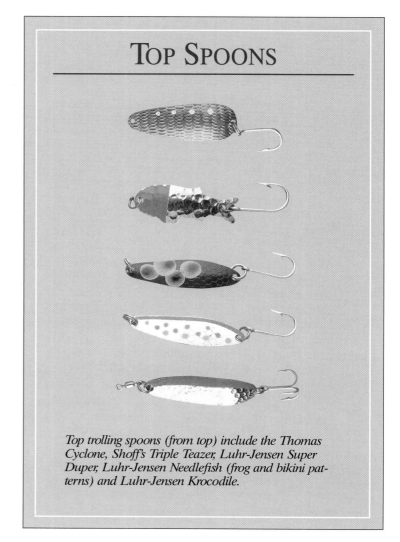

TOP SPOONS

Top trolling spoons (from top) include the Thomas Cyclone, Shoff's Triple Teazer, Luhr-Jensen Super Duper, Luhr-Jensen Needlefish (frog and bikini patterns) and Luhr-Jensen Krocodile.

DEEP AND WIDE

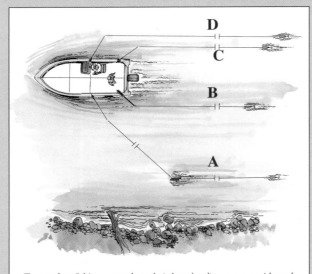

Two anglers fishing two rods each (where legal) can cut a wide and deep swathe through the water. A planer board carries the inside line (A) near shore, about 50 feet from the boat. A light spoon or surface plug trails 100 feet behind the board. Rod two (B) dredges the depths with a downrigger, quickly adjusting to changes in bottom and the depth at which fish are marked. Lure trails 25 to 75 feet behind the cannonball. The third rod (C) starts with two colors of lead-core, but may let out six or more, depending on the depth. A 30-foot mono leader and any one of a variety of lures complete the rig. The fourth rod (D) long-lines a surface bait 150 feet behind the boat, picking up high-riding browns and rainbows overlooked by sonar.

50 feet down, stick with lead-core on one rod, but add gang trolls or cowbells in front of the lure to increase its attraction value. And go to four or five colors of lead-core to get the extra depth you need.

Instead of splicing specific lengths of lead-core into the line, another option is to spool up 100 yards on the reel. That way, you can go from three to five colors very easily. Just remember that when setting the running depth, count only those colors that are actually in the water.

Reaching the strike zone of the deepest fish requires the use of diving planers and/or downriggers. Diving planers like Luhr-Jensen's Dipsy Diver and Deep Six, Big John's Diver Disks, Fish Seeker Divers and others, are easy to rig and fish. They come in various sizes so you can pinpoint different depths, up to about 90 feet with the largest Deep Six.

When targeting trout, standard rigging includes a 4- to 6-foot monofilament leader between the diver and lure. Your main line must be stout enough—20-pound test or better—to stand up to stress from the diver.

Downriggers are another option for taking spoons, spinners and minnow baits down to suspended trout. One of the most productive rigs, however, combines a size 00 silver dodger and one of the fly angler's favorite imitations—a Muddler Minnow.

Tie the Muddler about 18 inches behind the dodger, then tip it with a lively nightcrawler. The dodger provides flash and action, while the 'crawler adds a touch of scent and flavor.

Run the rig about 30 feet behind the 'rigger ball and just above the fish's level. I've found the best presentation is to troll about 1.2 mph in a lazy figure-8 pattern.

"Most times fish strike as soon as you get the lures in front of their faces."

Most times fish strike as soon as you get the lures in front of their faces, but if not, I usually spend about an hour making minor changes to boat speed, lure styles and running depths. If the fish are totally turned off, I mark the school with GPS, marker buoys or triangulation, before moving on. Sometimes you can come back to find actively

---

If you're marking fish but not getting strikes, you know what to do—swap lures, play with colors and sizes and/or modify your trolling speed until you spark a reaction. When you can see fish on the screen, it just takes perseverance and experimentation to get them to the boat. It's when you don't see fish that things get tricky.

Instead of jerking your lines and moving on, remember that there may be trout suspending farther offshore. Gradually shift your trolling passes outward and explore the depths before giving up. This is where deep-trolling techniques come into play.

If your screen shows hooks anywhere from 20 to

BEST BAITS FOR TROLLING

Light Spoons ⅛- to ½-Ounce	Heavy Spoons ½- to 1-Ounce	Plugs 1½- to 5-inch	Spinners Up to size 3	Trolling Flies 1- to 2½-inch
Needlefish Triple Teazer Thomas Cyclone Super Duper Dick Nite	Krocodile Dardevle Pixee Little Cleo	Rapala Flatfish Rebel Jointed Minnow Kwikfish	Mepps Vibrax Panther Martin Wedding Ring Super Wedding Ring Rooster Tail	Muddler Minnow Woolly Worm Woolly Bugger Carey Special
Color: Rainbow, bikini, brass, silver body/red head, frog, gold, perch	Color: Rainbow, brown, trout, hammered nickel, red-and-white, hammered brass/firestripe	Color: Yellow polka dot, frog, silver/black, gold/black, blue/silver, perch, rainbow	Color: Silver or gold blade, variety of tails	Color: Brown, gray, black, green, silver/gold body

feeding trout.

Another important consideration, and one that a lot of anglers forget: most of the fish could be holding closer to the surface than you realize. If you mark a few fish at, say, 10 or 15 feet, your boat could be spooking the rest out of sonar range.

The solution is an in-line side planer. There are a number of good ones on the market, but if you're fishing out of my boat you'll be using a Yellow Bird Mini Trolling Board. I run spoons 50 to 100 feet behind the boards, and anywhere from 25 to 75 feet away from the boat, depending on wind, wave and current conditions, and the distance from shore.

Eyes Open

Trolling success depends as much on your powers of observation as anything else. Watch for rising fish with one eye, scan your sonar screen for structure and trout below the boat with the other.

Be aware of wind direction, and changes in water temperature and clarity. Pay attention to other anglers. Glean what you can from anyone catching fish.

Finally, remember to document your success for future reference. When you hook a fish, note all the variables. Record which rod the fish hit, as well as lure type, size, color and running depth; trolling speed and whether you were on a straight course or in the middle of a turn; location on the lake, including distance from shore; and time of day.

Small Water Treasures

Don't let their diminutive size fool you; many small lakes are loaded with trout. If the majority of the fish are under 15 inches in length, I generally go with spinning tackle loaded with 6- to 8-pound test monofilament.

"Many small lakes are loaded with trout. Leave the downriggers at home but bring your lead-core."

Leave the downriggers at home but bring your lead-core. Troll spoons like Krocodiles or Dardevles about 60 to 100 feet behind the boat. Set a fairly light drag, put your spinning rods in their holders and troll at 1 to 1.5 mph.

Troll as close as you dare to fish-attracting cover such as fallen trees, stumps, overhanging bushes and around points.

ESTABLISHING A HOT DEPTH LEVEL

Trout often coexist in lakes that harbor warm-water species such as pike, walleye, bass or even muskies. In "two story" lakes like this, two distinct fisheries often exist—a shallower, warm-water fishery and a deeper, colder water zone that holds trout. By taking a temperature profile with an electronic thermometer (dropping a probe slowly down into the depths), an angler can zero in on the preferred temperature band a particular species of trout prefers. Then it's a matter of fishing this zone, targeting structure and baitfish schools that appear at the correct depth level. Remember, different trout species have different ideal temperature ranges.

In cold weather, trolling an F-4 Flatfish or No. 9 Rapala on the surface can be deadly. A silver No. 2 Mepps spinner or a black Rooster Tail can also be very effective. In the spring and fall, focus on shallow water—5 to 15 feet. During the summer, especially at midday, you'll probably be better off fishing lead-core in depths of 20 to 40 feet.

Trout spend a fair amount of time feeding on the bottom of small lakes (and large waters, too); that's where lead-core can be your best friend. Try trolling a Needlefish, Triple Teazer or a trolling fly right off the bottom. You will snag up once in a while, but that may be what it takes to get strikes.

Trolling Hardware

A top troller has dozens of lures to pick from, but you can be successful with a small, carefully-selected arsenal. Here are my favorites.

For flatlining, 3/8-ounce Krocodiles, No. 9 and 11 Original Floating Rapalas, trout-size Dardevles and Rooster Tails are hard to beat. You can use these lures with lead-core line, too, as well as size 1 and 2 Needlefish, Mepps spinners and Muddler Minnow flies. I also like Super Wedding Ring spinners with a nightcrawler or standard-size Wedding Rings tipped with maggots and Thomas spoons.

A variety of lures work well with downriggers. To boost your odds, add a size 00 chrome dodger 12 to 24 inches up from the lure. A dodger is especially effective when paired with a fly-and-'crawler combo, but it also works with spoons, plugs and other lures.

A 61/2-foot, light-action spinning rod with matching reel will do nicely for light trolling on small to mid-size waters. For larger lakes and bigger trout, an 8-foot, medium- or medium-light action graphite or glass trolling rod and levelwind reel are the perfect combo, and can also be used with a downrigger.

Lead-core line, diving planers, lake trolls, dodgers and flashers call for heavier tackle. A medium to medium-heavy action rod is required with all that drag in the water. Depending on how many colors you want to spool, a large-capacity trolling reel may be needed.

"Trolling for trout is a fine art that takes time to master."

Fine Art

Some trout purists sneer at trolling as a mindless game of riding around in a boat, waiting for a strike. In truth, trolling for trout is a fine art that takes time to master.

We've shown you how to do it, the rest is up to you. Give these tactics a try next time you're on the water—I guarantee they'll put you into trout.

Steelhead East & West

by Ed Park

What better way to expand your fishing knowledge than to learn how others are also catching your favorite fish.

are approximately 2,000 miles apart and the two cultures often do not mix, and 2) a few open-minded anglers have helped spread "new" ideas.

A few of the many who have helped this exchange include Buzz Ramsey, Lance Hinatsu, Dick Swan, Gary Loomis and Frank Amato.

Buzz Ramsey is a manager of outside sales and promotion for Luhr-Jensen and Sons, the Hood River, Oregon, manufacturer of fishing tackle. Buzz is noted as an outstanding angler and has fished extensively for steelhead in the Northwest. When the Great Lakes fishery exploded, he went there to learn and teach.

Lance Hinatsu of Sterling Heights, Michigan, is a steelhead fanatic who visited the Northwest in the late 1970s. He fished from a drift boat and saw the tremendous advantages of this specialized craft. He became the first to use a drift boat in Michigan.

Dick Swan of Clare, Michigan, one of that state's most highly respected anglers, is the number one advocate of the "Michigan system," which he helped develop. The long, limber noodle rods, combined with ultra-light 2- and 4-pound test lines, have become his trademark. Through his work as a guide, charter boat operator and well-known maker of custom rods, he has helped others learn this system.

Gary Loomis, of Woodland, Washington, is considered to be one of the country's top designers and manufacturers of fishing rods. He is also an avid steelheader and has worked closely with Swan in developing noodle rods.

Frank Amato, editor and publisher of Salmon Trout Steelheader magazine in Portland, Oregon, has been a leader in publishing magazines and books about salmonids. As one example of the intermixing of regional ideas, Frank's magazine went national in 1981. The October-November issue reported on his first trip to Michigan for steelhead.

Great Lakes anglers shook their collective heads and burst into laughter when they learned veteran Pacific Northwest steelheaders just discovered the "Michigan system," using noodle rods, cobweb lines, fine hooks and small baits a few years ago. That's old stuff; Great Lakes anglers have done that for years.

Likewise, Northwest steelheaders (where it all began) shook their own heads and burst into laughter when they heard Great Lakes fishermen finally began to use drift boats for Hotshotting. That's old stuff; Northwest steelheaders have done that for decades.

All this transcontinental grinning stems from two facts: 1) The Great Lakes and the Pacific Ocean

"A few open-minded anglers have helped spread 'new' steelheading ideas."

Through the efforts of such persons, knowledge has spread to benefit anglers in both regions. We now know the differences and similarities between the two fisheries.

The waters of the two regions are quite different. Streams in the Great Lakes region are generally smaller, shorter and slower moving. Many are regulated by dams. Northwest rivers are bigger, longer, faster and have fewer dams to regulate runoff. In addition, there is an excellent fishery for steelhead in the Great Lakes themselves, where fish are caught using techniques common to trolling for many lake species. Although some steelhead are caught in saltwater in the Pacific Northwest, the West does not really have a comparable fishery.

The Northwest is much wetter. While the total precipitation for Detroit for November, December and January is about 6½ inches, many coastal areas of Oregon and Washington will record more than 50 inches of rain during those same three months.

With greater rainfall and fewer dams, Northwest rivers often run wild, deep and broad, compared with smaller, more controlled rivers of the East.

The species of fish is the same—rainbow trout (Oncorhynchus mykiss)—though you can get into an argument. In the past the accepted definition of a steelhead was a rainbow trout that is hatched in freshwater, goes to the ocean for part of its life, then returns to freshwater to spawn. Since the Great Lakes are not oceans, many feel fish in the Great Lakes are not really steelhead but lake-run rainbows.

Steelhead, lake-run rainbow … no matter what you call them, fishing them is a challenge.

Others claim that since the parents were steelhead, the fish are indeed steelhead. Counterclaims insist "steelhead" is not a species but merely a condition of a species (rainbow trout), and the condition is that they have gone to sea. Change that condition and they are no longer steelhead.

Some fisheries biologists agree the rainbows of

the Great Lakes should correctly be called lake-run rainbows, not steelhead, but also admit the word steelhead has a special magic, and there is little they can do to change a word commonly used. So correct or not, these Great Lakes fish will continue to be known as steelhead.

There are definite differences in the fish from the two regions. Those from the Great Lakes are heavier for a given length. Food is more abundant in the Great Lakes, and life is easier without predators such as seals and sea lions.

Great Lakes runs return 20 to 25 percent, while Pacific Coast runs return less than 10 percent. Great Lakes runs are heavier with fish commonly stacking up below barrier dams. Northwest fish return more scattered and spread out through a river system.

The Northwest is mild, and many coastal stations rarely dip below freezing, while the Great Lakes often get subzero weather. Consequently, the rivers are colder in the East where water below dams may be only slightly above brittle. A steelhead's activity level is greatly influenced by water temperature. A fish in 50-degree water will be more active, run farther, jump higher and fight harder than that same fish in 34-degree water.

Another variable is angler concentration. It is common for crowds to stand shoulder-to-shoulder below a dam on popular Eastern rivers. Such crowding is rare in the Northwest.

Great Lakes rivers are generally smaller, so fishing is commonly done by wading. Northwest anglers often must fish from the bank or from a boat.

All these differences influenced the development of tackle and techniques suited to each region.

The heavy, stout tackle developed in the Northwest is necessary because a fresh 20-pound steelhead, with the power of a flood-stage river to help, is not going to be held with light line. Bank anglers must tighten down and hope everything holds.

Because of the heavier, siltier water and lack of crowds that spook fish, ultralight tackle is not needed. Northwest steelhead are not as leader-shy.

In the East, rivers are smaller and clearer and crowds are common, and this tends to make fish spooky; they get very leader-shy and they will not take a bait hung on the end of a 15-pound "rope." Anglers must use light lines.

But you don't fish 2-pound line with a stout 8½-foot West Coast drift rod. You need a more delicate

touch. So anglers such as Dick Swan developed rods so long and limber it is difficult to break even a thin 2-pound line.

And, according to Gary Loomis, "There is nothing that works better than a long, limber parabolic rod for catching big fish on light line."

The fishing conditions both dictated light lines (spooky fish) and allowed their use (less active fish, smaller, wadable rivers). The light lines dictated limber rods. From these conditions, the "Michigan system" was born. To complement the rods and line, Eastern anglers also use small, light hooks and smaller baits or lures.

Both regions have learned much. The Great Lakes angler learned to use heavier gear, drift boats and Northwest techniques so he can continue to fish during high water. As the rivers rise and get off-color, he finds that the fish are less leader-shy and can be hooked—and held—with heavier rods and lines.

Northwesterners are well versed in "Hotshotting"—working a diving plug downstream behind a drift boat that is held in the current by the man on the oars. Other plugs are used, but since the Hot Shot plug is the most common, the name "Hotshotting" has become the common expression for this fishing method. Many Eastern anglers now use this system from an anchored boat, letting the lures dance in a downcurrent deep run or pool. With the introduction of the drift boat, Eastern anglers are finding this is an extremely deadly way to catch steelhead in rivers fished from a boat.

Northwest steelheaders have long known the problems of catching steelhead when rivers are low and clear. The fish get spooky and will not hit a big bait or lure on a heavy line. Until the invention of very limber rods, ultra-light lines could not be used. The "Michigan system" now makes it possible for Northwest steelheaders to take fish in low, clear summer water.

Although each region has favored lures, the anglers who fish both areas have learned most spoons, plugs, drifters, flies and other lures work in both places. Presentation, adapted for the water conditions, is more important.

Steelhead are native to the Pacific coast, but their introduction into Eastern streams is one of the big fisheries success stories of the past couple of decades. This nation now has many outstanding steelhead waters.

Top Washington names include the Humptulips, Quinault, Hoh, Bogachiel, Washougal, Lewis, Kalama, Cowlitz, Green, Snohomish, Skagit and dozens of others. Oregon rivers of fame include the Alsea, Coquille, Kilchis, Nehalem, Nestucca, Rogue, Siletz, Siuslaw, Trask, Umpqua, Wilson, Clackamas, Deschutes, Sandy, Santiam and many others.

In the Great Lakes region, top Minnesota rivers are the Knife and the Upper Brule or Arrowhead. Wisconsin's most popular rivers are the Kewaunee, Root, Oconto, Manitowoc, Menominee, Milwaukee, East Twin, Peshtigo, Ahnapee and West Twin. Peshtigo, Ahnapee and West Twin. Illinois' main fishery is in the Waukegan River. Indiana has summer-run steelhead in Trail creek and the Little Calumet River.

> "Anglers in the Great Lakes and the Northwest will probably continue a friendly feud about which area, tackle and techniques are best."

Michigan's top rivers are the Little Manistee, Betsie, Platte, Pere Marquette, Pentwater, White, Grand, St. Joseph and AuSable. Ohio's top steelhead waters are the Chagrin, Grand and Rocky rivers and Conneaut Creek. Pennsylvania lists two significant steelhead creeks, Elk and Walnut. New York's best waters are Black, Salmon, Oswego, Genesee and lower Niagara rivers, and Maxwell, Skinner, Catfish and Irondequoit creeks.

Anglers in the Great Lakes and the Northwest will probably continue a friendly feud about which area, tackle and techniques are best. But many of us just want to learn what we can from both areas and adapting tackle and techniques to various water conditions.

Anglers who try new techniques will eventually bring more steelhead to the net.

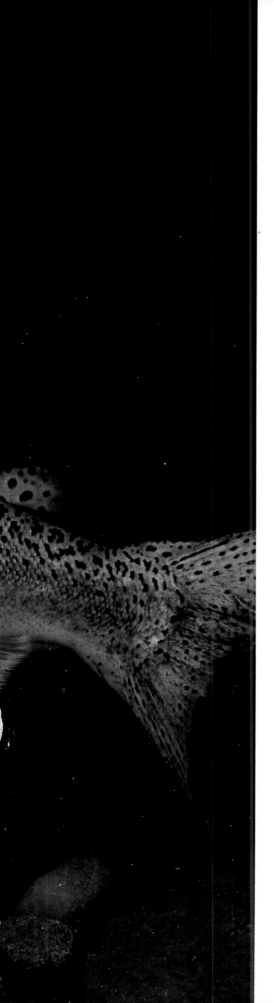

chapter 11

Salmon

Once thought of as a fish for only the rich or the elite, stocking has brought salmon (chiefly cohos and chinooks) within reach of many North American anglers, from the West Coast to the huge prairie reservoirs to the Great Lakes. And don't forget about the East Coast and its Atlantics, which are making a comeback from historic lows.

Here are a few of *North American Fisherman's* ideas for tangling with these silvery, streamlined fish — unlocking secrets so you can join in on the action.

Comeback Kings

by Dave Mull

There are more of these big salmon available than there has been in recent years, and here's the latest and hottest information on how to catch them.

You can always tell when a king eats your lure. The downrigger release pops, the rod throbs briefly, then the drag sizzles as the fish breaks hell-bent for the horizon. No jumping like a steelhead or deep dogfighting like a lake trout—just a screaming drag.

Such sizzling runs were common on Lake Michigan during its salmon heyday in the late '70s and early '80s. The big lake supported a healthy population of king salmon, and anglers from across the country flocked to its shores to dance with royalty.

By the mid 1980s, however, things began to change. Salmon numbers and sizes mysteriously declined, and with them, anglers' catch rates.

For example, Michigan anglers harvested 404,035 kings in 1986, with an angler success rate of 10.26 fish per 100 hours of effort. Within two years, however, a healthy fish in the 20-pound class had become a rarity—and remained so. The 1994 Michigan salmon harvest was down to a paltry 24,501 fish. Only 1.82 salmon were caught per 100 hours of fishing.

Not surprisingly, angler numbers—and the millions of dollars in revenue they generated—plummeted, sending states like Michigan, Illinois and Wisconsin scrambling for answers. The news wasn't good.

Two-Part Problem

The big lake's salmon were suffering from an affliction known as Bacterial Kidney Disease, or BKD for short. But according to scientists, BKD alone doesn't usually kill fish. Healthy salmon can often harbor the bacteria without suffering ill effects.

"It's like I might have a cold virus, but not have a cold," explains Jim Francis, Lake Michigan research biologist for the Indiana Department of Natural

Resources. The problem was compounded, however, by a serious decline in the salmon's main forage, alewives. Researchers theorized that malnutrition stressed the fish enough to allow the bacteria to gain a stronger foothold and eventually kill the fish.

The near-deadly one-two punch had sent salmon populations reeling.

The Road Back

When evidence suggested lower alewife populations were hurting chinook survival, Wisconsin acted by curtailing commercial alewife netting. The state then joined with Illinois and Indiana to reduce king salmon stockings by 25 percent.

"Major [salmon] die-offs in 1988 and 1989 occurred at a point when the alewife numbers were low lake-wide," Francis says. "Now we've just had a couple of really good back-to-back year-classes of alewives. We have no hard numbers, but it looks like there's definitely a correlation between more alewives and the comeback of the chinook fishery."

Biologists have also had success developing ways to control BKD in the salmon population. For example, Michigan, which supplies eggs to Indiana and Illinois, now mixes eggs and milt from numbered pairs of male and female fish. If either fish later tests positive for BKD, those eggs are destroyed.

King salmon may still be the premier species on Lake Michigan, but it's worthwhile to check out the steelhead fishing, as well as the brown trout and coho action.

"There's definitely a correlation between more alewives and the comeback of the chinook fishery."

Wisconsin takes a different tack. Before fertilization, hatchery workers drain the ovarian fluid (which carries the BKD bacteria) from around the collected eggs. Afterward, the eggs are treated with an antibiotic.

Hatcheries in all four states also feed young salmon pellets containing the antibiotic.

The treatment appears to be working. In the late '80s, 67 percent of the fish returning to Wisconsin waters had BKD. By the late 1990s the number had dropped to just 2 percent.

"BKD is under control, let's put it that way," says Francis. "It's still out there, but it's not nearly as prevalent—not causing the mortality [among kings] like it used to. Right now we have a healthy alewife

Target offshore summer kings by locating temperature breaks. Look for the thermocline on your sonar screen, or scum lines on the surface.

population, which means there's more forage, and the chinook are doing better than they have in the past."

Connecting With Kings

Lake Michigan's continually improving king salmon numbers have sparked renewed angler interest. Charter service bookings are way up from years past, and more privately-owned craft are plying the water.

However, NAFC members who haven't fished since the early boom years will find the fishing tactics have changed.

During the previously mentioned heyday, most anglers relied upon crankbaits such as Rebel Fastracs and J-Plugs to target kings. These crankbaits can still be extremely productive, but like most other tactics and baits, they have been niched for specific applications. If the fish are riding high in the water column, above 30 feet during cold-water situations,

or shallow on their fall spawning runs, look to cranks to be the primary weapon. During the deep-water times of summer, however, spoons and dodger/fly combos are the most consistent producers of big catches. Although tactics and preferences may vary from port to port, don't get talked into fishing just one way. Stay open minded and versatile to be consistent.

Carlson, Mauler, Diamond King, Pro-King and Stinger spoons are the ones most often heard about over the VHF radios of charter captains and fishermen. In dodger/flies, stick with a Luhr-Jensen size 0, silver or silver prism, with a pearl, white or green tinsel fly trailing behind. Popular flies include Howies, Cheddars, and Stanley Stingers.

"I'm trying to make my trolling spread look like a school of bait," adds Butch Bradshaw, who operates Sea King Charters out of St. Joseph, Michigan. "I run a lot of green-and-chartreuse combos, and silver-plated spoons with green and black tape.

RIGGING FOR TROLLING

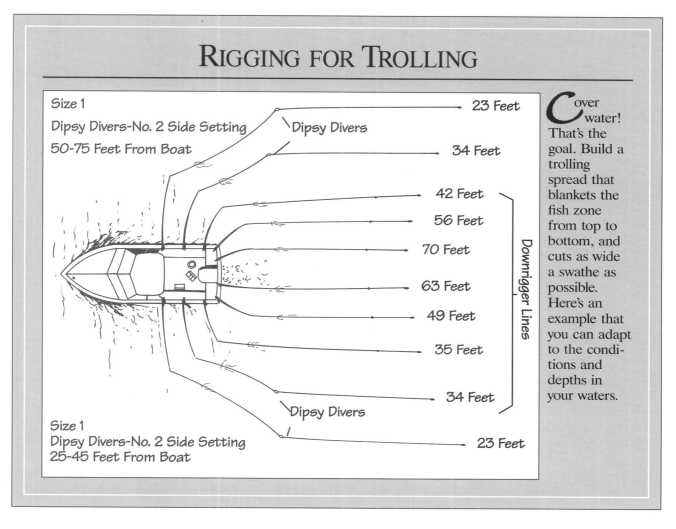

Size 1
Dipsy Divers-No. 2 Side Setting
50-75 Feet From Boat

Dipsy Divers

23 Feet

34 Feet

42 Feet

56 Feet

70 Feet

63 Feet

49 Feet

35 Feet

Downrigger Lines

Dipsy Divers

34 Feet

Size 1
Dipsy Divers-No. 2 Side Setting
25-45 Feet From Boat

23 Feet

Cover water! That's the goal. Build a trolling spread that blankets the fish zone from top to bottom, and cuts as wide a swathe as possible. Here's an example that you can adapt to the conditions and depths in your waters.

"If I'm looking for fish, I'll put a hodgepodge of different spoons out there until I find the color and type that works best."

A typical productive summer trolling speed will be anywhere from 2.2 to 2.7 knots. When starting a day, set the table with a smorgasbord of different spoons and dodger/flies, and vary their depths. With a 60 degree water temperature, kings will hover between 30 and 60 feet, with adjustments up for colder water and down for warmer water. Don't be surprised if the early morning spread of spoons cools down once the sun comes up. The fish quite often will change lure and color preferences as the sun rises in the sky and again when it sets. Once you dial into a pattern, begin changing over to those spoon or fly styles and colors and really make the most of your trolling passes.

Along with downrigging, make Dipsy Divers an important piece of your tools. Shallow "Dipsies" are typically run with smaller spoons and set out with 70 to 90 feet of line and run on a 3 setting using 25-lb. test mono as the mainline. Deeper Dipsies are set at 2 and string the reels with a thin diameter 30-lb. super braid like Gorilla Braid to help them dive deeper with less line out. Run a dodger/fly and a mid or larger spoon on your two

"Kings are easiest to catch when temperature breaks set up in summer."

Although the J-Plug (top) is a viable lure, spoons have largely taken over the chinook spotlight. There are hundreds from which to choose, but some of the most popular among Lake Michigan anglers include the: Carlson Spoon, Stinger, Evil Eye and Northern King. At left is a Dipsy Diver.

deep Dipsies with anywhere from 135 to 200 feet of line out.

King salmon are catchable throughout the year, but are probably the easiest to target when temperature breaks—both horizontal thermoclines and vertical columns of cooler water—set up in the summer.

"During the spring, look for spots with warmer surface temps and start fishing them," says Bradshaw. Warm water could be around river mouths, warm-water discharges, or farther out if the wind is blowing warm surface water away from shore."

After a long, cold winter, the warmer waters offer a comfort zone for baitfish—alewives, smelt and other forage species. And where baitfish go, salmon are sure to follow.

Clear, shallow water means spooky fish, so break out the trolling boards, side planers and Dipsys to get your lures away from the boat. While you're at it, string out a long flatline. A high-riding lure is

often the ticket for early-season salmon cruising near the surface.

During summer periods, the kings move deeper and will generally relate to two different forms of structure and edges. Typical bottom structure would be a feeding flat of 30 to 60 feet deep that quickly drops off to over 100 feet, or bottom contour reef areas that rise out of deep water and top off at 70 to 100 feet. The best edge is water-borne and is known as a slick. This is an extreme and abrupt temperature break that originates on the surface and can be quite easily detected with the naked eye or a surface temperature gauge. Kings will hug the cold-water side of this temperature break, feeding on the alewives that have come to pick off the photoplankton and zooplankton that the slick collects.

A baitfish ball on your sonar screen should also cause your mental fish alarm to sound. Work it by trolling the edges where the predators will be waiting for a baitfish to stray from the pack. And

don't be surprised if two or three rods pop at the same time.

Once in a while, however, you can work around a tightly-packed bait school without getting so much as a false release. When that happens, try this trick: Run your trolling spread right through the middle of the school. The cables, 'rigger balls and mono lines will scatter the forage. You'll know you've hit it because you can see the rodtips and 'rigger arms thumping as the baitfish bounce off the cables and lines.

Scattering the baitfish this way often triggers the salmon, which up till then were loitering around the edges, into a flurry of feeding activity.

Although they're not actively feeding, kings that are staging near river mouths, or have already moved upstream, can offer fall fishing opportunities— especially for anglers in smaller boats.

"Don't be surprised if two or three rods pop at the same time."

But fall fishing action can be spotty, depending on the weather and the fishes' mood. The salmon aren't concentrating on feeding at this time of year because their instincts are focused on the coming spawning run. Still, they can be caught.

Although spoons are certainly productive in the fall, Bradshaw says J-Plugs can also shine. His pattern of choice is a chrome plug with a green ladderback. Sometimes a magnum-size spoon trolled with J-Plugs at a fairly fast clip (2.5 to 3.5 mph) is the way to go.

Pre-spawn salmon will hold in a discernible school as they prepare to enter the river. When you locate a school, work it. If you can't get a release, change lure colors and/or styles, increase the letback from the 'rigger ball, or stack your lines to get more lures into the water.

The point is to alter your presentation until you establish the combination that hits paydirt. Since the salmon aren't in a feeding mood, you're really trying to make them mad.

Trolling speed is a critical factor no matter what the season. The magic number will change from day to day, Bradshaw says, but there's always a place to start—and that's in the 2- to 2.5-mph range. In the spring, cool waters may call for a little less speed. In the summer and fall, you might have to crank it up as high as 3.5 mph.

Although few anglers or biologists expect the chinook fishery to ever attain the same quality as the pre-crash days of the early 1980s, recent success rates are encouraging. The improvements have once again given anglers ample reason to expect rebounding king action during their next trip on the big lake.

The Spell Of The Atlantic Salmon

by Jim Bashline

Many anglers consider the Atlantic salmon to be the ultimate freshwater gamefish.
Hook one and you're hooked for life.

O ther fish species may jump higher, swim faster, have more endurance, more color and even taste better (although I doubt it), but none combine all of these attributes in a more beautiful package than does the Atlantic salmon. If an angler wants to experience the apex of fly fishing, the mysterious Salmo salar is already on his list of must-do adventures, or soon will be.

Members of the NAFC who live in the northeast quadrant of the U.S. and in Quebec and the Maritime Provinces seem to know, by osmosis,

what the lure and lore of Atlantic salmon fishing is all about. These anglers are geographically closer to the species. But many sportfishermen who pursue the salmon of the West Coast of North America have an understanding of this migratory blue blood for an entirely different reason: It is often compared with their steelhead.

The Atlantic salmon and the various species of Pacific salmon are not even of the same genus. The Pacific fish are Oncorhynchus while the Atlantics are Salmos. The steelhead is a Salmo and so are

The Ultimate Fishing Book: Strategies for Success

brown, rainbow and cutthroat trout. Pacific salmon die after spawning duties. Salmos do not. There's some attrition at spawning time among Atlantic salmon, but unlike their distant Western cousins, they are not biologically programmed to die.

There is some fair fishing to be had for Atlantics in Great Britain, Ireland, Norway and in a handful of other European nations. Icelandic fishing can be super at times, but the mother lode of angling for this historic fish is in eastern Canada. A half dozen rivers in Maine are becoming more productive after a long dry spell, but for every one of these rivers, Canada can count two dozen or more. The first-timer can be overwhelmed by choices. Where should I go? What tackle do I need? What time of year is best? What will it cost? How do I fish for Atlantics?

All of these questions, especially the last, have been the basis for many books and will no doubt lead to many more. I can't begin to answer each in great depth, but I'd like to try answering them in a way that will be helpful to NAFC members who want to sample this superstar of the finned world.

There are two kinds of Atlantic salmon destinations. The first is the remote camp where you will have the pools mostly to yourself. These are leased or privately held stretches of river where a package price includes food, lodging, guides and transportation. You'll find package trips to a variety of remote locations on Labrador and the Ungava Region of Quebec, as well as Quebec's North Shore of the St. Lawrence River.

There are some semi-remote rivers in Newfoundland, New Brunswick, Nova Scotia, Quebec's Gaspe Peninsula and the state of Maine. You can drive to most of these rivers.

Generally, the more remote the river, the more you pay per day of fishing. Atlantic salmon fishing may run $400 to $500 or more per day for the remote camp and about half that at "civilized" locations. These are only guidelines, mind you, since there are many degrees of luxury and service. Some renowned pools are pegged at $1,000 or more per day.

The odds are, you'll see and hook more fish at the remote camps (but not necessarily bigger ones) simply because there are fewer anglers. But some of the largest Atlantic salmon taken each year are caught in pools that flow beside public highways in New Brunswick and Quebec. In an attempt to put

the matter of location into perspective, let me tell you about two of my favorite salmon fishing target areas.

The first is the Mecatina River of Quebec's North Shore. To get there requires a commercial or charter flight to Chevry-Harrington Airport and then a 20-minute floatplane or helicopter hop to the camp. The camp is located at the mouth of the river, and you must travel upstream via small boat to reach the fishing pools.

Six or eight anglers are the usual complement for the week with a guide for each pair. During a normal week each angler can expect to hook an average of two fish per day. That doesn't sound like many, but remember, we're talking about averages. Some will hook a lot more and some a lot less.

You won't see any other fishermen on the river except members of your group. The food is terrific at the Mecatina Lodge, and since it's a family operation, employee turnover is not great.

The guides know the river intimately and can coach the beginner on placing his fly in the right spot. For the beginner or experienced angler who enjoys being with his own group, such a location should be considered—if he can get along without a television and telephone.

An entirely different sort of fishing is found on Nova Scotia's Margaree River. My headquarters there was the Normaway Inn, a charming country hotel with all the amenities, including a lavish menu and choice of private cabin or main lodge accommodations. Guide service can be arranged at the front desk, and your guide will pick you up at the front door.

It's a short drive from the Normaway to three dozen salmon pools on one of the prettiest rivers in the world. By law, there is no private water in Nova Scotia so you'll probably have to share the pools with other anglers. This is seldom a problem because the locals are most obliging in "rotating" the pools. A visitor soon learns that he must also move on after a dozen casts or so.

Actually, having a pool to one's self is possible most of the time. But the camaraderie on the Margaree is so much fun that to not share it is to miss one of the reasons for being there.

If an angler hooks a fish every other day on the Margaree, he's done well. During the peak of the fall run, mid-September to mid-October, a fish per day or better is possible for the savvy angler. And

The Atlantic salmon is the superstar of the finned world. "These incredible leapers just have it all," says Bashline.

Last-minute cancellations sometime create an opening in a prime location at prime time but reservations usually must be made several months in advance. Right now would be an excellent time to begin.

On some salmon rivers it's traditional to fish from a boat. This is most often the case if a river is wide and deep. While I'll fish from a boat when I must, to experience the essence of Atlantic salmon fishing requires one to spend some time wading. Felt-soled waders are a must since most salmon rivers have slippery rocks. A $9\frac{1}{2}$-foot fly rod capable of tossing an 8- or 9-weight-forward line is ideal. A lighter rod will seldom present the fly correctly. A line heavier than a 9 will usually offer too much air resistance, causing the same problem. The reel should hold a full fly line and 150 yards of backing.

As a rule, Atlantic salmon enter coastal rivers a bit earlier in the extreme southern reaches of their range. Salmon can show up in Maine rivers as early as late April, and some bright salmon are in the New Brunswick rivers about a month later. But most years the better fishing won't begin until June or July. As we travel farther north, the arrival times are later, with some fish in northern Quebec not reaching freshwater until mid-August. Regardless of where you seek them, Atlantics aren't available for much more than four months (which is a good thing—I'd be broke if they were).

About 75 percent of all Atlantics hooked fall for a standard wet fly fished across and downstream. The traditional approach calls for a cast of 45 or 50 feet at a point almost straight away from the angler. If all goes well, the fly drifts along naturally without much manipulation, and then, just before it reaches the point of maximum swing with the current, Sir Salmon rises up and gulps it with confidence.

Sometimes stripping or retrieving line is necessary to make this happen, but regardless of how it comes about, the rise of a salmon to a wet fly is the trickiest facet of the game. Unless the beginner has nerves of steel, he'll probably miss the first half dozen rises.

In moving water, a salmon usually times its rise in order to be beneath and just to one side of the drifting fly. It takes with a "curl" of the body, and once the fly is in its mouth, the salmon attempts to return to precisely where it was before rising. In doing all this, it usually shows part of its body, the dorsal fin and sometimes the tail.

some of the autumn fish of the Margaree are impressive—30 pounds and bigger!

Yes, you'll see other anglers on all of Nova Scotia's rivers, as you will on the public waters in New Brunswick and Quebec. If you're a gregarious sort, you'll enjoy it. If you're a "lone wolf" type, head for Labrador or Ungava Bay. You won't be bothered by crowds.

Travel agents, booking agencies and the lodges themselves are happy to answer questions by mail or phone, as are the travel departments of each province. Prices, fishing seasons and regulations change, so make sure you get current information.

It's a deliberate set of movements, not at all like the swift rush of a small trout. The quick-reflexed trout angler almost always strikes too quickly. The best rule to follow when fishing for Atlantic salmon is: Never strike when you see a hump or bulge on the water or even a mighty splash.

> *"About 75 percent of all Atlantics hooked fall for a standard wet fly fished across and downstream."*

Wait, wait, wait, until you feel pressure on the line or until the rodtip bends. Then lift the rod smoothly but firmly. Do not jab with a lightning reaction as you would with trout. Just tighten up, and you've got him!

I wish I could offer some magic advice that would make playing your first Atlantic salmon a more professional act. But I'm not sure it would be right even if I could. Oh sure, the conventional wisdom passed on by so many angling scribes includes: play the fish from the reel, keep the rodtip high, lower the rod (bow to the fish) when it jumps and all that.

But the truth is, you'll be so excited watching that silver torpedo run and jump that you'll promptly forget all good fishing advice you've received. And that's the way it should be. Lessons learned from experience stick better than those learned from advice.

Salmon rivers are all beautiful, as befits a fish of such exquisite strength and grace. And so are the flies used for catching this trophy. It generally is accepted that Atlantic salmon do not eat when on their spawning run. In fact, they are unable to (at least they are unable to swallow solid food) because upon entering freshwater their stomach opening closes.

For centuries, anglers have speculated about what salmon believe their fanciful flies are. The discussion will not end with me, but I choose to

Classic flies tied specifically for Atlantic salmon are a beautiful part of the spell.

believe the salmon's response was learned in the river of its birth.

There, as fingerlings (parr) the young fish spent the days of summer snatching insects from the surface. This learned reaction is rekindled when they see something drift over them. But as we know from looking at pictures of fly patterns, not all salmon will rise for the same fly or the same size fly. And that's what keeps those of us who tie flies hunched over the vise into the wee hours of the off-season. Since salmon don't talk, we have to experiment.

> "Salmon rivers are all beautiful, as befits a fish of such exquisite strength and grace."

If I had to be restricted to one fly pattern for Atlantic salmon—anywhere—I'd select a Black Bear-green butt. This is nothing more than a basic black fly with a little tag of bright green at the bend of the hook. It has a black hair wing, black floss or wool body, silver rib and is most often tied on a size 6 hook. (On different rivers, salmon flies as large as 5/0 can be useful as well as tiny ones down to size 14. Check with your guide, camp owner, outfitter or salmon fishing pals about this.) After the black fly the choices open up considerably.

I would certainly want a Rusty Rat in my box and a Blue Charm (which is mostly black, too). I'd also want a silver-bodied fly, such as the Silver Rat

or the Silver Doctor. A yellow-hackled Cosseboom ought to be there and at least one fully dressed traditional pattern, such as the Jock Scott, Dusty Miller or Torrish.

To top it off, a few high-riding dry flies like the Royal Wulff, Humpy or Adams in sizes 8 and 10 would be good insurance, as would a Bomber or two. The Bomber isn't really a dry fly but more of a long "bass bug" that salmon often will rise to when they won't look at anything else. Have most of your flies tied on single hooks but carry just a few on doubles for those days when you must sink the fly for good results. In spite of their appearance, double hooks don't seem to hook fish any more securely than do singles.

My leaders for salmon are pretty simple, and I've never found any reason to tie them otherwise. A leader of 36 inches of 30-pound, 24 inches of 25-pound, 24 inches of 20-pound, 20 inches of 15-pound and 30 inches of 12-pound works well.

If I want a finer tippet I reduce the last two sections of leader material to 15 inches and tie on a section of 8- or 10-pound. My preferred leader material for salmon fishing is Maxima. It's tough, takes a knot well and the chameleon color is about the same shade as most peat-stained salmon rivers.

I'll bet some NAFC members have guessed by now that I'm slightly hung up on Atlantic salmon. I've never met a fish I didn't like, but these incredible leapers just have it all. They're fished in beautiful places, rise to grab beautiful flies and then put on a show of reckless bravado. I must warn you, though, casting at Atlantic salmon can be addictive. You can "just say no" after one experience... but I'll bet you won't want to.

Index

fishing, 79
Hamilton, Robert, 46
Hannon, Doug, 48–49, 55
Hellgrammite baits in small
mouth bass fishing, 70
Hibdon, Guido, 38, 40, 41, 42
Hinatsu, Lance, 296
Holes, walleye fishing in, 161
Hybrid striper fishing, 236–40
crankbaits for, 240
downriggers for, 240
lures for, 239, 244–45
tailwater fishing for, 239
topwater rigs for, 239, 240–45
trolling for, 240
weather temperature in, 242–44
Hypolimnion, 190, 191

I

Ice fishing
in bluegill fishing, 83
for crappies, 124–27
for northern pike, 213–17
Ice-out equipment in northern
pike fishing, 203–4

J

Jerkbaits
in largemouth bass fishing,
25, 41–42
in striped bass fishing, 249–50
Jerkworm rigs in northern pike
fishing, 209
Jig-and-grub combo in
smallmouth bass fishing, 69
Jig-and-pig for largemouth bass
fishing, 18, 25, 30, 47, 55, 57
Jig and worm in largemouth
bass fishing, 25
Jigging
in crappie fishing, 113, 114, 116
in largemouth bass fishing,
10–12, 47
in muskie fishing, 226, 227–28
in northern pike fishing, 213,
216–17
in walleye fishing, 185–89

Jig heads in northern pike
fishing, 212
Jig-n-plastic rigs in northern pike
fishing, 209–10, 211
Johnson, E. F., 102, 105
Jumbo jigs in walleye fishing,
185–89

K

Kellar, Fritz, 124, 125
Kleve, Dennis, 175, 179
King salmon, 302–7
Klein, Gary, 33, 34
Korsgaden, Gary, 107, 124

L

Laden, Gary, 112, 114, 115, 116
Largemouth bass
color vision of, 49
Florida-strain, 16
migration of, 54
overhead predators for, 49
as sight feeders, 54–55
spawning, 39
Largemouth bass fishing, 7–57
backwater pits and ponds in,
31–32
bankside shades in, 50–51
boat control in, 32
boat positioning in, 10, 40–41
buzzbaits in, 36
Carolina-rigged soft plastics
for, 37
crankbaits in, 12–14, 17, 18,
37, 55, 57
cross-sun conditions in, 51
cruising in, 41
current conditions in, 31–32, 54
developing game plan, 15–17
double anchoring of boat, 9
Duclos' tips on, 8–14
effects of sunlight in, 48–51
fishing pressure in, 28–29
floating worms in, 42
forage in, 31
hunting for trophies, 9–10
impact of cold fronts on, 15–19

jigs for, 10–12
live crayfish bait for, 12
lures in, 10, 17–18, 19, 25, 30
in muddy water, 52–57
in natural lakes, 18–19
patience in, 9
pitching in, 32
plowing, 11–12
in ponds, 20–25
presentation in, 9, 13, 32
quietness in, 9
reactionary strikes in, 17, 18
researching locale, 9–10
in reservoirs, 18
river bars in, 32
in rivers, 26–32
and sandgrass bottoms, 22, 24
scents in, 9, 12, 55
shallow water in, 32, 38–42, 56
short-line techniques in, 56
slack water sites in, 31–32
spinnerbaits in, 18, 36, 55
stationary, 40–41
targeting stream, 29
target zones for, 14
timber habitat in, 7, 31
topwater baits in, 55
trolling speed in, 14
water-level changes in, 33–37
water temperature in, 21–22
weedbeds in, 18, 31
worms for, 10–11
Larson, Roy, 131
Lawson, Bud, 30–31
Leadhead jigs
in largemouth bass fishing, 30
in smallmouth bass fishing, 69
Leapfrog fishing for northern
pike, 216
Ledges, smallmouth bass
fishing by, 67
Leeches
in bluegill fishing, 87
in walleye fishing, 172–75, 177
Liquid-crystal display (LCD) in
bluegill fishing, 92
Little, George, 36
Live bait rigs in walleye fishing,
169–70
Long flies in trout fishing, 274–79
Loomis, Gary, 296, 298

water conditions in, 267
water depth in, 267
Tube jigs
in bluegill fishing, 93
in crappie fishing, 112, 114,
120–21
Tucker, Tim, 33, 38, 43, 48
Tuma, Terry, 86
Twitch baits for striped bass
fishing, 254

V

Vance, Randy, 236
VanDam, Kevin, 15, 35, 36, 89,
143
Verrusio, George, 29
Vertical fishing in crappie fishing,
123
Vertical hovering in crappie
fishing, 114–15
Vertical jigging in walleye fishing,
163
Von Haeger, Arden, 259–60

W

Walleye fishing, 149–95
baitfish in, 181, 183, 192
boat position in, 195
breakline in, 152
crankbaits in, 166–71, 194–95
do-nothing rigs in, 170
electronic locators in, 191–92
emerald shiners in, 181, 182
fathead minnows in, 179–80,
182
forage base in lake in, 167
jumbo jigs for, 185–89
leech & crawler rigging option
in, 177
live bait rigs in, 169–70
lunar effect in, 157, 170
lures for, 154–57
mud leeches in, 175
muskie crankbaits in, 170–71
nightcrawlers in, 175–77
nightfishing in, 150–57, 167
night gear in, 153, 155–57

pH level in, 191–92
presentations in, 163–65
quarter-pitching in, 165
quick-change rigs in, 157
redtail chubs in, 182, 184
ribbon leeches in, 172–74
river fishing for, 158–65
shad in, 181, 182, 183
signs of walleye in, 168–69
slipping in, 163–65
sonar screen in, 152
spottail shiners in, 180–81, 182
stratification in, 190–95
suspended walleyes in, 167
tackle and techniques in,
169–71
three-way rigs in, 161, 165
tiger leeches in, 174–75
trolling in, 194
for trophies, 151, 153
water temperature in, 190–95
weather conditions in, 167, 193
willow cats in, 182, 183–84
Walleye plugs in smallmouth
bass fishing, 77
Walleyes, stratified, 190–95
Wassink, Ryan, 142
Water conditions in trout fishing,
267
Water depth in trout fishing, 267
Water-level changes in large
mouth bass fishing, 33–37
Water temperature
in bluegill fishing, 91
in catfishing, 143–47
in largemouth bass fishing,
21–22
in northern pike fishing,
199–201
in shellcracker fishing, 95, 97
in smallmouth bass fishing,
60–65
in walleye fishing, 190–95
Weather conditions. *See also*
Cold fronts
in bluegill fishing, 91
in muskie fishing, 220–21, 223,
229
in walleye fishing, 167, 193

Weedbeds
in largemouth bass fishing,
18, 31
in muskie fishing, 221, 222–23
in smallmouth bass fishing, 79
White, Guy, 191
White bass, 237, 240
Willow cats in walleye fishing,
182, 183–84
Wind conditions in smallmouth
bass fishing, 78
Wing dams, walleye fishing in,
162–63
Wirth, Don, 52, 66, 76, 241, 246,
251, 258
Worms in largemouth bass
fishing, 10–11